T0373352

THE
OPEN-
ENDED
CITY

David Dillon at the Nasher Sculpture Center.
Photograph by Tadd Myers, www.taddmyers.com.

Roger Fullington Series in Architecture
University of Texas Press

The David Dillon Center for Texas Architecture
University of Texas at Arlington

THE OPEN- ENDED CITY

David Dillon on Texas Architecture

Edited by
Kathryn E. Holliday

UNIVERSITY OF TEXAS PRESS   AUSTIN

Publication of this book was made possible in part by support from
Roger Fullington and a challenge grant from the National Endowment
for the Humanities.

Requests for permission to reproduce material from this work should
be sent to:
 Permissions
 University of Texas Press
 P.O. Box 7819
 Austin, TX 78713-7819
 utpress.utexas.edu/rp-form

♾ The paper used in this book meets the minimum requirements of
ANSI/NISO Z39.48-1992 (R1997) (Permanence of Paper).

LIBRARY OF CONGRESS CATALOGING-IN-PUBLICATION DATA

Names: Dillon, David, 1941–2010, author. | Holliday, Kathryn E., editor.
Title: The open-ended city : David Dillon on Texas architecture / edited
 by Kathryn E. Holliday.
Description: First edition. | Austin : University of Texas Press, 2019. |
 Includes bibliographical references and index.
Identifiers: LCCN 2018034575
ISBN 978-1-4773-1761-7 (cloth : alk. paper)
ISBN 978-1-4773-1862-1 (library e-book)
ISBN 978-1-4773-1863-8 (nonlibrary e-book)
Subjects: LCSH: Architecture—Texas—Dallas—History—20th century. |
 Dillon, David, 1941–2010—Philosophy.
Classification: LCC NA735.D2 D55 2019 | DDC 720.9764/2812—dc23
LC record available at https://lccn.loc.gov/2018034575

doi:10.7560/317617

CONTENTS

CONTENTS

7. AESTHETICS AND ARCHITECTURE 328

CONTENTS

FOREWORD

Robert Decherd

David Dillon was a master of architecture criticism. Equally important, he was a master of the varied disciplines that form the foundation of great urban areas: design, planning, and policy. His range of interests was extraordinary, and he continually educated himself about new issues and disciplines across his career. His gift was an ability to apply this intelligence to critique the physical world created by the decisions people make every day about architecture, landscape architecture, urban planning, infrastructure, amenities, and human behavior. A truly talented writer, he deftly used prose and metaphors to make complex interrelationships understandable to regular folks and experts alike. He was a catalyst and a dreamer embodied in one person.

David joined the *Dallas Morning News* in 1981 as its first full-time architecture critic. The paper had previously relied on the talents of John Rosenfield and others, who had multiple duties, to cover architecture and urban affairs from time to time. But it had been a long time since those critics had written for the *News*, and there had never been a staff member whose sole duty was to write about these matters.

Burl Osborne came to the *News* as editor in 1980 with the goal of establishing the paper as a home for journalistic distinction. Burl and I soon realized that, among other things, this would require the *News* to assume a leading role in helping readers understand the importance of their physical environment and how its development was essential to Dallas's aspiration to become one of America's great cities. David's role was pivotal in this initiative, which extended across many parts of the paper—the daily news report, extensive long-form features and investigative work, occasional large-scale projects involving third-party experts hired by the *News*, and, of course, the editorial and op-ed pages.

David's work as a critic soon evolved into a de facto agenda for the Dallas architecture, planning, and development worlds. This agenda touched upon both the public and private sectors with uneven effect. David wrote about, and argued in favor of, significantly greater public investment in urban planning at the City of Dallas, without much success. His well-documented pieces supporting the need for development policies to be imposed on developers and property owners never garnered the political support needed to establish rules that had proven so effective in great cities around the world. Still, David's never-give-up approach laid the groundwork for the much more forward-looking investment and policy framework that has taken hold in Dallas since the turn of the twenty-first century.

Within the private sector, David's influence was much more immediate and widely felt. His dogged insistence that high design standards become the expectation rather than the exception for property owners, developers, and the design community had a lasting impact on the fabric of the city. The cumulative results are seen today throughout the physical center of Dallas as defined by the "eight-mile" circumference of Loop 12.

The intersection of criticism, architecture, public policy, and politics can be confusing to a newspaper audience. David stood out in his ability to make it less so. Employing his logical and coherent style, he made the big projects like Fair Park, the Trinity River, the Arts District, Central Expressway, DART, and the trails system feel approachable. He wrote about small projects and emerging architects in the same accessible way. And he always incorporated the historical value and importance of structures and places, ranging from the grandest to the funkiest. He made architecture less of an insider's conversation and more of a public dialogue.

David was tough-minded about matters he deemed to be lacking. His investigative reporting helped keep I. M. Pei's magnificent symphony hall on track, much to the chagrin of the very able citizen committee formed to oversee the project. His constant lament of Dallas's de-emphasis of great parks angered many at City Hall, but ultimately helped bring about a dramatic change in attitude. His conviction about the city's duty to build and preserve neighborhoods was a cause célèbre.

But David was not anti-establishment. He wanted great design and sensible urban planning, and when he saw it, he was on board—as with the Dallas Plan, created in 1992 and still the framework for much of the truly ambitious thinking among Dallas leaders. He sought wins for the people who populated Dallas, throughout Dallas.

It wasn't easy to know David Dillon until you had earned his respect, which he gave judiciously. Nobody ever conned David when it came to the subjects of his reporting or criticism. He was regarded as an intellect who traveled well with the common man or woman—a high-minded scholar who could translate and interpret complex ideas for his readers and students. Because of David, Dallas and Texas are far better. And because of his good works over the course of twenty-nine years, the *Dallas Morning News* achieved distinction in the realm of architectural criticism and urban reporting that continues today.

You will find elements of all David's interests, passions, and quirks in this inspiring anthology. I am proud to have counted him as a friend, a colleague, and one of the best journalists I've ever known.

ACKNOWLEDGMENTS

Selecting, gathering, and editing these essays took many years and involved many people. The process began in 2010 at the memorial service dedicated to celebrating David Dillon's life and influence. As friends and colleagues gathered at the Nasher Sculpture Center to remember his influence, Sally Dillon approached landscape architect Kevin Sloan about donating her husband's papers to the University of Texas at Arlington (UTA). By spring 2011, with the support of Dean Donald F. Gatzke and Special Collections archivist Brenda McClurkin, I was in Amherst, Massachusetts, helping Sally sort and box David's papers and recordings to ship back to Texas. Those papers formed the nucleus of the new David Dillon Center for Texas Architecture at the university's School of Architecture.

The next spring, as the Dillon Center's founding director I organized the first David Dillon Symposium, focused on the theme "Architecture Criticism Today." Writers from across the country assembled, again at the Nasher, to discuss Dillon's impact and the state of architecture criticism. From those discussions emerged a partnership between the Center and the university and the *Dallas Morning News*, which led to the hiring of Mark Lamster, a new architecture critic for the paper and a visiting professor for the school in 2013.

Since those first steps, the work of the Dillon Center, including its symposium and its engagement with public discussions about architecture and urbanism in Texas, has solidified the larger perception that greater attention to issues of planning and design is critical to adjust the course of growth and development. This collection stems from those discussions and provides a foundation for the continuing engagement of an ever-growing readership in the long-standing issues that affect the places we all call home.

None of this would have been possible without the support of Sally Dillon, whose generosity of spirit and whose confidence in me have been humbling and inspiring. She was truly David's partner and her understanding of his impact and passion for architecture was the impetus for the Dillon Center and this book. Her support, along with that of friends and family members including John and Susan Albach, Antonio de Mambro and Ruth Kolodny, Giuliana di Mambro, Victoria Dowling, Sallie Rawlings, Chris Wilson, and Sally Yeatman, has been essential. The Dillon Center's publication fund has also benefited from generous support from Diane Cheatham, Steven Daniels, Wendy Evans Joseph, Duncan Fulton, Ralph Hawkins, Lisa Lamkin, Michael Malone, Allen and Cynthia Mondell, Marcel Quimby, Katherine Seale, and Bryce and Patricia Weigand.

At the UTA School of Architecture, Dean Don Gatzke allowed the Dillon Center to take root as a means to connect the pragmatic architecture profession with the ideals of the ivory tower. Brad Bell, as interim director of the School of Architecture, continued that support.

This book would not exist without the discussions and debates that take place at the Dillon Symposium. The Dallas Architecture Forum, led by Nate Eudaly, and the Nasher Sculpture Center, particularly its director Jeremy Strick and Jill Magnuson, director for external affairs, nurtured this fledgling effort, as did Jan Blackmon, executive director, and Greg Brown, programs director, at the Dallas Center for Architecture. Their collaboration ensured that the symposium could reach the broad audience required for engaged architecture criticism to thrive.

At the *Dallas Morning News*, Robert Decherd and Jim Moroney pursued the partnership with the School of Architecture, and editor Bob Mong and deputy editor Lisa Kresl put the plan in place. Mark Konradi was central to the licensing of David's articles for this volume. Mark Lamster assumed the dual identity of critic and part-time professor in a completely new city with much appreciated wit and intelligence.

ACKNOWLEDGMENTS

At UT Press, Robert Devens, editor-in-chief, believed in this project from the beginning and provided wise counsel; Sarah McGavick, Lynne Chapman, and Sally Furgeson kept it on the straight and narrow.

The Dillon Center advisory committee members shared their expertise and time in preparing this collection and selecting its contents. I never knew David Dillon personally, but many committee members did, and discussing articles and themes with them made this book all the better. My thanks to Willis Winters, chair of the committee, as well as members Virginia McAlester, Nancy McCoy, Kevin Sloan, and Robert Fairbanks. David's friends and colleagues Stephen Fox, Larry Good, Greg Ibañez, Maxy Levy, and John Mullen also generously shared their memories and their expertise, and I am especially grateful for their support.

The contractions, reorganizations, and technological changes in the newspaper industry meant that the *Dallas Morning News* did not have access to the original photographs and illustrations that accompanied many of Dillon's articles while this book was being prepared. While many contributed to this effort, I would especially like to thank David Preziosi of Preservation Dallas, photographer Carolyn Brown, and Larry Good of Good, Fulton, Farrell for their efforts to track down photographs that correspond roughly to the original dates of publication. Brenda McClurkin, Ben Huseman, Cathy Spitzenberger, and Mitch Stepanovich from the UTA Libraries were also indispensible.

I have also been fortunate to work with fantastic UTA architecture and landscape architecture students who read Dillon's articles in my history classes and whose comments helped me understand his impact in new ways. Maria Capota and Kate Kosut prepared invaluable inventories and bibliographies from the Dillon Papers at the UTA Special Collections. Daniel Eudaly continued that process by beginning a finding aid. Estefania Barreto spent countless hours locating articles, looking through scrapbooks, organizing files, and searching for photographs. Graduate student Molly Plummer helped push the editorial process, Karis Bishop organized and provided illustrations, and Lilia Corral exhibited intrepid detective skills, tracking down obscure photographs from sources all over Dallas-Fort Worth. Their energy and dedication are an inspiration. I cannot say enough good things about the positive influence they will all have as future designers of our world.

Finally, to my husband David Dibble and son William Dibble, I offer my heartfelt thanks and love. They gamely embark with me on road trips, peering at overpasses and railcars, ascending skyscrapers, tromping through riverbeds, and seeking out suburban office parks and small-town city halls. I could not ask for better company on this journey.

INTRODUCTION

Kathryn E. Holliday

In a 1980 essay, David Dillon asked a provocative question: "Why is Dallas architecture so bad?" The question was startling, a slap in the face to a generation of city builders flush with cash and high on success. The essay ran as the cover story for *D Magazine*, and it took architects, real estate developers, and city planners to task for their fundamental neglect of design as a tool for enriching not just private pocketbooks but also public life in the city. Dillon offered both a diagnosis—too much self-interest, too little leadership—and a solution—look to more successful cities like Houston and Minneapolis. Architecture criticism wasn't just about giving the finished product a thumbs up or thumbs down. Instead, it was about people, money, government, and policy.

Dillon's article hit a nerve in early 1980s Dallas, then at the peak of an enormous building boom that reflected the city's growing sense of self-confidence. Within a year, Dillon became the architecture critic for *Dallas Morning News*, one of two major dailies that served the city. His first column, published August 23, 1981, on a page filled with advertisements for movies and movie theaters, encouraged downtown office workers to use their lunch hours to engage with the city. He suggested touring the restored Adolphus Hotel to develop an appreciation for its "Anheuser-Busch baroque" design.[1] That first column set the standard for Dillon's work for the newspaper over the next twenty-five years: write for everyday readers and open their eyes to the ways that good architecture could enrich their lives.

Dillon joined the staff of the *Dallas Morning News* at a critical moment in the paper's and the city's history. Since the tragedy of the Kennedy assassination in 1963 had thrust the city into the international spotlight, Dallas had embarked on a campaign to erase that hateful act and reinvent itself as a symbol of progressive city building. Under Mayor Erik Jonsson, the city created its ambitious Goals for Dallas program in 1965, bringing together civic leaders from a wide cross section of professions including business, technology, transportation, education, and architecture to create a shared strategy for civic reinvention. Jonsson, the former CEO of Texas Instruments, believed partnerships between private industry and public service would transform Dallas into a model postwar city. Unburdened by an extensive history, Dallas could quickly pivot and promote itself as a laboratory for innovative civic engagement, planning, and policy, driven by the expertise of the private sector.[2] Jonsson's Goals for Dallas project was an extension and repositioning of what is known as the "Dallas Way," a civic culture that placed authority in the hands of a business elite to make decisions about public policy that were, in the words of policy researcher Royce Hanson, "public spirited but not public-regarding."[3]

Goals for Dallas focused extensively on the need to rebuild downtown to attract business and promote civic investment. Recommendations included proposals for a new civic center and city hall, a new convention center, and improved highway circulation to and from downtown. The building campaigns of the 1970s followed this blueprint and began to redefine the city through a series of developer-driven projects that, despite involvement by city officials and lofty Goals for Dallas rhetoric about citizen engagement, proceeded with little public input or oversight. Dallas largely avoided federally funded urban renewal projects and instead cultivated private investment backed by a host of deep-pocketed investors.[4] A *Dallas Morning News* article from 1974 outlined nineteen projects either being planned or under construction for downtown, ranging from the development of the Reunion Tower entertainment complex around the historic Union Station train terminal to the construction of a new city hall, convention center, and public library.[5]

Other big plans were also afoot for a new downtown arts district.

Plans to remake the flood plain of the Trinity River into an urban park and Town Lake, for regional transit and rail, and for reinventing Fair Park, the state fairgrounds east of downtown, percolated as well. Dallas was awash with ideas about architecture and urban planning, but it very much lacked an open, public culture empowered to evaluate and sift through those ideas, separating overheated and self-interested ambition from ideas that could truly transform the city for all.

Dillon began writing about Dallas at exactly this moment, when some dreams surged forward and others fizzled. Before he joined the *News*, art critic Janet Kutner covered some aspects of architecture; business and real estate reporters covered others. They followed in the tradition of excellence established through decades of arts reporting by John Rosenfield, who championed music and theater from the 1920s to the 1950s. At the *Dallas Times Herald*, Bill Marvel covered art and some architecture on the side. There was no one whose beat was architecture—and, more broadly, the city itself.

The *Dallas Morning News* hired Dillon in 1981 as part of a larger restructuring of the paper led by Robert Decherd, a vice president at the Belo Corporation and executive vice president of the paper, and managed by newly appointed editor Burl Osborne, a veteran of the Associated Press. Under their leadership, the paper engaged in a relentless competition with the *Dallas Times Herald* that ultimately helped lead to the demise of the *Herald* in 1991.[6] A 1979 marketing study commissioned by Decherd indicated that the paper should focus on "cosmopolites," a "young, upwardly mobile" target demographic.[7] In this competitive landscape, the *News* marketed their new critic as an asset who gave their readers something available nowhere else (fig. 0.1). Dillon quickly set about claiming that territory. As an architecture critic, he connected the dots between art, culture, commerce, history, and public life in ways that few columnists and reporters ever get the opportunity to pursue, and his writing opened the door to the possibility of a new kind of public scrutiny.

As much as Dallasites today groan and dismiss the TV show with its cowboy hats and big hair, *Dallas* and Cowboys football were the central cultural touchstones in the early 1980s that defined the city and Texas as a whole to an increasingly international community.[8] Dillon, by contrast, asked the city to look inward and consider what development could do for the internal, local audience that actually called Texas home. He expanded the conversation about Dallas urban

CRITICS' CORNER

DAVID DILLON

ARCHITECTURE CRITIC

As one of the few architecture critics in the country working for a major newspaper, David Dillon's expertise and insight offer you a solid foundation into the world of architectural design.

For a glimpse at how Dallas' and the nation's skylines are taking shape, don't miss David Dillon — in the Today and Arts & Entertainment sections.

From City Hall to Market Hall...

NOBODY BEATS The Dallas Morning News IN THE MORNING

0.1. *In 1982, the* Dallas Morning News *ran advertisements highlighting the work of their new architecture critic as a draw for subscribers. Clipping from scrapbooks in the David Dillon Papers, Special Collections, University of Texas at Arlington. Courtesy* Dallas Morning News.

planning to encourage a greater understanding of the challenges facing the region, its suburbs, and its relationship with Fort Worth and other Texas cities. He reported on zoning changes, highway design, preservation challenges, and local history to contribute to the larger civic conversations about growth and policy. He followed the city through cycles of boom, oil bust, and boom again. He embraced some of the less lovable aspects of the North Texas region—the highways, the driving, and the vast open spaces—as symbols of the limitless possibilities embodied in the sprawling metropolitan area. While he rejected the term "metroplex" to describe the interconnected yet fragmented relationships among North Texas cities, suburbs, and exurbs, he embraced the reality that he was writing about a region as much as a well-defined city.[9]

In her 1985 nomination letter for the Pulitzer Prize, Arts and Entertainment editor Lindsay Heinsen described Dillon's writing as the work of "an advocate and a concerned citizen."[10] That sense of service, of serious self-analysis, became the central theme of his career as an architecture critic and journalist across the next twenty-five years. During that time, he wrote more than one thousand articles for the *Dallas Morning News* "in service of good design." A strong sense of civic responsibility is reflected throughout the essays collected here.[11] As Paul Goldberger, long-time architecture critic for the *New York Times*, observes, "To say that Dallas is a better city because of his voice is to speak the obvious. If the phrase 'conscience of a city' is a bit of a cliché, I can't think of an alternative that describes David's role in Dallas any better."[12]

A central mission of this collection is to illustrate the critical value of this kind of deeply embedded local writing to the growth and maturation of cities. The essays included here have been carefully selected to touch on themes that drove Dillon's writing and the region's development across twenty-five years: downtown redevelopment, suburban sprawl, arts and culture, historic preservation, and the necessity of aesthetic quality in architecture as a baseline for thriving communities. Selecting these themes was about more than representing the scope of his work. Many of the articles he wrote for the paper covered current events and a high percentage documented conferences, exhibits, awards—those kinds of articles are largely not included here.

Instead, the selection process focused on identifying the major issues that confronted Dallas—and other American cities—in the 1980s and the ways that Dillon covered those issues, often across the entire twenty-five years of his career as a critic. As a result, while the specifics of these essays will resonate with those who live in and care about Dallas, Fort Worth, and Texas, they are also deeply relevant to all architects, urbanists, and citizens who engage in the public life and planning of cities. All American cities struggled with empty downtowns in the 1980s, all cities have struggled to develop cultures that balance new development with historic preservation, all cities struggle with issues of racial and economic equity, and all cities have tried, with varying success, to use architecture as a magic bullet to cure issues of blight and economic redevelopment. Not every story is positive, and not every issue is resolved, but through these themes Dillon's continuous and evolving approach as a critic of the city emerges.

It is in these shared themes that Dillon's essays are relevant for readers across the United States, especially those who live in cities that lack a strong local press and vigorous local discussions about architecture and planning. Dillon did not practice criticism as a purely intellectual or theoretical endeavor; he eschewed the academic models of criticism that flourished in publications like *Assemblage*, *Oppositions*, or *ANY* during the 1980s and 1990s.[13] Instead, his fundamental strategy was to make information readily available in order to open public discussion of often obscure issues. He was a reporter, doing interviews and conducting research, as well as a critic (fig. 0.2). There is much to be learned from this straightforward approach. As Chicago-based architecture critic Blair Kamin observes, the image of the architecture critic is often associated with the global perspective of New York-based critics writing about high-end international design, but its strongest and most impactful traditions are located in local and regional newspapers.[14] Nancy Levinson, editor of *Places Journal*, amplifies that same theme: "[T]he liveliest and most influential architecture criticism has been largely local."[15]

These local architecture critics facilitate public engagement in conversations about planning and city building, and they are a crucial ingredient in the creation of a culture of enlightened design. The National

0.2. *Dillon kept his notes in traditional reporter's notebooks, with a running table of contents that he wrote on the cover. Several dozen of his notebooks are preserved in the David Dillon Papers, Special Collections, University of Texas at Arlington.*

Arts Journalism Program cited local engagement as the most important contribution that newspaper-based critics make to larger public understanding and engagement with issues of architecture and urban planning: "While high-profile architecture is thriving in the United States . . . the sprawl of generic construction that is engulfing most communities nationwide underscores the news media's responsibility to nurture a thorough critique of the new built environment."[16]

Those critiques take place not in a handful of quick articles, but across years and decades. Dillon began writing about the plans for a downtown Dallas arts district in 1981 and was still writing about it when he retired in 2006. He also first wrote about the need for a comprehensive plan for downtown revitalization in 1981 in a piece about the uncontrolled development in Oak Lawn, where "street life is more than just a catch phrase used by Bostonians and New Yorkers."[17] That focus continued: he helped write a series for the paper called "Downtown's Pivotal Decade" in 1991, contributed an essay in 2004 that compared Dallas to the failing city of Detroit, and projected a "taller, denser Dallas" in 2006.[18] The length of these public debates and developments proves not that the critic's voice has no immediate impact, but that sustained attention is crucial.

Dillon's writing is particularly relevant for Sunbelt cities that continue to deal with urban sprawl, civic fragmentation, rapid cycles of economic bust and boom, and real estate development that often proceeds without a clear civic benefit. He wrote not to impress other critics or to curry favor with architects, but for readers of the daily newspaper. As Dillon himself pointed out, he could not always be sure that he influenced decisions, but he did believe that he helped people speak up and engage in a process that often seemed opaque: "We all prod and provoke and praise in hopes that, over time, others will join the chorus."[19]

While these overarching issues of urbanism and civic life drove Dillon's agenda, the more intangible nature of quality in design was equally important. He wrote during the 1980s and 1990s, the heyday of postmodernism, and he turned his attention to understanding the best and worst of its scenographic impulses. He critiqued both high postmodernism—at Disney headquarters and in Celebration, Florida—and, more importantly, the everyday postmodernism of downtowns and suburban sprawl. Promoting visual literacy and engagement in the public meant writing detailed critical analyses of places that readers could actually visit, testing their own sensibilities about color, materials, scale, and landscape (fig. 0.3). If Dillon was not quite a "tastemaker," he did still aspire to educate readers about "good design."[20]

More than being a critic, Dillon was a *writer*. He was enormously prolific and he published books and hundreds of magazine articles in addition to his articles for the *Dallas Morning News*.[21] Not every piece was about architecture—he also occasionally covered theater, music,

0.3. *"How to Read the New Buildings" was a handy guide to postmodern frills and it accompanied the article "Bye Bye Boring Buildings," published September 30, 1984. Clipping from scrapbooks in the David Dillon Papers, Special Collections, University of Texas at Arlington.* **Courtesy** *Dallas Morning News.*

and art. He wrote reflective, poignant essays, like his remembrance of his mother and their journey together to buy a painting in Boston. The essay, which centers on a landscape painting of a winter scene in New Hampshire, is deeply personal and allows a glimpse of how important art can be in defining people's lives and relationships.[22]

Dillon did not start out as a writer about architecture. Instead, he began his career writing about writing. He grew up in Fitchburg, Massachusetts, earned a PhD in literature from Harvard, and moved to Dallas in 1969 to teach in the English department at Southern Methodist

University.[23] His first book was a primer on creative writing called *Writing: Experience and Expression*. The down-to-earth instructions found there formed the foundation for his career writing about cities and design: how to write metaphors, how to make comparisons, how to describe

> the arrangement of physical details in space, appeal[ing] to the intellect through the senses. By presenting pictures to the imagination it connects ideas to concrete objects and sensations. . . . Good description comes from meticulous, loving attention to the world around us, not from some innate creative spark. It is a basic tool for discovering and rediscovering that world and for sharing our findings with a reader.[24]

Dillon first learned to write about architecture by studying John Updike's writing about Central Park and Mark Twain's writing about the Mississippi River—in other words, architecture, landscapes, and city streets formed the setting for the stories of our lives.[25]

Dillon's nuanced and literary perspective on writing enabled him to shift his voice easily to suit different audiences. He wrote for magazines aimed at professional architects, like *Architectural Record*, *Domus*, and *Texas Architect*. His tone there was clearly didactic, providing incisive commentary intended to shape designers' thinking about their own work. But when writing for *Southern Accents*, the tone changed and focused more on travel and the value of experiencing buildings and neighborhoods. His monograph on the architect O'Neil Ford is an approachable portrait of a man, his architecture, and Texas itself that contrasts Mary Carolyn Hollers George's more minute documentary biography of the same man. His book on Dallas architecture is a breezy, accessible portrait of a city as much as it is a discussion of individual buildings.[26] On a more personal level, Dillon's colleagues described him as a "crusty" New Englander and Kamin deemed him as a combination of Emily Dickinson and a hockey player, acerbic and direct.[27]

This collection, however, intentionally focuses on Dillon's newspaper writing, a format that demands short, precise, accessible, and timely writing. It is this format, more than the others, that defines his voice and sets him apart from other architectural writers. Ada Louise Huxtable, who wrote for the *New York Times* between 1963 and 1982, provided the model for modern newspaper architecture criticism. She was a powerful advocate for historic preservation and for quality in design that contributed to the larger construction of the urban social environment. Her writing was fierce, evocative, and often funny, peppered with phrases that referred metaphorically to a "gilded turkey" and the bones of an "expressway brontosaurus."[28] She called developers, architects, and politicians to task for sloppy, self-serving decisions that undermined the creation of a better city for all.[29]

While Huxtable provided a persuasive model for the invaluable public service provided by architectural criticism in newspapers, the number of critics was always small. A 2000 survey of one hundred and forty major daily newspapers with daily circulations of more than seventy-five thousand indicated that only forty had an architecture critic. Of those, only thirteen were full time like Dillon.[30] Perhaps because of the complex nature of architectural writing, which cuts across finance, public policy, art, construction, and current events, architecture criticism remains a tiny field whose practitioners tend to be located in "metropoles," major population centers with cultural pretensions and large pools of readers interested in this interdisciplinary dynamic.[31] During the 1990s, Dillon counted Robert Campbell at the *Boston Globe*, Paul Goldberger at the *New York Times*, Blair Kamin at the *Chicago Tribune*, Inga Saffron at the *Philadelphia Inquirer*, and Allan Temko at the *San Francisco Chronicle* among his peers, all critics who combined journalism with pointed commentary on local policy and design.[32] By 2010, though, Thomas Fisher, former editor for *Progressive Architecture*, could speculate about the "professional extinction" of architecture critics who wrote for local papers as more papers laid off the already miniscule number of critics in the face of shrinking circulations and revenues.[33]

Dillon's trajectory at the *News* reflects this larger national narrative. He began in the early 1980s; spent the 1986–1987 academic year at Harvard, sponsored by a Loeb Fellowship; and by the mid-1990s, he and his wife Sally had moved to Amherst, Massachusetts. Dillon taught courses on architecture and writing at the University of Massachusetts-Amherst and wrote remotely for the paper, traveling to Dallas for events and relying on the fax machine and email for research services. He continued to cover Texas architecture, but more of his writing focused on art, theater, and architecture on the national and international stage, and he spent more time freelancing for national publications. While this collection focuses intentionally on Dallas and Texas, Dillon by the 1990s had a global beat. He covered the massive redevelopment of Barcelona for the 1992 Olympics, as well as redevelopment plans for New Orleans after Hurricane Katrina and for the World Trade Center site after 9/11.[34] Dallas architecture, by the 1990s, had also become more global, as both Dallas and Fort Worth sought the services of celebrity "starchitects" to reinvent their civic images.

In 2001, when Bob Mong became editor-in-chief, Dillon began to write as a member of a team investigating connected themes across departments. The Tipping Point series, a 2004 investigative editorial endeavor about multiple crises in Dallas's politics and economy, placed Dillon's pieces "Community" and "Decision Time" alongside articles on policing and education. The paper's editorial responses to *Forward Dallas*, the new city plan adopted in 2006, show the influence of his thinking and engagement with planning across the previous twenty-five years.[35] More of Dillon's writing for the paper focused on issues of policy that led to fragmentation and division that undermined building a healthy and equitable network of cities across the region. Ironically, at the moment that his hard-earned depth of perspective as a critic became more publicly and seamlessly integrated into the paper's overall editorial stance—his articles moved from the arts page to the front page—the paper also began a series of layoffs that resulted in the loss of its most experienced staff. In 2004, the *News* executed the first of a series of downsizing efforts, and in 2006, Dillon accepted a buyout in the next round. His departure left a void. He had contributed to occasional special features and he was not immediately replaced. Instead, Scott Cantrell, the paper's eloquent classical music critic, took on building reviews.

Across that twenty-five years of writing about Dallas, Fort Worth, and Texas, Dillon claimed his own territory, expertise, and readership, taking Huxtable's engaged civic model and applying it to a completely different kind of metropolitan context. Dillon's local newspaper readers inhabited a seemingly endless landscape of skyscrapers, highways, and low-rise prairie suburbs that defied traditional assumptions about city-building. He reveled in this context and adored explaining its idiosyncrasies to natives of more traditional cities. A visitor from Dusseldorf once told him, "When I see Dallas, I see only today." The comment heard most often from European visitors was "so clean" and "so quiet," damning compliments that suggested that North Texas failed to connect on a more visceral, personal level with its citizens and visitors.[36] For Dillon, these comments were opportunities to talk about highways, cars, suburbs, and private real estate as realizations of American ambition and optimism unimaginable in the confines of older, more mature places.

At the same time, Dillon recognized the excesses and failures of this system. He identified private real estate developers large and small as the linchpins of Texas architectural culture, writing about Gerald Hines in Houston, the Bass family in Fort Worth, and Ross Perot Jr. and Diane Cheatham in Dallas.[37] The *News* valued these contributions to their business coverage and nominated him for a Pulitzer for his feature article, "The Education of Harlan Crow," which created a portrait of the developer through changes in the design of the buildings he financed. This is a classic Dillon essay that introduces architecture in the context of a people story, while educating readers about the private, behind-the-scenes process that shaped the city's future.[38] Dillon was a reporter on architecture as well as a critic: he wrote to explain, categorize, critique, and reinvent the Texas city both to himself and to an audience that was as eager to understand the amorphous, sprawling landscapes they inhabited. Dillon promoted his own views, but he also championed the work of others, from small, insightful projects by his friend, the architect John Mullen, to visionary planning schemes like James Pratt's *Dallas Vision,* exhibited at the Dallas Museum of Art in 1990.[39] Even though he was not always right—and readers definitely wrote to complain—he provided a model of engaged civic and architectural journalism.

Alexandra Lange describes four kinds of critical writing about architecture: formal, experiential, historical, and activist.[40] Dillon's writing touched on all these modes, but he most often settled into the formal and historical forms when describing the elements of good design, as displayed at the Kimbell Art Museum or the Nasher Sculpture Center, or when shifting into education mode to share stories about architects like O'Neil Ford. Dillon was frequently very funny. His essay "Need a Plan? Have a Pastry!" compared a proposed renovation at the Dallas Plaza of the Americas complex on Pearl Street to a "cinnamon chocolate cake with a white Hansel and Gretel doorway straight from a pastry tube."[41]

Dillon was sparing in his use of the activist's voice, saving his sharpest columns for issues that really mattered. Perhaps reflecting the larger political culture of North Texas, he avoided stridency, and, more often than not, he attempted to strike a balance that showed readers his position while accommodating dissent. In Dallas, simply pointing publicly to an issue decided in private can be far more controversial than it might at first appear. Dillon's early articles critiquing plans for the Arts District, which read as straightforward accounts of the planning process, ruffled feathers. By January 1985, after Dillon had been writing for the *News* for a little more than three years, Arts and Entertainment editor Lindsay Heinsen could report that "[h]e has taken strong, at times extremely controversial stands on major public issues."[42] This calmly nuanced tone allowed Dillon to address topics that, in Dallas, rarely received public coverage. In discussing heated debates over local arts funding for minority arts groups in 1990, for example, he could critique the new idea of multiculturalism while still suggesting that groups like Teatro Dallas and Dallas Black Dance Theatre deserved a greater piece of the city's funding.[43] His review of Bass Concert Hall in Fort Worth acknowledged both the enormous public affection for the building and its monumental trumpet-blowing angels as well as architects' disdain for it.[44]

Ultimately, this collection of essays is about Dallas itself—the policies, personalities, and projects that have shaped its ascent to the global architectural stage. While at moments it provides something of a capsule urban and planning history of the city in the last decades of the twentieth century, it should not be read as a history. Instead, Dillon's essays provide insight into the culture of public discourse in Texas, suggesting which topics were acceptable and which were not. While Dillon could skewer civic boosters who "believed their own press releases," it is also true that the dialogue in Dallas and many other Texas cities was, and still is, driven by those press releases and by big plans. Questions about the mechanisms and effects of growth and policy decisions remain unanswered and even unaddressed, and appreciation for the consequences of past actions upon the present remains a difficult subject. As scholars Patricia Everidge Hill, Royce Hanson, Robert Fairbanks, and Harvey Graff have all observed, Dallas has long claimed (erroneously) not to have a history at all—and this collection provides further proof that there are many histories waiting to be written.[45] Dillon described Dallas as an "open-ended city," unconstrained by history, tradition, or geography and propelled by the creation of its own distinct model of optimistically market-driven sprawl and inter-metropolitan consumption.

Architectural and urban histories in the United States have primarily focused on the stories of its largest cities, and architecture critics focus on an even smaller subset. Take a look at the bookshelves in any substantial academic library; they are lined with books on New York, Chicago, Los Angeles, Boston, and Washington, DC, but the volume drops off quickly as focus turns to cities outside the national centers of political, economic, and cultural power. Urban historian Alan Lessoff, in his history of Corpus Christi, Texas, aptly summed up the lopsided focus on "primary" and "secondary" cities, with large metropolises providing the dominant narrative for how we understand both architecture and urban history. For Dallas and all Texas cities, there is a more complex equation. Within Texas, Dallas functions as a primary city—but in the world of architecture and planning, it is decidedly secondary. When Lessoff describes Corpus Christi's "ruminations, conversations, and debates [that reflect] an acute . . . awareness of second-tier status," he is also describing Dallas's sense that its aspirations to culture and urban success must measure up against the models provided by the traditional centers of architectural power.[46] The questions, debates, and successes that play out in Texas cities and other major "secondary" cities like Atlanta, Nashville, and Phoenix provide a much-needed context for understanding how the culture of architecture, urban design, and planning adapts and evolves when confronted with a constantly shifting set of localized political and economic conditions.

Looking back to that first question, "Why is Dallas architecture so bad?" with hindsight, it is clear that Dillon did not really think that all Dallas architecture was bad. He deplored its missed opportunities, its bad decisions about big projects, its reluctance to learn quickly, and its missteps in planning Fair Park, the Arts District, and the Trinity River Park. But he maintained a persistent belief in the ability of an engaged citizenry to demand higher quality and greater accountability for urban context. He looked to the work of other cities—examples in Houston, San Antonio, Austin, and El Paso, and beyond—that could provide comparative perspective on decisions made in North Texas. He understood his audience, and for them, he championed the work of small practitioners and the successes of major designers when they came. That success was not just about aesthetic judgment but also, in the tradition of Jane Jacobs and William Whyte, about incrementally creating a richer social life for the city as a whole. As the stakes for urban development continue to soar and issues of equity, gentrification, and the balance between civic ambition and everyday livability continue to occupy the public dialogue across the United States, the argument for the importance of architecture critics has never been stronger.

NOTES

1. David Dillon, "A Brief Walking Tour of the Adolphus Hotel," *DMN*, August 23, 1981.
2. The Goals for Dallas program produced a series of publications beginning in 1966, the first titled simply *Goals for Dallas* (Dallas: Graduate Research Center of the Southwest, 1966). On Jonsson, see Darwin Payne, *No Small Dreams: J. Erik Jonsson—Texas Visionary* (Dallas: DeGolyer Library, 2014) and Richard Tuck, "J. Erik Jonsson: The Practical Dreamer," *Legacies* 15 (Fall 2003): 66–79, as well as the interviews with Jonsson conducted in 1980 and 1981 by the Dallas Mayors' Oral History Project, sponsored by the Dallas Public Library. Royce Hanson, *Civic Culture and Urban Change: Governing Dallas* (Detroit: Wayne State University Press, 2003) discusses Goals for Dallas in the larger context of Dallas political and business culture.
3. Hanson, *Civic Culture*, 19.
4. Robert Fairbanks, *The War on Slums in the Southwest* (Philadelphia: Temple University Press, 2014), 131–140. Fairbanks outlines the complex local, state, and federal politics behind urban renewal policy in Dallas and the decisions that moved toward a mix of private, federal, and state funds for "urban rehabilitation."
5. Dotty Griffith, "Back to Where It Started," *DMN*, July 7, 1974. "Ray Hunt Details History of Union Terminal Project," *DMN*, June 30, 1974.
6. David Gelsanliter provides an inside look into the operations of the *Dallas Morning News* and some perspective on its relationship with the *Dallas Times Herald* in *Fresh Ink: Behind the Scenes at a Major Metropolitan Newspaper* (Denton: University of North Texas Press, 1995), and Judith Segura puts the *DMN* in context within the Belo Corporation's media holdings in *Belo: From Newspapers to New Media* (Austin: University of Texas Press, 2008). See also Jim Schutze's personal remembrance of the demise of the *Herald*, "What Really Killed the *Herald*," *D Magazine* (February 1992).
7. Segura, *Belo*, 187. The marketing study was conducted by Yankelovich, Skelly, and White.
8. Harvey J. Graff, *The Dallas Myth: The Making and Unmaking of an American City* (Minneapolis: University of Minnesota Press, 2010), especially chapter 1, "Locating the City: Three Icons and Images of 'Big D.'"

9. Dillon, "It's the Rocket Ship. No, the Green Building. No, the One with the Hole on Top," *DMN*, December 18, 1988. In an article filled with wordplay, Dillon wrote, "In 1973, Dallas-Fort Worth became a 'metroplex,' for reasons only the North Texas Commission, our regional chamber of commerce, knows for sure. Out of the accidental collision of 'metropolitan' and 'complex,' two honorable, upstanding English words, came nonsense. The Dallas-Fort Worth metroplex turns up in marketing brochures, not in dictionaries. Webster is mute on the subject."

10. Lindsay Heinsen to Pulitzer Jury, January 18, 1985, Dillon Papers, Box 21, Special Collections, University of Texas at Arlington. A frustration of Dillon's career was that he did not receive a Pulitzer Prize for criticism, despite being nominated by the paper several times.

11. Dillon, "Architecture Criticism and the Public," *Texas Architect* 2009 (reprinted in this volume, page 34).

12. Paul Goldberger, "Criticism Today" (keynote address, David Dillon Symposium, David Dillon Center for Texas Architecture and Dallas Museum of Art, April 26, 2012).

13. Mary McLeod's brief essay for the final issue of *Assemblage* is an apt summary of the rise of theory during the 1980s and 1990s. Mary McLeod, "Theory and Practice," *Assemblage* 41 (April 2000): 51.

14. Blair Kamin, "Architecture Criticism: Dead or Alive?" (address, Society of Architectural Historians annual meeting, April 16, 2015). Edited transcription available through *Nieman Reports*, http://niemanreports.org/articles/architecture-criticism-dead-or-alive/.

15. Nancy Levinson, "Critical Beats," *Places Journal* (March 2010), https://doi.org/10.22269/100306.

16. András Szántó, Ray Rinaldi, and Eric Fredericksen, *The Architecture Critic: A Survey of Newspaper Architecture Critics in America* (New York: National Arts Journalism Program, Columbia University, 2001), 8.

17. Dillon, "Crisis in Oak Lawn: Dallas's Most Liveable Area Is Living on Borrowed Time," *DMN*, November 15, 1981.

18. Dillon, "Community," *DMN*, April 18, 2004, in a special section of the *Dallas Morning News* dedicated to "Dallas at the Tipping Point." "Down the Road—Future Will Force Dallas to Become Part of Something Bigger," *DMN*, January 29, 2006.

19. Dillon, "An Anchor in the Real World Is Necessary to Stimulate a Public Dialogue," *Nieman Reports* 46, n. 3 (Fall 1992): 74.

20. Dillon, "Mickeyville. Celebration, Walt Disney's tightly crafted dream village, is taking shape near Orlando," *DMN*, November 26, 1995, and "Disney's Grand Design: Hotels and Resorts Complete the Fantasy World," *DMN*, February 24, 1991. On the idea of consumer taste and the media that shape it, see Monica Penick, *Tastemaker: Elizabeth Gordon, House Beautiful, and the Postwar American Home* (New York: Yale University Press, 2017).

21. He also wrote the annual essay on architecture for the World Book Encyclopedia.

22. Dillon, "With This 'Winter,' Mother Was Content," *DMN*, March 2, 1997.

23. Stephen Fox, "David Dillon, 1941–2010," *OffCite*, July 7, 2010, http://offcite.org/david-dillon-1941–2010/, and Scott Cantrell, "David Dillon, 1941–2010: Architecture Critic Cultivated Respect," *DMN*, June 4, 2010, provide biographic narrative and testimony to Dillon's lasting importance from friends and colleagues.

24. Dillon, *Writing: Experience and Expression* (Lexington, MA: D. C. Heath and Company, 1976), 14.

25. Dillon, *Writing*, 33–39.

26. Dillon, *Dallas Architecture 1936–1986* (Austin: Texas Monthly Press, 1985), with Doug Tomlinson's photographs; Dillon, *The Architecture of O'Neil Ford: Celebrating Place* (Austin: University of Texas Press, 1999); and Mary Carolyn Hollers George, *O'Neil Ford, Architect* (College Station: Texas A&M University Press, 1992). Dillon began the book in the early 1980s, conducting a series of interviews with Ford shortly before the architect died in 1982. Portions of those interviews are preserved in the Dillon Papers, Special Collections, University of Texas at Arlington. The initial book was sidelined because of issues finding a publisher; he returned to the project in the mid-1990s after moving back to Amherst. Editorial materials and research related to the book are in the Dillon Papers, Special Collections, University of Texas at Arlington.

27. Cantrell, "David Dillon," and Blair Kamin, conversation with author, October 4, 2016.

28. Ada Louise Huxtable, *Kicked a Building Lately?* (Berkeley: University of California Press, 1976), xi, 83.

29. David Dunlap's obituary provides a succinct overview of Huxtable's work and impact: "Ada Louise Huxtable, Champion of Liable Architecture, Dies at 91," *New York Times*, January 7, 2013. After her death, an outpouring of testimonials to her impact appeared in newspapers and architecture magazines.

30. Szántó, Rinaldi, and Fredericksen, *The Architecture Critic*, 9–10.

31. Dennis Sharp and Trevor Boddy provided contextual commentary on newspaper criticism relative to other forums at a 2005 seminar organized by the Aga Khan Award for Architecture: Dennis Sharp, "Architectural Criticism: History, Context and Roles," and Trevor Boddy, "The Conundrums of Architectural Criticism," in *Architectural Criticism and Journalism: Global Perspectives*, ed. Mohammad Al-Asad and Majd Musa (Turin: Umberto Allemandi/Aga Khan Award for Architecture, 2006). Sharp refers especially to the association of metropoles with newspaper criticism but also fails to name Ada Louise Huxtable in his listing of important twentieth-century architectural critics (p. 31).

32. For their work, see Allan Temko, *No Way to Build a Ballpark: And Other*

Irreverent Essays on Architecture (San Francisco: Chronicle Books, 1993); Robert Campbell and Peter Vanderwarker, *Cityscapes of Boston: An American City through Time* (Boston: Mariner Books, 1994); and Blair Kamin, *Why Architecture Matters: Lessons from Chicago* (Chicago: University of Chicago Press, 2003).

33. Thomas Fisher, "The Death and Life of Great Architecture Criticism," *Places Journal* (December 2011), https://doi.org/10.22269/111201.

34. From a special section on design at the Barcelona Olympics, see especially the front-page story, "A City Reborn—Olympic Bid Helps Barcelona Reinvent Itself as Pacesetter," *DMN*, May 10, 1992; "Filling the Void—Compromise Must Be the Foundation for World Trade Center Site," *DMN*, July 28, 2002; and "Rise and Fall—Dallas Builds Bridges to the Future, while a Devastated New Orleans Faces its Greatest Challenge," *DMN*, December 26, 2005. Dillon's coverage of the World Trade Center was informed by his earlier coverage of the Oklahoma City bombing, from the initial tragedy to the completion of the memorial. See, for example, "Blast Alters Face of City Forever," *DMN*, April 25, 1995, and "Memorial—On April 19, 2000, a Memorial Will Open to the Public on the Site of the Explosion. Spare Design Creates Churchlike Setting," *DMN*, April 16, 2000.

35. Dillon, "Community" and "Decision Time," *DMN*, April 18, 2004, and "Forward Dallas—A Plan Before the City Council Would Change the Way this City Lives, Works and Moves. Here's Why It Matters to You," *DMN*, May 7, 2006.

36. Dillon, "Impressions of Dallas: A Foreign *Object*," *DMN*, June 30, 1991.

37. See for example, Dillon, "Fort Worth: Where Sundance West Begins—The Mixed-Use Project Shows How to Start Revitalizing a City's Core," *DMN*, June 14, 1992; "Uptown's Victory in the Making—After Early Struggles, Perot Jr. Presides over Urban Boomtown," *DMN*, June 21, 2006; and "Dallas Developer Builds Reputation for Creativity—Cheatham's Eclectic Mix of Modernity Has Trusted Foundation," *DMN*, June 23, 2002.

38. Audio of Dillon's interview with Crow is preserved in the Dillon Papers, Special Collections, University of Texas at Arlington. The controlling impact of developers on urban architecture remains little studied and was of particular interest to Dillon. The manuscript for his unpublished book on the Boston-based developer John Rouse is also in the Dillon Papers, University of Texas at Arlington. Current scholarship that expands our understanding of developers includes Sara Stevens, *Developing Expertise: Architecture and Real Estate in Metropolitan America* (New York: Yale University Press, 2016), and Charles Rice, *Interior Urbanism: Architecture, John Portman and Downtown America* (London: Bloomsbury, 2016).

39. Dillon, "A Pratt's Eye View—The Architect Depicts a Future Dallas that's Pulled Itself Together," *DMN*, November 18, 1990. Pratt's plan was published as *Dallas Visions for Community: Toward a 21st Century Urban Design* (Dallas: Dallas Institute of Humanities and Culture, 1992). Mullen's work

was featured in "Tough Houses—Three Architects Buck the Traditional with Unconventional, Well-Defined Houses," *DMN*, March 1, 1988. Dillon later noted that a short piece on houses designed by architect Edward Baum received more reader response than many of his articles on big planning issues: "Readers Root for Baum's Simplicity," *DMN*, July 25, 2004.

40. Alexandra Lange, *Writing About Architecture: Mastering the Language of Buildings and Cities* (New York: Princeton Architectural Press, 2012), 10–11.

41. Dillon, "Need a Plan? Have a Pastry," *DMN*, March 3, 1991.

42. Heinsen to Pulitzer Jury, January 18, 1985.

43. Dillon, "Cultural Divide," *DMN*, October 18, 1992.

44. Dillon, "Classical Concoction: Performance Hall Design Delights in Days Long Gone," *DMN*, May 9, 1998.

45. Hanson, *Civic Culture and Urban Change*—see especially chapter 2, "The City That Invented Itself"—and Graff, *The Dallas Myth*, as well as Patricia Everidge Hill, *Dallas: The Making of a Modern City* (Austin: University of Texas Press, 1996), xvi–xxii.

46. Alan Lessoff, *Where Texas Meets the Sea: Corpus Christi and Its History* (Austin: University of Texas Press, 2015), 2, 12.

1

THE
CRITIC'S
VOICE

This collection contains only two of David Dillon's essays from sources other than the *Dallas Morning News*. Together, these two pieces form bookends for Dillon's career and show a consistency of purpose even across the years of development and change that separate them.

The first is the 1980 essay that put him on the map in Dallas architecture circles—"Why Is Dallas Architecture So Bad?" While Dillon does not explicitly answer his own question, he points to one of the major weaknesses in architecture culture in Dallas: leadership. While the audience for this *D Magazine* piece was certainly the general public, secondary and intended audiences were the developers and architecture executives responsible for much of the Dallas commercial landscape in 1980. Those developers and CEOs remained both the subject and the object of Dillon's criticism, the key to improving the dialogue and the quality of architecture in North Texas.

From that early shot across the bow, Dillon continued to hammer away at the same issues, asking the public to hold leaders accountable for decisions that affected their own neighborhoods and quality of life. He defined architecture criticism broadly, to encompass the intertwined issues of planning, preservation, and economic development that are critical to the daily lives of a broad citizenry. In the latter essay, "Architecture Criticism and the Public," published in *Texas*

Architect, Dillon specifically considers the fate of public discussion of these issues, given the decline of newspaper criticism, and supports the development of new local and regional publications, both in print and online, to take its place. When Dillon wrote this piece in 2008, blogs were on the rise and social media barely existed. Given how quickly platforms and audiences change in the online world, with the popularity of blogs expanding and shrinking and entire websites, such as the city-focused Gothamist, first deleted on a whim, then later restored, Dillon's advice to cultivate professional and local networks to create audiences remains evergreen.

Why is Dallas architecture so bad? Because we're trying to look like too many other cities: big and boring

D MAGAZINE, MAY 1980

As originally published, "Why Is Dallas Architecture So Bad?" (fig. 1.1) included short individual building reviews of good and bad buildings, inside and outside Dallas. Those mini-reviews are not included here; instead, the focus is on Dillon's synthetic take on Dallas architecture culture.

"Dallas is a 'gimme another one of those' city when it comes to architecture. Very conservative, uneasy with anything new. I couldn't sell an angle there to save my life." The vice president of one of Houston's top architectural firms said it, and few people in Dallas who know anything about architecture would disagree. Although there is an estimated $300 million in new construction in downtown Dallas, there are few good buildings. When you ask why, you get various explanations: The average Dallas client cares about location, plumbing, and air conditioning, not design; no Dallas architectural firms are sufficiently strong and self-confident to do good work in spite of dull clients; Dallas is a new city, with little architectural heritage to refer to; no one at the top of business and banking is willing to blaze the trail for good design; the general public doesn't know anything about good architecture and consequently doesn't insist on it.

The last is popular among architects and developers, and highly

Routes: Mapping the Odd History of Dallas' Street Names

Real Estate Roulette: Pay Too Much Now or Pay Even More Later

Bogus Burgundy: The Wine You're Drinking May Be a Fraud

All in the Familia: The Medranos' Master Plan to Run Dallas Politics

DALLAS / FORT WORTH

MAY 1980 / $1.75

WHY IS DALLAS ARCHITECTURE SO BAD?

1.1. *"Why Is Dallas Architecture So Bad?" was the cover story for* D Magazine *in May 1980. Image courtesy* D Magazine.

questionable. Regardless of what the public "knows" about architecture, it certainly isn't indifferent.

Before Reunion Tower and the Hyatt Regency Hotel, Dallas's skyline consisted of a flying red horse and a glowing phallic column atop the Republic National Bank, which put it in roughly the same category as

1.2. *Philip Johnson, Thanks-Giving Square, Dallas, 1976. Photograph by Carol Highsmith. The Lyda Hill Texas Collection of Photographs in Carol M. Highsmith's America Project, Library of Congress, Prints and Photographs Division.*

Omaha and Indianapolis. When Dallasites talked about their sublime skyline, it was more from wishful thinking than direct observation. Reunion and the Hyatt changed all that by giving the city a genuine landmark building, a civic symbol that expresses visually many of the things Dallasites like to think are true of the city as a whole. It is chic, glittery, futuristic, a bold anchor for the entire west end of downtown; it calls up images of affluence, high fashion, and self-confidence, things the rest of the country imagines Dallas to be. A few months after it was completed, the Hyatt had passed the postcard test—and worked itself onto menus, corporate logos, party decorations, even the credits for the ten o'clock news. Today it is difficult to remember what the skyline looked like without it. When friends come from out of town, the obvious move is to drive them past the Hyatt or take them up to the ball for a drink, not simply because this is a pleasant way to pass a few hours but because the experience answers the inevitable question, "What is Dallas really like?" As architecture, the Hyatt matters because it's a clear statement about the city. It's a good quick read.

Philip Johnson's Thanks-Giving Square also matters, although for different reasons (fig. 1.2). As a design it is far less successful than his Water Garden in Fort Worth, which functions as a true public square. In contrast, Thanks-Giving Square's high walls back people off instead of inviting them in, the way a roadblock diverts cars. And the attempt to combine a water garden with a chapel, restaurants, and truck terminal reflects a distressing Dallas tendency to get as much as possible out of every square foot of ground. If a skating rink could have been worked into the plan, one suspects it would have.

And yet, Thanks-Giving Square works, as anyone who's tried to get in on a warm spring day realizes. Secretaries and stockbrokers jostle one another for a spot on the sloping concrete walls, while children slap at the cascading water (No Wading Allowed!), and older people, with nothing particular to do, sun themselves on the grass. It is tempting to say that Thanks-Giving Square is popular by default, because it is virtually the only green space downtown. But that is only part of its appeal. It is a triangle in a sea of squares and rectangles, an intimate space in the midst of cavernous, impersonal ones. It provides a change of pace in an otherwise monotonous downtown, and together with Reunion says something basic about what people want a downtown to be: a place with variety, a sense of proportion and human scale, surprising views mixed with familiar reference points, a place with some drama, some uplift, yet in which the observer is not intimidated. The public understands these things as well as the architects and planners, and responds enthusiastically when given half a chance.

Downtown Dallas currently provides few such opportunities. A city that gives tickets for jaywalking and sleeping on benches in front of City Hall and forces street vendors to sell food prepared and wrapped in some sanitary kitchen ten miles away doesn't really understand urban life, however well it may understand ordinances. People come to city centers to talk, argue, window-shop, and show off. But right now, most people go to downtown Dallas to work and shop, period. It's a one-shift area. Many Dallasites would probably agree with the executive who admitted that the only time he went downtown was to sign a note at the bank, and that now that interest rates were so high he probably wouldn't be doing that very often.

Pedestrian shopping malls, so successful in Boston, Minneapolis, San Francisco, and Philadelphia, are still opposed by downtown merchants because, among other things, they eliminate parking spaces. Like most Southwestern cities, Dallas has developed an unnatural dependency on the automobile, generally at the expense of street life. Historically, downtown Dallas was a highly urban place, with shops, hotels, and offices organized into a tight, cohesive fabric. At the moment, Dallas is mainly a series of towering glass boxes interrupted by parking lots. Visitors are constantly surprised to find sidewalks suddenly playing out in mid-stride, or else being sliced in two by a major traffic artery. It's a major logistical problem to walk from, say, Union Terminal to the warehouse district, or from City Hall across town to the Southland Center. Downtown sidewalks are simply part of the street grid, not places for people. They provide few opportunities to pause and rest—thus the popularity of Thanks-Giving Square—few inducements, in fact, to do anything except trudge on from one block to the next.

Dallasites also like to boast about the climate and the tradition of great open space, although as Edmund Bacon, former executive director of the Philadelphia Planning Commission, pointed out several years ago, they usually experience both from the comfort of their air-conditioned sedans. Ours is not an ideal climate. Much of the year it is too hot, too bright, too windy; it's a climate of sudden shifts and extremes, for which downtown offers few compensations in the form of arcades and plazas and tree-lined malls. Dallas could learn a lot from Mediterranean cities about how to protect pedestrians and shoppers from sun and heat—except, of course, that this might mean giving up a certain amount of prime retail and commercial space at street level. And if there is one principle that is followed religiously by Dallas developers, it is this: Use every square inch you can. Build right to the sidewalk, and collect as much rent as possible. You can count on the fingers of one hand the number of downtown commercial buildings that acknowledge the existence of a pedestrian public. One Main Place has a large, sunken plaza that could use a lot more landscaping and a lot less concrete; the plaza in front of One Dallas Centre could turn out to be an important public place, as could the enclosed garden/atrium in Plaza of the Americas. But that's about all. Marbled bank lobbies do not count as public spaces.

Other cities are well ahead of Dallas on this point. In Houston, for example, I. M. Pei's new Texas Commerce Tower will occupy only the back third of its lot, the remainder being given over to public park and plaza. The result promises to be considerably less intimidating than Pennzoil Place across the street, which is not at its best at ground level. In New York City, the Office of Midtown Planning has devised a series of zoning incentives to increase pedestrian use of all new buildings in the area. In return for a few more floors of rentable space, developers are being required to create public spaces on the lower floors of the new buildings, including indoor plazas and malls. The Citicorp building now has a retail mall on the lower three floors, and the Philip Morris Building, designed by Ulrich Franzen, will house a branch of the Whitney Museum. Even the Tandy Center in Fort Worth, in most respects a dull, off-the-shelf project, has a branch of the public library in the shopping mall. There are presently few incentives for this kind of development in Dallas. "We're still overly concerned with punitive measures here," says architect and planner Dave Braden. "The city likes to read the rule book to developers instead of giving them incentives to do something really good."

Dallas has begun construction of an all-weather skybridge system, following the lead of Minneapolis, Philadelphia, and other cities. As one might expect, the bridges now connect only office buildings and parking garages, but plans call for them to be tied into the retail core; as the experience of other cities has shown, they work best in areas of high density, much less successfully on the fringes. Edmund Bacon proposed a skyway system that would begin at the Convention Center, run through City Hall and the library, and spill into the second floor of Neiman Marcus. The idea, Bacon explained, is to direct the "golden flow" of convention traffic into the retail core instead of allowing it to be dispelled aimlessly around the periphery. While Neiman's would undoubtedly endorse the idea, it's unclear how other merchants would react, particularly those at street level. But at least the skyway system is a means of tying the downtown together without adding more traffic islands and one-way streets.

It's far more difficult to do anything about scale and texture downtown, even though both are extremely important to the overall experience of cities. Every summer friends return from Europe with stories about this quaint little city or that, by which they usually mean a city of narrow, crooked streets, sidewalk cafes, and old, humanly scaled buildings—terribly inefficient by American standards, yet obviously alive. At $50 a square foot, it's difficult to convince a developer to think small, just as the predominance of the International Style in high-rise buildings, with its emphasis on smooth finishes and high gloss, makes it difficult to think in terms of texture and ornamentation. We have to rely upon older buildings for that, and occasionally a newer one, like Republic Bank. Like most new cities, Dallas has systematically bulldozed most of its older buildings, leaving the Adolphus and the Wilson block and "Big Red" to remind us of the delights of ornamentation and detailing, all the glorious excess that somehow says "manmade." What we do have is a warehouse district that is largely intact. Most of the buildings date from 1900 to 1920, are constructed of brick or reinforced concrete, and are four or five stories tall. If properly developed, this area could become a significant architectural counterpoint to downtown, along the lines of Boston's Quincy Market or Minneapolis's warehouse district. What's lacking is some cooperative commitment from banks, developers, and the city. Five years ago, bond money was appropriated for the development of a mall along Market Street, but it wasn't until March 1980 that bricks were laid. At this rate, the warehouse district will be completed at about the same time that Plaza of the Americas makes the National Register.

It's easier, of course, to point out what's missing architecturally in a city than to explain how to go about filling the gaps. Bad architecture frequently just happens, whereas good architecture requires planning, commitment, pride, and a conceptual reach that goes beyond the bottom line and the fluctuations of the economy. Dallas undoubtedly has these qualities, but with a few notable exceptions they aren't showing up in its architecture. "Well, we're a young city," apologists say. True enough, compared to Boston and New York. But Dallas is approximately the same age as San Francisco, Houston, and Atlanta, all of which have attained a high degree of architectural excellence in spite of their youth. It's interesting that Dallas thinks of itself as young, tough, and aggressive when it comes to business, and merely adolescent when it comes to design. At 140 years old, the rhetoric sounds a bit tired.

Most cities with national reputations for architecture and planning also have strong and vocal schools of architecture nearby. Boston has Harvard and MIT, Philadelphia has the University of Pennsylvania, Minneapolis has the University of Minnesota, Houston has Rice, and so on. Whether the teachers are practitioners or the molders of practitioners, the presence of these schools raises the level of discourse about the built environment in ways that are unknown in Dallas. Here, architecture surfaces as a public issue mainly in connection with zoning; the talk is largely about quantity rather than quality. By and large, the Dallas Museum of Fine Arts ignores architecture as a subject for exhibition. Last fall, the AIA-sponsored "Celebration" fizzled through a combination of bad timing and general apathy, although a similar event has been going on in Houston for four years, getting larger and more popular each time. The closest school of architecture is at the University of Texas at Arlington, a new school that is just beginning to find a direction. Its impact on Dallas architecture so far has been minimal and will probably stay that way for several years to come. Among the local architectural community, it has the reputation for being a source of competent technicians rather than fresh thinking about design.

One often hears the complaint from Dallas architects, including the very best ones, that most of the important commissions go to outsiders. This is probably true, though no truer than in Denver or Minneapolis or many other cities. But statistics are not the issue—quality is. If a city gets second-rate work from imported, nationally known architects, it should kick itself, but if the buildings are good, responsive to local needs, it makes no difference who did them. A city can't have too many good buildings, and the local architects who live with them can be inspired in the same way that painters can be inspired: by seeing other paintings. Dallas's record on this issue is mixed. I. M. Pei, for example, has done two first-rate buildings in Dallas, and Welton Becket probably transcended himself with the Hyatt Regency. Philip Johnson, on the other hand, has done far better work in Houston and Fort Worth than in Dallas. Thanks-Giving Square might have been done more successfully by a local architect, one with more feeling for the city and the climate, but it's just as important to keep in mind that the majority of downtown buildings, old and new, have been designed by local architects.

What Dallas architects need far more than patronage and a pat on the back is strong—one is tempted to say "inspired"—leadership at the highest levels: from the major banks, which could be the Medici of Dallas and aren't, from someone with sufficient taste and clout to go after the very best work possible. Any building is a collaboration between architect, client, and available resources. Assuming enough of the latter, then whether a building turns out to be good or bad depends on how well architect and client communicate. Theoretically, the client defines the needs and the objectives of a project, and the architect interprets and translates them into a design. In actual fact, one is usually in control. Someone once asked Houston developer Gerald Hines how far he pushes the architect on his projects. "Until he says that he's going to quit. Then I know I've pushed far enough."

Architectural history contains numerous examples of how the taste and determination of one client brought a great building into existence. When Mrs. Phyllis Lambert, daughter of the president of Seagram Distilling Company, saw the initial drawings for the company's new headquarters in Manhattan, she threw up her hands in disgust, convinced her father to put the project on hold, and then set out on a world-wide search for the best architect and design she could find. She found both in Mies van der Rohe, who, because he didn't have a license to practice in New York State, hired Philip Johnson as his associate. The result was possibly the finest metal and glass skyscraper ever built, the Seagram Building.

In Minneapolis, Kenneth Dayton, president of Dayton-Hudson Corporation (Target Stores), almost single-handedly brought in Johnson/Burgee to design the IDS Center, and was instrumental in the selection of Kenzo Tange to design the Minneapolis Institute of Art and Hardy Holzman Pfeiffer to design Orchestra Hall, recognized as one of the finest performance halls in the country. The de Menil family has worked more quietly for the arts and architecture in Houston (the

Rothko Chapel), as has Ruth Carter Johnson in Fort Worth (Amon Carter Museum, Fort Worth Water Garden).

Dallas is still waiting for this kind of leadership. The closest it's come is Erik Jonsson, who concentrated on the large public and institutional buildings that tell the rest of the country that Dallas is a city—City Hall, the regional airport, a public library. The first is a masterpiece and the second far-sighted; one can only speculate about what might have happened had Jonsson turned his attention to downtown. Vincent Carrozza's One Dallas Centre is an outstanding building, but only one, and probably not prominent enough to start a revolution. Raymond Nasher has done several tasteful shopping centers and excellent small office buildings, but has yet to move into larger projects. Stanley Marcus, a national taste maker in fashion and retailing, has shown little interest in architecture.

The one person in Dallas with enough clout and money to change the shape of downtown is developer Trammell Crow. Like his Houston counterpart, Gerald Hines, Crow started out after World War II building warehouses, then moved into apartments, hotels, and shopping centers (Peachtree Center, Embarcadero Center in San Francisco). Anticipating the growth of Dallas as a fashion and merchandising center, he built the Dallas Apparel Mart and the World Trade Center, two of the most successful facilities of their type in the country. And the Loews Anatole is, by Crow's and others' estimates, one of the most successful new hotels in the country. Crow is a man of great energy and determination and considerable personal charm, who has yet to raise the quality of Dallas's architecture. His local buildings range from gruesome to competent, but never rise to the standards of Pennzoil Place or One Shell Plaza, both Hines projects.

Among architects Crow has the reputation of being a meddler who insists on drawing the plans and specifying the materials on many of his projects, including the brick on the Anatole. "I love the timeless quality of brick," he says. "It reminds me of Rome." Says one designer who's worked for both Hines and Crow: "Hines is very exacting and watches the numbers very closely, but he's willing to let the architect be the architect. Trammell, on the other hand, likes to work the whole concept out himself and then tell the architect, 'Put a little finish on this, will you?' The results speak for themselves."

Crow agrees that he and his staff participate actively in the design of his projects and says it's the only way to get them finished. "I'm only interested in projects that get built, and that means staying on top of things all the time. If you just turn a building over to an architect, he'll ruin it on you. Hines may do more spectacular buildings, but I'll take my organization over his any day."

On the subject of hiring local architects, which he does often, Crow is equally emphatic: "There's plenty of talent right here in Dallas. There's no need to run off to New York every time you want to put up a new building. I feel a responsibility to support the local firms, give something back to the community."

In addition to the nearly completed Diamond Shamrock Tower (Jarvis Putty Jarvis), Crow has plans for a 900,000-square-foot office tower across from Catedral Santuario de Guadalupe on Ross (to be designed by Beran and Shelmire, architects for the Anatole and the World Trade Center), and a forty-story, 1.3-million-square-foot building at the corner of Ross and Harwood, overlooking the site for the new Dallas Museum of Fine Arts. He's also recently purchased a tract of land in the northeast section of Woodall Rodgers, near the proposed site for Symphony Hall. In other words, Trammell Crow has a great deal to say about how the proposed downtown arts district will look. This is small consolation to arts supporters, who privately mock Crow's taste while standing in awe of his power. Crow, in turn, asks impatiently why he and other developers should sit on projects indefinitely while the arts groups decide if they want to buy this plot of land or that. One moment he'll refer to them as the "artsy-fartsies"; the next he'll reiterate his love for Dallas and say that he wants to see something good happen in the arts district. At the moment, however, it's unclear what the solution will be.

The situation surrounding the new museum and the arts district only underscores how unsettled things still are in downtown Dallas. As Henry Cobb, architect of One Dallas Centre, pointed out at the dedication last year, "Dallas is now at a crossroads in its development. On the one hand, it has to avoid purely arbitrary invention, mere thingery; on the other, it has to avoid creating dozens of homogenized buildings that are simply dropped onto a site and left. The goal is to create a true urban context."

Unlike most large cities in the United States, Dallas has a chance to do this. It is not locked in. Options remain. An estimated 20 percent of the nine hundred acres within the central core are undeveloped. The economy is strong, the corporate base is growing rapidly. The city is up for grabs architecturally.

Louis Kahn, designer of the Kimbell Art Museum, once described a city as "a place where a small boy, as he walks through it, may see something that will tell him what he wants to do his whole life." Perhaps in a few years, if the choices that are made now are enlightened instead of expedient, a small boy will look up at the Dallas skyline and decide that he wants to become an architect.

Architecture criticism and the public

TEXAS ARCHITECT, 2009

Dillon gave this talk to architecture professionals in 2008, address-ing the decline of print architecture criticism in the United States and the potential for local and regional publications, in print and online, to take their place. Dillon spoke specifically to the idea that the architecture profession could sponsor these publications, through organizations like the American Institute of Architects (AIA) and its local and state chapters. The recommendations that come at the end of the essay were intended for architects, but they apply to anyone wishing to start a blog, newsletter, or magazine about architecture.

This version has been edited and adapted from the print version published in Texas Architect, *a professional magazine published by the Texas Society of Architects. The original address was to the Council of Architectural Component Executives, who met in Richmond, Virginia, in 2008.*

I've just returned from a trip to Amsterdam and Paris and one of the things that surprised me—besides twenty-dollar chicken salad sand-wiches washed down with fifteen-dollar glasses of *vin ordinaires*—was the number of architecture and design magazines for sale in airports, train stations, bookstores, and sidewalk newsstands. They were everywhere, all the major ones—*Architectural Record, Architecture Review, El Croquis, Architectura, Viva, Domus, Casa Bella*—plus dozens of smaller, more technical publications and a few academic journals.

This, obviously, is not the situation here in the United States, where right now we have only one national architecture magazine, *Architectural Record*, one national celebrity interiors magazine, *Architectural Digest*, and a handful of smaller design or trade publications with geographical or topical emphasis, such as *Dwell, Metropolis*, and *Contract*.

Progressive Architecture has been gone for fifteen years. *Architecture* folded several years ago, to be succeeded by *Architect*, which seems like *People* magazine for designers, though it may evolve into something more substantial. What's left is a collection of shelter and lifestyle magazines aimed at interior decorators, furniture manufacturers, and readers with an unhealthy interest in wicker furniture and throw pillows.

The result of all this publishing activity is a huge vacuum in serious design commentary, in which architecture, the most public of the arts, is losing touch with its public—its customer base, if you like—and has less and less influence on how our communities are planned and designed.

Yet as we all know, vacuums exist to be filled and savvy design magazines, including AIA chapter magazines, help to shape the design discussion in their regions, provided they understand what is happening in the larger publishing world and where they fit in that volatile environment.

NEWSPAPERS IN DECLINE

To restate the obvious, American newspapers are in a meltdown mode, with revenues dropping and market share shrinking. And one of the most endangered areas of coverage is art and architecture.

This coverage is being marginalized or eliminated across the country. To give you an idea of what this means, three years ago my paper, the *Dallas Morning News*, had seventeen full-time arts writers, one of the largest arts staffs in the country. Now it has only five, and that number will likely drop further. I took a buyout a year ago and now do only special projects for the paper, which means that I write six or eight times a year compared with between eighty and one hundred times before. And I will not be replaced. The architecture beat will disappear, ironically at a time when Dallas and Fort Worth are rising to international prominence in the arts.

The same thing is happening in other cities. As far as I know, Washington, Atlanta, Houston, and Miami no longer have full-time architecture critics. Minneapolis recently sacked its long-time architecture writer, and New York City is down to one full-time architecture critic, Nicolai Ouroussoff at the *Times*, whereas a few years ago it had three or four.

This is disastrous because newspaper critics are the front line of architecture coverage, always more timely and often more comprehensive than design magazines. Newspapers are where the public gets most of its architectural information, as well as most of its information about planning, community development, neighborhood preservation, and other matters that it cares about. Online sources can't begin to plug this gap, which means that conversation has virtually stopped on most of these critical issues. Dialogue and debate have given way to deafening silence.

The justification from publishers is economics. The price of newsprint is skyrocketing; the Internet is killing ad revenue; people aren't reading anymore; architecture coverage is too specialized, too esoteric, for a time of shrinking resources and shrinking readership. These justifications are heard less often in discussions of sports or fashion coverage, which seem to be exempt from cuts in many papers.

However, I don't believe for a second that the public no longer cares about architecture and planning, that it's become a niche subject. Just look at the proliferation of design and planning review boards around the country. Most communities have at least one—my home town of Amherst, Massachusetts, has three. Whether this indicates that the public is passionate about design or scared to death of what architects might do to them is a different matter.

The same can be said of the growth of architecture support groups, patterned in some ways after the Museum League in New York or the Chicago Architectural Foundation. Texas, where I've spent most of my career, has two exemplary community design organizations: the Rice Design Alliance in Houston, which has a broad civic agenda encompassing parks and urban planning as well as architecture, and the Dallas Architecture Forum, which for ten years has been bringing architects from around the world to talk and teach, and in the process has raised the design consciousness of the entire city.

What's lacking everywhere, however, is a common language and shared frame of reference for talking about these issues. Architects and the public inhabit different worlds when it comes to identifying and analyzing what really matters in communities.

Architectural Record, for which I've written for fifteen years, recently polled six national critics about what was most important to residents in their part of the country. And almost without exception the key issues were public and civic—affordable housing, regional planning, access to transit, neighborhood preservation, congestion, sprawl, open space. Architecture with a capital *A,* as in what are Rem Koolhaas or Frank Gehry up to now, barely made the list. Which is to say that there is a big disconnect these days between what architects are doing and what the magazines are publishing, and what the public is doing and interested in.

If you doubt that, drive around any new suburb or subdivision and see what's being built. The new houses are mostly imitations of traditional styles, grotesquely done in many cases, but still worlds away from what turns up in the architecture magazines and trendy style sections.

Correctly or not, the public perceives the profession to be largely indifferent to its concerns. They think architects are interested mainly in architecture as art, in architecture as a business, or in defending the autonomy of the profession, which has been largely squandered, whereas they see themselves as custodians of the public realm and the social and communal elements of architecture and design.

This is a very simplistic division, I admit, but the communication gap is real, and architects and architectural journalists bear much of the responsibility for creating it, and for closing it.

So what might we do? Here are a few ideas.

- Exploit the possibilities of the Internet because that's where the biggest gains in readership are going to occur. One great advantage of the Web is that it is boundless, with no space constraints. You may be restricted to one or two photos of a project in the magazine, but you can put up twenty on the Web. You can also include interviews, reader surveys, resources lists, and so on.
- Most architecture magazines are too project driven and too object driven. We all enjoy looking at stunning images, but by themselves they're not going to get you where you want to go. To have influence

in your communities, you've got to be more issue driven and topic driven. Local, local, local is the new publishing mantra in our instant access age.

- Architecture magazines written exclusively, or nearly so, by practitioners are a bad idea because most architects can't write, and those who can tend to write for one another, not for the wider public you want to reach.
- Be vocal and out front editorially on issues of local and regional importance. Be willing to take a stand. If you want to raise community design awareness, to start a dialogue, you've got to take some chances and speak out editorially.
- To become more visible, sponsor community forums, small design competitions, guest speakers, and lecture series. This may require partnering with other organizations, such as schools of architecture, friends of the library, the local museum league. Become conveners.

Another way to put this is that architects and architecture magazines are looking for a way to regain influence and establish authority, which is not the same thing as power.

Power is the ability to make something happen, or not happen, or happen differently. Authority is a different matter. Authority means that your work is read, listened to, talked about, paid attention to. Influence or authority comes not from stopping Project X in its tracks, but from being able to gradually sharpen community perceptions about good design, and thereby raise public expectations about what is acceptable and what is not.

The great critic Ada Louise Huxtable once said that the public knows its rights when it comes to the law, or Social Security, or Medicare; it's up on all the entitlement programs. But it does not know what it is entitled to in terms of architecture, urban design, or environmental policy.

One job of a good design magazine is to help educate the public about its rights in these matters because in the end its biggest ally is a concerned public and its most powerful weapon is the ability to arouse public opinion in the service of good design.

2

RETHINKING DOWNTOWN

The emptying of American downtowns began in the post–World War II years as businesses and residents began their steady flow to the newly exploding suburbs. When Dillon began writing about Dallas and Texas cities in the 1980s, the full impact of that decades-long exodus had begun to settle in: empty streets, empty office buildings, thoughtless demolitions, and negative growth defined downtowns across the state. Dillon's writing on the subject of civic identity and urban development is defined by these problems as they existed primarily in Dallas, with a healthy dose of skeptical comparison with how other cities had handled similar challenges. Recurring themes include the roles of private industry, real estate developers, and local government in determining the goals and pace of downtown redevelopment. Equally important were public attitudes toward downtown. Dillon noted that Dallasites had not traditionally been "plaza people" but that those attitudes were beginning to change.* The need to balance housing, public space, transit, and commercial development cried out for clear planning priorities and policies, but as Dillon's coverage clearly

---

* Dillon, "Plazas with a Pulse: Havens for the Harried Bring Workers out of Their Offices," *DMN*, October 6, 1987.

shows, Texas cities were led by private property rights more than by the idealistic *communitas* of city planning.

The articles gathered here provide an overview of ideas and approaches that have reshaped downtowns since the 1980s, beginning with Dillon's synopsis of Mayor Erik Jonsson's ambitious planning that fueled growth in the 1970s and early 1980s. The oil bust of 1986 and subsequent recession slowed redevelopment to a snail's pace, leading to a period of renewed planning. An unregulated building boom followed in the 1990s, prompting Dillon to call Dallas "Comeback City" in 1993. In 2002, a seven-part series, written with urban planner Antonio DiMambro, created the "Go Dallas" catchphrase, identifying the projects and attitudes needed to continue the city's attention on remaking downtown.* Dillon catalogs these strategies and approaches, often with the benefit of hindsight, and focuses on lessons that could propel cities toward smarter decision-making and planning in the twenty-first century.

By his final columns as a full-time critic, in 2005 and 2006, Dillon's take on city planning and urban development was fully mature, honed across years of watching Texas cities grapple with big, ambitious designs that left underlying social and economic problems untouched. His consistent takeaway was to stay focused and think small: "What's lacking are innovative small plans, tailored to the special qualities of individual places, plans that recognize that cities and towns develop slowly, incrementally. The big-bang, one-shot solution dies hard everywhere."[†]

---

[*] The series included articles by rival mayoral candidates Laura Miller and Tom Dunning, published under the headline "Visions for Downtown," as well as a series of editorials spearheaded by Dillon and DiMambro, beginning with "Go Dallas—A Vision. Of the City. For the City." *DMN*, February 10, 2002.

[†] Dillon, "In Looking to the Big Picture, Cities Overlook Much of Importance," *DMN*, March 5, 1989.

Erik Jonsson: Contemporary Dallas is a testament to his grand vision as mayor

AUGUST 17, 1986

Dillon excelled at telling stories about architecture and cities through focusing on stories about people. This profile of legendary Dallas mayor Erik Jonsson came early in his career at the newspaper, and he used Jonsson's ambitions as a foil for discussing Dallas's civic aspirations.

"Dallas's major challenge is to create and shape the future instead of being run over by it."

Thus spake Mayor Erik Jonsson when announcing his candidacy for a third term in 1967. It is the kind of statement that usually induces public snoring, but in Jonsson's case the rhetoric was flying on more than wind. Planning for a new City Hall and a new regional airport was under way. The library system was expanding to distant corners of the city. The first phase of the ambitious Goals for Dallas program had been completed.

From all appearances, the future seemed as likely to be run over by Jonsson as he by it.

Erik Jonsson was mayor of Dallas from 1964 to 1971, and, by any reasonable estimate, he is the most worldly and visionary person ever to hold the job. From the day he took office, fewer than three months after the Kennedy assassination, he trained his eye on the far horizon, a prairie Columbus who knew that the greatest opportunities are those that nobody can yet see.

He envisioned the city as a gigantic, integrated circuit in which everything from City Council meetings to ambulance service and traffic lights would run with computerized precision. It was a grand vision of the City Efficient, shaped by an engineer's fascination with order and precision, yet without the chilly narrowness that such terms often imply. As mayor he combined the roles of elder statesman and *pater familias*, someone entitled by reputation and circumstance to stand above routine political squabbling and dream grand dreams.

"Erik represented what Dallas wanted to be and feared that it might never become because of the assassination," says former city manager George Schrader, who toiled for fifteen years to implement Jonsson's dreams. "He was gracious, genial, a successful and unblemished entrepreneur. The public was willing to let him be the city for a time."

Erik Jonsson was born in Brooklyn on September 6, 1901, the only son of Swedish immigrants. He studied engineering at Rensselaer Polytechnic Institute and moved to Dallas in 1934 to be the secretary for Geophysical Service Inc., which did seismographic surveys for major oil companies. To keep its crews busy during slack times, GSI began exploring for oil on its own. It was so successful that it split off from the seismographic division and was eventually bought by a larger oil company in 1941.

Jonsson and three other GSI employees—Eugene McDermott, Cecil Green, and H. B. Peacock—were given a ten-day option to purchase the seismographic division. They spent nine days frantically patching together the necessary financing, calling in every chit they had, and on the tenth day—Saturday, December 6—closed the deal.

"There was a recession in oil exploration about that time," Jonsson explained years later. "So we were buying a business that was almost junk. But we took our chances on this because we did know how to run the business. I decided on Sunday afternoon I'd go play a game of golf, and on my way out to the course I heard the Pearl Harbor news. I thought maybe we had lost everything that we'd put up yesterday—in my case a lot of money that I didn't have. So maybe I was broke again."

There were more opportunities for oil exploration than Jonsson anticipated, and GSI turned a modest profit for the rest of the war. Then the familiar boom-and-bust cycle resumed. The company needed another product to offset the inevitable slumps in the oil and gas business. The initial solution was an electronic submarine-hunting device, the extension of seismographic technology to a different kind of quarry. This led in turn to transistors and semiconductors for the suddenly exploding electronics industry.

In 1950 a new parent company known as Texas Instruments was formed, with GSI as a subsidiary. From a modest beginning on Lemmon Avenue, TI has grown to net sales of $5 billion, with a remarkable string of electronic breakthroughs: the first pocket transistor radio, the first handheld calculator, single-chip microcomputers, 3-D seismic surveying, and, not least, E.T.'s English teacher, Speak & Spell.

Keeping the company on track during the turbulent early years of high tech required not only intense research but also strategic planning. In 1952 Jonsson and his colleagues began regular planning conferences, at which executives, scientists, and technicians established policy and set long-range goals for the company. The objective was not only fresh ideas but also developing a sense of common purpose. Jonsson brought the TI model of corporate planning with him to Dallas City Hall.

Jonsson became mayor in February 1964, succeeding Earl Cabell, who had resigned to run for the US House of Representatives. The city had been drained of its pride and self-confidence by the Kennedy assassination. Books and articles were appearing from all quarters portraying Dallas as a backwater of hatred and bigotry. Jonsson's first job was to rebuild the city's self-esteem, and he chose to do it without the public relations experts recommended by City Hall pundits. He relied instead on his own commanding presence and a faith in Dallas rooted in his early experiences here.

"The people were different from those I was used to. They weren't so crowded in that they became impolite. Shopkeepers said 'thank you' and 'hurry back.' I saw people in the middle of a depression who were still able to smile, who had just added a few hours of work to a day and still committed themselves to an installment plan for a new truck or automobile. They weren't afraid, and they took you at your word.

"The whole city was depressed by [the assassination]. We were being criticized by the whole planet and took it on the chin very generously. I would have thought that people would be sympathetic to us. Presidents had been assassinated in other cities."

"Jonsson is not an aloof man," says Nelle Johnston, his secretary for nearly forty years, "and that ability to communicate was a soothing balm on an inflamed and not very rational set of emotions."

Jonsson also understood that the circumstances called for more than civic pep talks. Yet during his first months at City Hall, he found himself little more than a glorified caretaker.

"He complained that he was just fighting fires, not dealing with issues," recalls Bryghte Godbold, then president of the Southwest Center for Advanced Studies, an institute supported heavily by the TI founders that eventually became the University of Texas at Dallas. "He was very frustrated because he thought he should be clarifying what the city could be."

Like a good engineer, he saw the city as a system of interlocking parts, in which what happened in one place invariably affected what happened in others. He wanted to re-examine Dallas from the ground up, starting with basic institutions such as city government and the library system, then moving outward to unexplored territory. The city was accustomed to thinking only in terms of the next budget; Jonsson wanted the city to think ahead ten and twenty years.

As he chided the Central Business District Association in December 1984, "Rather than talk about hanging flower baskets on Main Street or building landscaped malls between X and Y streets, Dallas should devise a bold and comprehensive set of goals for the future."

Out of these convictions and frustrations came the first Goals for Dallas program, the most ambitious exercise in participatory democracy that the city has ever seen. It marked the first time that whites, blacks, and Hispanics rolled up their sleeves and worked on the problems of the city together.

The Goals program started with approximately twenty Dallas leaders, who selected a sponsoring organization (the Southwest Center for Advanced Studies) and raised the initial funds. This group gradually expanded to eighty-seven, representing a generous cross section of the Dallas population. It met regularly to discuss the future of the city, often in consort with national consultants brought in by Jonsson to keep the intellectual sparks flying. Among the visitors were John Gardner, author of *Excellence*; philosopher Barbara Ward; and urban planners Constantin Doxiadis and Edmund Bacon. Texas Instruments had thrived on bold ideas, and, consequently, Jonsson was unafraid of scholars and intellectuals, even those who were 180 degrees from him politically. He urged Dallas to develop its own MIT and promised to help finance it.

In June 1966 the group gathered in Salado, Texas, to hammer out the original goals and discuss strategies for implementing them. A list of thirty possibilities was narrowed to twelve, covering everything from the government and design of the city to transportation, public safety, graduate education, even family planning. Today we might describe such an approach as synergistic or holistic, but for Jonsson it was merely a practical vehicle for getting done what he wanted to get done.

Jonsson was an ex-officio member of the Goals committee, but from all accounts made no attempt to impose his will on the group. "Erik never interfered with the process," says Floyd Norman, a Dallas physician who became executive director of the Goals program in the late 1970s. "He left you alone because he believed that bad ideas wouldn't be implemented anyway. He wasn't afraid of the outcome."

The goals were then presented to the public in twenty-five neighborhood meetings, often chaired by bankers and developers who knew South and West Dallas only as red-lined areas. The president of a major bank found himself explaining the goals to an all-black audience in a Forest Avenue church.

The goals were later published as a book that was distributed, often free, throughout the city.

"The program didn't achieve everything that Erik envisioned," says Stanley Marcus, one of the original conferees, "but it was a fascinating exercise in civic introspection. It made it possible for citizens to look at what they had and evaluate it."

The first fruits of the process showed up in the 1967 Crossroads bond election, which provided money for branch libraries, a new City Hall, land for D/FW Airport, a renovation of Fair Park, and an assortment of road and sewer projects. Crossroads was three times larger than any previous bond issue, some $175 million, and called for a hefty tax increase.

Despite all this, it passed overwhelmingly, largely because Jonsson sold it at every Rotary luncheon and church social he could attend. The neighborhood public meeting, now a mainstay of Dallas political life, began in this campaign. These were not simply public works projects, he reminded the voters, but their legacy to next generations.

To those who objected to the cost, he said repeatedly, "We can't afford not to tax ourselves more."

And if that didn't work, he'd fall back on dramatic exaggeration reminiscent of an Old Testament prophet: "We must have the airport and these other projects, and we must have them without a moment's delay, or we will wither on the vine."

Jonsson's first and most controversial undertaking was building the new City Hall. It wasn't that Dallas didn't need one. He and others described the old City Hall on Harwood Street as a "box with a dog-house and a henhouse on the back." The issue was, what kind of City Hall? The prevailing view was that Dallas needed a no-nonsense office building that would house city offices together with courts, police department, and jail. That's the way city halls were usually built.

But Jonsson had another model in mind—the city hall in Stock-holm, Sweden. In 1964 he led a delegation of Dallas leaders on a tour of Scandinavian cities to observe transportation systems, greenbelts, and other manifestations of sound planning. He also impressed upon them the importance of having a building, like Stockholm's, that was at once administrative and ceremonial and that created a symbolic center for the city, like the cathedrals in medieval times.

A citizens' committee was appointed to select an architect, with advice from the dean of the school of architecture at MIT. No Dallas architects were considered, a decision that still rankles local design-ers. After working through a list that included Philip Johnson, Edward Durrell Stone, Skidmore, Owings and Merrill, and several other firms, the committee chose I. M. Pei.

Pei's signature projects, such as the East Wing of the National Gal-lery of Art and the Kennedy Library in Boston, still lay ahead. But on the strength of his designs for the Boston Government Center and the Cecil and Ida Green Center for the Earth Sciences at MIT, he was gaining recognition as an important contemporary architect. The "contemporary" part appealed to Jonsson, as did Pei's obvious flair for the bold, sculptural forms that Jonsson wanted in the new City Hall. They made an ideal team.

"Jonsson contributed greatly to the spirit of the design," says archi-tect Ted Amberg, who spent more than a decade supervising construc-tion of City Hall. "The building responded to Jonsson's challenge to build for the future of Dallas and to be a symbol for the city."

Pei produced a bold, cantilevered structure, with a slanting front that sailed out over a public plaza like the prow of a gigantic ocean liner. It was not the first cantilevered city hall. Frank Lloyd Wright had designed one for Tempe, Arizona, and the Boston City Hall, with its slanting facade and grand civic plaza, was also under way. But Pei's design clearly met Jonsson's criterion that the new building be "a monument to the city's pride, a symbol of a first-class city that is reaching for greatness."

Pei, with Jonsson's backing, insisted that the city double the size of the site to make room for both the plaza and future expansion. The City Council, slightly dazed, went along by purchasing land along Canton and Young Streets, a portion of which would eventually accommodate the Central Library. It was a dramatic illustration of a basic Jonsson planning principle: Always buy more land than you think you need, because you undoubtedly will need it.

No sooner was the project launched than it began to take on water. Initial construction bids were as much as 50 percent over budget. The plans were redrawn, eliminating the jail, courts, and half of the underground parking garage, and sent out for bids once more. The results were the same, forcing Jonsson to put the project on hold.

The longer the delay, the more intense the criticism of Pei's design and Jonsson's support of it. Jonsson, to his credit, stuck by the design through a succession of strikes, suits, and countersuits, all the time reiterating his belief that the design "connotes the strength and power that are to me symbolic of the fast-growing yet solid city that we are."*

The building opened in 1978, seven years after Jonsson left office (fig. 2.1).

Of all Jonsson's civic undertakings, the most significant was the single-minded shepherding of the construction of Dallas/Fort Worth Regional Airport.

His passion was at once personal and high-minded. As a boy he once spent his last dollar on a biplane ride and claimed later that he got a good glimpse of the future from the cockpit. In the '50s and early '60s, as president and chairman of Texas Instruments, he virtually commuted between Love Field and New York. With each year, he saw

---

* While Dillon was not the paper's architecture critic when City Hall opened, he did later write several short pieces on the building, including "Despite Plans, Plaza Still Lacks Activity," *DMN*, September 1, 1981, and "City Hall Turns Twenty and You Can't Beat It," *DMN*, March 20, 1998.

2.1. *I. M. Pei, Dallas City Hall, completed 1978. Photograph by Carol Highsmith. The Lyda Hill Texas Collection of Photographs in Carol M. Highsmith's America Project, Library of Congress, Prints and Photographs Division.*

parking get worse and waiting lines longer. Love Field was becoming overcrowded and potentially unsafe.

In 1964 the Civil Aeronautics Board sent a blunt telegram to Dallas and Fort Worth telling them that if they didn't select a site for a regional airport, the CAB would do it for them. Dallas had recently spent millions on remodeling Love Field, and Fort Worth was preparing to do the same at Greater Southwest International Airport, so the prospect of a joint venture was not warmly received. Some of Jonsson's close friends in the Citizens Charter Association wanted to fight the government order. Jonsson, however, interpreted it as a terse statement of the inevitable, and thus an opportunity to be seized rather than ignored.

The trick was getting Dallas and Fort Worth to agree on a design and a method of operation, which at the time was about as plausible as getting a cobra to share quarters with a mongoose.

Fort Worth and the Dallas City Council felt that 6,000 to 8,000 acres would be sufficient. Jonsson, relying on the first computer-generated model of an airport, recommended 25,000 acres. They compromised at 17,500.

In mid-1967, Fort Worth voters approved the creation of a regional transportation authority, only to have Dallas voters turn it down. Jonsson publicly blamed himself for not working hard enough on the election. George Schrader recalls that at seven o'clock the morning after the defeat, Jonsson turned up at a meeting of the Crossroads Bond Committee and lectured the committee members on their political responsibilities.

"He told us that we had let Dallas down, and that if we didn't get moving we'd lose the airport, and that would mean losing the future," Schrader says.

The bond issue passed, but the crises were not over. A few years later, the newly created Environmental Protection Agency threatened to stop work on the airport until the cities filed environmental impact statements. That would have meant a delay of as much as five years, which meant, in all probability, that the airport couldn't have been built. Jonsson and others asked the EPA to let the project go ahead, provided the airport authority would file all the necessary studies along the way. The EPA agreed.

The Dallas/Fort Worth Regional Airport opened in September 1973, on a gust of superlatives. It was the biggest airport in the world, the most expensive, and the most highly automated, with a computerized baggage system and an experimental people mover known as Airtrans. It was efficient, far-sighted, and an engineering triumph, just what one would expect from Erik Jonsson. The master plan projected that by the year 2000, D/FW would have 235 gates serving 50 million passengers annually. Yet it would be so efficient that the average distance from curb to plane would be 120 feet, half the length of a 747.

Some of the projections have come true, and others have not. Several other airports are larger, and at least four carry more passengers. Parking has become a major problem. But the economic benefits are inescapable.

Jonsson said at the dedication that the sky would be Dallas's ocean, and that has turned out to be the case. Without D/FW there would be no Las Colinas, nor the steady influx of new companies from more congested parts of the country. It is our most solid claim to being an "international city." Jonsson's only complaint is that it is already too small.

"We're not far from saturation now, maybe another decade," he says solemnly. "Then we'll confront the same problem as New York City in the 1950s. They ran out of air space and tried to go out to the boondocks in Long Island and New Jersey. But nobody wanted an airport near them. We should be gathering land for two or three satellite airports. Otherwise the environmental guardians will overwhelm us, and we won't be able to buy enough land."

Erik Jonsson became mayor at Dallas's bleakest hour. By the time he left office in 1971, he had established an agenda for civic and social improvements that, he hoped, would carry the city into the late twentieth century. It hasn't, of course, but it's still a good map to travel by.

Jonsson was fortunate to have a custom-designed city council that marched to his tune, as well as a citizenry that needed to feel good about itself and was willing to be shown the way. He made no pretense of being a populist mayor or one of the guys. Discussions of city problems were likely to turn into Platonic dialogues involving speculation about ideal urban form. He was more at home with the Greek philosophers than with zoning boards and task forces. Some found him autocratic and patronizing, too much the Swedish papa, while most admired his ability to be firm and decisive without being cutting.

"He wielded great power without appearing to," recalls a former council member. "All he had to do was look at you, and you fell into line. He made a big thing of being a modest man, but all you had to do was see him in action to realize that he loved those public appearances."

"Erik is one of the few businessmen I've seen who knew how to get along in the political arena," says Stanley Marcus, one of Jonsson's Democratic allies. "Business is autocratic, and politics is democratic. The quickest way isn't always the best. Erik got impatient at times, but he got over it pretty well. He was far better than the average Republican who runs for public office."

Jonsson's contributions are clearest in the public institutions that he nurtured: City Hall, the airport, the library system, the University of Texas at Dallas. He envisioned them larger and better than most people at the time were willing to, and in many instances that confidence has been repaid.

D/FW Airport—too small or not—planted the seed of the "international city" tag that publicists since have turned into a numbing cliché. City Hall remains an architectural tour de force and a dramatic symbol of progressive city government, though it has not become the public gathering place that Jonsson hoped for. Less architecture in this case might well have been more.

But Jonsson was as concerned with building ideas as monuments.

Goals for Dallas was his most impressive achievement in this sphere, though it survives today only in attenuated form. It was an expensive program to operate (Jonsson himself contributed more than $1 million) and depended for its success on unwavering support from city government. That support has dried up, yet the program's influence is still visible in the scope of many city projects, such as the Arts District and the decision to build a regional transit system. However confused both of these efforts may currently appear, they reflect Jonsson's adventurous spirit.

"He was always at his best describing how things might be," says George Schrader, "and as a result he gave the city an ambition that it never would have had otherwise."

What hasn't carried over is Jonsson's comprehensive urban vision. Current debates about zoning and planning policies, for example, are taking place in a vacuum. Planners, developers, and homeowners all have agendas, which are expressed mainly through the particulars of setbacks, height restrictions, and kinds of land use. What's missing is any vision of the possible futures that might grow out of all this tinkering with details. Without such an overriding vision, Dallas will likely end up with the same old mess created by a whole new set of well-intentioned guidelines.

Jonsson, ever diplomatic and genial, is reluctant to criticize his planning successors, though he admits to being dismayed by the chaos in North Dallas and the proposed cuts in city services, such as libraries. He insists, however, that there is no shortage of talent for dealing with these problems in 1986. What's lacking, Jonsson says, is people who will take the time.

"We say, 'We can do that tomorrow, next year, when we need it more,'" he says. "But somebody must be concerned for laying the background for what must be done. It's possible with most problems to see them coming, to assess them, to know how much time and money it will take to fix them. But somebody has to be thinking about it. It won't happen by itself."

How best-laid plans of '60s helped create urban division

DECEMBER 8, 1991

This essay begins with a quick overview of the Dallas skybridge and tunnel system, a largely failed urban plan from the 1960s that helped create empty downtown streets. * Dillon, using a frequent strategy, brings in examples from San Diego, Denver, and Phoenix as workable models for fixing Dallas. The connecting thread is housing and entertainment combined with office and commercial space—something that would come to Dallas about a decade later (see "Shock of the NEW," 2001).

Each weekday the intersection of Elm and Griffin streets is jammed with students and shoppers—mostly black and Hispanic—waiting for crosstown buses spewing clouds of diesel smoke. Below, on the underground concourses, office workers—mostly white—pause for ravioli or moo goo gai pan on their way to the bank, the cleaners, or the travel agent.

This two-tier system is a legacy of the 1960s, when Mayor Erik Jonsson and planner Vincent Ponte teamed up to create their version of the City Efficient. Instead of a melting pot or an urban carnival, they

---

*   See Dillon's essay, "Dallas: A Case Study in Skyway Economics," *Design Quarterly* n. 129 (1985), 25–28.

saw downtown as a streamlined machine with computerized traffic signals, underground truck terminals, and a network of tunnels and skybridges through which pedestrians zipped unimpeded.

But what seemed like progressive planning in the 1960s has become regressive in the 1990s. Instead of the center of civic life, downtown has become a collection of discrete worlds, where each project looks out for itself and nobody looks out for the whole.

One-third of downtown's retail space (about 650,000 square feet) now sits underground, mostly invisible from the street and inaccessible to those who don't already know where it is. "The city that has done the most to kill off its streets is Dallas," wrote William Whyte in *City: Rediscovering the Center.* "One gathers that the proponents [of the tunnel and skybridge system] would be delighted if pedestrians could be eliminated from the streets altogether." The proponents may get their wish. Increasingly, downtown streets belong to the poor, the homeless, and the politically disenfranchised, while office workers retreat to a sanitized, air-conditioned rialto from which all vestiges of urban diversity have been banished. "The general economic outlook for the region is very positive," says Bernard Weinstein, director of the Center for Economic Development and Research at the University of North Texas. "But the outlook for downtown is very problematic." Over the past twenty years, downtown Dallas has become so obsessed with office construction—real or speculative—that housing, shopping, and public space seemed like trivial pursuits. In relying so heavily on private enterprise, the city often forgot to act in the public interest. Planning became piecemeal and ad hoc—a district here, a special project there. Now that the boom has ended, downtown is struggling to become a real place again, without the political and planning tools of many of its competitors, including Denver, Phoenix, and San Diego.

For the first half of the twentieth century, downtown was Dallas's heart—the place everyone went to shop, to eat, to mingle with the larger community. Elm Street had thirteen movie theaters in the 1950s, and nearly every block held a quirky shop or restaurant, or at least a memorable sign. The *Dallas Then and Now* photography exhibit at the J. Erik Jonsson Central Library reveals a diverse and vigorous downtown, the "little New York" of countless tourist testimonials.

That downtown began to disappear in the late 1950s, as the interstate highway system siphoned off residents, jobs, and shopping to the suburbs. From 1960 to 1980, Dallas's population grew from 680,000 to 900,000, and most of that expansion occurred beyond downtown, around the new freeways, interchanges, and shopping centers.

The city grew another 10 percent in the 1980s, but the suburbs expanded by 20 percent and captured most of the new jobs.

While downtown still contains 25 percent of Dallas's office space, it produces less than 3 percent of its retail sales. Even with 115,000 workers, only one marquee specialty store survives—Neiman Marcus—and no theaters. Twenty-six percent of its office space sits vacant, along with 37 percent of its land. The trees are dying, and the fountains don't work. "The city ought to embalm downtown for the next twenty-five years to keep it from decaying any further," says Stanley Marcus, who recently moved his office from downtown to the Crescent. "I just don't see a way out for it. We have to reconcile ourselves to its being one of the larger office parks in the country." And yet high up, and from a distance, downtown Dallas appears almost physically correct. Few skylines can top its blend of architectural bravura and entrepreneurial chutzpah. And in every corner stands at least one monument to bold municipal planning: City Hall, the Dallas Convention Center, Reunion Arena, the West End Historic District, the Arts District. The current $92 million expansion of the convention center and the proposed $20 million renovation of the Farmer's Market reflect the same kind of "big fix" thinking.

Yet in assembling the big pieces, Dallas regularly overlooked the small ones. In their recent report on Dallas, national urban affairs consultants Neil Peirce and Curtis Johnson noted that "across the United States we have not seen a downtown as comparatively devoid of street-level activity, of tone and texture and interest." Thirteen years ago, Philadelphia planning czar Edmund Bacon urged Dallas leaders—only half in jest—to construct a skybridge linking the convention center with City Hall and Neiman Marcus. His point was that without attractive routes to stores and museums downtown, Dallas would never capture the "golden flow" of conventioneers. They would either hole up in their hotel rooms or else jump in a cab and head for NorthPark. "I'm talking about a gut economic issue, not some eccentric art project," Mr. Bacon warned at the time.

Nobody listened.

The latest attempt to correct this situation is Pegasus Plaza at the intersection of Akard and Main Streets. Named for the winged horse whose hoofs caused springs magically to flow, the plaza is the centerpiece of a $3.5 million Dallas Main District project that includes wider sidewalks, more trees, new pavement, more art, and fewer buses.

Its supporters see it as the beginning of a downtown renaissance; others view it more skeptically as just another fragment, too little and too late.

Two blocks north, on Pacific Avenue, DART will soon construct a one-mile, $40 million transit mall. In the early 1900s, the Texas and Pacific railroad tracks were considered the major obstacle to downtown development; this time, DART is hoping that a transit mall will spark new shopping and restaurant development, in the manner of Denver's 16th Street Mall. What's unclear—and currently unexamined—is whether the transit mall will complement Main Street or kill it.

DART also hopes to locate a bus transfer center to mesh with its light rail system. A sound idea, but so far, downtown property owners can't agree on where to put the center. Sites in the West End, the east end, and smack in the middle of downtown have all been proposed and rejected as inappropriate. "Everyone wants the transfer facility, but two or three blocks from where they are located," says DART's director of planning, Ron Thorstad.

The hidden agenda once again appears to be the "undesirables" and what to do about them. "Dallas is spending an enormous amount of energy these days on negative things," William Whyte noted on a recent visit. "It seems to think that if panhandlers and street people were eliminated, downtown's problems would be over." Though no two cities are ever identical, some comparisons are more instructive than others. Denver, San Diego, and Phoenix are all young, sprawling Western communities, politically conservative and afflicted with boom- and-bust economies—much like Dallas, in other words.

But the similarities end there. In rescuing their downtowns, all have used tactics that Dallas is only beginning to consider, including land banking, low-interest loans, and other economic incentives. Each has some form of redevelopment agency empowered to make things happen downtown. All have comprehensive plans to guide future growth. San Diego even has a city architect and a city landscape architect.

San Diego also has a temperate climate, a resort atmosphere and—to the astonishment of many visitors—a bustling downtown. More than ten thousand people live there, including one thousand working poor housed in attractive, single-room-occupancy hotels. Downtown

Dallas, by comparison, has approximately two hundred and fifty residents, most of them in one building.

The area between the convention center and Horton Plaza, downtown San Diego's Hollywood stage-set shopping mall, is packed with cafes, restaurants, and small hotels. The scale is intimate and the mood wildly eclectic. An adult theater, a hardware store, and a fashionable Italian restaurant coexist in a single block—as good an example of healthy urban diversity as one could wish.

The keys to this resurgence were strategic planning coupled with far-sighted political leadership. In the mid-1970s downtown San Diego was a wasteland, so Mayor Pete Wilson—now Governor Wilson—made downtown revitalization a crusade. He created the Centre City Development Corp. and gave it the necessary powers, including eminent domain and low-interest loans, to stimulate housing and shopping. "San Diego is not a regional hub like Dallas," explains the corporation's vice president for planning, Max Schmidt. "The demand for office space is limited. So we decided early on to focus on housing and retail, to create a neighborhood within the city and bring people to it." The corporation supports itself with income from tax increment financing districts, which last year generated $15 million in revenue. The money supports a wide range of downtown development projects, including new parks and affordable housing. "The overriding concern here has been to worry as much about the small stuff as the big stuff," says city architect Mike Stepner.

Equally important was a 1974 report on San Diego's special landscape by renowned planner Kevin Lynch, who also prepared the original report on the Dallas Arts District. Called "Temporary Paradise?" the report has been reprinted numerous times and provides the philosophical and aesthetic framework for all planning discussions in San Diego. James Pratt's exhibit *Dallas Visions for Community* draws on Mr. Lynch's work, but has yet to receive the same kind of political endorsement.

Denver also has a plan, and a redevelopment agency, and roughly eight thousand downtown residents. But its most conspicuous planning success to date has been its $25 million transit mall on 16th Street.

Designed by I. M. Pei & Partners, architects for Dallas City Hall and the Morton H. Meyerson Symphony Center, the mall halted the decline of downtown Denver in the late 1970s. Department stores were fleeing, fear of crime was high, and many downtown streets, including 16th, had become cruising strips. "The mall helped turn all that around," says Don Turner, director of mall operations for the Denver Partnership Inc., which manages, maintains, and promotes the 16th Street Mall. "Now everybody wants to develop against it." The mall bustles with restaurants, cafes, and stores ranging from Woolworth's to Brookstone. It was a decisive factor in the construction of Tabor Center, a large office, hotel, and shopping complex that opened in 1984. Macy's has announced a new store for downtown Denver, and several vacated department stores have been successfully converted into apartments and condominiums. All this activity is fed by free shuttle buses that run between two transfer centers at opposite ends of the mall.

The mall works so well, in fact, that city officials worry that it is sucking the life out of adjacent streets.

Whereas both Denver and San Diego had definable centers, Phoenix only sprawled. And it did so despite the absence of freeways, the villains in most downtown-decimation stories.

So, six years ago, Phoenix divided itself into nine urban villages, each with a business center and several concentric rings of commercial and residential development. The plan acknowledged that Phoenix had become a city of independent satellites, of which downtown was only the first among equals.

To make downtown competitive, Phoenix—like Dallas—tried to pack it with splashy, one-of-a-kind attractions: convention center, concert hall, theater complex, all within a few blocks of one another. A new arena for the Phoenix Suns basketball team opens next season. "Downtown is finally starting to be identified as the kingpin," says former planning director Rick Counts. "We are far more optimistic about it than we were ten years ago." Yet even Mr. Counts admits that downtown Phoenix still has a long way to go. Although five thousand people live there, it remains as devoid of color and texture as downtown Dallas. The streets are broad, largely deserted on weekends and after five o'clock. A new Mexican crafts market near the convention center, called the Mercado, is half-empty and survives mostly on subsidies.

The one exception is Arizona Center, a new retail and office complex across the street. According to the developer, the Rouse Co., the center drew more than 2 million visitors in its first year.

A hotel, a movie complex, and a third office tower are being planned. "People kept telling me that they wouldn't go downtown for fifty dollars," says Andrew Conlin of the Rouse Co. "Now, I see them here a couple of times a week." The city assembled the land for Arizona Center. But the real source of the development's success, in the minds of some downtown observers, is Phoenix's new freeway system, which cuts the driving time from north Scottsdale to downtown from an hour to twenty-five minutes.

Phoenix may become the only American city to use freeways to colonize downtown instead of empty it. "The freeways are the best thing that ever happened to downtown," says Margaret Mullen, executive director of the Downtown Phoenix Partnership. "They've made us the hub of everything in the region." The flight to the fringe will continue into the twenty-first century.

Putting her faith in people, not systems: Author Jane Jacobs talks of how city planning fails, and offers some solutions

MAY 14, 1993

This brief profile of Jane Jacobs is more of a curiosity than a serious interview, but it is indicative of the Dallas tendency to invite celebrity experts in to deliver a diagnosis and issue a report card. Jacobs's assessment of Dallas is at once apt and completely off base, and Dillon smartly focuses on her desire for a more pedestrian entrepreneurship to enliven the city's economic streetscape.

When Jane Jacobs saw downtown Dallas the other day, it reminded her of Hong Kong. That's not a connection most people would make, but then Jane Jacobs doesn't look at cities the way most people do. At seventy-six, she has built a career on spotting surprising juxtapositions and telling details, and then spinning them into compelling narratives about how cities really work.

"In Hong Kong and Dallas, you have wonderful towers that somehow compose themselves into works of art," says Ms. Jacobs, who is in Dallas for Friday's "What Makes a City" conference at City Hall. "In Hong Kong, the space between the towers is humanized by all sorts of street activity, but it lacks the oases that Dallas has. You have basically a wonderful downtown here. It's too bad there aren't more people enjoying it."

Density, variety, disorder—these are the essential ingredients of

Jane Jacobs's urban vision. In 1961, she rocked the planning world with the publication of *The Death and Life of Great American Cities*. This fiery assault on urban renewal and the theories that spawned it, by a woman with no planning background and only two years of college, has become an American classic—so certified by its appearance in a new Modern Library edition.

While experts decried her as a churlish amateur prescribing home remedies for urban ills, the public cheered her as a street-smart observer who used her senses and her daily experience to describe the ballet of urban life. She saw cities as complex organisms composed of millions of tiny, interrelated cells that never show up on the abstract maps and charts of professional planners.

"I like looking at old settlements and arrangements of living and working," she explains, "not to be with it, or trendy, but because they work. Select what works, and the heck with theoretical things that don't work."

The 1980s were tough on cities everywhere, eviscerating downtowns and turning established neighborhoods into slums. Yet, sounding more Republican than radical, Ms. Jacobs rejects government programs as a way out of the morass.

"Government should set the policy and take responsibility for what is public," she says, "and then allow private developers a lot of freedom in interpreting the rules. Government should not get into the development business as much as it has, and developers should not make public decisions as much as they have."

Informed that downtown Dallas is now 38 percent vacant land, she thinks immediately of a small-scale entrepreneurial response.

"You have lots of Asian immigrants here," she replies, "who know how to put up markets faster than anyone in the world, and be successful at it. Show them the vacant land and say, 'Go to it.' Every advantage should be taken of this skill that Americans have forgotten or had beaten out of them."

She dismisses the objection that such activity would be inappropriate in a business and banking center. "The fact that it's not in keeping with everything else is the reason to do it. If banks can't understand that cities are created economically, and by everybody, we're in an even worse mess than I thought we were."

Instead of federal mass transit plans, which she calls "magic carpets that hop over the fabric of the city," she argues for transit that is stitched into the fabric of the city. She thinks extending the McKinney Avenue trolley is a great idea and suggests creating an entire network of vans and jitneys, operated by individuals who know who needs to go where, and when. "It's a great way to find out where more ambitious kinds of transit will work," she adds.

The downtown Asian markets and the jitney network are archetypal Jane Jacobs. Think small, she urges. Be flexible. Trust people rather than systems. Don't genuflect before experts.

"What a miraculous thing it is," she reflects, "when you have a body politic with all different kinds of people that works, that everybody feels they have a stake in. And how tenuous and fragile, too."

DART-chitecture: Light-rail system's clean design enhances Dallas

JUNE 18, 1996

Public mass transit came late to the North Texas region and is plagued with problems balancing the needs of the fragmented metropolitan area. The Dallas Area Rapid Transit system, or DART, had its origins in the Dallas Transit System, but officially formed in 1983 as an alliance between Dallas and fourteen surrounding incorporated cities. While one of DART's primary missions was the creation of a regional light-rail system, it took decades to open the first lines. Dillon's article celebrates that opening and points to the importance of public design as a celebration of shared civic ambition.

No doubt about it. Cities look different from trains. Cities look different with trains. Watching a line of gleaming yellow-and-white cars swing down Pacific Avenue, bells clanging, is like falling into a time warp. Is this 1996 or 1896? Is this Dallas?

DART's new light-rail line gives a shot of urbanity to a city that has consistently resisted it. Even if this first phase tells us nothing about DART's future, we should celebrate it anyway. It represents an $850 million gamble that Dallas can still save its downtown, make peace with its suburbs, and generally pull itself together.

The first leg of the new line, which opened Friday, covers eleven miles from South Oak Cliff to downtown. By December, it will stretch to Park Lane in near North Dallas, with further extensions planned for Richardson, Plano, Carrollton, Garland, and other communities in the next century.

As design, the new line is generally clean, crisp, and pragmatic. Durability and low maintenance are the goals, which means no exotic materials and no cute postmodern touches that in a few years will scream "late 1990s." Yet compared with the early park-and-ride facilities, which were designed to withstand a shock of ten on the Richter scale, the design of the new line seems lightness itself. The engineers obviously learned something in six years.

The centerpiece of the new system is the Downtown Transit Mall, which unfolds like a scroll from the West End Historic District to the Plaza of the Americas at Pearl and Bryan Streets. Light-rail enthusiasts call this the "spinal cord of the central business district" and believe that eventually it will be lined with shops and sidewalk cafes. Few takers so far, though, realistically, such transformations take years and rarely occur until the city becomes a developer.

The challenge for the mall's designers, Sasaki Associates, was to transform a pair of back streets into an urban boulevard, while simultaneously dispelling fears that light rail is only for poor people and minorities. DART spent $45 million on the mall and its four stations. Sidewalks are wide and surfaced with colored paving blocks instead of raw concrete. The transit way is lined with single and double rows of magnolia, crape myrtle, red bud, and maple trees, which supply both visual continuity and welcome shade. Each station has a signature clock—moon, sunflowers, etc.—as well as a bronze map sculpture by Dallas artist Brad Goldberg depicting the surrounding neighborhood (fig. 2.2). Even the light poles have sporty steel caps.

The stations are simple low platforms, three hundred feet long, with arcing steel canopies cantilevered from thick piers. The arc is a design motif that reappears on columns, kiosks, and art up and down the mall. Except for the West End stop, with its red brick columns, Victorian street lights, and other period bric-a-brac, the stations (by the Oglesby Group) are clean and contemporary. Finishes include aluminum, concrete, limestone, and polished granite. Each has a welcome mat of brick, granite, or limestone, along with benches, kiosks, and route maps. If things occasionally get overwrought—a few blocks of Pacific are nearly solid with poles, signals, and benches; the moon

2.2. *Brad Goldberg, map sculpture for the Central Business District Transitway, Dallas Area Rapid Transit (DART), 1996. Photograph courtesy Brad Goldberg.*

clock at Bryan and St. Paul is virtually eclipsed by flying steel—the overall effect is upbeat and welcoming.

The one regressive gesture is the absence of toilets and water fountains and the introduction of benches designed to keep the homeless from stretching out. Paranoia about "undesirables" has led DART—and many other transit agencies—to eliminate basic public services. Public transit succeeds to the degree that it becomes classless, as it has in Portland, Toronto, and Boston, where everyone from CEOs to students rides the trains.

This unspoken social agenda has also influenced the design of the bus transfer centers. DART eliminated buses from the mall to reduce congestion and pollution, and also to prevent passengers from milling about in front of stores and office buildings. Instead, it constructed bus transfer centers at opposite ends of downtown, where eighty thousand passengers a day will switch to and from rail. These new gateways present marvelous opportunities for civic architecture. Unfortunately, they are little more than bus parking lots, without shops and restaurants, places to pass through rather than pause.

Using such valuable urban land so one-dimensionally is foolish, particularly given expectations that rail will revive Bryan and Pacific

Streets. They are ideal sites for mixed development. The main transfer station in downtown Portland, Oregon, features a Starbucks coffee pavilion and a flower market. Many stations along the Washington Metro contain restaurants, convenience stores, and produce stalls. What do these cities know that we don't?

The downtown transit mall accounts for only 1.2 miles of the twenty-mile starter line. Elsewhere, DART has opted for clarity and utility, relieved by splashes of color, pattern, and art.

The Eighth and Corinth Station, for example, has a simple corrugated metal canopy with copper trim, some decorative paving, and an open, transparent layout that is both pleasant and easy to monitor. Murals by Dallas artist Johnice I. Parker tell the story of the African-American community that surrounds the station. One chapter in an evolving linear narrative.

Union Station, on the other hand, appropriately recalls Dallas's railroading past, using drumheads from historic trains (Lone Star, Texas Eagle) and white glazed brick such as that used in the original 1916 terminal. The architecture is tough and industrial—lots of steel and cable—while the art, twelve terrazzo panels by Philip Lamb, tells the story of transportation in Dallas. Whether one likes all the art or not, the fact that DART has commissioned so much of it, from so many local artists, deserves applause.

If one bonus of train travel is speed and convenience, another is the opportunity to view a familiar landscape from a new perspective. The views of downtown from across the Trinity are spectacular, especially at night, when the city's skyline sparkles. The trains run through lush Trinity bottomland that many Dallasites have never seen and that evokes settings in the stories of William Faulkner or Eudora Welty. Even riding the surface line along Central Expressway should induce a sense of moral superiority as one gazes down at ten lanes of gridlock.

Design is only one aspect of light rail, less important than the overall service plan, but indispensable to wooing a public that believes transit is dirty and dangerous, something one does from necessity, perhaps, but never for fun. In this context, good design serves an evangelical purpose; it can raise hopes and make converts.

DART has succeeded in making the first phase of its rail system attractive, inviting, and comprehensible. You want to take a ride. Whether initial curiosity will blossom into mature affection is another matter, and another story.

Urban salvage: The loft life is transforming downtown

MARCH 8, 1998

Five years ago, two hundred and fifty people lived in downtown Dallas, most of them in a single building—the Manor House on Commerce Street. To everyone else, downtown was terra incognita, to be explored only on weekends with visiting relatives. The Sixth Floor, a trip up to the Reunion ball, maybe dinner in the West End—that was urban adventuring.

Downtown may seem hard, hot, and hostile, but to a growing number of people it feels like home. Since the early 1990s nearly ten thousand lofts, apartments, and condominiums have been completed, started, or announced within a mile radius of Akard and Main, an astonishing number considering the stampede to the suburbs that began in the 1950s.

Even more astonishing is that much of this new urban energy is concentrated in renovated factories and warehouses that used to appeal only to starving artists. Now they are filling up with lawyers, accountants, and computer programmers, who have been lured by the romance of wide-open interiors and spectacular views.

"Downtown Dallas may finally be achieving critical mass," says planner John Gosling, who prepared the master plan for the State-Thomas neighborhood north of downtown. "There's now an established market, developers can get financing, and anxiety-ridden suburbanites have an option they didn't have before." That's the rosy picture. The darker one is that downtown has a stagnant job base, few services, and no street life. It may be more of a destination than before, but it is not yet a place. Suburbs are located north and west of downtown—this exodus has paradoxically made downtown housing possible by depressing land values.

Instead of $150 a square foot, good sites can be found for $20 to $30 a square foot, the range within which housing makes economic sense. Developers who used to dream of skyscrapers on every parking lot now find consolation in futons and wet bars.

"With housing coming back and retail following, we may eventually get the lively downtown people say they want," says developer Robert Shaw, whose Columbus Realty Trust has sparked the current boom by building twenty-seven hundred apartments in the McKinney Avenue/State-Thomas area, also known as "Uptown."

Mr. Shaw points to the hallmarks of the "New Urbanism"—streets for people rather than cars, public spaces, apartments upstairs over shops—as reasons for Uptown's success. Some projects, such as Mr. Shaw's Columbus Square, follow this model while others are merely suburban garden apartments in downtown drag.

But New Urbanism is a somewhat trendy wrapper for more basic social and demographic changes. The "back to the city movement" that swept the country in the 1970s and early '80s was led by yuppies, who gentrified faded historic neighborhoods close to downtown (Swiss Avenue and Munger Place, for example), then moved on as the economy soured and, more importantly, city schools deteriorated.

The urban pioneers of the 1990s have gone beyond the fringes to the center of the city, where they occupy buildings that won't show up on *This Old House*. While few families with young children are moving back, most other constituencies are represented: singles, young marrieds, middle-aged professionals, and empty-nesters who are tired of yard work, no longer need the good schools, and want to be close to museums, theaters, and cafes with sidewalk tables.

"I wanted to downsize my life," says realtor Kitty Dusek, who after a divorce traded in a three-bedroom house in Rockwall for a loft apartment at 1900 Elm, formerly the Titche-Goettinger department store. "Six acres of mowing was too much for me, so now I'm living in what used to be Titche's linen and fine china department. I feel so 'in.'"

"People are getting more for their money in the city than in a suburban tract house," says John Keith-Tetrault, director of the Community Partners Program of the National Trust for Historic Preservation. "There is a discernible difference in value and that is beginning to be recognized all across the country."

However, more for your money doesn't mean cheap. Downtown apartments are averaging $1.10 per square foot, which means nearly $900 a month for a typical 800-square-foot unit, plus parking and other fees. Pioneering isn't the bargain it used to be.

Dallas and many other cities have been encouraging this migration by offering tax abatements, low-interest loans, and other incentives to create in-town housing. The incentives not only provide cash, they also express the city's commitment to downtown renewal, which bankers like even more.

Although roughly two-thirds of the ten thousand apartments and condos are in new buildings, the most spectacular spaces are in salvaged warehouses and factories. With their tall ceilings and dramatic skyline views, lofts have epitomized urban living from *La Bohème* to *Seinfeld*. And thanks to a handful of courageous developers, the supply has increased dramatically.

Bennett Miller turned the Magnolia Station petroleum depot in Little Mexico into sixty-nine loft apartments, then added twenty new townhouses ($250,000 and up) that have been snapped up by investment bankers and computer consultants from Plano, Las Colinas, and the Park Cities. He and Columbus's Robert Shaw have now teamed up to renovate the American Beauty Flour Mill in the Cedars, just south of City Hall.

Along Buena Vista and Travis Streets north of downtown, developer Alan McDonald and architect Ron Wommack have recycled hundreds of 1960s garden apartments into contemporary lofts and condos, reusing materials and restoring the fabric of the neighborhood along with its buildings. Architect Graham Greene's renovation of the old Titche's store is an epicenter of downtown housing. A few blocks to the west, the historic Wilson and Kirby buildings are about to be converted to housing, while the Magnolia Building, with its landmark flying red horse, will become a hotel.

Over in Deep Ellum, Mr. Greene's 3200 Main, one of the earliest loft conversions, has been joined on the east by the Continental, the Farm and Ranch, and the Murray—all by Pan American Capital Corp.—and

2.3. *Adam Hats lofts, a renovation of the former Ford Model T Production Plant (1914) and Adam Hats factory (1955) into residential lofts by Corgan. Image courtesy Corgan Associates.*

on the west by the Adam Hats Building and 2220 Canton, both carved out of old factories by Corgan Architects (fig. 2.3).

In all, more than two dozen warehouses and industrial buildings containing nearly three thousand housing units have been renovated in the past four years. They've filled up so quickly that developers are complaining about running out of old buildings. To which preservationists would say, "Where were you ten years ago when the bulldozers arrived?" Yet with the exception of the Wilson, Magnolia, and Kirby buildings, none of these renovated structures is architecturally distinguished. Preservation with a capital *P* is not the issue; urban resettlement is. These older buildings matter because they stand in the heart of the city, where they can serve as anchors for streets, blocks, and eventually entire neighborhoods. By recycling them, developers have given the stamp of approval to so-called "marginal" neighborhoods.

The area around Magnolia Station was an industrial wasteland before Mr. Miller arrived. The explosion of new apartments at Woodall Rodgers and Harry Hines shows the power of his good example. Likewise, Gaston Yards in Deep Ellum wouldn't have happened without the earlier wave of warehouse conversions.

If you build it . . .

The boom in downtown lofts, apartments, and condos has surprised the real estate experts.

"There's a huge latent demand here for something a little different," says Steve Kanoff. "Dallas housing is so homogeneous that, when an interesting product comes along, people flock to it." John and Maribel Pieper had lived in downtown Milwaukee and Atlanta and expected to do the same in Dallas, but they were temporarily rerouted to Valley Ranch in Irving.

"The real estate people told us Valley Ranch was quiet and friendly," says Mrs. Pieper, "but it wasn't anything. Everybody kept to themselves." Within a few weeks, they had found a loft in the Continental on Elm Street. "The minute we saw it, we said, 'This is it,'" Mrs. Pieper says.

Like most loft dwellers, the Piepers like the openness, the views of downtown, and the satisfaction of living in a building with a past. And they're willing to put up with driving to the grocery store and the movies.

Architect John Higgs is more intrigued by the opportunity to do what he wants with his space. He and his wife, Danni, are moving into the American Beauty Flour Mill on South Ervay, where the walls are concrete, ceilings soar to twenty feet, and there are railroad tracks and a steel mill next door. "We just don't build that way anymore," he says excitedly. "Every apartment is unique." Justin and Ann Ford, professionals in their early forties, could have lived anywhere but decided on a townhouse in Magnolia Hills, the upscale wing of Magnolia Station, "because we wanted to be part of a reviving neighborhood." He commutes to Plano, and she works at home. In the evenings they attend concerts and frequent the restaurants along McKinney. They'd prefer less driving and more neighborhood services but enjoy being part of a tight urban community.

"Out in the suburbs we didn't even know our next-door neighbors," Mr. Ford says. "Here we tend to band together because we're trying to build a neighborhood. We're all in this together."

LOOKING AHEAD

If downtown Dallas has indeed turned a corner, it's still unclear where it is headed. Thriving downtowns have at least three things in common: unique attractions that lure suburbanites back to the city, a resident population with money to spend, and enough stores and restaurants for them to spend it regularly.

Downtown Dallas has a leg up on the first with the Museum of Art, the Morton H. Meyerson Symphony Center, the West End, and its stock of older buildings. That can't be duplicated in Plano or McKinney. Its resident population is growing, though it will probably take thirty thousand residents rather than ten thousand to create a real constituency for downtown. Grocery stores and dry cleaners are still mostly rumors.

Yet along with these pluses come some serious minuses.

Residents and jobs go hand in hand in a healthy downtown, and right now most of the new jobs are in the suburbs. One-third to one-half of Uptown residents work in Las Colinas and along LBJ Freeway. If this trend continues, cautions University of North Texas economist Bernard Weinstein, "downtown could emerge as a bedroom community for the suburbs." While this might sound intriguing, he adds, it would be bad for the city because housing never generates the tax revenue that office buildings do.

A flourishing downtown needs not only ethnic and economic diversity, but also many types of housing. Lofts are hot now, but they are also typically an experiment. As the hip singles marry and have children, they usually seek more conventional apartments, condominiums, and single-family homes. Downtown is short on all three.

More residents means more services, such as banks, grocery stores, dry cleaners, and pharmacies. Most downtowners still drive to shop, eat, and be entertained, even though the idea of urban living is to stash the car and do these things on foot or by public transit.

More residents will demand more greenery. Not vast parks, but small landscaped spaces where it's possible to walk the dog or watch the birds. At a grander scale, a truly civic Trinity riverfront, lined with parks, promenades, and playing fields, would be an enormous boost for downtown.

Downtown is beginning to come together around DART rail. Office workers now ride it to lunch, sometimes just for fun. But more connections of all kinds are needed. An adult version of the McKinney Avenue Trolley, for example; real walking streets, especially north and south; and improved links to the West End, the Farmers Market, and the proposed arena.

The new Katy hike-and-bike trail from Mockingbird to Turtle

Creek could be a lush green thread uniting diverse neighborhoods and making the dream of a carless environment momentarily possible.

Together these improvements could provide the connective tissue that would make scattered housing projects into neighborhoods, where residents could feel part of something bigger than their own building.

REINVENTING DOWNTOWN

If these changes occur, the current housing boom could be a prelude to a reinvented downtown. Instead of a service district populated mainly by lawyers, bankers, and government workers, or a tourist and convention district aimed at dentists from New Jersey, downtown could expand into a mixed-use urban neighborhood with its own voice and its own agenda.

In this reinvented downtown, the old distinction between a white-collar core and a blue-collar fringe would dissolve.

Warehouses and small factories might coexist with housing, shopping, and entertainment. An apartment building next to a produce market would no longer be an anomaly. Struggling areas such as the Cedars and North Oak Cliff would emerge as areas of great opportunity, supplying not only workers and services for the core but also housing and recreation.

The rediscovery and reinvention of downtown will take several decades, with inevitable shifts in priorities and momentum. The housing boom is encouraging, and DART may turn out to be Dallas's new life-support system.

But few of the big urban problems have been solved—here or anywhere. The 1990 census confirms that the flight to the suburbs is continuing, with more African-Americans, Hispanics, and Asians joining the parade. And while many American downtowns are reporting dramatic decreases in crime, few are touting similar improvements in their public schools. To attract and hold the middle class, the schools will have to come back as well.

Downtown living has never been for everyone. Parents with young children will still flock to the suburbs. But if only a fraction of those who abandoned downtown return—as little as 10 percent, according to some observers—it can develop a new life. Five years ago, such a statement would have been delusional; today, it sounds quite plausible.

Arts magnet: Fort Worth is trading its "Cowtown" image for one geared more toward culture

MAY 3, 1998

At the same moment that Dillon wrote about Dallas's new resurgence of downtown living options, he summarized a different approach to downtown revitalization in Fort Worth. Spearheaded by the Bass family's investments, the northern end of Fort Worth's downtown transformed in the early 1990s with the assistance of a PID or "public improvement district" created in 1986, which provided a funding safety net for private downtown investment.

In the mid-1980s, the downtown entertainment district consisted of the Caravan of Dreams and a handful of bars. Today it includes three live theaters, twenty movie screens, a museum, a mega-bookstore, several dozen restaurants and clubs, and a general atmosphere of upwardly mobile exuberance.

On weekends the streets are crowded with moviegoers and bar-hoppers and people playing chess at sidewalk tables. It is neoned and noisy and nothing like the rolled-up, shuttered place of a few years ago.

"The cinemas and the restaurants have returned vitality to the streets," says former planning director James Toal. "People are proud to be downtown again."

Fort Worth's success has attracted envious glances from mayors and managers in other cities, who want to work the same magic in their own downtowns.

The appeal is understandable, particularly in downtowns that were run over and left for dead by the real estate crash of the '80s. What do you do with a half-filled shopping center or 20 million square feet of empty office space?

But the risks are great as well. Entertainment makes a good appetizer or dessert but rarely a main course. Almost by definition it is mutable, unpredictable, prone to enormous changes at a moment's notice. Whatever happened to festival markets, those sure-fire cures for ailing downtowns? Are paint-balling and video arcades the foundation of an economic development plan?

"The danger is focusing everything on entertainment and not paying attention to other things," says Pat Faux, a planning consultant from Annapolis, Maryland. "Building a stadium before you've got a team. Discovering that you're not quite the destination you thought you were. For places that have something nice to start with, entertainment may help, but not every city does."

While downtown Fort Worth's resurgence is dramatic, it also derives from unusual circumstances, the most important of which begins with *B*. The Basses, Sid and Ed, have been the Medici of Fort Worth, pouring millions into renovating old commercial buildings, then filling them with lofts, restaurants, and offbeat commercial ventures that less committed developers would shun. Sundance Square survived several nosedives before finding the right combination of shopping, dining, and entertainment.

"In the mid-1980s, Sundance Square was two blocks," says Bill Boecker, the president of its management company. "How much activity can you get into two blocks? So we expanded, brought in movies and other entertainment, and that gave us the boost we needed. A majority of the people who go to movies eat out before or after. Entertainment attracts those complementary activities that make for a complete evening out."

The success of Sundance Square shows the value of patience, deep pockets, and total control. The ten blocks of Sundance Square are a private world in the middle of the public realm, where cleanliness and orderliness are paramount and where the Bass gendarmes are more conspicuous, and more aggressive, than the city's. Getting bounced from Sundance Square is nearly the equivalent of getting bounced from downtown.

But geography and history also have a great deal to do with

2.4. *Sundance Square in the 1990s, shortly after the completion of Sundance West in 1991. The northern section of downtown mixed some historic fabric along Houston Street and Main Street with new construction in historic styles. Courtesy Sundance Square Corporation.*

downtown Fort Worth's revival. It is barely nine blocks long, which means that it is walkable and immediately comprehensible in ways that downtown Houston and downtown Dallas are not. Such concentration encourages street activity ("synergy" in plannerese) and, like holding a news conference in a small room, creates the impression that more is going on than really is.

Unlike downtown Dallas, downtown Fort Worth doesn't have to compete with a Las Colinas or a Galleria for affection and loyalty. It's the only downtown around, to which everyone pledges allegiance.

Even more important, it wasn't nuked by urban renewers in the 1950s and '60s. As a result, it is remarkably intact, with blocks of turn-of-the-century masonry buildings awaiting new ideas from enterprising entrepreneurs (fig. 2.4). Compare this with the situation in Dallas's Arts District, where two gleaming cultural monuments are separated by sterile parking lots and freeway ramps. No old buildings to convert to lofts or studios. No street life. No real streets. All the urban texture will have to be trucked in.

The Bass Performance Hall has the luxury of being the capstone of the entertainment boom rather than its catalyst. Had it come earlier, it might have been burdened with unrealistic and unrealizable public expectations: "The Hall that Saved the City!" One unarguable truth in urban development is that there are no quick fixes. No single building—arena, shopping mall, concert hall—can revive a downtown. Vitality resides in the nurturing and coordination of hundreds of ordinary daily events.

What's happening in downtown Fort Worth is encouraging and instructive. But not even the most rabid civic booster would claim that downtown's future is assured. Many questions remain.

Most of the entertainment activity is concentrated on the northern end of downtown, around the Basses' Sundance Square and Worthington Hotel. Comparatively little is happening south of Fifth Street, where parking lots and empty buildings predominate. The demolition of the Interstate 30 overpass may change this, but not tomorrow.

The once blank and windowless Tandy Center has reopened as an outlet mall and reportedly is prospering. But downtown still needs more back-to-basics retail to go along with the cappuccino and the T-shirts. The few remaining Western wear stores and mom-and-pop cafes, authentic links to Fort Worth's past and an antidote to preciousness, should be retained.

Downtown Fort Worth, like most downtowns, needs residents to become a community instead of just a weekend destination. Right now it has roughly five hundred apartments and condominiums. Another five hundred are under way. It needs five thousand.

Other items on the agenda include renovating the spaceship Fort Worth Convention Center, which has irradiated street life for blocks around, and creating a memorable link between downtown and the museums, which are still the city's premier tourist attraction.

But the overarching question, which residents tend not to ask in public, is what happens if the prince gets bored and turns his attention elsewhere? The Basses almost single-handedly launched the renaissance in downtown, and as the owners of some thirty blocks of its real estate, their participation is critical to the future. But so is the participation of others, outsiders, even Dallasites, who can broaden and diversify the original vision, maybe give it a more contemporary spin.

According to architect David Schwarz, who has designed the performance hall and most other Bass projects, the prince's goal is "to get downtown to the point where others start to build." That's beginning to happen. Marriott is renovating the historic Blackstone Hotel on Main Street. The new housing on the east and west sides of downtown is being built by outsiders. All encouraging.

The great contribution the Basses have made to Fort Worth is to articulate a vision of downtown, even if it's a vision that not everyone likes, and to try to build it as thoughtfully as possible. The proof of their success would be for them to become dispensable.

Shock of the NEW:
The downtown-housing boom
has forged winners and losers

JANUARY 14, 2001

After fifteen years of encouraging more residential development in downtown, Dillon began to assess the quality of the buildings that finally began to fulfill this mission and came back largely disappointed. Dallas had never truly had dense downtown housing, and the new designs of the 1990s were largely inventing a whole new typology. Dillon argued for higher quality and a more "urban" feel to the designs, something that could distinguish diverse downtown housing from apartments in far-flung urban sprawl.

Let's get one thing straight: Nothing invigorates a downtown more than housing. It puts people on the streets, attracts food stores, dry cleaners, and copy shops, enlivens the restaurant and bar scene, and generally energizes urban life.

Downtown Dallas hasn't been truly urban for fifty years, yet thanks to the current housing boom it could be again. The boom started five years ago with the conversion of old warehouses and industrial buildings to lofts. When the supply ran out, the focus shifted to new apartments and condominiums—from Deep Ellum and the West End to Uptown, Oak Lawn, and the Central Expressway corridor. It's the best thing to happen to downtown in a generation.

At the same time, the boom has a dark side—two in fact.

The quality of many new apartments and condos is appalling. Constructed of cheap materials in a slipshod fashion, they are incipient slums—and no amount of market babble about efficiency and economic necessity can disguise that. Too much of the new housing is designed for newcomers with short memories.

The downtown market is also split between luxury condominiums for the overprivileged and pricey apartments for yuppies. Affordable housing is hard to find, and attractive low-income housing virtually nonexistent. This situation promises trouble down the road, when the metropolitan population is projected to reach 7 million—around 2025, according to demographers—and most of those aren't software designers or investment bankers.

The good news first. In the early 1990s, downtown Dallas had only two hundred and fifty residents, most of them living in one building; today, there are approximately ten thousand apartments, lofts, and condos, and eighteen thousand residents, within a mile or so of Akard and Main. That's a huge jump in a short time. Downtown may soon cross the critical 4 percent threshold, meaning that when 4 percent of a city's population lives in and around downtown, it probably won't dry up and blow away. That works out to roughly another twenty thousand urban pioneers to patronize stores, restaurants, theaters, and museums.

IN THE FLOW

What's happening in downtown Dallas is happening in Seattle, Chicago, Cleveland, and other cities, and for many of the same reasons: Violent crime has been decreasing steadily for a decade, and with it the perception that cities in general, and downtowns in particular, are dangerous.

Conversely, the suburbs are no longer the drug-free, crime-free, smog-free utopias they were once thought to be. There are choices to be made.

Couples are having children later and staying in the city longer, soaking up urban energy until they have to emigrate for good schools and Little League.

Empty-nesters, no longer needing schools and tired of mowing grass, are trading in their tract villas for high-rise roosts. An urban ZIP code now has cachet.

Perpetual gridlock has made commuting costlier and more stressful, and daily life more of a grind. Nobody wants to spend two hours a day stuck in traffic or drive half an hour for a cappuccino.

This is not, of course, the end of suburbia as we know it—the latest census indicates that it is alive and well, despite the emergence of anti-sprawl vigilantes—but only a slight adjustment to the traditional urban-suburban equation.

For young, adventurous, and well-educated people, the suburbs are no longer the promised land. Increasingly, they prefer living in an urban neighborhood of shops and sidewalk cafes rather than manicured cul-de-sacs. Ironically, some suburbs—Addison and Richardson among them—are rushing to urbanize themselves by creating new downtowns with shops at street level, apartments above, and plenty of historical veneer for resonance.

HERE TODAY, GONE TOMORROW

While it's easy to cheer this renewed interest in downtown, it's hard not to be dismayed by some of the results. A few architects and developers are working hard to understand and fit into the city, while others are pulling plans out of bottom drawers and hoping nobody notices until they've left town.

Corgan Architects' 2011 Cedar Springs is a new brick-and-concrete loft building designed to look like the old brick-and-concrete loft buildings that have been torn down. It has some odd features, such as a virtual lobby and open corridors, but the floor plans are sensible and the views of the downtown skyline spectacular. It looks as if it belongs in the city, not in Plano or McKinney.

On the other hand, The Phoenix, on Mockingbird Lane, is a mishmash of flakeboard, fake stucco, and cartoonish art deco details that mock the historic Dr Pepper building that was demolished to make room for it. Rents average $1.25 a square foot, which translates to roughly $1,000 a month for a modest one-bedroom apartment. The Phoenix boasts that it has "redefined timeless," which it certainly has if "timeless" means "five years." From balconies barely deep enough for potted plants to hunkering parking garages that block light and views, it is rote architecture at its shabbiest.

Appalling on a far grander scale is 3225 Turtle Creek, a twenty-two-story, fake stucco behemoth that shows what happens when the main objective is cramming as many apartments onto a site as possible. Strip away the decorative balconies and you have 1930s worker housing in

Berlin or Budapest. Even the dumbest of the older Turtle Creek towers achieved a certain graciousness by preserving views and fragments of the lush landscape. Ignoring even those modest precedents, 3225 Turtle Creek looms over adjacent streets and sidewalks.

"Many of these developers were doing garden apartments five years ago," says Mike Puls, a Dallas real estate consultant. "To go from that to urban density is really hard. They say they can do it, but often they can't."

Mr. Puls insists that Dallas buyers and renters have grown more sophisticated and that in general the better projects outperform the mediocre ones. Yet in this context "better" usually means finishes and accessories, not design.

The Mayfair, an architecturally unclassifiable condominium tower overlooking Lee Park, offers coffered ceilings, granite countertops, cavernous walk-in closets, a putting green, and a master bathtub big enough to float a Pontiac. Yet except for the views and the prices—about $250,000 to $2 million—the units are unremarkable. And the building is pure theme park: arched entrances, corner towers with curving iron balconies rising to a forest of mansard roofs with pediments and finials. If architecture were psychiatry, the Mayfair would get a diagnosis of multiple personality disorder.

Apartment dwellers have "amenity packages," including pools, fitness centers, crown moldings, cooking islands, concierge services, and business suites with computers and teleconferencing equipment. The Phoenix and the Quarters at Cityplace have stage-set courtyards with palm trees and dancing water jets. The Park at Farmers Market, an eleven-building suburban apartment project in urban drag, contains its own basketball court and a movie theater with arena seating, no less. Many of these projects are gated enclaves rather than extensions of the surrounding city.

MORE SIGNS OF INTELLIGENT DESIGN

Fortunately, there are also projects that clearly belong in the city, that know they belong in the city, and are happy to be there.

One of the most intriguing of these is Mockingbird Station, by RTKL, under construction at the intersection of Mockingbird and Central. It is an ambitious blend of apartments, offices, restaurants, a hotel, and an art movie house, all located on a DART line and interconnected by bridges and landscaped plazas. It is too early to tell whether its industrial chic will seem fresh or merely trendy. But the effort to concentrate so many different uses in one spot is precisely what Dallas needs along its transit lines.

Downtown Dallas has almost no middle scale, only big and little, the skyscraper and the McDonald's. At eleven stories with 127 apartments, Block 588, also by RTKL, helps to fill that gap. It exploits its urban setting by using a curving glass wall to frame views of downtown and exhibiting a certain industrial swagger that would be out of place in the hinterlands. It is less impressive on the backside, where gates and security fences give it a more institutional look; yet compared to its neighbors, with their kitschy facades and acres of bad stonework, it is very smart and sophisticated.

WHERE DO WE GO FROM HERE?

If the metropolitan population does rise to 7 million during the next twenty-five years, downtown housing will have to get denser and more diverse—eight stories instead of two, affordable and subsidized as well as luxury. Otherwise, downtown will attract only a narrow segment of newcomers.

Little of the new housing serves families, for example, or the many different kinds of households that now fall under that heading: single parents, gay and lesbian couples, elderly, and disabled people living alone.

Likewise, much has been written about the explosion of jobs in technology and finance, and the new Dallas housing certainly tracks that curve. Yet statistically, the biggest job increases will be in so-called service jobs: cooks, carpenters, janitors, bus drivers. These people keep the new economy humming, but $1,500-a-month apartments are far beyond their means.

"If downtown Dallas is going to succeed, it will have to have mixed housing," says Bennett Miller, who pioneered the development of downtown lofts. "You can't cater only to people with disposable income. You need those who have to work for a living."

In Seattle, Chicago, Kansas City, Toronto, and other cities, such housing is available, often tucked inconspicuously into buildings that also include expensive apartments and fancy restaurants. They are microcosms of the larger community, not precious enclaves. Little of this exists in Dallas, in part because the city's housing incentives are still modest, and in part because it is extremely difficult to achieve.

The profit on affordable housing is small compared to market-rate apartments and condos, and the regulations and paperwork are onerous.

"It takes a very committed individual to do that kind of work," says Terry Clower, associate director of the Center for Economic Development at the University of North Texas. "You can't be in it for the short haul and the quick buck. On the other hand, if we can't provide that kind of housing in a boom economy with low inflation and low unemployment, when can we do it?"

Dallas has reason to feel good about the downtown revival. The combination of new housing, DART, and a revamped Central Expressway has made it more attractive and more accessible. At the same time, the revival remains fragile. The economy could go south; priorities could shift. Instead of a lively mixed urban neighborhood, downtown could end up as just another business and government center or a sprawling tourist and convention district of interest mainly to visiting cardiologists and fly fishermen.

The first phase of the downtown revival has been led by private developers and investors with very specific agendas. The next phase will likely require more government participation, as well as a different kind of developer—someone interested in neighborhood- and community-building and willing to take on the tough small projects as well as the lucrative big ones.

"Dallas has neglected the inner city for so long that it will take twenty years or more to bring it back," cautions Mr. Miller. "And it's going to be a hard birth. We've done the easy stuff. Now we have to start on the rest."

Quick-fix syndrome: To revitalize downtown, the whole must outweigh the parts

MARCH 31, 2002

Dillon provides a quick summary of the previous twenty years of planning strategies, or "big fixes," used to revitalize struggling downtowns: performing arts centers, pedestrian malls, festival marketplaces, convention centers, and sports arenas. He encourages Dallas to focus instead on smaller-scale interventions like landscape design and pedestrian experience to create "connective tissue."

With its proposed $250 million Center for the Performing Arts, Dallas has caught the latest urban wave, along with Philadelphia, Miami, Houston, Los Angeles, and a dozen other American cities. Performing arts centers have become the new fixe du jour for ailing downtowns, succeeding the pedestrian mall, festival market, convention center, cultural district, sports arena—and presaging who knows what. Dallas has built or toyed with all of these and has now set its sights on the Trinity River and the massive Victory development.

Former mayor Ron Kirk called the Trinity plan "the key to Dallas's economic future," while Ross Perot Jr. referred to his Victory development as the future "Times Square" of Dallas and "the new front door for the city." With the threatened withdrawal last week of partner Tom Hicks, and resistance to additional public subsidies at City Hall, that door may be closing.

The premise of the big fix is that the way to lure disaffected urbanites back downtown is to create a constellation of special attractions that the suburbs can't duplicate, such as ballparks, concert halls, and blockbuster exhibitions.

It's theme-park thinking, but with understandable appeal. Most people like to eat and shop and be entertained, and historically, downtown has been the place to do such things, whether it's a Greek agora, a Renaissance piazza, or a Disneyfied Times Square. The trick is to persuade the visitors to stick around or to come back when there isn't an important game or special show. That takes more than one or two big fixes, as generations of American planners have discovered.

One of the most popular urban-design nostrums of the 1960s and early '70s was the pedestrian mall, of which Dallas's Akard Street is a tiny remnant (fig. 2.5). This was the era of urban renewal and the interstate highway boom, when planners became convinced that the car was the enemy of public life. One remedy was to close streets to create tranquil, traffic-less zones where shoppers and tourists could stroll contentedly among flowering shrubs and antique street lamps. (Dallas's extensive sky-bridge-and-tunnel system sprang from the same desire to separate people and cars.)

But the typical result was a wasteland of shuttered stores and empty plazas. Most cities that built pedestrian malls eventually ripped them out. The few that flourished, such as Nicollet Mall in Minneapolis and the Third Street Promenade in Santa Monica, California, accommodated cars and buses. Cars, it turns out, are an essential element of the urban experience, part of our mental map of how cities work. Banishing them entirely creates eerie, alien landscapes where nobody feels comfortable.

FAILED FESTIVALS

The pedestrian mall bug was followed by festival market flu. Dallas caught a mild case in the '80s when it poured millions into public improvements around the Farmers Market in hopes of creating a new commercial cornucopia.

This phenomenon was driven by the spectacular success of Boston's Quincy Market and Harborplace in Baltimore, Maryland, both developed by the Rouse Co. America's downtowns were on the ropes, and any sign of life was greeted with wild enthusiasm. Quincy Market attracted nearly 10 million visitors its first year, persuading mayors

2.5. *Akard Street pedestrian mall shortly after its completion, with the Adolphus Hotel in the background, as designed by Myrick, Newman, Dahlberg landscape architects. Image from the Schrickel, Rollins and Associates slide collections, University of Texas at Arlington.*

and city managers that a savvy blend of food, shopping, and entertainment, cleverly choreographed and tightly policed, was just the thing to revive the center city.

But the concept didn't travel well. Except in Boston and Baltimore, festival marketplaces bombed. New Yorkers preferred the real Manhattan to the concocted version provided by South Street Seaport; residents of Toledo, Ohio; Tampa, Florida; and Flint, Michigan, were equally underwhelmed by their ersatz town squares.

The devil was in the details. The marketplaces required large public subsidies, were formulaically designed, and often featured the same mix of stores and restaurants as the regional malls to which they were allegedly an alternative. The Dallas version would have contained a replica of the San Antonio River Walk, complete with riverboats and strolling musicians. Dallas dodged that silver bullet when Rouse pulled out, though some of the spirit of the marketplace survives in popular consumerist warrens such as Mockingbird Station and West Village.

CONVENTIONAL WISDOM

No fix was bigger in the 1980s and '90s than a convention center, in small towns as well as major cities. In 1992, for example, an urban design SWAT team from the University of Minnesota traveled up and down the Mississippi River advising mayors and city managers on how to perk up their moribund downtowns. What they wanted to talk about most was a convention center, even when the best they could hope for was an occasional tractor pull or fly-fishing tournament. They had seen the future over in St. Louis or St. Paul, and they were going to build it.

The Dallas Convention Center has been expanded so many times that it's more like an artificial mountain range than a building. These expansions have enabled the city to attract home builders and cardiologists and other expense-account philanthropists and to keep its top ten ranking in the national convention sweepstakes, significantly below New York, Las Vegas, and Orlando, Florida, but roughly even with Atlanta, New Orleans, and Washington, DC.

Yet whatever this golden flow of tourists has done for Dallas's economy, it has done little to energize downtown. The convention center remains inscrutably vast and disconnected from the rest of the city. No stores, restaurants, and chic hotels line Young Street; weary conventioneers exit into bleak parking lots and empty streets. Some of them pile into cabs and head for downtown Fort Worth, where an old-fashioned urbanism of street, block, and square still prevails. The Wild West theming gets a bit thick, but the scale is comfortable, the sidewalks are jumping, and one thing connects to another. Even the locals show up.

Sports arenas generate stronger feelings than convention centers because they offer the cachet of being big league instead of merely convenient. Yet the economic evidence is overwhelming that with a few exceptions—Washington's MCI Center, for one—arenas and ballparks generate little new money or new development, particularly when located on the fringe of downtown like Reunion Arena or the new American Airlines Center. There's no synergy in a remote site. Fans drive in and out without setting foot in the city.

A LIVABLE CITY

In a special report on Dallas published eleven years ago in the *Dallas Morning News*, urban historian Neal Peirce noted that while from a helicopter downtown looked stunning, "when we got to street level, we found astounding inactivity, a place so vacant you'd have thought the neutron bomb exploded there, removing the people."

Much has changed since then. Fifteen thousand people now live in downtown lofts and apartments compared to a few hundred in the early '90s. DART rail has arrived to pick them up and drop them off in aerodynamic comfort. The Arts District, after a decade in intensive care, is showing signs of sustainable life, with a sculpture garden, a performing arts center, and possibly a new natural history museum by Frank Gehry in the works. Santiago Calatrava has been commissioned to design a dramatic new bridge connecting downtown and West Dallas, and plans are under way, however muddled, to reclaim the Trinity River that flows beneath it.

What hasn't changed since Mr. Peirce's report is that downtown Dallas remains a stark, abstract place, far more appealing from a distance than up close. In its fascination with big fixes it has neglected the small, everyday ones that make downtowns livable: parks, trees, walkable streets, places to buy a good baguette or a $3 shine.

The late sociologist William Whyte—no stranger to Dallas—referred to such things as "tremendous trifles" and pointed out that, though apparently trivial, they can have a dramatic cumulative effect on cities and landscapes. They were his potent antidotes to "the grand-sweep approach to regional design" and the big-fix approach to urban development.

Paris has more monuments than any capital in the world, yet it is also a city of cafes, gardens, parks, surprising views, and an inexhaustible supply of great walks. It is this interplay between big and little, grand and ordinary that makes it such a memorable place.

Similar things could be said about London, Boston, New York, Montreal, Chicago, San Francisco, Seattle, and Vancouver, all cities rich in grain and texture. Barcelona, Spain, used the 1992 Olympics to reinvent itself, not just by building arenas and stadiums but also by investing simultaneously in neighborhoods, parks, gardens, beaches, public art—the condiments of urban living.

Downtown Dallas still needs big ideas, but it also needs greening and softening and more connective tissue to pull its fragments together. Instead of one fifty-story building, it needs five ten-story buildings. Not only more housing, but also a broader range of housing to attract a more diverse urban population. And nothing would draw the middle class back quicker than a couple of first-rate public schools. The arts magnet is terrific, but it's not enough.

Downtown's next monument could be the Dallas Center for the Performing Arts, which is being touted as both the city's cultural showpiece and the exclamation point for the Arts District. Norman Foster and Rem Koolhaas are outstanding architects, and there's an excellent chance that their designs for the opera house and theater will be stunning. But architecture alone won't produce the civic triumph the public is hoping for. It will take all the other stuff—shops, cafes, parks, housing, that elusive element known as "ambience"—to turn the Arts District into a place instead of a collection of discrete cultural destinations. The goal is a bouillabaisse instead of a buffet.

This won't happen overnight. It took twenty-five years for New York's Lincoln Center to become a cultural mecca; Yerba Buena in San Francisco is still a work in progress after nearly thirty years. A building, even a great building, is only a first step.

Dallas at the tipping point: Community

APRIL 18, 2004

Dillon was a key writer for the Dallas Morning News *Tipping Point series (fig. 2.6). Based on a report commissioned by the paper and completed by consulting firm, Booz Allen Hamilton, the series led with the stark declaration: "Dallas calls itself the city that works. Dallas is wrong." The report looked at economics, demographics, education, and crime and came to pessimistic conclusions about the city's prospects for major change. Dillon contributed research and analysis to many Tipping Point articles and wrote "Community" and "Decision Time." These pieces reflect his immersion in issues of policy, public administration, and economic development beyond the traditional confines of architectural aesthetics and point to the accumulation of experience gained over twenty years of reporting.*

The Tipping Point series and the Booz Allen report generated conversation and controversy but few results. In 2005, the city held a special election to consider replacing the city charter, vesting more power in the mayor and less in the city manager, as the report recommended. That vote failed. Forward Dallas, *the city's new strategic plan appeared in 2006, but its goals of improved public education and increased middle-class population have failed to materialize.*

90

2.6. *The "Tipping Point" was a special investigative report by the* Dallas Morning News, *published in 2004. The special section's cover emphasized the critical nature of the issues that faced the city.* Courtesy *Dallas Morning News.*

The Booz Allen Hamilton report concludes with a recommendation that is easy to express but hard to follow. "Creating the type of change Dallas needs to stem [its] decline requires an act of bold political leadership. What remains unclear is who, if anyone, will provide the sustaining leadership to help the city change course." Ordinarily, city government would provide that leadership by setting an agenda, gathering resources, and mustering public support to achieve it. But Booz Allen found that City Hall is broken and questioned whether Dallas's other institutions are strong enough to drive change.

The business oligarchs who once ran the city, Mayor R. L. Thornton's famous "dynamic men of Dallas," are gone, and their successors are more committed to their own companies than to traditional ideas of public service.

Dallas's grass-roots organizations are weak, and its voters apathetic. Turnout in the May 2003 municipal election was barely 10 percent. Even Detroit, the urban abyss into which Dallas vows never to fall, drew 33 percent in its last mayoral contest.

The evidence notwithstanding, Mayor Laura Miller believes that the city could be mobilized on behalf of dramatic civic change.

"We have a huge, untapped resource out there with business leaders, the faith community, all these people out there who are frustrated with what they see," Ms. Miller said. "And they want changes, and they're willing to help, to spend their money and their time and their energy fixing the problem."

There is no question that Dallas is a more diverse, demanding, and dissenting place than it was forty years ago, harder to handicap, with new constituencies and new priorities.

So the key question may not be "Who will lead Dallas?" but "Who is Dallas?"

"We lack a sense of identity, of who we are as a city," said Andres Ruzo, former chairman of the Greater Dallas Hispanic Chamber of Commerce. "Dallas is a multicultural city, but we haven't embraced that richness."

Race is the unacknowledged driver of Dallas's civic agenda, the not-so-secret ingredient in how the city works and looks.

"It is a factor in every decision that is made in the city of Dallas," said Ben Click, who was police chief from 1993 to 1999. "I don't know if there is another city in the country with racial divisions as pronounced. That makes it very difficult day in and day out to make decisions. You walk on eggshells [and] are afraid to make decisions that need to be made."

In the last ten years, Dallas has had a black mayor, a black police chief, and black and Hispanic school superintendents. Yet these breakthroughs, significant as they were, came later than in other big cities.

And some of Dallas's most important political and legal victories—single-member council districts, an end to court supervision of schools and public housing—were won only after bruising legal battles. Bitter memories from those past struggles shadow and shape today's Dallas.

Civil rights lawyer Michael Daniel, who forced the city and federal government to confront institutionalized segregation in the city's public housing, said Dallas still resists honest talk about race.

"White people hate it because they always feel like they get mau-maued into talking about things that don't fit with their reality," he said. "Black people hate it because they feel like they get pressured to say things aren't as bad as they are."

To City Council member Elba Garcia, the faces at the council horseshoe offer proof of a city pulling together since the arrival of 14–1.

"We finally have elected officials that look like the city of Dallas. And that's why I believe that the city is going forward with diversity," Dr. Garcia said.

A Dallas discussion about racial divides is not just a black-white issue. The city is 36 percent Hispanic, and the Dallas Independent School District is nearly 60 percent Hispanic, with many new immigrants arriving unprepared for school.

Geography matters, too. A demographic and economic barrier splits the northern and southern halves of the city like a geological fault line.

The southern sector accounts for roughly half of Dallas's land area, but development there lags so badly that "that it would take over thirty years at aggressive growth rates for the south to catch up with the north," Booz Allen said.

Projects such as Pinnacle Park, much touted by the city's economic development department, have barely made a dent.

"South Dallas is your curse and your great opportunity," said Antonio DiMambro, a Boston planner and urban designer who is working on community-redevelopment projects in southern Dallas.

"A curse because the extraordinary level of decay and degeneration contributes to the negative image that people have of the city. It's your ugly racial divide, though you don't talk about it quite that way.

"Yet if you are going to have any additional growth in the city, you have no choice but to put it there. Dallas needs a big change of attitude about this sector. Some enlightened leader has to stand up and say, 'Enough with exporting development to the suburbs. We're going south.' And mean it."

Not so long ago, a city leader would have emerged from a Dallas business establishment that was all-male, all-white, and all-business. It had only one agenda—"What's good for business is good for Dallas"— and only a handful of people to push it.

But that was then and this is now.

"The business guys can't run the city anymore," said political scientist Royce Hanson, author of the 2003 book *Civic Culture and Urban Change: Governing Dallas*. "They don't have a clue to what's going on. They're flummoxed even when they're trying to do good."

And memories of Dallas's exclusionary politics complicate any involvement by business people in public life. "Suspicion attaches to them, often without reason," Dr. Hanson said.

Recent interviews with two dozen area business executives revealed that the business-city gap had become so wide that some CEOs couldn't even name the mayor of Dallas. One consequence has been a drop in civic volunteerism, the backbone of the old "Dallas way."

"When we get good people involved, we tend to kill them," said former mayor Ron Kirk, referring to the daunting workload that often burdens volunteers such as Walt Humann and Don Williams. "We need to come up with a new structure for tapping our best talent."

But like others interviewed for this article, Mr. Kirk had no idea what such a structure might look like.

If the main problem were simply overcrowded calendars, the solution might be more Palm Pilots and savvy administrative assistants. But business has changed, becoming less local, more global.

Dallas's largest banks are owned by financial conglomerates based elsewhere. Even big companies with local roots face shareholder pressure over their balance sheets, which don't include a line item for civic service.

"We squeezed it out of corporate America," said one executive who spoke on condition of anonymity. "Employees think, 'You've given us two jobs.'"

It's rare, this executive explained, to find someone with enough time and energy to run a major business and also give back to the city.

These problems are hardly unique to Dallas. Yet in the best-performing peer cities, such as San Jose and Phoenix, the lines of communication between business and government are clear and open. In Dallas, they are filled with static.

Asked to name the institution most influential today in city life, one Dallas business leader heaved a sigh and named the city government.

"I do so reluctantly, because I wish it wasn't true," this executive said. "I wish the answer had been business people, again. Right now, that's not really the case."

"It's really important to create a system of government where voting matters," Dr. Hanson observed.

Dallas doesn't have one.

The May 2003 election featured a trifecta of electoral bounty—campaigns for the mayor and council, for the school board, and a $555 million city bond proposal.

Yet scarcely one in ten registered Dallas voters turned out. Five incumbent council members ran unopposed; one was elected with barely one thousand votes. Several candidates who lost City Council races in Arlington polled more support.

With the exception of San Antonio, every peer city in the Booz Allen study had higher turnout in its most recent mayoral election.

In the last thirty-five years, turnout in a Dallas mayoral election has cracked 26 percent just once—the 1991 election that marked the city's first under 14–1.

"The numbers say either that people are not upset with what they're getting, or else that they see no chance for real change so they aren't bothering to vote," said Dan Weiser, the Dallas political analyst and demographer.

The 2003 *Dallas Morning News* poll found support for both hypotheses.

When asked about city services, residents were less satisfied than they were ten years earlier. But they said they were more positive about the city as a whole and their neighborhood in particular.

At the same time, they also expressed no consensus on who is most important in shaping the city's future, and by a large margin they believed they have little influence on what happens there.

A more hopeful view of residents' feelings about their city emerged in a group interview with five City Council members.

Looking past the anemic turnout, they cited the ballot box endorsements given to the city's 2003 bond package.

"That tells you something. For a city that is about to tip the wrong way, that wouldn't happen," Dr. Garcia said.

Except in cities such as Boston and Chicago, Americans typically don't organize around municipal politics. Schools, traffic, security, and property taxes are more likely to be the issues that galvanize residents and draw neighborhoods together.

But it's hard for this to happen when neighborhoods are in constant flux. Booz Allen found that Dallas's population is remarkably transient, with almost one in five residents moving to the suburbs between 1995 and 2000.

In many cities, broadly focused community organizations help compensate for sprawl and neighborhood volatility.

"Producing a good active set of community organizations is as important as anything you can do on the economic front," Dr. Hanson said.

Dallas would seem to have plenty of grass-roots organizations—linked to schools, churches, neighborhoods—that could stitch together the city's fragmented constituencies. Compared with similar groups in other peer cities, though, they are much more narrowly focused, according to social scientist Patricia Evridge Hill, author of *Dallas: The Making of a Modern City*.

"Dallas's neighborhood groups are very inward focused on specific needs," she said. In San Jose, by contrast, these groups "are deeply involved in framing citywide issues such as growth management. They're not parochial in the way Dallas groups are."

The best of these groups are involved with the community as well as one another, and for long periods of time, so that they develop the credibility and trust needed to produce civic capital, and ultimately to shape government.

The tri-ethnic Dallas Alliance, which dissolved in the mid-1990s, had some of those attributes. Spinoff groups such as Dallas Together were more ad hoc and short-lived. Minorities often dismissed them as public relations stunts rather than serious attempts to resolve serious problems.

Phoenix, a sprawling, multicentered city like Dallas, has tried to address both neighborhood stability and a sense of community by supporting construction of thousands of middle-class homes—about four thousand last year alone—within a few miles of downtown.

While the architecture is generic Spanish Colonial hodgepodge—innovative design is not a staple of boomtowns—the sheer number of units allows the city to attract and keep middle-class families that are the foundation of urban stability.

Phoenix also subdivides itself into fourteen urban villages, each with some type of civic center—usually a shopping mall or a library—plus a village planning committee that reviews major zoning and land-use matters.

"The committees were created because people got tired of a [downtown] elite making all the decisions," said Ray Quay, a planner for the city. "They provided broad public representation in a city that did not have much of an ethic about creating place and community."

The committees cut across council districts so that they aren't under the thumb of a single politician. They meet regularly with the city's planning staff. Although the committees' roles are only advisory, their recommendations are taken seriously by City Hall and developers.

Dallas's most ambitious effort at public consciousness-raising was the first Goals for Dallas program in the mid-1960s. It was the last hurrah for the Dallas oligarchs, initiated and orchestrated by Mayor Erik Jonsson and staffed by recruits from Texas Instruments and other leading corporations.

It was a product of its time, built around dynamic leadership, ample funding, a sense of common purpose, and a feeling of urgency—and, in the beginning, a need for civic therapy.

"Erik felt the need to do something to get Dallas out of its depression after the Kennedy assassination," recalled Bryghte Godbold, who was recruited from the Ford Foundation to run the program. "And what he decided on was to plan our future as a city."

Residents met in small groups to develop one hundred goals on a broad range of topics: improved public transportation; better schools, including a research university; economic development; and environmental quality.

Out of this process eventually came an expanded library and community college system, a retooled University of Texas Southwestern

Medical Center, and a research center that became the University of Texas at Dallas.

But the process didn't satisfy everyone politically, nor did it achieve some of its most critical goals.

Black leaders felt sufficiently shortchanged that they created Goals for Black Dallas.

And if the unfinished business from Goals for Dallas—regional transit and environmental planning, for example—sounds familiar, that's because it is. Dallas continues to revisit these issues over and again.

The city must find a way to break this cycle, Booz Allen said, "because the consequence of business-as-usual will be to see Dallas go the way of declining cities like Detroit."

Forward Dallas: Would it work? Yes, if the city finds the money and leaders to see it through, says architecture critic David Dillon

MAY 7, 2006

The city's Forward Dallas plan followed hard on the heels of the Dallas Morning News *diagnostic Tipping Point series. The paper's editorial board endorsed the plan but registered skepticism about its implementation. Dillon's editorial provided context for how to think about yet another big plan for Dallas—one that set ambitious goals that have yet to be implemented today as the city continuously rediscovers the difficulty in managing public resources in a political environment that favors private development and minimal taxes. Dillon wrote three of the paper's short policy responses to the plan; this one provided the most general overview. They were among his final pieces written for the paper as a full-time critic. ***

It's hard to argue with the basic premises of Forward Dallas, the comprehensive plan making its way through City Hall. It calls for a denser community built around mass transit, mixed-use development, housing close to jobs, and significant investment in new infrastructure,

---

* The other two pieces included "Forward Dallas: A Plan Before the City Council Would Change the Way this City Lives, Works, and Moves. Here's Why It Matters to You," and "Forward Dallas: Land Use. The Zoning Code Is Handcuffing Dallas, Which Needs a Smarter Guide to Development," both published May 7, 2006.

particularly in the disenfranchised southern sector. It talks about protecting stable neighborhoods and stabilizing fragile ones, streamlining Dallas's Byzantine development code, and persuading public officials to stop dithering and take charge of the city's future before it is too late.

Density, mobility, equity, clarity, accountability—what's not to like? At a conceptual level, Forward Dallas strikes all the right chords. It is pragmatic, solidly researched, farsighted, and deserving of broad public support.

Where it sometimes falters is in connecting the dots—explaining how Dallas is going to get from A to B, who's leading the parade, and where the money will come from to pay for it. This is a common weakness of comprehensive plans, which almost by definition have to focus on the big picture and the long-term instead of the day-to-day.

Yet in a city that is nearly broke and without a planning tradition, the day-to-day matters enormously. Right now, Dallas doesn't have the money to implement this plan or to hire enough professional staff to monitor it. It will have to solve these problems soon, probably before the November bond election, so that good policy can become good practice.

The solid stuff first:

Forward Dallas recognizes that the world is running out of cheap energy, which will make sprawl unsupportable and force irresponsibly expansive cities to recycle and redevelop, or else. Dallas is one of those cities, founded by a real estate speculator and sustained by the conviction that there always would be cheaper land farther out.

Well, cheap land has gone the way of cheap energy. There is virtually none left in the northern half of the city, and even the seemingly virginal southern sector has at best a fourteen-year supply.

With oil reaching $75 a barrel and likely to go higher, redevelopment is no longer an option; it is an imperative. Most successful cities know this. Even Los Angeles, the citadel of sprawl, is redeveloping its downtown at a furious pace. As the plan suggests, Dallasites are going to have to live closer together and like it because the alternatives are unacceptable.

Dallas is also a quintessential freeway city, where the car is king and the interstate a surrogate public space. Ninety percent of Dallas residents commute to work. Yet despite decades of compulsive road building, congestion is worse, commutes are longer, and life is increasingly frantic. Building more highways is not the answer, whereas developing efficient, economical alternatives to the automobile could be.

Forward Dallas proposes investing in light rail, commuter rail, transit centers, and bike and hiking trails. The word "choice" runs through the document like a mantra. It is a comforting word, a virtuous word, yet for at least the next decade, Dallas's first choice should be investing in mass transit.

Why? Because Dallas is so far behind other major cities—we don't even have rail connections to the airports—and because trains and trolleys are the keys to creating more dense, Mockingbird Station-like developments at the University of North Texas Dallas campus, Fair Park, the Stemmons Corridor, and other strategic locations throughout the city.

Density means shorter trips, more efficient use of land, and opportunities to live, work, and play in the same neighborhood. If current development trends continue, new growth would be concentrated in and just north of downtown. The Forward Dallas vision, on the other hand, would distribute growth more equitably around the city, including South Dallas, frequently in smaller parcels that would attract new developers.

Dallas is also a single-family-house-on-a-quarter-acre-lot city, to the point that any talk of multifamily housing produces apocalyptic visions of crack houses and swarms of Dumpster divers. But Forward Dallas is correct in calling for more housing options throughout the city, ranging from apartments to luxury condos and single-family attached units.

Uptown's victory in the making: After early struggles, Perot Jr. presides over urban boomtown

JUNE 21, 2006

Dillon wrote many articles chronicling the creation of Victory Park on the far northern boundary of downtown Dallas and was critical of the site selection, the political process, and the design of American Airlines Center, a neo-traditional sports arena that anchors the development. In this piece, however, Dillon makes peace with the final product as representative of a typically Texan method of competitive city-making that lets private development lead the way.

Five years ago Victory Park was on life support, a casualty of 9/11, the tech bust, and investor hysteria about both. Hotels pulled out, retailers fled—a stampede and a nightmare all in one.

"It shot everything down; the whole program died," recalls its developer, Ross Perot Jr. "All we could do was hunker down and wait it out." The strategy worked. Victory Park, which includes American Airlines Center, is now a 75-acre boomtown, with a 251-room superluxurious W Hotel, opening today, plus condos, restaurants, shops, and bars sprouting like mushrooms after a spring rain. There is $850 million in construction at the moment and a projected $3 billion in the next decade.

The W, a one-letter code for hip, will feature the famed Ghostbar on the top floor.

102

Sitting jacketless in the Victory Park marketing center, starched shirt and American flag lapel pin catching the light from a nearby window, Mr. Perot is taller, blockier, and more guarded than his twangy quote-machine father. His tight smile says, "Glad to meet you" and "I'm in charge."

He calls Victory "an urban neighborhood," and an extremely upscale one at that, with small condos starting around $200,000 and grown-up versions, such as Mr. Perot's own aerie plus heliport in the W, topping out at $6 million.

"We wanted to create a place where people can live, work, and play and never have to use an automobile," he says. "Texans will never give up their cars completely, of course, but we've tried to create an attractive environment. No question, it's going to be on the high end. Even if you rent, you'll have to be a professional to live here."

THE VISION

Victory is the latest and largest chapter in the Uptown development saga, though it is more west than north of downtown and far denser and more contemporary than its neighbors.

Implausible as it seems, Victory is the offspring of American Airlines Center, the retro red-brick hulk that is home to the Dallas Stars and Dallas Mavericks. Opened in 2001, AAC is being surrounded by slick metal and glass buildings and by the time Victory is finished may be totally camouflaged.

This has prompted speculation that between then and now Mr. Perot had an architectural epiphany and that if he could figure out a way he'd airlift the arena to a remote corner of the site.

He says no, that if he had it to do over again he'd hire the same architect, David Schwarz, and embrace the same art deco-cum-airline hangar design.

"I like the comfortable feeling you get when you're next to it," he says. "Even when there isn't an event, it's a pleasant place to be. You can't say that about a lot of modern buildings."

He likes all kinds of architecture, he continues, from the futuristic control tower at Fort Worth's Alliance Airport to the vintage mill house he and his family—wife Sarah and four children—occupy in London. The design competition for AAC, he points out, also included I. M. Pei, Helmut Jahn, and Ricardo Legorreta, all card-carrying modernists.

"Ross is a businessman, not an architecture critic," says Jonas

Woods, president of Hillwood Capital, which oversees Victory. "He could see that the whole Dallas market was starting to go modern, and he wanted to create a project for his new city within a city."

TRANSFORMATION BEGINS

American Airlines Center made Victory viable by changing the public's expectations about what could be done with a polluted site on the edge of a twelve-lane freeway.

"It went from being a blighted area to a place where you could go see the Stars and Mavericks and spend several hundred dollars in a night," says Mr. Woods.

But the transformation wasn't quick or easy. All development is at least half politics, and in the early 1990s it was all politics all the time.

"Those were the toughest negotiations I've ever been involved in," says former Dallas mayor Ron Kirk. "The egos were huge; there were times when we didn't think we could get Ross and [Stars owner] Tom Hicks to agree on anything. But in the end, they buried their differences and we got a deal."

Dallas officials were apoplectic about all the high-dollar, high-tax revenue development that was moving west toward Alliance Airport, including Federal Express, Intel, Texas Motor Speedway, and American Airlines. They reminded Mr. Kirk that Fort Worth had a vibrant downtown because the Basses were pouring money into it, whereas Ross Perot Jr. was punting. Maybe he'd like to do something for his hometown, too. A splashy civic project, an arena perhaps.

Although Mr. Perot cared little about ice hockey and basketball, he saw at once that an arena was a tool for leveraging a major downtown land deal. "It was my anchor tenant to attract several million people a year to the development."

Yet to build an arena you need a team, so Mr. Perot bought, then subsequently sold, a majority interest in the Mavericks. And then he turned his attention to acquiring the 75-acre brownfield that TXU Energy wanted to dump and that the city was willing to subsidize with $135 million in bond money.

"It was the kind of big, one-off project that Ross likes to do," says Isaac Manning, a longtime Hillwood associate and now president of Trinity Works in Fort Worth. "He works hard, he's very methodical, and he doesn't like to repeat himself. It was perfect."

Mr. Manning was his fraternity brother at Vanderbilt from 1977 to 1981, spending summers waiting tables and digging ditches while Mr. Perot fulfilled his ROTC obligations with Navy cruises, jump-school training at Fort Benning, Georgia, and Marine officer candidate school at Quantico, Virginia. He later flew F-4 jets for the Air Force and in 1982 completed the first round-the-world helicopter flight.

The military has shaped Mr. Perot's view of the world, from his methodical approach to development (long lists, weekend team meetings) to the names of his projects (Victory, Alliance) to the way he runs his life.

"It gave me confidence and discipline. You have to know a lot of engineering to be a pilot, and to think out front of a problem because of the speeds you're traveling at. Plus the world looks different from up there. Much smaller," he says.

Friends add that the military was his own form of grounding, a way of staying connected to the real world while living in the shadow of an eccentric billionaire father.

TURNING TO REAL ESTATE

Ross Jr. grew up watching his father turn EDS from a backyard computer service company into a high-tech behemoth with a global reach. He planted trees at the former company headquarters on Forest Lane, camped out there with the Boy Scouts, and when his father and his partners sold the company to General Motors for $2.6 billion in 1984 became an instant real estate tycoon.

"I had four sisters, an aunt, and a grandmother," he says, "so literally it was just Dad and me looking for something to do together. Now computer service is pretty complex for a young guy. But we both liked real estate, and it was much easier for a father and son to work on."

So in the 1980s they began buying thousands of acres of undeveloped land in Plano and other suburban communities, just as the real estate market was crashing.

"If the market hadn't turned down, we would never have become developers," he recalls. "We spent a lot of time in bankruptcy court." They developed Legacy in Plano, Circle T Ranch in Westlake, and several more residential developments.

Twenty years later Alliance Airport is still only 25 percent complete, while Victory Park will take fifteen more years to finish. Yet

2.7. *The view from Victory Park Plaza south toward downtown. Photograph by Kathryn Holliday.*

Mr. Perot is looking for new projects. He's starting a hotel company in India, is "watching" Dubai, and at the request of the royal family may take a second look at Abu Dhabi in the United Arab Emirates.

Suddenly he tips back in his chair and stares at the ceiling, as if trying to picture working in such far-flung outposts. Then, just as suddenly, he's back in Texas, in the ozone this time. He says he hasn't been able to ride his bike lately because of all the red and orange alerts.

"Our big issue here is going to be air quality," he says. "We're in trouble. I'm shocked that the citizens of North Texas don't push environmentalism more and that our political leadership hasn't forced us to clean up the air."

He says that the new W is going to be "pretty green" and that Hillwood is building green warehouses at Alliance. "We're doing OK, but we could be doing better."

Time is running out, and there's still a photo to take. He points toward a black Hummer in the parking lot and slips behind the wheel for the three hundred-yard trip to the new Victory Plaza, a grand public space with some of the qualities of a pinball machine.

From here, the shape of Mr. Perot's "city within a city" starts to come into focus: Victory Park Lane, lined with condos and apartments, curving toward Reunion Tower in the distance, the ball sitting atop its stem like a gigantic cocktail onion (fig. 2.7). And in the other direction, the W, its helipad peeking over the edge like an eyebrow, lines up regimentally with other downtown skyscrapers, as though Victory were just an extension of an established pattern.

"Come back to Dallas in ten years and it will be a whole new city," he says confidently, as though he's already got the plans in hand. "With the price of gas and the increase in congestion, it is going to develop an East Coast, European lifestyle. People will have a place in Victory, walk back and forth to work during the week, then go out to the country for the weekend. I can see it."

3

THE METROPOLITAN LANDSCAPE

Dillon never defined his role as an architecture critic to focus solely on buildings or the urban center—and while he returned over and over to downtown Dallas as a subject, he never neglected the much larger sprawling metropolitan landscape that surrounded it. Dallas and Fort Worth are the largest twin centers in a polynucleated urban region defined by a vast accumulation of more than two hundred separately incorporated suburban cities over more than nine thousand square miles. Many of those cities began as nineteenth-century farming towns, some began as railroad whistle stops, others sprang up as newly invented bedroom communities after World War II, and still others incorporated as late as the 1970s and 1980s, the result of continued white flight and economic segregation. Dillon wrote with some ambivalence about the challenges of creating a distinct civic identity in the midst of this metropolitan jumble that sprawls across the Texas prairie and the flood plains of the Trinity River. On the one hand, he embraced the romantic tradition of the westward-facing American pioneer and celebrated the wide open possibilities of the seemingly endless prairie landscape. He appreciated the allure of the open highway and intuitively understood its appeal to the thousands of people who lived in and loved Dallas-Fort Worth's exurban landscapes: the freeway "extended the democratic fluidity of the grid, allowing the city to run on and on."* On the other hand, Dillon critiqued the isolation of suburban corporate campuses and gated communities that led to thoughtless waste and social fragmentation.

In the decades in which *Learning from Las Vegas* generated both controversy and admiration for the vernacular of the automobile-oriented commercial strip, Dillon used his columns to promote a little learning about Dallas-Fort Worth and the pathways that connected them: the Trinity River, Highway 80, and railroad viaducts.† While opponents of sprawl focus on cars and highways as destructive influences on urban development, Dillon could join that critique while still embracing the highway as essential to the identity of the metropolitan landscape: "This is a car city and a freeway city, and nothing is likely to change that."‡ He cataloged the attempts of suburban cities to create a sense of identity within this suburban sprawl, allowing cities like Addison, Richardson, Grand Prairie, Grapevine, and Arlington to carve out distinctive footprints that kept them from being swallowed up into the expanding metroplex. This enclave mentality posed direct challenges to issues of equitable housing and shared public space.

Another recurring theme is the landscape itself. While the rolling topography of North Texas offers little dramatic terrain, Dillon saw the potential of the prairie, the Trinity, and its tributaries to create a shared sense of environment among the highways and suburban territorial boundaries. His recurring coverage of the long and bitter debates over master plans for developing the Trinity River consistently focused on creating "a soft, green place in a hard, dry land" that could allow greater access to shared public space. Dillon's coverage of these plans began in the 1980s and the three essays included here provide much needed context for the development of those plans today. While he loved highways, he did not love the idea of a highway within the levees of the river. From the beginning, he argued passionately against pairing the river with an "urban expressway," and in August 2017, the Dallas City Council finally voted against building a toll road in the Trinity's flood plain.

The essays gathered here cover this sprawling, divided conception

---

* See "Why We Should Love Freeways," 1990.

† Robert Venturi, Denise Scott Brown, and Steven Izenour, *Learning from Las Vegas* (Cambridge, MA: MIT Press, 1972).

‡ See "Stream Dreams," 1999.

of the city, where public spaces and landmarks like water towers, neon signs, bridges, public parks, and overpasses are the most identifiable public landmarks that can help root communities in shared public spaces. These anonymous and often overlooked cultural landscapes were essential to Dillon's larger sense of Texas architecture: the "small and fragile parts of the city are as important as the arenas and skyscrapers."*

---

* See "Shelter and Shade," 2008.

A trip down memory four-lane: Highway 80 once carried travelers from coast to coast. Super highways put an end to that, but not to its vintage charms

APRIL 7, 1985

While some of the landmarks that Dillon celebrates in this love let-
ter to vintage Highway 80 have now fallen by the wayside—most
notably the Alamo Plaza Hotel in Dallas—remarkably, Theo's
Drive-In and the Yello Belly drag racing track and a handful of oth-
ers survive. The overall blue-collar and rural time warp this ride
down Highway 80 provides is intact today. Dillon celebrates its
nostalgia, but the slow-paced, stop-and-start highway ride from
Dallas through Grand Prairie, Arlington, and Handley to Fort
Worth remains a critical piece of the metropolitan landscape.

It never got the good press of Route 66. Pop singers couldn't seem to
find their kicks on it; Martin Milner and George Maharis didn't cruise
it every Friday night in their sleek Corvette. And yet, in its way, Highway 80 has as valid a claim to being called America's main street as
its more northerly cousin. It is a gaudy, cacophonous, and sometimes
humorous reminder of what cross-country travel was like before there
were interstates and ring roads and other romance-less circumnavi-
gational aids.

Highway 80 begins on the Georgia coast near Savannah, humps up
briefly toward Macon and the prehistoric Indian mounds at Ocmul-
gee, then slides down again to Montgomery and Selma, Alabama,

battlegrounds from another war. From there, it runs arrow-like toward Vicksburg, Mississippi, where Grant and Sherman starved out the Confederate Army and turned the tide of the Civil War, then on to Monroe and Shreveport, Louisiana, and into Texas.

On its Lone Star leg, Highway 80 wraps over and around Interstate 20, which superseded it in the mid-sixties, slicing through Marshall, Kilgore, Longview, and other vestiges of the East Texas oil boom. In Dallas, it is briefly West Commerce and Fort Worth Avenue, turning into Main Street in Grand Prairie, Division in Arlington, and East Lancaster in Fort Worth. There, it merges once again with Highways 20 and 30, after which it slowly loses its identity and sense of direction as it winds through New Mexico, Arizona, and California, terminating in San Diego.

The Dallas-Fort Worth stretch of Highway 80, though barely forty miles long, contains much of the kaleidoscopic variety of the rest of the road. It is rural and urban, sophisticated and kicker, a meandering four-lane strip of gas stations, trailer parks, and optimistically named tourist courts—Shangri-La, Mt. Vernon—that once enticed weary travelers with promises of private showers and "refrigerated air."

For decades, Highway 80 was the busiest stretch of highway in North Texas, carrying nearly fourteen thousand cars a day, more than 4 million a year in the early 1950s. These numbers are roughly a tenth of what major expressways such as Central and Stemmons carry today, but in the '30s and '40s they were sufficient to make Highway 80 one of the most prized strips of blacktop in the Southwest. In the early 1940s, before Oak Cliff went dry, it was home to Pappy's Showland and the big bands of Glenn Miller and Guy Lombardo. One bombastic Arlington mayor went so far as to describe it as the "Broadway of America." Seldom beautiful and almost never coherent, Highway 80 was nevertheless a vital strand of raw, blue-collar Americana that underscored in neon and bold graphics that most durable of American themes—the open road and the possibility of a wondrous new frontier waiting just over the horizon.

That Highway 80 is largely a memory now, a crumbling parenthesis between the freeways and interstates that long ago surrounded it. Driving it today is like falling into a time warp in which some colorful bits of regional history have been temporarily preserved.

We roll beneath the triple underpass on West Commerce, then creep past the new Lew Sterrett Justice Center, a superb architectural deterrent to crime, cross the viaduct with its period street lamps, and immediately find ourselves among used car lots and mobile home parks. This is the strip architecture of the 1980s, yet not so far removed from what was there decades ago. Off to one side, like museum exhibits, sit the Mission Motel and Alamo Plaza Hotel Courts, colorful relics of a tourist court row that once included some thirty complexes designed in the popular vernacular styles of the time—from the predictable Mission and Spanish Colonial styles of the Southwest to less indigenous species such as the Cotswold cottage.

In 1985, the distinction between motel and hotel is sometimes hard to grasp. What is the Hilton Inn at Central and Mockingbird, for example? But in the 1920s and '30s, when most of the Highway 80 units were built, the situation was simpler. A tourist court was simply the next phase of the stagecoach inn—a small, modest building that offered rudimentary lodging for highway travelers. If sometimes uncomfortable, many were colorful and welcoming, with individual carports next to each unit, covered porches, flower boxes, and, in the really posh versions, "refrigerated air." With the decline of Highway 80's fortunes, most of the remaining tourist courts have turned residential, charging about $75 a week for what used to be a standard unit.

Architectural conformity is never an issue along Highway 80. The buildings are mostly small and cheap, the signs large and expensive, with the startling juxtaposition being almost de rigueur. Beyond the first rise, where Highway 80 turns into Fort Worth Avenue, we come upon El Taco Illegal, La Estrallita Ballroom, the recently closed Torch restaurant, and Last Frontier and Palace Courts motels, the latter featuring pitched Hansel and Gretel roofs and rugged fieldstone walls (fig. 3.1). Clyde Barrow is buried close by in the Western Heights Cemetery, not far from Luchea's Psychic World.

From 1915 to 1927, the enterprising Victor Clifford Bilbo tied this area together with his Bilbo Jitney line. For five cents, a person could ride from the Dallas County Courthouse on Commerce to the fringes of West Dallas, which at that time included Irving, Cement City—where the Portland Cement plant is now—and such long-forgotten destinations as Sowers and Gates.

The traditional pulse of Highway 80 is strongest on weekends. Scattered up and down the sides of the road are station wagons and battered pickup trucks weighted down to the tire rims with oranges and grapefruit, sacks of pecans, stuffed toy animals, rolls of carpet—

3.1. *The Palace Courts, built in 1930, still survive at 4054 W. Davis Street in West Dallas near Cockrell Hill and Grand Prairie on the old Highway 80, also known as the Bankhead Highway. They are a lingering reminder of the motor courts, motels, and gas stations that used to dominate the highway landscape. Photograph by Carol Highsmith. The Lyda Hill Texas Collection of Photographs in Carol M. Highsmith's America Project, Library of Congress, Prints and Photographs Division.*

a moveable feast of non-essential consumer goods arranged, more or less, to catch the wandering eye of the tourist.

On Saturdays and Sundays, the Yello Belly drag strip is in operation, the squeal and the smell of burning rubber floating cloud-like over the grounds. As many spectators seem to catch the action from the lip of the highway as from the stands. Nearby is a gun range and an automobile auction, and not too far away a drive-in pawn shop, perhaps the only one in the world. As an expression of Highway 80's blue-collar, gimme-cap character, it is perfect.

Through downtown Grand Prairie, Highway 80 becomes Main Street. The mix of businesses changes little: gas stations and auto body shops, interspersed with hardware stores, supermarkets, a gigantic drive-in movie screen, and a cluster of antique stores. The United Auto Workers union hall is here, along with a scattering of Rodeway Inns and Pizza Huts. Some sidewalks are covered by canopies, a sensible if somewhat labored allusion to the western town that Grand Prairie never really was. And running down the middle of Main Street is the quintessential symbol of the American West, a railroad track—with a string of flat cars waiting in anticipation of who knows what—running off toward an infinitely receding horizon.

Between Grand Prairie and Arlington, Highway 80 peters out into nondescript strip architecture once again. It loops around behind Six Flags Over Texas and Six Flags Mall, past long rows of cookie-cutter warehouses and familiar fast-food restaurants. The vast General Motors plant, the source of most of the area's prosperity, looms off to the south. But there are bright spots, such as the sign for Zolon's Courts beckoning us to linger for "A Day or a Lifetime." And a vintage 1950s drive-in called Theo's, with its neon sign and zigzag metal canopy suggesting the possibility, if not the fact, of carhops on roller skates. The vast and gloomily mysterious Eastern Star Home is here, not far from the Home for Aged Masons, set amid one of the few remaining large pecan groves along this length of Highway 80.

As it crosses into Fort Worth, the highway slips briefly back into character: the West Begins Motel, a sign for a minnow shack, with the second *n* painted in after the fact, and clusters of pawn shops and antique stores, some of the latter featuring wagons, wheels, and other bits of regional bric-a-brac plopped shamelessly out in front. Here and there, the highway bites at the edges of old neighborhoods, mostly black and Hispanic, built up of small frame houses including a few long, narrow "shotguns." There's a deep country feel to some of these blocks, even though they lie within sight of downtown Fort Worth, its skyline now dominated by the futuristic City Center towers designed by Paul Rudolph. Just east of downtown, Highway 80 becomes orderly and businesslike again, merging invisibly with efficient, six-lane Interstates 30 and 20.

Before progress caught up with it, Highway 80 was the economic spine that connected Dallas both to Fort Worth and to the piney vastness of East Texas. More money flowed into these cities on Highway 80 than on any other route. Yet at its height, the Dallas-Fort Worth stretch of Highway 80 had fifty-three traffic lights and nearly that many cross streets. A forty-mile trip could take two hours. To merchants along the strip, the sluggish traffic was a godsend. But it was not a highly prized value among transportation experts concerned with speeding a truckload of seedless grapes from Anaheim to Atlanta in two days.

In the early 1950s, the crush of traffic got so heavy that proposals for widening, straightening, extending, and otherwise improving this precious slice of real estate appeared almost monthly. One called for making Highway 80 one-way and constructing a companion expressway to the south. Merchants managed to beat down this proposal, but not for long. The wedge of progress had arrived.

In 1957, the state finally opened the Dallas/Fort Worth Turnpike. And with it the vitality, if not the raw, indigenous character of Highway 80 began to change. In the mid-1960s, I-20 was completed, another of Texas's many legacies from the 1956 National Highway Act, which eventually put 90 percent of America's cities on one vast and largely colorless highway system.

Over the next decade, Highway 80 became a vehicular backwater, an eddy in the powerful current of commercial traffic. Nothing is going to revive Highway 80 because no one really has to drive it anymore. Nostalgia rather than business is the appeal now. And history.

Why we should love freeways: Dallas was built not only by freeways but for them—made to be seen at 60 mph with the top down

JUNE 3, 1990

From its opening lines, Dillon's essay evokes the fast and often hard-to-navigate world of North Texas freeways with its cryptic nicknames and internal logic. Dillon was both a critic and fan of the open highway and wrote about it repeatedly over the years. This particular article best captures the ways in which Dillon connected the spirit of the highway to its creation of an "open-ended city."

From the peaks of LBJ—the flyover to Stemmons Freeway, for example—Dallas unfolds like a gigantic topographic map, with clumps of trees marking rivers and creeks and the towers of downtown and Las Colinas erupting through the surface like magma.

Overviews are hard to come by on this flat, tabletop landscape, unless you have an office on the fiftieth floor—or drive the freeways. The freeways lift us momentarily out of the urban sprawl and expose the abstract, infinitely receding drama of prairie and sky. In this largely featureless terrain, freeways are lines of force that establish boundaries and structure the way we live.

Every city has its cachet. New Orleans has the French Quarter, San Francisco the Golden Gate Bridge. Dallas is a city of rides: two-ticket rides, three-ticket rides, and a clutch of exhilarating, indelible four-ticket rides that rival anything Disneyland and Six Flags have to offer.

117

Like most western cities, Dallas is made for the sweeping panoramic view, made to be seen at 60 miles an hour with the top down.

This is not how Dallas likes to think of itself, even though nearly everyone here drives and it is difficult to get anywhere without using the freeways. Implicit in our rush to be a "world-class" city is a nostalgia for a turn-of-the-century urbanism of row houses and boulevards and bustling civic squares; a longing for the Paris of Hemingway and the expatriates, or the London of *Upstairs, Downstairs*.

But instead of the Rue de Rivoli or Trafalgar Square, Dallas has freeways, three hundred miles of them, coiling about the city like a necklace—or a noose, depending on one's point of view.

A sure way to jump-start a stalled conversation is to mention rush hour on Central Expressway (US Highway 75). A chorus of commiserative groans swells up where only awkward silence was before. And the chorus is bound to grow louder and shriller as the billion-dollar expansion of Central gets under way this week.

Freeway bashing has become part of American conversational culture, like complaining about taxes or the weather. We load onto freeways many of our ambivalences about cities, so that they have become synonyms for urban misery.

And yet freeways are as compelling a symbol of the modern American city as skyscrapers, particularly in the West, where space routinely pulls people apart instead of drawing them together.

LIFE, LIBERTY, AND THE PURSUIT OF ASPHALT

While freeways generate their share of problems—pollution, noise, sprawl—they also make it possible to go where we want, when we want, alone if we like, and cheaper and faster than almost any other means of transport. They are among the most democratic of modern technologies, a Bill of Rights for wheels.

To understand what freeways mean to Dallas, it is necessary only to observe them at night, from above, when the red glow of taillights turns them into immense veins and arteries. The language of freeways is laced with biological terms—circulation, bypasses, feeders, arterials—that only underscore their life-sustaining role. An estimated 22 million vehicle miles are racked up daily on Dallas area freeways, which translates into 2.5 million cars on an average day.

Like it or not, Los Angeles is Dallas's parent, and Houston, Denver, and Albuquerque its next of kin.

In these cities freeways are more than conveniences for getting from A to B; they are public spaces, distinct from the world of streets and sidewalks, yet possessing their own order and etiquette. When it is working well, a freeway is an invisibly choreographed dance. To sweep onto Stemmons from Woodall Rodgers, then slice diagonally across six lanes of traffic to catch Interstate 30 to Fort Worth, all without braking or losing the beat on the radio, demands flawless timing and a fine understanding of freeway protocol.

For many people, the rush-hour commutes are the only private, un-interrupted intervals of the day, times to fantasize, meditate, practice one's sales pitch or basso profundo. On the freeway we can be alone while remaining part of the grand flow, participant and observer both.

The better freeways are linear art galleries, with the buildings and bridges and murals arranged like exhibits. Stretches of Stemmons (Interstate 35E) and the Dallas North Tollway qualify, although they can't compare to the Hollywood or San Diego freeways in Los Angeles, which abound with murals and sculptural curiosities.

The best freeways are in themselves works of art. Frank Lloyd Wright, no slouch as a prophet, once observed that "as new and greater road systems are added year by year they are more splendidly built. I foresee that roads will soon be architecture too ... great architecture."

Mr. Wright was correct, as usual. Freeways are paradigms of form following function, far clearer and more instructive than buildings, particularly over-decorated postmodern buildings. Freeways are concatenations of curves, slopes, and tangents, enlarged diagrams from geometry textbooks. The roadways represent the triumph of the horizontal line over the accidents of topography, while the inter-changes and overpasses are heroic minimalist sculptures, the modern equivalent of the Roman aqueducts.

From downtown, Dallas's freeways radiate outward to the suburbs like spokes on a wheel, paralleling old rail lines and commercial routes, occasionally representing the apotheosis of a trail. At their extremities the spokes join LBJ and I-20, which mark the boundary between city and suburb, the way medieval walls separated town and countryside.

At key points these great walls are pierced by interchanges that resemble the civic gateways to ancient cities. These monumental entrances—Interstate 20 and US Highway 67, LBJ (Interstate 635) and Stemmons—become frames for the downtown skyline, conveying a sense of civic importance that is uplifting, worthy of celebration.

THANK YOU, MR. TURNER

Until the 1940s Dallas had a few parkways and boulevards, including Swiss Avenue and Turtle Creek Boulevard, but like most American cities, no freeways. With the completion of Central Expressway in 1949, Texas's first freeway, Dallas began to ooze north as Richardson and Plano became exits instead of remote prairie outposts. But it was the passage of the Federal-Aid Highway Act in 1956, abetted by cheap FHA mortgages, that started the stampede for the suburbs. From the late 1950s, when Stemmons and the Dallas/Fort Worth Turnpike (I-30) were opened, to the early 1970s, which saw the substantial completion of LBJ and I-20, Dallas grew by 179 square miles. The city's population almost tripled from 300,000 in 1940 to 885,000 in 1970.

The Sun Belt boom didn't start in the late 1970s, with the wholesale emigration of Cleveland and Buffalo to the Southwest, but in the 1950s, with the inauguration of the Interstate Highway System.

Appropriately, perhaps prophetically, the key man at the Federal Highway Administration during these years was Francis "Frank" Turner, a native of Dallas and a graduate of Texas A&M. He helped build the Alaska-Canada highway in the 1940s and then went to Washington as President Eisenhower's point man on the federal highway program. He was so committed to the interstate cause that he refused to pull strings even for his parents when they were displaced by Interstate 35W in Fort Worth.

"They said, 'Son, can't you do anything?'" Mr. Turner told a reporter later. "And of course I couldn't. Well, they didn't want to leave the old place, but when they got settled into the new house, all brick, they were happy."

Frank Turner's freeway program changed the cosmography of Dallas, redirecting energy and resources from the center to the periphery. It extended the democratic fluidity of the grid, allowing the city to run on and on, mostly across abandoned cotton fields beyond Loop 12. Once considered Dallas's northern boundary, psychologically at least, Loop 12 (Northwest Highway) quickly became synonymous with downtown Dallas for residents of Plano and McKinney.

Instead of one downtown, Dallas suddenly had half a dozen, each with its own skyscrapers and shopping mall and continental restaurant. Main Street was no longer main street; Central and LBJ were. By the late '70s, Dallas was a loose constellation of satellites linked by freeways, rather than the contained radial city of earlier decades.

In many, particularly older cities, freeways were superimposed with an awesome disregard for existing boundaries and topography. Lying down in front of the road graders became a staple of '60s activism.

But Dallas built most of its freeways when land was cheap and the potential disruption minimal. Overall, they stimulated development instead of disrupting it.

Even so, there are scars, most of them borne by the poorer, minority communities. Central Expressway cut through the heart of historic Freedman's Town and further isolated Deep Ellum from downtown. Woodall Rodgers did the same thing to the State-Thomas district.

And even enthusiasts acknowledge that freeways can be sclerotic. Central Expressway, designed for 80,000 cars a day, now carries an average of 153,000. LBJ groans under 207,000 cars a day, despite predictions that its peak would be 85,000. Congestion lasts all day instead of only in the morning and evening.

The new engineering term for maxed-out freeways is "hyperactive," which means that even though they regularly exceed capacity—2,200 cars per lane per hour—they keep on flowing. No one is sure how this happens, although one theory attributes it to a combination of smaller cars and savvy drivers who can tailgate at 65 miles an hour, like A. J. Foyt.

Yet it is doubtful that, even if it wanted to, Dallas could survive without its freeways. In 1980, the freeways carried half of its daily traffic and 70 percent of its rush-hour volume. In 1987, the average automobile commute was 23 minutes, compared to 38.5 minutes for public transportation.

Imagine driving from Dallas to Arlington daily on US Highway 80. Even as a change of pace it is excruciating. North Park is ten minutes from downtown on Central, but thirty minutes and thirteen lights via McKinney and Hillcrest. For lack of a freeway, driving crosstown from Buckner Boulevard to the Dallas Market Center can take forty minutes.

THE ROAD AHEAD

In America "the road" always has been about the future, an emblem of change, a promise of possibility. From Whitman to Steinbeck, Kerouac, and Joan Didion, it has communicated a message of freedom and untapped potential. To "hit the road" means not just to move on, but to move toward something better. The freeway expresses these values in a more dramatic form.

In his 1922 drawings for La Ville Contemporaine, or the modern city, the great Swiss architect Le Corbusier showed freeways flying across the urban landscape on stilts, penetrating the centers of buildings and liberating the ground beneath for parks and gardens. Le Corbusier hated crowded conventional cities and would have demolished half of Paris to accommodate his streamlined futuristic vision. Nevertheless, his ideas exerted powerful influence on urban freeway designers for decades.

So did those of industrial designer Norman Bel Geddes, whose *Futurama* exhibit at the 1939 World's Fair introduced 10 million dazzled visitors to the concept of "superroads," twelve-lane expressways on which cars sped at 120 miles an hour.

There is plenty of Corbu and Bel Geddes in the intersection of I-20 and Highway 67, and even more on the Dallas North Tollway near the Galleria.

Here is a *Blade Runner* landscape of triumphal arches and snake-like curves and twenty-story knife edges, all arranged like sculpture on a vast coffee table. For one extraordinary stretch the roadway and the buildings seem to be one, as in Le Corbusier's drawings, though without the parks and gardens below. Europeans applaud this brash display of American chutzpah, even as the locals moan, "Why us, Lord?"

Whatever Dallas's urban future may be, we're all going to drive to it. This is a car city and a freeway city, and nothing is likely to change that.

The rebuilding of Central is only the controversial centerpiece of a ten-year, $3 billion road program for Dallas. Growth will continue to be centrifugal, as it is in most American cities. Twice as many Americans commute from suburb to suburb as from suburb to downtown. In Dallas County, only an estimated 10 percent of the commuters work downtown.

Such sprawl presents insurmountable obstacles to rail transit, which requires high densities and a simple linear pattern to survive. Train into town in the morning, train out again in the evening. There are no models for a successful suburb-to-suburb rail system of the kind that Dallas requires.

The fear that orbiting satellite cities will kill the old-fashioned downtowns has been exaggerated, as visits to Baltimore, Boston, Chicago, Columbus, Ohio, and dozens of other cities confirm. Even downtown Los Angeles is booming.

What the satellites have done is make traditional downtowns more

specialized. Downtown Dallas may end up as a convention and entertainment center, with no housing, little shopping, and only banks and
government offices for ballast.

Faced with the often chaotic growth of the satellite cities, it is easy
to forget that the older organic cities evolved slowly, and after much
trial and error. Dallas needs a broader urban vision that accommo-
dates the satellite cities and that acknowledges not only the necessity
but the virtues of freeways.

RIDE OF RIDES

To get in the right frame of mind, take a run south down Stemmons on
a clear morning when rush hour is ebbing. The freeway unfurls like
a long ribbon, fluttering side to side and up and down on its rush to
downtown.

On its northern fringes, around LBJ, it is little more than a strip,
flanked by hamburger stands and miniature golf courses.

Closer to town, the images start to bunch up and overlap, and Stemmons changes from a slide show to a movie (fig. 3.2). Buildings grow

3.2. *The Stemmons Freeway, winding its way southeast toward downtown Dallas
in 1994, with the Trinity River flood plain at right. Photograph by Squire Haskins
Photography, Special Collections, University of Texas at Arlington.*

larger and more athletic. The Stouffer Hotel advances and recedes like a dancing tube of lipstick. The Reunion ball bounces now to the right of the center lane, now to the left, then lands dead-ahead like the bull's eye in a target.

Then comes the Loews Anatole hotel, hunkering down like a sumo wrestler, and the Infomart, London's Crystal Palace reborn as an electronics warehouse. These forms make no sense except as freeway exhibits.

Beyond are the Katy freight yards, bracketed by grain elevators and the strutting Dallas Power & Light substation, a collection of relics mounting up through the warehouses of the West End to the pirouetting prism of the First Interstate Bank Tower—an architectural time line in 3-D.

And then the big payoff: a jog to the right . . . the arcing, gravity-defying leap to Woodall Rodgers . . . the Trinity flood plain spread out to the right . . . the West End straight ahead . . . a shudder of anticipation . . . and a quick veer to the left, like the final surge of the roller coaster.

It is Dallas's ultimate thrill ride, impressive enough to sell the producers of *RoboCop* on Dallas—and memorable enough, perhaps, to make us celebrate the open-ended city the freeways make possible.

Tower power: Water tanks rise to provide scenery, a sense of place, ad space, islands of roadside whimsy

JANUARY 20, 1991

For simple, utilitarian structures, water towers come in spectacular disguises: hamburgers, champagne corks, golf tees, candles, thermos bottles, rocket ships, even the Tin Man's hat.

Though too industrial to be true pop art, they certainly qualify as inadvertent public sculpture, for which the local tabletop landscape provides the spacious setting.

Water towers are mainly flatland phenomena, a way of ensuring that residents of topographically deprived areas such as Dallas have enough water pressure to keep their lawn sprinklers clicking and their fire insurance rates down. The flatter the landscape, the more visible the towers become.

There is hardly a city or town in Texas without at least one aerial water tower out on the highway, telling travelers where they are and why they should be happy to be there.

Who could locate Farmers Branch without its white water tower, erupting from the flatlands off LBJ Freeway like a gigantic vanilla ice cream cone? Plano would be just another clump of anonymous sub-divisions along Central Expressway if it weren't for its scattering of bulbous water towers, set out like onions, each inscribed with the red, white, and blue Plano logo.

This is the most obvious symbolic function of the towers, as landmarks. In West Texas, water towers and grain elevators are the principal navigational aids, often the only measure of "middle distance" on an infinitely extended landscape.

Yet names and logos are rarely enough for aspiring municipalities. There is invariably the urge to boost and advertise, to welcome visitors to the home of the Red Delicious apple or the site of this year's PGA Championship. For this purpose, the tanks become spherical billboards.

Lewisville is a northern suburb of Dallas. More important, it is the stomping ground of the "Fighting Farmers" football team, a fact underscored by a pitchfork-brandishing farmer on the municipal water tower on Interstate 35. Golden arches and revolving chicken buckets are no match for this aerial display.

Some towns paint their water towers like checkerboards; others prefer candy stripes or chevrons. The more aesthetically attuned use them as canvases for the work of local artists.

Las Cruces, New Mexico, used two of its water tanks as canvases for scenographic paintings of American Indian and Spanish history by local artist Tony Pennock. Germantown, Maryland, took a *National Geographic* approach by turning its water tower into a view of the Earth, as seen by the *Apollo* astronauts from twenty thousand miles. Gaffney, South Carolina, deep in the American Peach Belt, gave its water tank a ripe blush and a steel stem and leaf. Designed by CBI of Chicago, it could just as easily have been created by sculptor Claes Oldenburg.

And for anyone with an interest in urban history, water towers provide a handy three-dimensional time line on which to plot how far and how fast a town has grown.

The oldest surviving water tower in University Park, erected in 1934, has a homely, erector-set quality, with narrow steel ladders and catwalks, the SMU mustang on the tank, and a tiny tots playground at the base. It is a small town, pre-freeway relic, a piece of municipal archaeology.

The town's other water tower, near Northwest Highway and Hillcrest Avenue, is four times larger and bursting with swagger.

When it was built in 1949, it marked the northern edge of Dallas's development; now it looms over subdivisions and shopping centers like an errant spaceship.

The town of Allen, a few miles north of Plano on I-75, offers a more condensed version of the same story. On one side of the highway stands a slender, Buck Rogers-ish tower with the word "Allen" fading slowly away. On the opposite side of Central stands the new tower, white and massive, with "Town of Allen" written in crisp red and white letters. (Patriotic color schemes are never out of style on water towers.) The difference between the two is the difference between cotton town and commuter suburb.

To the pioneer modernists of the early twentieth century, American water towers and grain silos were paradigms for a new world architecture. Le Corbusier and others traveled the country admiring their stark simplicity and purity of form. All surface and mass, without a hint of period decoration, they represented architecture reduced to its essentials.

Some artists and photographers of the period made the celebration of simple industrial forms the basis of an entire aesthetic. Charles Sheeler—a tower man if ever there was one—followed much the same route as Le Corbusier, painting pictures of steel mills and silos. Berenice Abbott and Margaret Bourke-White took memorable photographs of urban towers and tanks, of which the neon-striped tanks atop the West End MarketPlace might be colorized re-creations.

In our time, Bernd and Hilla Becher have devoted their careers to photographing industrial architecture, spending years on a book on water towers. In their photographs, the towers have a stark, abstract quality, as though they had been painted onto a neutral backdrop—the way we see them in West Texas.

The engineers who design the towers think of them less poetically. They are spheroids, ellipsoids, hydropillars, hydropeds, waterspheres. The Gaffney "Peachoid" and the Germantown "Earthoid" reveal a sense of humor that is seldom associated with the concatenation of vents, valves, and risers that make the towers work.

So much stark monumentality and industrial clarity sometimes gets the better of residents, who don't enjoy being loomed over by an ellipsoid that resembles E.T. In response to neighborhood uneasiness, Dallas Water Utilities is trying to put more of its storage tanks underground, with only a fraction of their enormous bulk visible to nearby residents.

Near Forest Lane and Abrams Road, the city has constructed a 10 million-gallon underground tank with a veneer of Georgian respectability. The exterior is covered with bands of colored brick and has faux windows and doors, several with pediments, as well as a crisp cornice line. It is positively chirpy and would have nauseated Le Corbusier. The only clues to its real function are a steel ladder attached to the roof and a collection of steel vents and pipes off in one corner. "People think it's an indoor arena, and all those windows are where you buy tickets," says Greg Kuchy, assistant director of Dallas Water Utilities. "Maybe that's the kind of response we're looking for. We want to be good neighbors." On Jim Miller Road, this neighborliness is expressed by a landscape earth wall that surrounds the storage tank, on top of which are fourteen public tennis courts. The city recently redesigned the pump station as well, adding arched windows, glass block, and a veneer of vaguely Southwestern brick and stucco.

A new storage tank on Sorcey Road, in far southwest Dallas, also will get the residential treatment, including a pitched roof and decorative trim that fits the neighborhood. It will be surrounded by a park and soccer fields.

The city maintains that the underground tanks are cheaper, easier to maintain, and friendlier to neighborhoods. This is probably true. But to the unreconstructed modernist and the highway sculpture enthusiast, the domestication of the water tower also involves a certain loss.

The aerial towers are the surrogate hills and bluffs that nature chose not to bestow on North Texas. The bold landmark, visible for miles, shrinks to a discreet bump in the earth.

A Georgian storage tank doesn't inspire the same kind of awe as 2 million gallons of water sloshing around 150 feet in the air. It's easy to drive by the first without noticing it, while the second usually brings us up short, like a conjuring trick that we have to see just one more time.

All surface and mass, without a hint of period decoration, they represented architecture reduced to its essentials.

Building a city's future: Habitat for Humanity has an answer for urban blight

OCTOBER 4, 1992

Much of Dillon's coverage of housing issues focused on high-end and luxury housing, from gated suburban communities to downtown lofts. But affordable housing increasingly became a public problem in Dallas, and discussions of models of affordable housing became more frequent. This is an early piece on the subject, highlighting Habitat for Humanity's entrée into the issues of suburban housing; Habitat's practices have changed since this essay was written.

On Friday afternoons, Rosalia Serrato leaves work at a downtown hotel, changes quickly into jeans and a sweatshirt, and climbs up on a roof or under a porch (soon to be her roof and her porch). The house is a modest bungalow, like hundreds of others in East Dallas. But for someone who has been living with three children in a one-bedroom apartment, it looks like Versailles. It has a small kitchen with a new stove and refrigerator, a living room with a vaulted ceiling, three bedrooms and a backyard shaded by a massive oak tree for climbing.

"My fourteen-year-old son keeps asking me, 'When am I going to have my own room?'" Ms. Serrato says, "and I keep saying, 'Some day, some day.'"

"Some day" now means November 14, when Ms. Serrato will put on her best Mexican dress, cook up mole and ranchero beans for her

129

neighbors, and move her family onto Lindell Avenue, between Greenville and Live Oak.

Habitat for Humanity, an international volunteer organization, and the Junior League of Dallas are providing the money and the labor for the house. Dallas architect Paige Close designed it in conjunction with a local American Institute of Architects affordable housing competition. And Ms. Serrato has put in four hundred hours of sweat equity to cover part of her down payment. She'd put in four thousand hours if she had to.

"I've never owned a house," she says excitedly. "In Mexico I lived with my mother and father, and in America I've always lived in small apartments. So this is my dream, this house for me and my children."

Ms. Serrato, thirty-four and divorced, found out about Habitat from a girlfriend at the hotel who urged her to apply. She says she was skeptical that anyone "would take a poor girl with three children." But in February she filed an application for a house, accompanied by copies of her income tax return, her employment and credit history, and other personal information to prove that she would be a solid and upstanding homeowner. Members of Habitat's Family Review Committee visited her apartment twice. Then nothing. For weeks, no calls. "You lied to me," she told her friend. "They'll never call."

But they did. In May, she went to Dallas Habitat's office on Hudson Street to meet the Junior League women who had volunteered to build her house. Because she was first to qualify, she got her choice of house plans and could pick the siding (blue and white), the carpet (rust), and the light fixtures (brass with a bit of etched glass).

"We were all impressed by her strength," says Jody Lyke, chair of Habitat's Family Review Committee. "She's been through a lot, but she doesn't dwell on it. She believes that things will get better if she works hard."

Like most Habitat houses, Ms. Serrato's is compact (one thousand square feet) and efficient rather than fancy. The basic structure consists of large prefabricated panels that volunteers can put up in a day. The kitchen contains a counter so the living room won't have to be used for eating. Hallways are narrow so rooms can be larger. Her oldest son will sleep in the middle bedroom; the younger sons will share the front bedroom, and she will take the one in back, looking out on the yard. "Private," she says peeking between the studs, "very private." She repeats the word half a dozen times, like a mantra.

Mr. Close, the architect, made his design fit the neighborhood by adding a large front porch and a double gable that allows for a tall living room. With a backyard, Ms. Serrato will no longer have to drive her children to the park to play.

Habitat for Humanity has received glowing press in the wake of Hurricane Andrew. Amid the residential rubble of South Florida, Habitat's houses emerged structurally sound, with only a few broken windows and ripped shingles. Instead of cheap construction, Habitat had used prefabricated polystyrene and wire panels sprayed with concrete that were designed to withstand winds of up to 120 mph. News of durable affordable housing made headlines around the country, bringing Habitat International, the parent organization based in Americus, Georgia, thousands of new applications and more than $4 million in contributions. Habitat's US affiliates have built more than sixteen thousand houses from Dallas to Appalachia, making the organization the nation's twenty-seventh biggest home builder.

The Dallas branch was founded in 1985 and for the last three years has been focusing on Garret Park East, a marginal neighborhood of bungalows and apartments bounded by Ross, Greenville, and Live Oak. Most were owned by absentee landlords who put off improvements in anticipation of a condo boom that never happened. Three years ago, Habitat received thirty properties from a bankrupt developer in return for paying $130,000 in back taxes. So far, it has built or renovated twenty-seven houses and sold them at cost (approximately $35,000) to such qualified buyers as Rosalia Serrato. Her mortgage payment will be about $250 a month, less than she pays for her cramped apartment. And now she will be part of a neighborhood instead of just a number on a hall mailbox. Habitat formed a neighborhood association and a crime watch group and used its volunteers to paint and patch another seventy-five houses that are not officially its responsibility. Executive director Wink Dickey estimates that neighborhood crime has dropped 60 percent in three years and that absentee ownership is down from 80 percent to roughly half. Some absentee landlords have even begun repairing their houses to keep pace with the local market.

"Home ownership stabilizes a neighborhood," he says. "Working on your own house, or one down the street, brings people together."

Considering its bleak past, Garret Park East is undergoing a dramatic renaissance. But many problems remain, Mr. Dickey says, among them the city's glacial progress in providing curbs, sidewalks, and other public improvements. Some neighborhood streets still have a semirural character. Mr. Dickey also tells of paying $1,000 to have a block replatted for Habitat's five new houses and then having to pay $35,000 for a new water main because, according to city logic, five houses make you a developer while four leaves you still a builder. Habitat hopes to pay for the water main out of federal block-grant funds it will receive next year.

"We're not looking for special treatment," Mr. Dickey says, "but if the city wants to have affordable housing, it needs to waive some of the permit and connection fees. Last year, we spent over $20,000 on these, and that's almost another house."

Yet for all the familiar urban complaints, Garrett Park East is no longer the bleak and disheartening place it was a few years ago. A settling and ordering is taking place, accompanied by occasional dramatic bursts of neighborhood pride. Just up the street from Rosalia Serrato's new house stand two elaborately landscaped cottages, one displaying a sign that says "Yard of the Month," and the other obviously the home of the first runner-up.

The spectacle of dueling begonias is both amusing and as clear a sign as one could want of residents laying claim to a place. Earlier pioneers did it by planting lilacs or grapevines. The urban pioneers of Garrett Park—such as Rosalia Serrato—are doing it with azaleas and Bermuda grass. But the message is the same: "We're staying."

This idea won't hold water: Trinity River Parks Plan will only create a river of concrete

MAY 30, 1993

Dillon's critique of the Trinity River Parks Plan put him at odds with many in the architecture profession, but it was prophetic. In 2017, the Dallas City Council finally voted to eliminate funding for the highway that had been bundled into the plan for decades.

The only thing to do with the Trinity River Parks Plan is deep-six it. Or considering the normal water flow in the Trinity, maybe deep-three it. In its current form, the plan will cut off the city from the river by interposing ten lanes of new highway between downtown and the water's edge. That's two hundred feet of steel and concrete, another Stemmons Freeway, a new Maginot line.

And that's just for openers. The new plan, presented at Thursday's Greater Dallas Planning Council meeting, shows a chain of small recreational lakes running approximately from Westmoreland Road to Corinth Street. They represent the latest incarnation of the Town Lake and Chain of Lakes proposals that have been around since the late 1970s. They cover 677 acres, half the size of White Rock Lake, which is hardly Lake Superior. How much serious recreating can be done on these "ponds" is unclear. But a glance at the plan shows that most of it—softball, soccer, hiking and biking trails—will be on the east or downtown side of the river, with comparatively little for West Dallas and Oak Cliff. Sound familiar?

Moreover, the playing fields and trails will be located in the Trinity River flood plain, which turns into the Nile about fifteen to twenty times a year. Even with a deeper channel, they often will be under water and mud. How will Parks and Recreation handle this maintenance nightmare, when it can barely pay to mow median strips?

But that's not the most troublesome part. The sponsors of the plan, a loose consortium of developers, politicos, and business leaders known as the New Trinity Coalition, admit they have no idea how much the proposal will cost. Nor have they done any economic analysis to determine what kinds of development could, or should, occur along the banks of Dallas's most precious natural resource. The plan has been created in a vacuum, driven not by any vision of the city's future economic health but by the desire to build a high-speed road as fast as possible, for the benefit of a handful of powerful developers. It's a highway scheme masquerading as a parks and recreation plan.

The clock is ticking on the coalition. To bolster its credibility, it needs to join hands with the Army Corps of Engineers and the North Texas Council of Governments, both of which are working on major transportation and environmental plans for the Trinity corridor. And it needs the endorsement of the Dallas City Council to have a shot at $57 million in federal highway money to be distributed to Texas later this year.

"It's essential that the plan be adopted quickly so that we can get in line for those funds," coalition president Bill Ceverha told the meeting on Thursday.

But that's no reason to endorse this simplistic, crude, and environmentally dubious proposal. Many American cities, in fact, are dismantling urban freeways like the one the coalition is promoting. Boston is depressing Southeast Expressway to reconnect itself to its waterfront. San Francisco is doing the same thing with the Embarcadero Freeway, and Fort Worth with Interstate 30 through downtown. Seattle has been building parks and public buildings over its interstates for decades in order to tame them.

If there is a need for another north-south freeway in Dallas—hardly clear-cut at the moment—it can be more sensitively designed and sited than this. It doesn't have to wall off the river and kill one of downtown's few remaining chances for renewal.

The New Trinity Coalition has been meeting with architects, planners, and environmentalists for months about its plan, though evidence of rethinking is slight. But surely this much talent can come up with something better than the current half-baked scheme. The Trinity could be a prime location for new housing and recreation, as well as for new businesses to replace the warehouses and distribution centers that are slowly moving out of the area. Simultaneously, the city needs to develop a land use plan for the river that encourages sound development and prevents the mishmash of jails and transmission towers and concrete cows that occurs now.

In opening Thursday's program, Dallas architect Lawrence Good asked whether the Trinity might finally "become our Central Park, our city living room?" Not with the current plan it won't.

Mr. Ceverha stressed on Thursday that the plan is still "conceptual." Good. Let's put it in the city archives, stamped "Bad Ideas," and get on with the real work of reclaiming the Trinity.

Big mess on the prairie: The ubiquitous "North Dallas Special" becomes a Texas tradition

OCTOBER 2, 1994

Ask Dallas architects to name a favorite Dillon article and this is the one they recall—a tongue-in-cheek critique of the postmodern McMansion as built in the prosperous suburbs north of Dallas. Dillon created an entire syntax for the unlikely combination of speculative suburban housing and pretentious quotations from a cornucopia of European palazzos. While definitely funny, Dillon's critique also sought answers for why the high-end suburbs had such powerful market appeal.

Some cities are as famous for their houses as for their topography or climate. San Francisco is identified with its Victorian "Painted Ladies." And Santa Fe is synonymous with thick-walled adobes. And Dallas is celebrated for—well—the "North Dallas Special" (fig. 3.3).

You know the ones—hulking two-story brick houses, with Arc de Triomphe entrances and enough gables and hip roofs to be scale models of an avalanche. The North Dallas Special dominates the local landscape, gobbling up the prairie from Plano to Southlake. One is probably going up on your block right now. The sound you hear is good taste being dashed.

"Specials," as they're known in the real estate biz, appear in various guises, Country French to Baronial Brit. But there's really only one house, the pieces of which builders reshuffle constantly.

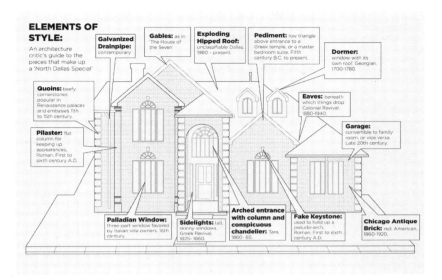

ELEMENTS OF STYLE:
An architecture critic's guide to the pieces that make up a "North Dallas Special"

Galvanized Drainpipe: contemporary

Gables: as in 'The House of the Seven'

Exploding Hipped Roof: unclassifiable Dallas. 1980 - present.

Pediment: low triangle above entrance to a Greek temple, or a master bedroom suite. Fifth century B.C. to present.

Dormer: window with its own roof. Georgian. 1700-1780.

Quoins: beefy cornerstones popular in Renaissance palaces and embassies 11th to 15th century.

Eaves: beneath which things drop. Colonial Revival. 1880-1940.

Garage: convertible to family room, or vice versa. Late 20th century.

Pilaster: flat column for keeping up appearances. Roman. First to sixth century A.D.

Palladian Window: three-part window favored by Italian villa owners. 16th century.

Sidelights: tall, skinny windows. Greek Revival. 1825- 1860.

Arched entrance with column and conspicuous chandelier: Tara. 1860- 65.

Fake Keystone: used to hold up a pseudo-arch. Roman. First to sixth century A.D.

Chicago Antique Brick: red. American. 1860-1920.

3.3. *The "North Dallas Special" was Dillon's satirical take on the increasingly outsized pretensions of the historicizing McMansions of the far north suburbs in Dallas County. He created an entire lexicon for the potpourri of historical details and their reapplication in novel contexts. Illustration by Karis Bishop, based on the original* Dallas Morning News *illustration.*

A typical $200,000 model contains roughly 3,000 square feet and is covered in red brick—Chicago antique preferred—though stucco support groups are popping up in a few renegade neighborhoods. It features a soaring arched entry—brass lanterns bracketing the door, fan light overhead, maybe a slice of etched glass—flanked by gabled forms with curtained Palladian windows that could be bedrooms, but may also be three-car garages. Square columns—inscrutably proportioned—rise through a forest of pediments, dormers, and half-round windows to a roof with at least sixteen different pitches. From above it resembles a flapping tent, but to builders it represents tradition.

Other cities have their own versions, of course. Atlanta showcases plantation modern; San Diego is one big hacienda; Boston is home to the pseudo-saltbox. But at least these examples of postmodern kitsch have a recognizable local pedigree and usually a modicum of authenticity. Where does the North Dallas Special come from? A block of them is like a cocktail party at which all the guests are speaking in fake foreign accents.

Mostly, they're whipped up by builders and marketers, who are interested primarily in the street facade, which they treat as a gigantic board on which columns, dormers, arches, porches, and other decorative bric-a-brac can be hung like Christmas ornaments. The decorations are the architecture.

Inside, a chandeliered foyer leads to a "great room" in which den, dining room, kitchen, island, fireplace, and wet bar have been conflated into a set from *Dynasty*. Media room, game room, exercise room, and other vestiges of the consumptive '80s are then packed around this central space like so much architectural batting. Diversity without variety or intimacy. And customizing is only one delusion away. One builder touts "a free-standing circular stairway that leads to a Juliet balcony"; another offers a grand staircase, down which the owners are to "imagine their daughter walking on prom night."

"Fifties traditional houses on steroids," is *Texas Architect* editor Joel Barna's felicitous summary of this phenomenon.

HEMMED IN

Ideally, these North Dallas behemoths would be surrounded by acres of grounds, like the great country houses on *Masterpiece Theatre*. But around Dallas—the Vatican of land speculation—they are typically crammed like row houses onto 70 × 120-foot lots, (50 × 150 in the Park Cities) with only a ribbon of turf between them. Unable to spread out, they go up and up and up.

In older neighborhoods they resemble teenagers whose clothes suddenly no longer fit. Out on the prairie they cluster around cul-de-sacs, often so tightly that some communities have passed ordinances forbidding side windows so that neighbors can't peer into one another's bedrooms. Imagine fleeing the pandemonium of the city for a master-planned Arcadia, only to end up with less privacy than you'd have in a downtown apartment house.

So why would people plop down $200,000 and more for a house that looks just like the one next door? And across the street? And across town? Do they really like these pumped-up tract houses? Or do they buy them because there's nothing else available?

"Buyers like these houses because they give them the most glitz for the money and the size of the lot," says Dallas custom home builder Bob Thompson.

Certainly the exploding roof creates the impression of twice as much floor space as there really is. And all the brick and brass evoke images of mahogany sideboards and vintage port, instant venerability for buyers who may be only in their thirties or early forties. One couple told me that their "special" symbolized their achievements and gave them something to show for all their years of work.

Such aspirations can't be dismissed. Yet compared to other cities, the Dallas housing market offers few ways to satisfy them.

"Who would have the nerve to build a modest, individually oriented house in the middle of all that stuff?" asks architect Frank Welch. "The pressures to keep on doing the same thing are enormous."

MASS PRODUCTION

Gone is the architectural variety of Dallas's older neighborhoods, replaced by houses that, to paraphrase Dorothy Parker, run the gamut from A to B. Economics is one reason. Builders used to do four or five houses at a time and keep a close eye on details. Now they might construct fifty or more in a mad dash to "maximize" the profits on their land.

Complacency is another. Production builders stick to stock plans—three or four to a development, which they have their draftsmen (architects are rarely involved) tweak this way and that in response to customer desires or the latest bleats from the marketing department. Even custom builders, who have bigger budgets and occasionally employ design architects, keep such a tight rein on innovation that their houses are often indistinguishable from the tract versions in everything except price.

"In Dallas, it's usually a case of 'We need this plan drawn up, and we want it to look like such-and-such because that's what's selling,'" explains architect Mark Humphreys. "In other parts of the country, builders are more willing to take chances."

Hiring your own builder would seem to be a way around this creative impasse, except that it's not easy to do, especially in large master-planned communities. Here developers work from an "approved" list, and one gets on it by (a) having a healthy balance sheet, (b) displaying a flair for "North Dallas Specialness" and (c) agreeing to prepurchase a certain number of lots. As a reward for such loyalty, the developer keeps unapproved builders out.

"It would take such a long time to get approval for an outside builder that you probably couldn't afford to wait," says Lucia Bone, marketing director for Highland Shores.

These builders are not strictly a club or a fraternity, although many of them have worked together in the past and have offices together on "Builders Row" near Belt Line Road and the Dallas North Tollway. They are more like a repertory company whose members have been doing the same play for so long that they know one another's lines by heart.

SMALLER IS BETTER

But even excess has its limits. In other parts of the country a "small is beautiful" movement is emerging, as home buyers rediscover the joys of 1,200 square feet and low mortgage payments. The wave hasn't hit Dallas yet. But here and there one notices subtle deviations from the monotonous norm. A few builders have begun inserting "stone accents" into their brick facades, creating a rustic Sherwood Forest look. Others are adding vestibules with sloping Hansel and Gretel roofs, like a Cotswold cottage.

One Dallas architect has gone even farther out on a limb by predicting a decisive shift to things Italian.

"Weary of Georgian and French influences," he announced in a press release, "clients are expressing a strong preference for Italianate over other architectural styles. It is becoming the most sought-after look in affluent neighborhoods throughout Dallas."

Anyone who hopes to stay ahead of the design curve is therefore on notice. Instead of rows of overstuffed brick and brass houses, Dallas home buyers can look forward to an invasion of Adriatically themed homes, featuring loggias and campaniles and striped silk pennants fluttering from rooftops. "Ciao, y'all."

Safe havens: Gated communities are appealing to today's yearning for security

JUNE 19, 1994

"Safe Havens" was one of two articles by Dillon about the grow-ing market for gated communities published on the same day. "Security for Sale," published on the front page, broadly outlined the arguments for and against the developments; the two articles were also accompanied by a map and detailed listing of gated com-munities in the Dallas-Fort Worth region.

Promoted as the latest advance in luxury living, gated communities date back at least to the Middle Ages and the Renaissance. Princes built them to shelter their families and loyal retainers in times of siege and pestilence, often surrounding them with towers, moats, and drawbridges.

The titans of American industry have created gated enclaves from Newport, Rhode Island, to St. Louis and Beverly Hills, sometimes copying the architectural style of their historical predecessors.

Yet these early versions were few in number and limited in ef-fect. Their contemporary offspring, on the other hand, are popping up everywhere, attracting middle-class families as well as CEOs, and presenting unprecedented challenges to city planners.

Few cities have ordinances governing gated communities, other than requiring that developers build and maintain the private streets and keep them accessible to emergency vehicles. "There were so few of them in the past that it just wasn't much of an issue," says V. C. Seth of Dallas's planning department.

Though the largest gated communities are being constructed in the suburbs, where assembling substantial tracts of land is still comparatively easy and cheap, residents of urban neighborhoods are trying to achieve similar effects by petitioning cities to barricade local streets.

Until last fall Dallas had no policy about such requests. Each was considered on its merits; and, according to senior traffic engineer Ken Melston, only one or two came up per year. But public pressure has intensified to the point that last October the city drafted a street-closing ordinance. Residents must pay for the closings, up to $10,000 per street depending on the type of barricade, but the city still takes care of maintenance and utilities.

So far the city has received seventy-five serious inquiries and has closed one street, Willow Wood Lane in North Dallas. Three more are pending. The city also has "abandoned" several streets—turning them over to private owners—including Excelsior Way near Forest and Preston.

Planners say they expect more closings and abandonments this year.

"Fear of crime and nonresidents using the streets—those are the justifications," says Mr. Melston. "Crime statistics on residential streets are not that high, but the residents say they feel safer with the barriers."

CLOSING CONTROVERSY

Street closings have become a controversial issue in many cities. Dayton, Ohio, recently erected sixty gates in the urban Fair Oaks neighborhood, rerouting traffic and creating a series of suburban cul-de-sacs. Police say violent crime has dropped 50 percent since the barricades went up. Critics attribute the decline to the closing of a notorious crack house and say that crime is otherwise unchanged.

"Cul-de-sacs have never cured crime problems," says Daniel Lauber, president of the American Institute of Certified Planners. "At best, they might shift crime to another street. At worst, they make pedestrians more susceptible to street crime."

Chief among the criticisms of gating is that it is anti-democratic in spirit and divisive in effect.

US Labor Secretary Robert Reich, writing in the *New York Times*, sees gated communities as part of the "secession of the fortunate fifth."

"The secession is taking several forms," he explains. "In many cities and towns the wealthy have in effect withdrawn their dollars from the support of public spaces and institutions shared by all and dedicated the savings to their own private services. As public parks and playgrounds deteriorate, there is a proliferation of private health clubs, golf clubs, tennis clubs, skating clubs, and every other type of recreational association in which costs are shared among members. . . . The new community of people with like incomes and with the power to tax and enforce the law is thus becoming a separate city within a city."

"Gating is an outgrowth of not wanting anything in our backyard that is different from us," adds Mr. Lauber. "Gates reinforce the tendency to categorize people by race and class, which only intensifies our social problems."

A CLASS ISSUE

Although overwhelmingly white, affluent, and professional, class is typically more an issue in gated communities than race. Anyone with $400,000 can buy a house in The Enclave in Plano, or in nearby Oakdale. Many professional athletes, black and white, live in various gated enclaves around Dallas. Asian and Hispanic families, though not numerous, are present as well.

"I grew up poor, one of fifteen kids," says Frank Simmons, an African-American businessman who recently moved into Regents Park, a thirty-acre wooded, gated community in DeSoto. "I wanted to have a nice house in a nice neighborhood, where my kids could go to a good school."

Mr. Simmons says that, though security and property values influenced his decision to move to Regents Park, he was equally attracted by its "entrepreneurial spirit."

"All the people in the neighborhood are entrepreneurs or professionals. That's a plus. We can all commiserate about business." Developers describe places like Regents Park as "lifestyle communities" or "common interest" communities, implying that residents are simply choosing one kind of life over another instead of consciously excluding certain groups or activities.

"Developers design more for lifestyle than from fear and anxiety," says Steve Harvill, executive manager of the Glen Lakes Homeowners Association. "What can we provide that will make us stand out? That's really the question they are asking."

So Stonebriar and The Cliffs of Gleneagles feature their eighteen-hole golf courses. Cottonwood Valley and Windsor Ridge in Las Colinas advertise their proximity to canals, hotels, and an equestrian center. The Downs of Hillcrest highlights its ponds and streams, only minutes from major freeways.

A PREMIER PLACE

"The gates and the grounds are a big plus for us," says Norman Campbell, who has lived in Glen Lakes since 1984, when his children finished college. "We're ten minutes from downtown Dallas, yet feel like we're in the country. There's openness but minimal care. Somebody looks after things when we're away. It's a premier place to live, but we could afford it, so why not?"

Amenities in these places—pools, tennis courts, golf courses—are restricted to residents, who pay for them through monthly assessments that range from $100 to $1,000 and more.

Many communities are subdivided into economic precincts that are far more precise and detailed than in conventional neighborhoods or subdivisions. There might be estate sections and family sections and starter sections. Stonebridge Ranch, a large master-planned community in McKinney, is organized into eight residential villages of different economic niches.

These economic distinctions are often reflected in the design of walls and gates (wood, brick, steel, and cut stone have different messages) or the species of tree planted along sidewalks and medians (pines for starter areas, maples and red oaks for more established ones) or the presence or absence of "water features."

"People are taking a risk," explains Susan Evans of Timarron, a new master-planned community in Southlake. "They want to know that the house next to them will be as appealing and of the same quality as their own."

Although gated communities are booming around Dallas, the area has not yet experienced the problems of some parts of California, where the proliferation of enclaves has put entire districts off limits to the public.

COURT DECISIONS

In 1991, a group called "Citizens Against Gated Enclaves" sued the city of Los Angeles for allowing Whitley Heights, an affluent neighborhood near the Hollywood Bowl, to gate public streets against outsiders. In January 1993, a Superior Court judge ruled in favor of the plaintiffs, saying that "the city owes a duty to the public not to allow gates on public streets." This decision was later upheld on appeal, throwing the city's nearly two hundred pending applications for barriers into legal limbo.

The city of Plano, having approved four gated communities in three years, is now taking a second look at the issue. The City Council declared a moratorium on new applications until it could develop guidelines, which it approved Monday. Among them are requirements that future gated communities be surrounded on three sides by natural areas, such as creeks and parks, and have no more than two gates per mile or roadway. The goal, say city officials, is to discourage gating without banning it completely.

Developers have complained that the moratorium was driving business to neighboring cities, while opponents, led by African-American Councilman David Perry, argued that more gates will mean a more segregated and fragmented city.

"I'm totally against them," he says. "Plano has an outstanding police force, the lowest crime rate of any city its size in Texas. We should have an open community. When people move here they should have Plano as a whole as their focus, not their own private utopias."

Mr. Perry's views are echoed by Plano's planning director, Frank Turner, who has urged the city to be cautious about approving gated communities.

"I see no compelling reason to create them for reasons of security," he says, "or to promote them that way."

ARE THEY EFFECTIVE?

Security experts generally agree that gates and walls keep out peeping toms, hubcap thieves, and other forms of so-called transient crime, though there is considerable debate over whether crime then spills over into adjacent neighborhoods. Shorecrest, a Miami neighborhood surrounded on three sides by gated communities, has seen its crime rate rise 59 percent in six years. It is now considering gates as well.

But the effectiveness of gates in preventing serious crime is more questionable. Rick Highfill, division president of Barton Protective Services in Irving, points out that many security companies pay guards little more than minimum wage, which can translate into low morale, poor training, and a turnover rate of 200 percent a year. Even at $10 an hour, a low figure, the annual cost for 24-hour security covering one gate and one guard is $87,000. Which is why many guardhouses are unoccupied after dark, and dummy cameras and bogus warning signs take the place of patrols.

"Security is more perception than reality," adds Frank Zaccanelli, executive vice president of the Perot Group's Hillwood Development Corp. "If a professional thief wants to break in, he'll find a way. But people perceive gated communities to be more secure, and from a developer's point of view that's a marketable commodity."

This thesis is hard to test because virtually all of the gated communities in Dallas are located in what police consider low-crime areas. Yet even when neighborhoods are tranquil and unthreatening, the perception of security is a powerful inducement. Victor Arias and his family moved from suburban Chicago to Hackberry Creek, the largest of Las Colinas's gated communities with nearly six hundred houses, because of what he calls its "small town feel."

CONTROL IS SOUGHT

"It seems like a secure, established neighborhood where our kids can run around without having to worry about traffic," Mr. Arias says. "We looked in Preston Hollow and the Park Cities, too, but you never know what's going to happen there. In a gated community you can control some of that."

Mr. Arias admits that having to check in and out all the time is "definitely a minus" for his family and friends, but like many people he is willing to trade inconvenience for peace of mind.

Peace of mind is a worthy goal, say critics, unless it is purchased at the expense of one's obligations to society in general. Citizenship has traditionally been defined as a contract involving obligations to the public welfare as well as one's own. But if everyone is looking out mainly for his own gated space, critics ask, who is looking out for the whole? And what becomes of the whole?

"It's a gang way of looking at life, the institutionalization of turf," says noted urban critic and historian Jane Jacobs. "And if it goes on indefinitely, and gets intensified, it practically means the end of civilization."

For those who live outside the walls and gates, the issue has become one of equity. Why should the public subsidize services for affluent communities from which they are excluded? Rita Walters, a council-woman from South Central Los Angeles, complains that affluent Los Angelenos in gated communities regularly vote "no" on tax and bond referenda for more police and better schools, while willingly taxing themselves to pay for gates and guards.

"If you're willing to pay the money it takes to wall off your com-munity (and) to pay for private security," she asks, "why not be willing to pay for an extra measure of tax, that may not be as much, and that will benefit the city as a whole? Then you won't have to have the guards and walls."

THE REAL WORLD

Sociologist Amitai Etzioni says that he would be in favor of affluent neighborhoods "reallocating" money to poorer neighborhoods to pay for basic services, but not at the expense of their own security or identity.

"In the best of all possible worlds, with no crime, I might say OK, take down the gates," he says. "But in the world we live in, upper-middle-class people don't want to rub shoulders with other classes of people. They haven't wanted to for two hundred years."

Jane Jacobs and others see the issue as more complex than tradi-tional class divisions. They view gated communities as the vanguard of a new urban tribalism that pits races and ethnic groups against one another and that will produce the same dire consequences as tribalism everywhere.

"The old notions of community mobility are being torn apart by these changes in community patterns," says Edward Blakely, head of the department of city and regional planning at UC-Berkeley. "What is the measure of nationhood when the divisions between neighbor-hoods require armed patrol and electric fencing to keep out other citi-zens? When public services and even local government are privatized? When the community of responsibility stops at the subdivision gates? What happens to the function and the very idea of democracy then?"

Stream dreams: The Trinity River Plan is huge; so are its potential problems

AUGUST 15, 1999

Plans for the Trinity River have percolated for decades. This 1999 update identifies the tensions between funding models and uses for the river and its flood plain. Confusion about how redevelopment of the river can benefit neighborhoods adjacent to it remains today. The five Calatrava bridges that Dillon references here have been reduced to two: The Margaret Hunt Hill Bridge opened in 2012; the Margaret McDermott Bridge is under construction with completion targeted for 2018.

At $1.2 billion, it would unleash the biggest public works blitz in Dallas history, bigger than Central Expressway, bigger than DART or D/FW International Airport. Mayor Ron Kirk has called it "the key to Dallas's economic future," and he may be right. Over the next thirty years, it proposes to control urban flooding, revitalize neighborhoods, create jobs and development, provide new parks, and ultimately re-center the city.

But along with the promise come many problems. The plan that the City Council is poised to approve on August 25—prepared by Halff Associates of Dallas—is still mainly an engineering diagram and hydrology report. It offers no compelling vision for the Trinity that will make everyone stand up and cheer; its design ideas are generic, and it lacks the rigorous economic analysis that would reassure the public that its $1.2 billion is being well spent. What exists is a collection of tempting but often self-contradictory fragments:

- A downtown lake that will be too small for anything except canoes and paddleboats.
- A toll road that may relieve congestion in the downtown "Mixmaster" but will also increase noise and pollution in the river park the plan is supposed to nourish.
- Five dramatic suspension bridges by Spanish architect Santiago Calatrava that may be too expensive to build.

These are not the customary confusions of any large public planning project; they reflect the back-to-front development of this one.

When the city asked voters to approve $246 million for the Trinity in May 1998, it had a wish list, not a plan, served up as a glossy slide show filled with romantic images and boosterish rhetoric. Trinity bond referendums having failed twice before, the city needed to show the Army Corp of Engineers, the Texas Department of Transportation, and other agencies that it could bring public money and a public mandate to the bargaining table. And it did, by the slimmest of margins. Only then did the city start focusing on the details.

The Trinity Plan, known officially as the *Trinity River Corridor Master Implementation Plan,* rests on four basic ideas: flood control, recreation, transportation, and economic development. For it to succeed, these ideas must be seamlessly integrated so that each reinforces and invigorates the other. Right now they are at war. The toll road is getting most of the attention, neighborhood revitalization and economic development virtually none.

THE LAKES

Lakes have been part of the Trinity dream since the early 1900s. They show up in the Kessler Plan of 1911 and the Springer Plan of the 1950s. They appear as a single large body of water, like Town Lake in Austin, and as a chain of smaller lakes strung out along the river like a necklace. Whatever their shape, they represent the deep psychic longing of a parched prairie city for liquid refreshment and renewal.

The current plan calls for a $32-million, 135-acre downtown lake, which would be slightly larger than Bachman but only one-ninth the size of White Rock. It would sit in the middle of the flood plain, with the main channel flowing to either side, and be fed by groundwater and treated effluent from the Central Wastewater Treatment plant downstream. A second 100-acre lake might eventually be built downstream if improvements are made to the Interstate 35E bridge.

Halff Associates, which is responsible for virtually everything in the floodway, has shown that the lakes can be built. A more basic question is, for what? Early sketches of them dotted with colorful sailboats were seductive fictions. They may be large enough for canoes and paddleboats, but nothing larger. And because the Trinity is classified as "suitable only for noncontact recreation," they will be off-limits to swimmers as well.

At the moment, the lakes' primary function seems to be ornamental rather than recreational, something to look down on from a skyscraper or a bridge but not much else. There are other options: Constructing a series of spectacular fountains and waterworks to celebrate the river or sculpting the landscape into a Dallas version of Memphis's Mud Island. A simple river park of nature trails, ponds, and wetlands might be more appealing, and easier to maintain.

THE ROAD

In drawings, the Trinity toll road appears only as a red line running inside the levees from Highway 183 near Irving to Highway 175 in southeast Dallas. It is intended to relieve the sclerosis of the Interstate 30/I-35E Mixmaster and the I-30 canyon south of downtown. The toll road would siphon through-traffic from these roadways and presumably liberate downtown from gridlock.

The toll road began as a 45-mph parkway, the preferred alternative of citizen advisory groups. But once it was clear that the Texas Department of Transportation couldn't build a parkway for at least twenty years, it became a toll road because the North Texas Tollway Authority has access to funding that the state does not. The authority believes that a 60-mph toll road is feasible, though no funding is allotted.

Yet feasibility has its price. Lost in the road discussion is the basic idea of the floodway as an oasis, a place to escape the noise and pollution of the city without having to drive one hundred miles.

As proposed, a toll road would bring whining tires and clouds of exhaust into the heart of the park. To accommodate it, the levees would have to be extended 120 feet into the floodway. Where it dips under bridges, it must be reinforced by concrete flood walls, which are seldom sublime. Ultimately, the toll road will further isolate the river by placing another barrier between it and the city. To reach the lake, the centerpiece of the project, visitors will have to cross a 30-foot levee, four lanes of traffic, a channel, and a bridge before getting to the water's edge.

The environmental impact study, also being done by Halff, will force the re-examination of alternatives, including Industrial Boulevard and a more easterly route roughly parallel to Stemmons Freeway. The main objection to these alternatives previously was cost, primarily buying right-of-way and reconstructing the sumps on the downtown side of the river. The Transportation Department estimates that these changes would double the expense to approximately $800 million.

But there are counter-arguments. Much of the additional cost might be recaptured from the federal government and from increased tax revenue from the new businesses fertilized by the road. Inside the levee, the toll road would bypass or limit much of this development; outside, it would energize it without intruding on precious green space. Not a simple issue, obviously, which is all the more reason for a thorough economic assessment of the entire riverfront.

Ultimately, a levee toll road represents outdated thinking. Other US cities are no longer building highways through greenbelts. They're dismantling them. Boston is burying the Central Artery along its waterfront; Fort Worth and San Francisco are removing elevated freeways in their downtowns. Washington, DC plans to eliminate the divisive Southeast/Southwest freeway through the heart of the capital. Can't Dallas find a better solution to its traffic problems than invading its potentially most significant parkland?

THE BRIDGES

Santiago Calatrava's five bridges are not the plan, but they are its boldest and most visionary element, the one feature that could raise it instantly from public works to public art.

These graceful arched spans include an extension of Woodall Rodgers Expressway to West Dallas, crossovers at the north and south ends of the proposed toll road, and replacements for the I-30 and I-35E bridges, which are scheduled to be rebuilt, though not yet funded.

The argument for these bridges is simple. Instead of replacing existing structures with fatter and uglier versions of the same design, Dallas could have an ensemble of dramatic gateways that would celebrate the entry into downtown and finally give Dallas some legitimate claim to being a river city. They might make commuting memorable instead of merely excruciating.

In briefing the City Council in June, Mr. Calatrava described the bridges as an opportunity to show that "the river can be a frontyard instead of a backyard where you put your prisons and your electrical lines."

His bridges would be expensive—approximately a third more than conventional pier-and-beam structures—but they would add poetry and drama to a river that has never sung. They would help reconnect two halves of the city, while creating genuine civic landmarks to compete with a revolving restaurant and a flying red horse.

As eleventh-hour additions to the plan, the bridges have been attacked as expensive frills that will require more taxpayer subsidies. Maybe they will. But the proper response to critics is that plans evolve. New opportunities arise that require more imaginative responses. Credit Halff with recognizing the ordinariness of their original effort and trying to do something about it.

THE LEVEES

Because of runaway development in Irving, Carrollton, and other upstream suburbs, downtown levees would likely burst during an eight-hundred-year flood. To reduce this danger, the Trinity Plan recommends creating a series of wetlands south of downtown and new levees at Lamar Street and Cadillac Heights.

The Lamar Street levee would protect a low-lying industrial area that could eventually become a prime development site. The Cadillac Heights levee is more problematic because a levee won't solve the neighborhood's biggest problem: toxic waste. Decades of dumping by lead smelters and plating companies and rendering plants have contaminated the area to the point that the Environmental Protection Agency must post warning signs to protect residents. A levee won't change that.

Many engineers and environmentalists advocate buying out such neighborhoods and allowing them to flood naturally. The city insists that buyouts don't make economic sense and that residents don't want to move anyway. Others contend that more generous buyouts would prompt most to leave.

A third levee, along Luna Road in northwest Dallas, would protect land for future industrial development. Yet this levee is so speculative that city officials can't say when or if it will ever be built. The Army Corps of Engineers hasn't even determined if it is needed.

THE ECONOMICS

It doesn't take an Alan Greenspan to see that the Trinity River Corridor could energize the redevelopment of downtown, the Stemmons Industrial District, and much of South and West Dallas. Such development would dramatically expand the city's tax base and make Dallas the center point of the booming North Texas economy.

But the Trinity Plan lacks an economic component. Except for a few pages in a 1997 study of the Trinity parkway—now the Trinity toll road—and assurances from city officials that the plan will produce a windfall, there has been no systematic investigation of what this enormous public investment could mean for downtown, the riverfront, the neighborhoods, and the region. This is basic information, and without it the plan won't work.

Halff Associates is responsible for everything between the levees; economic analysis is the city's obligation. Officials acknowledge that the information would be nice to have but have made few efforts to get it. And this in the Vatican of market analysis, where corporations survive on consumer surveys and demographic studies and focus groups.

The Stemmons Industrial District, for example, is in transition. Most of its warehousing has moved to the suburbs; many of its buildings are on life support. In twenty years, if the riverfront and the road are completed, this area will be redeveloped as an urban neighborhood surrounded by water and parks and easy connections to downtown. It is critical for the city to plan for this transformation.

At the moment, the city seems content to sit back and allow the market to answer these questions. That's a good way to get what you don't want. While the city shouldn't design the district, it ought to establish the ground rules and the framework. The price for inaction could be a free-enterprise version of the Dallas County Jail fiasco, where massive buildings have been air-dropped onto the banks of the Trinity without concern for scale, location, or effect on future development. The river can't absorb another hit like that.

CONCLUSION

By any standard, the Trinity Plan is a snag of overlapping and competing issues, which even the experts haven't been able to sort out. Equally obvious is that the plan has reached a critical stage when the right decisions will propel it forward and the wrong ones will kill it.

To scuttle the plan and do nothing would be irresponsible. Even its harshest critics concede that. Forward is the only way to go; yet plunging ahead without correcting the problems in the current version would be reckless.

Economic analysis has to anchor the plan. Building a lake or a bridge or a toll road without knowing how it might affect businesses, neighborhoods, and land values is absurd. And right now, nobody knows. The plan needs an outside economic consultant, with a fresh eye and no political baggage, to study each of these issues in depth.

Establishing an independent Trinity River development corporation, responsible for the riverfront and adjacent areas, would be a shrewd next step.

It's also time for a design transfusion. Halff Associates is solid on engineering, but the Trinity is more than an engineering project. It's an opportunity to create a unique work of civic art, which means it needs the best architects, landscape architects, and urban designers. Except for the Calatrava bridges, there's no energy in any of the proposed designs. They are flat, formulaic, and forgettable. For $1.2 billion, Dallas should get more.

The environmental impact study for the toll road now under way will buy the city eighteen months to reflect, re-examine, and possibly recapture the original vision for the river that has been lost in the angry public debate and landslide of impenetrable technical reports.

For all its pragmatic benefits, the Trinity project is also about making a soft, green place in a hard, dry land. It's about reconnecting West Dallas and South Dallas to the rest of the city, about allowing it to grow from within instead of scatter to the edges, about finding a heart that isn't all business.

The plan that the City Council will consider on August 25 takes tentative steps in these directions, but it still has a long way to go.

Set sail with the latest Trinity River Plan: With something for everyone, time to begin long-delayed project

MARCH 30, 2003

While the latest iteration of a Trinity River Plan, designed by Michael van Valkenburg and made public in 2016, makes some of the specifics of this essay obsolete, the general observations remain. Funding, execution, and management are key to making the park a reality more than fifty years after the first plans emerged. As this collection went to press, the Trinity Park Conservancy had begun a new series of studies to make Harold Simmons Park a reality.

There's something for everyone in the latest Trinity River Plan: parks, roads, lakes, levees, playing fields, perhaps an esplanade or two. It could not have been otherwise. When Alex Krieger, William Eager, and the other consultants were hired last September, the $1.2 billion Trinity project was in deep muck. The engineers weren't talking to the environmentalists; citizen groups had little good to say about City Hall, which was scrambling to find common ground, any common ground, on which all parties could stand.

The instructions to the consultants, therefore, were to produce a plan that everybody could live with—an old-fashioned political compromise, in other words, that neither repackaged the over-engineered, under-designed Halff plan nor offered such a radically new alternative that the project would have had to start over.

"We expect the consultants to be realistic and not come up with a proposal that is impossible to fund," says Karen Walz, director of the Dallas Plan, the organization that coordinated the review. "Nobody is interested in a dream scheme."

"Compromise" can be a code word for no nerve or vision, but not in this case. The old plan focused on an eight-lane tollway, four on each side of the river, plus a pair of off-channel lakes. The new version is significantly better—because a parkway is preferable to a tollway, meadows and wetlands more appealing than monolithic lakes. It is more varied, more environmentally sensitive, and in the long run better for the city.

At the same time, it includes a lot of roads, leaves many public access problems unresolved, and sidesteps key economic development issues. If it is no longer a highway plan masquerading as a park plan, it is still a bypass for the suburbs that slices through Dallas's most valuable natural resource at a time when many American cities are fighting to get highways out of parks and greenways altogether.

To their credit, the consultants have tried to soften the road's impact by splitting it into a six-lane tollway north of Continental; a four-lane, 45-mph parkway next to downtown; and possibly only a simple landscaped boulevard along Lamar. A four-lane collector road would run along the top of the east levee, connected to the downtown grid on one side and the river parkway on the other.

The consultants insist that they are only refining what has already been proposed. "We don't think that we're smarter than the people who have been working on this for years or that they were wrong," Mr. Eager, the transportation planner, told the City Council on March 5.

A parkway is certainly what the public thought it was voting for in the 1998 bond election; a version of the levee road was published in the Dallas Plan's 1994 final report. Yet the new proposal also recognizes, as the previous ones did not, that traffic volume is not uniform, that it is possible and desirable to tailor the road to the demand. Mr. Eager says that if he had his druthers, the entire road would be a parkway, without tolls.

"My main fear is that if we don't do a portion of the reliever road, we'd have a lot of trouble carrying the project forward."

Translation: The tollway portion is as much about politics as traffic. Without tolls, the North Texas Tollway Authority couldn't come up with its share of the road construction costs, estimated at between

$535 million and $658 million. Bond holders would balk, the Texas Department of Transportation and other agencies might pull out, and the entire project could crater.

Much depends on how sensitively the proposed tollway/parkway is designed. Preliminary sketches show the road tucked into the side of the downtown levee, which would be raised and widened. (Previously, the levees were considered untouchable.) This would reduce noise pollution and visual blight, without necessarily solving the access problem to the park. Pedestrians would have to cross the parkway on bridges, then descend staircases to the water.

In his public presentations, Mr. Krieger, a Harvard University urban designer, often referred to Memorial and Storrow Drives in Boston and Cambridge, Massachusetts, to show how roads and rivers can coexist. Yet there are no levees on the Charles River. Moreover, Memorial Drive is a four-lane road that can be crossed, cautiously, on foot, while Storrow Drive is a four- to six-lane divided roadway crossable mainly by overhead bridges. It effectively severs Back Bay from the Charles River; the fact that so many Bostonians end up there anyway is a tribute to their determination, or desperation, rather than to enlightened urban design.

The park portion of the Trinity Plan seems less problematic. The original chain-of-lakes concept was a product of bottom-line engineering rather than good planning. The new version, by Hargreaves Associates of Cambridge, proposes a sequence of terraced lakes linked to meadows and wetlands and fed by treated groundwater and sewage. The river channel would meander from side to side and have mostly soft, natural edges. This alignment would improve water quality and be more appealing to visitors.

The big unknown is flooding, which could pose serious maintenance problems and in extreme high water threaten structures. The landscape architects insist that these problems can be avoided by properly contouring the lakes and surrounding wetlands.

At the March 5 council briefing, Dallas mayor Laura Miller cautioned that the new Trinity Plan is still only a concept. "Nothing is finalized, nothing cast in stone," she noted. During the next twelve months the plan will be examined by city, state, and federal agencies, debated by community groups, scrutinized by budgeteers. Changes and refinements are inevitable.

A few other topics may not be on the table but should be:

- If the Trinity River is truly Dallas's most precious natural resource, attach a value to it, a dollar figure even, instead of thinking about it as just so much free land. Road builders have no incentive to do this, but the city has every reason to calculate its worth and incorporate that into its comprehensive land-use plan.
- It is time—beyond time, really—to create a Trinity River Development Corp. to coordinate the future of the riverfront before the best sites are lost. The city and county have already built a crime theme park along the Commerce Street levee, and Jerry Jones is talking about a football theme park farther downriver on land that would be perfect for housing.
- Such strategic planning requires an aggressive and involved planning department. The city planning staff has been largely shut out of the Trinity discussions, as though it were just another big public works project instead of a key to the city's economic future. When the consultants go home, Dallas will have to manage this vast resource on its own. It helps to have some practice.

In any case, it's time to move on, vigilantly. If earlier Trinity discussions had been smarter and the designs better, Dallas might have gotten its dream scheme after all. But they weren't, and it didn't. The current plan is a mix of good new ideas and residual mistakes. Even so, it is better than anyone could have expected six months ago.

Shelter and shade: A city project brings architecture to the people

MAY 1, 2008

It's spring, and architecture is popping up all over Dallas. Not just condos in Uptown and malls on the Tollway, but stunning pavilions in public parks. Eight have been completed so far, with another dozen on tap for this year. Eventually, there will be forty-three, including restorations of nine historic WPA pavilions from the 1930s, making this one of the most ambitious civic architecture initiatives in the city's history.

"Civic architecture" implies courthouses, libraries, and other high-minded monuments that remind us of our rights and responsibilities as citizens. But the pavilions are lowercase architecture for the people, simple utilitarian structures designed for picnics, birthday parties, and other celebrations of the ordinary and the everyday. They cost an average of $210,000, which works out to $9 million for the entire program, approximately one-fifteenth of what the city pumped into the American Airlines Center.

"We want to get distinguished architecture out into the neighbor-hoods, so that residents can feel good about themselves and their city," says Willis Winters, architect, assistant director of Dallas's Park and Recreation Department, and the vision behind the program.

"Distinguished architecture" is the operative phrase here, and one that is rarely applied to park pavilions—typically cookie-cutter

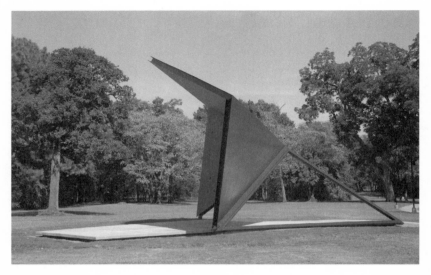

3.4. *Rand Elliott designed one of the first of a new generation of pavilions for Dallas public parks. This butterfly-like canopy of folded steel is in Opportunity Park off Malcolm X Boulevard. Image courtesy Dallas Park and Recreation Department. Photograph by Willis C. Winters, courtesy the Dallas Park and Recreation Department.*

structures, picked from a catalogue and thrown up fast and cheap. Better than nothing, but not by much.

The Park Department has taken a more imaginative approach by hiring some of the best architects in the region to design its pavilions, including Frank Welch, Ron Wommack, Joe McCall, and Pablo Laguarda, as well as recruits from New Orleans, New York, Oklahoma City, and Oslo, Norway. This is not a lottery; the architects were required to submit drawings and scale models and meet several times with neighborhood groups to win support for their designs.

"Willis challenged us to come up with fresh ideas, not pat solutions," says Oklahoma City architect Rand Elliott, who designed a performance shell for Opportunity Park in South Dallas. "He wanted our best work, which is not what you usually hear from City Hall."

Consequently, the new pavilions are more varied, sophisticated, and engaging than their tin-roof and pipe-column predecessors. Elliott's performance shell is a piece of steel origami, red on one side, silver on the other, that has been cut and folded to create an enclosure for singers, dancers, and musicians (fig. 3.4). Contoured benches and

160

community recognition plaques will be added this summer to complete the design.

Equally spare and abstract is Edward Baum's "chaise longue" for Ridgewood Park in East Dallas, featuring a thin wood and steel roof that hovers like a minimalist cloud above benches and picnic tables.

The Mexican-American community near Columbia Avenue's Randall Park asked for a shade structure where mothers could look after their small children while their sons and husbands played softball and soccer nearby. So Winters created a canopy of thin metal slats that flutters above a grassy play space like a gigantic tent, filtering the light while casting dramatic shadows on the ground.

Several pavilions are intentionally whimsical, such as Laguarda's tangle of leaves and branches in Hattie Rankin Moore Park and McCall's "leaning towers" at Brownwood Park, each struggling to stay upright in a metaphoric wind. A few are more straightforwardly contextual, like BRW's twin-peaked pavilion at Lindsley Park, which borrows its pitched roof and decorative brick columns from the English Tudor cottages in the adjacent neighborhood.

Community reaction to these pavilions has been overwhelmingly enthusiastic. There has been virtually no vandalism, a sure sign of public acceptance. When residents feel that they've had a say in a design, that it hasn't been imposed on them, they usually embrace it and look after it, like a gift from a good friend.

Though only half-finished, the project is being watched closely by other cities that, like Dallas, have thought of pavilions, bus shelters, and other humble structures as maintenance problems instead of design opportunities. Imagine the improvement in the Dallas streetscape if DART had hired a few good architects to design its bus shelters instead of buying them in bulk, like salt and sand, and spreading them around the city. A bad design replicated hundreds of times becomes publicly subsidized blight.

But the pavilion program may pay off in other ways down the road. Dallas's best architects often refuse to work for the city because of low fees and heavy bureaucratic meddling. The fees are still miserly, but by improving the program and the selection process, the city hopes to create a pool of local talent that it can draw on later for larger civic commissions. This is not an argument for parochialism, but a recognition that to create a robust architectural culture, or a robust local economy, you can't import everything; sooner or later, you have to grow your own. And it can work. Alvar Aalto's first commission was a bus shelter in Helsinki, and look what that led to.

Ultimately, great cities pay attention to the little things as well as monuments: trees, parks, sidewalks, views, what urbanist William Whyte memorably called "tremendous trifles." Individually, they may not amount to much, but collectively they have an enormous impact because they help make cities livable and memorable.

What sticks in our minds about, say, Seattle and San Francisco, is not great architecture, of which there is surprisingly little, but the quality of the places themselves, the richness of their public life. Just being there is pleasure enough. Barcelona, now an economic powerhouse, is a bouillabaisse of small sensory pleasures that includes everything from neighborhood plazas to fountains, street lamps, and manhole covers.

In its own modest way, the Dallas Pavilion Project is making a similar statement: that the small and fragile parts of the city are as important as the arenas and skyscrapers.

4

ARTS DISTRICTS

Dallas began discussion of moving its arts institutions—its museum, symphony, opera, and theater—out of Fair Park and into downtown in the 1960s. Those plans stemmed from growing concern about the decline of South Dallas during the age of urban renewal and white flight. They became firmer in 1977, when a commissioned report by Kevin Lynch and Stephen Carr of Cambridge, Massachusetts, laid the groundwork for the formation of a formal arts district on the north side of downtown in a battered area that had once been part of North Dallas, one of the city's thriving Freedman's Towns.* The plan progressed in 1982 with the Sasaki plan, which created a formal blueprint for consolidating blue-ribbon arts institutions into a district centered on a tree-lined Flora Street. The Dallas Museum of Art was the first institution to open at one end of that proposed promenade at the intersection of Harwood and Flora Streets in 1984 and the Dallas City Theater the last, so far, in 2012 (figs. 4.1a and b). Farther west, Fort Worth created the nucleus of its cultural district in the 1960s with the creation of the Amon Carter Museum adjacent to the 1936 rodeo grounds at the Will Rogers Memorial Center and catapulted to international attention with the completion of Louis Kahn's designs

---

* Carr, Lynch Associates, "A Comprehensive Arts Facilities Plan for Dallas: Prepared for the City of Dallas," 1977.

4.1a. *View down Flora Street toward the Dallas Museum of Art in the Arts District in about 1983, just after the museum's opening. The DMA was the sole arts institution with a permanent home in the district. Image courtesy Dallas Museum of Art Archives, Building Photography.*

4.1b. *View down Flora Street toward the Dallas Museum of Art in about 1985, with installation of the street furniture, lighting, and landscape continuing toward the east. Image courtesy Dallas Museum of Art Archives, Friends of the Dallas Arts District Records.*

for the Kimbell Art Museum in 1974. By the 1990s, arts and cultural districts became a major tool for economic and cultural development, allowing Texas cities to compete with each other to carve out a place as cultured, cosmopolitan cities on par with more mature cultural meccas like New York and Los Angeles.*

Dillon's long-term coverage of the Dallas Arts District and his periodic comparisons of its development with institutions across the state, but especially in Fort Worth, Houston, and San Antonio, is one of his most thoughtful and important contributions to the civic dialogue about architecture and public space. Arts districts present particular challenges in cities driven by private development rather than by public planning, and Dillon covered the development of each master plan for the Dallas Arts District and the opening of each new institution meticulously across three decades.

The articles collected here represent only a fraction of Dillon's writing on the subject. Issues of site acquisition, planning of public space and thoroughfares, the selection of internationally renowned architects, the balance of high art institutions with space for artists, and the general public returned again and again in new permutations. Dillon frequently called for more public, open discussion of decisions made in private and more public accountability for projects built with private money. While some of his criticism may seem mild, he wrote in an environment that lacked a robust culture that supported questioning the priorities of the civic and business elite. His repeated calls for more diversity and greater public engagement remain at the center of reforms for the Arts District today, as evidenced by the 2017 draft Dallas Arts District Master Plan calling for changes to allow the creation of a "bustling, livable, walkable, and more urbane neighborhood."†

---

* For more general treatments of the phenomenon of arts and cultural districts in US cities, see Arthur C. Brooks and Roland J. Kushner, "Cultural Districts and Urban Development," *International Journal of Arts Management* 3, n. 2 (Winter 2001): 4–15; Joni Maya Cherbo, Ruth Ann Stewart, and Margaret Jane Wyszomirski, eds., *Understanding the Arts and Creative Sector in the United States* (New Brunswick, NJ: Rutgers University Press, 2008); and Michael Rushton, ed., *Creative Communities: Art Works in Economic Development* (Washington, DC: Brookings Institution Press, 2013).

† "Connect: The Dallas Arts District Master Plan," draft report, June 7, 2017, *http://dallascityhall.com/departments/pnv/Documents/170608_DRAFT_DAD Master* Plan_v7.pdf.

Is there a place for the arts in the Arts District? Conceived as a downtown cultural oasis, it's developed into a real estate playground

OCTOBER 13, 1985

It may not look it, but the Dallas Arts District is eight years old.

Its birth is recorded in a 1977 arts facilities report, commissioned by the city and written by Stephen Carr and Kevin Lynch of Cambridge, Massachusetts. Without defining "arts district," the consultants recommended that Dallas's major arts organizations be relocated downtown, preferably within easy walking distance of one another. Such a concentration of facilities, the consultants said, would benefit the organizations involved and help to revitalize the central business district, then hard-hit by defections of stores and restaurants to the suburbs.

The Carr-Lynch report provided ammunition for moving the Dallas Museum of Fine Arts out of Fair Park and has remained part of the philosophical bedrock of the Arts District.

In addition to the new Dallas Museum of Art, which opened in January 1984, the Arts District currently consists of a temporary stage for the Dallas Theater Center and a partially completed ceremonial boulevard known as Flora Street. Construction has finally begun on the Dallas Symphony's Morton H. Meyerson Symphony Center, which is scheduled to open in mid-1989. These facilities are clustered in a twenty-block area bounded by Ross Avenue, Routh and St. Paul Streets, and Woodall Rodgers Freeway.

But if one asks what the Arts District is about these days, the answer is that it's mostly about office buildings and land speculation. The exciting blend of SoHo, Tivoli Gardens, and Centre Pompidou that the public thought it was getting when it approved funds for a new museum and concert hall has not materialized. Vendors, performers, street-corner evangelists, and other signs of street life are still hard to find among the slick corporate and institutional buildings. The impression is more of an office park with an arts theme than of a cultural district.

Backers reiterate that the Arts District is in its infancy, that its full character won't be visible for another fifteen years. True enough. Yet some of the same people will acknowledge privately that the original description of the district was fanciful, if not downright misleading.

Most of the basic conditions for messy vitality have not existed in the district. Land is exorbitant, having mushroomed in price to between $200 and $300 per square foot, from $20 to $30 a square foot eight years ago. There is no housing and no inventory of inexpensive older buildings in which artists and fledgling arts-related enterprises might find a home.

"The Arts District is a microcosm of arts support in Dallas and Texas," says Jerry Allen, the city's director of cultural affairs. "It will offer a good system for supporting major institutions. Small and emerging groups will have to scramble for leftovers, and individual artists will be left out in the cold. It would require a complete turnaround in attitude among people who control the arts in Dallas for things to be different."

"The major question right now is how do you put the arts in the arts district," says Bob Venuti of Metropolitan Structures, a major developer in the district. "I don't think we want just the museum and the symphony. We've got to make room for others."

In response to this growing concern, a task force of visual artists has been formed to advise about arts activities for the district. Chaired by Patricia Meadows of the D'Art Visual Art Center and Paula Peters of the Central Dallas Association, the task force has drafted a preliminary report that recommends, among other things, the identification of all suitable exhibition sites in the district and the creation of an "art panel" to review and recommend visual arts proposals for the district. The reason for these recommendations is spelled out candidly in the draft report:

"The focus of the Arts District on large institutions and massive real estate developments has made it evident that artists are on the verge of being shut out of the Arts District. . . .

"There has not been a serious effort made to involve artists in any of the planning or decision-making processes. This lack of trust has resulted in an adversarial cloud hanging over the Arts District."

Whatever sour grapes may lie beneath this statement, there is also abundant evidence of its basic validity. In an otherwise soft Dallas office market, developers continue to jockey for position and prestige in the Arts District, making it one of the premier real estate playgrounds in the country.

The first round of major commercial development began late last year with the opening of LTV Center, together with its performing arts pavilion and public sculpture garden. The developer, the Trammell Crow Co., is now considering building two mid-rise office towers on Harwood Street. The towers would be designed by DMA architect Edward Larrabee Barnes for a site that includes land leased from the museum.

Metropolitan Structures of Chicago will begin construction in January of a 1,650-car parking garage beneath Flora and Crockett Streets, above which it plans to erect a pair of fifty-two-story office towers and a shopping pavilion.

Next door, adjacent to Guadalupe Cathedral, architect Araldo Cossutta has proposed a forty-story office tower, as well as a small building along Flora Street to replace the rectory and parish center that would be demolished. The proposed tower would sit on gigantic stilts to allow glimpses of the cathedral from Ross Avenue and Crockett Street.

Scattered among the new and proposed buildings are three large parcels of land critical to the future development of the Arts District. The most significant is the 5.2-acre tract next to the new concert hall, formerly occupied by the Borden dairy. The city is asking voters to approve $28 million in the November 5 bond election to purchase it outright from the current owner, Dallas Central Business District Enterprises. City officials have mentioned it as an ideal location for an opera house or other performing arts facilities.

Diagonally across Flora Street is a large tract owned by SPG International and several other investors that is intended for unspecified future uses, most likely a combination of office and retail.

In the middle of the district, bisected by the Pearl Street exit of

Woodall Rodgers Freeway, sits the large Triland International tract, once mentioned as a likely hotel and office site and now on the market for a reported $300 a square foot.

Several developers have been ogling the remainder of the Belo Mansion property for a speculative office building, with additional space for the Dallas Bar Association.

With the physical character of the Arts District pretty well set, its success as a cultural center will depend largely on its arts programming.

At the moment, this is the responsibility of the Arts District Foundation, which is made up of major property owners and the heads of major arts organizations that are or want to be in the district. The foundation has a $500,000 endowment, virtually all of it the proceeds from the LTV Center opening gala last year. To date, it has helped fund gospel and jazz concerts, performances by the new music group Voices of Change and students at Arts Magnet High School, and summer workshops by the Children's Arts and Ideas Foundation.

While such programs have been well received, for the most part they represent the relocation of arts activity occurring elsewhere in the city rather than the initiation of something new. Yet one of the original hopes for the district was that it would function as an incubator of new artistic ventures.

"To do this, the Arts District needs a full-time programming person to work with the Arts District Foundation," says Jerry Allen. "It may think it isn't ready for this, but it is. The kind of programming that the district needs can't be done piecemeal by volunteers."

In this context, some revisions and amendments to Dallas's 1983 Arts District ordinance may be in order. In its present form, the ordinance focuses mainly on Flora Street building heights and setbacks, parking, and related architectural and urban design matters. Space for artists and performers is left to the discretion of the individual property owners, a recommendation rather than a requirement. Yet why shouldn't provision of such space be included in the ordinance, part of the price of admission to the Arts District?

The Arts District Management Association, made up of major property owners, already has the power to tax itself for street maintenance, security, and other expenses not covered by city funding. Why not a stipend for programming and street-level activity as well, again as part of the cost of doing business in such a lucrative environment? The

Trammell Crow Co. is doing this voluntarily at LTV, but with the cast of characters in the district changing regularly, it would be good to have the support guaranteed, no matter who buys what plot of land.

Many of the critical issues facing the Arts District come together on the Borden site, bounded by Fairmount, Flora, and Pearl Streets and Woodall Rodgers Freeway. The property was purchased in 1983 by CBD Enterprises to keep it in friendly hands until the city decided whether to buy it for additional arts facilities. The property, supporters say, is a steal at $135 per square foot, compared to the roughly $250 to $300 a square foot it would bring on the open market.

That's true as far as it goes. Yet one of the painful ironies of this situation is that eight years ago, Carr and Lynch urged the city to bank land throughout the Arts District in anticipation of just such needs. Land was then selling for around $20 per square foot, meaning that by judicious negotiating the city might have funded the entire Arts District without bond issues.

But that, as they say, is old news. At issue now is what to do with the Borden site should voters agree to buy it. Discussion so far has centered on using it for an opera house or for a second facility for the Dallas Theater Center. While this would be consistent with the institutional bias of the district, it might also represent a conventional and limited response to the opportunity.

If it buys the Borden site for less than half its market value, the city will have an extraordinary bargaining tool with private developers. The city would be in a position to offer the land in return for the promise to build what it wants in the Arts District: affordable housing, theaters, studio and exhibition space, "alternative" restaurant and retail space. The needs of established institutions ought not to preclude using the land for these purposes.

The Dallas Arts District will never be funky and offbeat. At best, it may turn out to be a Southwestern version of New York's upper Park Avenue, with expensive galleries and boutiques surrounded by office towers and, perhaps, apartment buildings. If that is not what was promised, it is not necessarily the worst of all possible worlds, either. Despite the hype, the Arts District cannot be all things to all people. Much of the creative activity that the public hoped would take place in the district will take place elsewhere, in the small buildings and overlooked neighborhoods where art traditionally is made.

Which doesn't mean that the Arts District can't be a forum and a catalyst for bold new work that transcends the safe and sane standards associated with corporations and institutions. Right now, the Arts District is being programmed a bit like a suburban shopping mall, in which the objective is to lure people downtown with special events in hopes that eventually they will come back on their own.

The message of much of this is that the arts are good for business, a fact that has been demonstrated dramatically by the escalation in real estate prices in the Arts District. What is unclear is whether in the long run business will be good for the arts.

Can sculpture keep its place in the sun? Giant skyscrapers threaten to overshadow DMA garden

JULY 2, 1985

Debates over skyscrapers, sunlight, and public space at the Dallas Museum of Art sculpture garden, designed by landscape architect Dan Kiley, and at Thanks-Giving Square pointed to the need to manage the relationship between commercial and public uses in the new Arts District. They also foreshadowed the later controversy that arose when Museum Tower's glass façade began to cast intense glare and reflection into the Nasher Sculpture Center's galleries and garden in 2012.

Sun is to sculpture what spotlights are to an actor—a source of drama, definition, that elusive element known as "presence."

Right now, the Dallas Museum of Art's sculpture garden has plenty of sun—probably more than it needs in the summer (fig. 4.2). But the character of the space could change radically with the construction of a massive office project immediately to the museum's west.

Last December, Lincoln Property Company announced plans to build a forty-five-story office tower, two fifty-story towers, a twenty-story hotel, and a large retail and restaurant pavilion on the current Southwestern Life Insurance site bordered by Ross, St. Paul, and Akard. The completed project would contain 4.3 million square feet of space, making it one of the densest developments in Dallas.

4.2. *Landscape architect Dan Kiley's Dallas Museum of Art sculpture garden, photographed in 1984. Photograph by Daniel Barsotti, courtesy Dallas Museum of Art Archives, Building Photography.*

It could also be one of the most oppressive. A preliminary shadow study by sociologist and Dallas design conscience William Whyte indicates that the 100-foot-high base alone would eliminate most of the museum's sculpture garden's midday sun from October to March. The three office towers would cast even larger and longer shadows, extending possibly as far as LTV Center, two blocks away.

At the moment, the DMA is taking a low-key, conciliatory position, hoping that good will and community pride will forestall a public confrontation.

Representatives of the DMA and Lincoln Property met Friday to discuss the situation further, but reached no firm agreement.

"It's not a legal issue or a planning issue," says DMA director Harry Parker. "At this point, it's a neighborly issue. We've instructed our architect to talk to their architect about ways to resolve the problem. We believe that we are dealing with reasonable people and that there is room for negotiation."

DMA architect Edward Larrabee Barnes sees the situation differently.

"That bustle (base) along St. Paul will mean no sun at all for much of the winter," Barnes says. "Worse than that, it introduces an enormous break in scale. There's no transition at all between the museum and the surrounding buildings. If this project gets built as designed, the museum board will be wringing its hands and saying, 'We didn't have to let it happen.'"

Lincoln Property partner William Duvall says that the project will happen, beginning in late fall, and that he is surprised that the shadow issue should surface only now.

"We went to the museum last fall and showed them our plans," he says. "We've spent millions of dollars on architect's fees, and not once has anyone from the museum come to us about a shadow problem. They've even suggested that shadows might be a real benefit. William Whyte may want to negotiate, but the museum and the city have not."

Until Whyte sounded the shadow alarm at a Dallas Institute of Humanities and Culture seminar on downtown in March, public discussion of the Lincoln Property project centered on the office towers. Designed by Kohn, Pedersen, Fox of New York City, the three towers are a sporty and highly decorative reprise of '30s skyscraper design, as much Chicago style as New York, but richly detailed and evocative. They will make stunning additions to the downtown skyline.

But the skyline isn't the issue here. It's the street and public spaces, and what happens to them when they are suddenly overpowered by 4.3 million square feet of development. The base of the proposed project, in addition to casting large shadows, overwhelms the street and treats the art museum as though it doesn't exist. It is a scaleless affront to traditional values of urban design, more surprising in that it comes from a firm with a deserved national reputation for sensitive and thoughtful responses to difficult downtown sites.

Lincoln may be justly miffed at being asked to make enormous design changes at the last minute. But that doesn't absolve the company or its architects for not considering these basic contextual issues in the first place. Kohn, Pedersen, Fox declined to comment.

"And where has the city been while all this has been going on?" Whyte asks incredulously.

Most cities are unprepared to deal with sun-and-shadow issues. Some, however, are beginning to recognize that the right to light is among the most important that large cities have.

New York City recently adopted a sun-and-shadow ordinance as part of its revised midtown zoning rules. This ordinance requires that 75 percent of the sky surrounding any new building remain open: If a person standing 250 feet away can see three-fourths of an imaginary sphere above and around a building's top, the building passes.

The ordinance is modeled on a sunlight preservation system developed in Great Britain, and in certain aspects marks a return to the spirit of the city's landmark 1916 zoning ordinance, enacted to prevent the streets of Manhattan from turning into dark canyons. Out of this ordinance came the distinctive wedding-cake skyscrapers that still mark the Manhattan skyline.

San Francisco has the nation's most sophisticated sun-and-shadow ordinance. Starting with the logical assumption that in a cool and windy city public spaces require sun, the city did an inventory of all public parks, squares, and plazas downtown. Then it created an ordinance that prohibits construction of any building that would shade these spaces from one hour after sunrise to one hour before sunset, 365 days a year.

The ordinance was overwhelmingly approved by San Francisco voters in a 1984 referendum, making it an expression of popular will as well as planning wisdom.

George Williams, assistant planning director for San Francisco, says that while the ordinance has generally been well received, the city still has to bring some architects and developers kicking and screaming to the negotiating table.

"I'm shocked by how insensitive architects are to this issue. They have no concern with the impact of their buildings on adjacent buildings or streets."

But Williams denies that the shadow ordinance has made good architecture more difficult or costly.

"If there is a lesson here for other cities, it's that once you require architects to address the shadow issue, it is not a real inhibition to design. You don't have to downzone the bejeezus out of everybody to get responsible buildings."

Peter Bosselman of the University of California at Berkeley's environmental simulation laboratory, whose research was the backbone of the San Francisco ordinance, agrees that the ordinance hasn't killed profits or good design.

"In case after case, we've found that the same density, the same floor-area ratio, can be achieved with a different building configuration," he says. "Some ingenuity is needed from the designers, however, and they will only do it if the policy makers demand it."

Dallas policy makers look upon such demands the way Luke Skywalker looked at the Sarlac pit—nervously.

The city flirted briefly with a shadow ordinance in 1982, following complaints that Thanks-Giving Square was literally being overshadowed by new office towers. Peter Stewart, benefactor and developer of Thanks-Giving Square, demonstrated then that it was in shadow 90 percent of the daylight hours during the fall and winter, compared to 50 percent in 1977, before construction of Thanks-Giving Tower. He urged the city to adopt a sun-and-shadow ordinance to preserve the remaining view corridors, but the proposal got such a cool reception from developers that it was quietly dropped.

Stewart subsequently used his computer data to persuade Cadillac-Fairview to make some light-preserving modifications in the siting of its First City Center project.

The Thanks-Giving Square, like the DMA sculpture garden, is a major public space adversely affected by insensitive new construction. It is shadowed at a time of year when sunlight matters most, and consequently, its public appeal has been significantly diminished. Worst of all, the loss of sunlight was unnecessary: Stewart showed that subtle reconfigurations of Thanks-Giving Tower would have increased the amount of available sunlight without diminishing the building's rentable space.

So the museum is partially correct in calling this a "neighborly" issue. Yet the resolution is not so simple as asking a neighbor to remove an offending fence. Lincoln Property officials have said that construction of the first tower, directly across from the sculpture garden, will start this fall. If this is true, then the opportunities for major changes are slim.

"There's no question that we should have acted sooner," Barnes says. "Time is running out. We should have nipped this in the bud." The massiveness of the base and the position of the towers are the key issues, not height. Three tall towers, generously spaced and pushed back from St. Paul Street, would be less damaging to the sculpture garden than the present scheme, in which the two tallest towers belly up to St. Paul Street. The key unknown, Whyte said in his report, is whether or not there will be any niches through which sun can reach the garden. "The positioning of the towers is crucial," he noted.

Redesigning the base is a trickier matter, though not an impossible one. The present version is overscaled and ponderous, rising straight up from the sidewalk to a height of one hundred feet, twice the height of the DMA's barrel vault.

Lincoln Property has said repeatedly, however, that it wants to be a good neighbor to the museum and to the Arts District. It plans to create a sculpture garden in the center of its project to complement the museum's; there also have been discussions between the respective architects about ways to link the two by means of a bridge or platforms.

But how much more neighborly it would be to reduce the scale of the base to more civilized proportions, giving the street and the garden a chance to breathe.

Harry Parker and members of the DMA board say they believe they are dealing with reasonable people, that friendly negotiations are still possible. Let's hope they're right, so that one of the city's best public spaces isn't compromised just as the public is really learning to enjoy it.

Donald Judd's austere kingdom: A sculptor driven by a powerful vision has made the southwest Texas landscape his own museum

FEBRUARY 12, 1989

Since Donald Judd's death in 1994, the draw of his art compound in Marfa has only intensified. Dillon's essay captures Judd's vision for the town and Fort Russell just as it began to draw a wider audience to the remote and romanticized landscapes of West Texas.

A little height goes a long way in Marfa.

In this land of craggy peaks and grassy plains, where there is no middle distance, only near and far, a water tower or a grain elevator becomes a skyscraper. Marfa has one of each, plus a courthouse with a mansard roof and an implausibly flamboyant cupola. Together they make a faint silhouette on the horizon that says "town here."

But nobody goes to Marfa (pop. 2,503) for its architecture. The only reason for art lovers to make the two hundred-mile drive southeast from El Paso, through the Sierra Blancas and the Davis Mountains, zig-zagging between two time zones, is to see the sculpture of Donald Judd. For nearly twenty years he has quietly, almost secretively, been transforming this tiny ranching town, the seat of Presidio County, into a mecca of modern art.

There are no billboards outside town announcing this, no "Home of Donald Judd" signs, no Judd Street. Yet Judd's Marfa project is unique in the history of American art—one of its peaks. In this high, austere place he is living out the ultimate artist's fantasy—making sculpture, and also controlling totally the conditions under which it is seen.

Hundreds of pieces are here, most installed permanently, never to be moved, sold, or lent. They are not the pieces that dealers couldn't sell; they are his best work, the legacy of a lifetime. Over the years he has complained bitterly that no comprehensive, permanent installations of the work of post–World War II artists—his generation—exist anywhere in the world. "You're lucky if you can find four Pollocks in New York City," he says.

Because of Marfa, nobody can say that about Donald Judd. The twenty-five-year retrospective of his work that opens Sunday at the Dallas Museum of Art is only a teaser.

Judd first saw Marfa in 1946 from the window of a bus, and something obviously stuck. In the 1960s, as his artistic star was rapidly ascending, he began scouting property in the Southwest. His parents were living in Tucson, Arizona, but he found nothing there, or in Baja California, to his liking. So he returned to the Pecos region of southwest Texas, only to find Alpine too big, Marathon too impoverished, and Presidio too seedy. He ended up in Marfa.

"I like open land, and cactus, and I'm not very interested in trees," he explains. "Marfa was perfect."

He bought a place to live and work, with enough space for his wife and two children. By the late 1970s he had acquired more property: a pair of Army commissary buildings two blocks from the courthouse, and 350 acres of land and buildings at Fort D. A. Russell, an abandoned Army base on the edge of town that had been a camp for German prisoners of war during World War II.

The first he surrounded with a high adobe wall and made into a studio. The second he gradually remodeled into permanent exhibition spaces for his own work and, eventually, that of fellow travelers Larry Bell and Dan Flavin. He also purchased the abandoned Wool & Mohair Company warehouse in downtown Marfa, beside the Southern Pacific tracks, and converted it into exhibition space for the crushed-automobile sculpture of his longtime friend John Chamberlain.

Judd went to Marfa to focus his life and his art, to escape New York's frantic and fractured SoHo scene. He wanted to get back to basics; to reduce sculpture to form, line, and color; to make clear, clean objects instead of convoluted personal statements in the manner of the Abstract Expressionists. What better place to do it than Marfa?

"This is a serious place about art," he says firmly. "It is not about art education. The public [attention] is simply a byproduct."

Initially Judd benefited from strong financial backing by the Dia Foundation in New York, founded by art dealer Heiner Friedrich and funded primarily by his wife Philippa de Menil of Houston, heiress to the Schlumberger oil field drilling business fortune. Dia poured an estimated $5 million into Judd's pristine, rectilinear vision in the form of commissions, real estate, exhibitions, and a monthly salary of about $17,000.

According to its charter, Dia exists to underwrite art projects "that cannot obtain sponsorship or support from other public or private sources because of their nature or scale." Judd had gallery and museum support, but only philanthropists could fund the creation of one hundred mill aluminum boxes, each of which cost $5,000 to fabricate.

As long as oil prices stayed high, Dia supported Judd's Marfa project in truly Florentine proportions; when oil slumped, so did Dia's funding. The relationship came to a bitter and litigious end in 1986, and Judd established the nonprofit Chinati Foundation, with himself as president and a board of directors that includes Annalee Newman, widow of sculptor Barnett Newman, and Brydon Smith, director of Canada's National Gallery.

Chinati—the name means either black bird or a small cup of coffee, but its origins are unclear—holds an open house every October at the fort, to which friends, collectors, curators, art historians, and townspeople are invited. There is music, dancing, and much polyglot conversation, topped off by a feast of barbecued cabrito and beer in the fort's old gymnasium.

The rest of the year, visitors are welcome Thursday through Saturday from two to six. Chinati occasionally mounts temporary exhibitions, such as last fall's first American exhibition of the abstract geometric paintings of the late Richard Paul Lohse. It also commissions individual works by artists Judd admires. Claes Oldenburg recently completed a model for a gigantic steel horseshoe, to be erected over the grave of the last cavalry horse, which just happens to be at Fort D. A. Russell.

"The Oldenburg piece is a step toward loosening things up a bit," Judd laughs. "We don't need another comprehensive exhibition of other people's work down here."

The exhibition that really counts, of course, is Judd's.

He spends at least six months a year in Marfa, mostly in his compound, making new pieces and quietly refining his assault on museums, galleries, the whole notion of art as commodity. In an era of fashion and flux, he is making an eloquent case for continuity and permanence.

"Museums have a very fashionable and parochial view of things," Judd says caustically. "This (the DMA exhibit) is my seventh show in the last two years. I'm running around the world like a gypsy. But that isn't reality. When an installation changes all the time, nobody pays any real attention to it, and you (the artist) lose the chance to do something really well. That's why I go back to Marfa."

At Marfa, art and architecture, object and space have been united in ways rarely seen in museums or galleries. The art is made for the space, the space is shaped to fit the art.

With lapidarian precision, Judd renovated the two artillery sheds at the fort to house one hundred of his mill aluminum boxes, each 41 × 51 × 72 inches. He replaced the original flat roofs with galvanized metal barrel vaults, similar to those on local barns, and replaced the roll-up garage doors with large aluminum windows, so that natural light washes the sculptures throughout the day (fig. 4.3).

4.3. *Donald Judd installed his one hundred untitled works in mill aluminum in two artillery sheds at his Marfa compound between 1982 and 1986. © 2017 Judd Foundation/Artists Rights Society (ARS), New York.*

Boxes made Judd's name—boxes in all sizes and materials, boxes that sat on the floor and hung from walls, icons of basic geometry. Judd did them first; so many imitators came along afterward that it became difficult to recall why the originals were so innovative.

The Marfa installation answers that question. Arranged in neat, soldierly rows on squares of scored concrete, the boxes appear infinitely varied, as changeable as the light: golden in the early morning, blue-black in the early afternoon, now blinding, now consumed by shadows. Weighty as they are, some seem to hover above their concrete pads. The installation erases any negative preconceptions about the sensory appeal of raw industrial materials and forms.

But at Marfa, Judd's vision is not confined to buildings. It spills out onto the landscape.

Directly outside the artillery sheds, surrounded by tall grass in which wild antelope graze, stand fifteen massive concrete sculptures, containing two to six pieces each. Critics have tried to read symbolic significance into the number fifteen, but Judd insists that was all he could fit onto the flat portion of the site.

At first glance, Judd's "concrete things," as the residents describe them, might be septic tanks or the remains of a highway project. They appear scattered over the landscape instead of placed with Judd's usual mathematical exactitude. But that is an illusion. They are precisely arranged in a line one-half mile long, each piece 98$\frac{7}{16}$ inches by 98$\frac{7}{16}$ inches by 196$\frac{7}{8}$ inches.

Some are open, like gigantic picture frames; others are dense and closed, like bunkers. They are as much about light and shadow and the rudiments of volume, form, and color as the aluminum boxes. And they are equally sensuous and tactile, with smooth, warm surfaces and spaces that children like to climb into.

The installations at Fort D. A. Russell show the public Judd. The compound in town represents the solitary, ruminative, private Judd—Judd the hermit and reclusive genius. There are no parties or public exhibitions here.

The entire complex of warehouses, studios, courtyards, and gardens is surrounded by a high adobe wall, like a small monastery. It is a still place, except when the Godbold feed mill next door is operating, and it is as rigorously laid out as any of Judd's sculptures. The adobe walls are a frame, within which other walls make other frames. The courtyard is a grid, with plum trees and cottonwoods planted in thin, straight lines. And in one corner stands a rectangular swimming pool, with a rough adobe wall behind it; beyond that, the metal towers of the feed mill. In these overlapping images is a mirror of Judd's world, the concept that becomes a place, the line of thought that extends into the real landscape, the life that is art.

Like his boxes, the commissary buildings are neatly partitioned. One contains a studio and a library, the other a small kitchen and bedroom flanked by two more permanent exhibition spaces. And in most of the spaces is a partially made bed, a disorderly counterpoint to Judd's pristine sculpture, a reminder of his presence even when he is absent.

Few townspeople ever enter the compound; it is doubtful that they realize what goes on inside. Judd employs local laborers on all his projects, which makes him one of the town's major employers. Residents seem to appreciate that. "Nice fellow. Keeps to himself," says the proprietor of the El Paisano Hotel on Highland Street.

But the appeal of his work mystifies some. "We think of those concrete things of his as eyesores," says an attendant at the downtown Fina station.

Judd can be critical of the town—until someone attacks it. Then he becomes a defender, even a booster.

"The general level of public interest in art is not high and broad enough that you would get much more of an audience for my work in New York City than in Marfa," he says.

Yet he denies that there are more than accidental connections between the place and his sculpture. Marfa is a place to work, to be alone; the ideas come from within.

"The land is the land and the art is the art," he says. "The pieces would look just as good in Switzerland."

They might look as good, but they wouldn't look the same. Driving across this landscape of simple, elemental shapes, on days when the light turns everything into a silhouette, when a mountain is reduced to crisp edges and deep shadows, it is hard not to see the place in the art somewhere.

Then again, maybe it is the journey that makes the difference. It's easier to get to Switzerland than to Marfa. The trip is a kind of pilgrimage, and what good is a pilgrimage if it's easy? The people who come to

Marfa come for a reason. They pay attention because there are so few distractions, and therefore they see more. To Judd, that's precisely as it should be.

"If you want to see the Giottos, you go to Padua," he says. "If you want to see Judds, you go to Marfa."

Remaking a masterpiece: The Kimbell should rethink its expansion plan

OCTOBER 29, 1989

Dillon's piece on the controversial plan to expand the Kimbell Art Museum in 1989 is a diplomatic rebuke of a project that was halted by international outcry. Romaldo Giurgola's doomed proposal to add on to Louis Kahn's masterpiece delayed the execution of the Kimbell's expansion until the completion of Renzo Piano's addition—a separate wing across the lawn—in 2013.

Intimate. Elegant. Refined. The words recur like a litany in descriptions of the Kimbell Art Museum. To many people it is the perfect marriage of form and content, a museum that is its own greatest work of art. Altering it would be like altering the Parthenon or the Pyramids.

Yet in late July the Kimbell announced an $8 million expansion of Louis Kahn's masterpiece, to be designed by his colleague and disciple Romaldo Giurgola and to open in 1992—the Kimbell's twentieth anniversary. The addition will contain galleries, sculpture courts, lecture and seminar rooms, and other spaces related to the museum's educational programs.

"We feel that we are compromising our mission to promote the appreciation of art by having to bundle up and put into storage our permanent collection whenever we have a major exhibition," explains director Edmund "Ted" Pillsbury. "The reason to have exhibitions is not to bring in crowds but to show the permanent collection in a new light. And we're not able to do that."

But not everyone is convinced that more is better at the Kimbell.

New York Times architecture critic Paul Goldberger wrote that the Kimbell was one of the few museums left with the resources to remain small and that perhaps it had not asked the right questions about its future.

Two weeks ago the *Times* published a scathing letter from Sue Ann Kahn, the architect's daughter, accusing the Kimbell of architectural vandalism.

"Why not add more bays to the Parthenon to accommodate more tourists?" she asked.

"Why not extend the Guggenheim Museum by adding a few more spirals? . . . In a country that has so few architectural monuments of true greatness, why does an art museum, of all institutions, choose to destroy the scale and diminish the perfection of one of the greatest?"

Greatness can be hard to live with. If the Kimbell were merely an average building, or just a very good one, nobody would care how many additions it had. But it is the masterwork of a giant of twentieth-century architecture, so every move a museum director or another architect makes is magnified a hundredfold.

It is hard to argue, on principle, that the Kimbell should remain inviolate, since so many revered landmarks have been built over repeatedly without loss of favor. St. Mark's, St. Peter's, the Louvre, the US Capitol—the list goes on and on.

The Kimbell opened in 1972 with a small permanent collection representing a choice cross section of Western, Asian, and African art. It was a connoisseur's museum, a world apart, offering—in the words of founding director Richard Brown—"a harmonious simplicity and human proportion between the visitor and the building and the art objects."

Mr. Brown specified natural light and warm natural materials as essential parts of the Kimbell experience, all contained in "a form so complete in its beauty that additions would spoil that form."

The Kimbell's collection has grown slowly rather than exponentially. Unlike the Whitney or the Guggenheim, its vault is not bursting with unexhibited masterpieces. Most of its best work is on view most of the time.

And in all of this, smallness has been the Kimbell's ally, forcing it to make tough aesthetic decisions that larger institutions rarely have to face. It has consistently sought out the "A" paintings because it could afford them, and because it had no room for the "B" works.

But director Pillsbury has also made it clear that he is no longer entirely comfortable with the Kimbell's precious, jewel-box status. He wants the museum to be more at the center of things, especially now that Fort Worth's long-delayed Cultural District is finally emerging. This means, among other things, importing and generating more large traveling exhibitions, for which the Kimbell is not always the ideal setting.

Several times in the last six years the Kimbell has had to store its permanent collection to accommodate a blockbuster show, including *Guido Reni: 1575–1642* and *The Bronze Age of China*. While it's hardly a chronic problem, Mr. Pillsbury doesn't want to live with it forever, either.

More urgent, it would seem, is the need for additional classrooms and meeting space. Thanks largely to Mr. Pillsbury, the Kimbell has become as popular as the Fat Stock Show, with a broad range of lectures, concerts, symposia, and other public programs. Neither Mr. Kahn nor Mr. Brown could have foreseen this change. The bigger surprise is that there isn't more educational space in the proposed addition, the bulk of which is galleries and parking.

But even granting that a modest addition might be justified, even farsighted, the Giurgola plan is not the way to go.

His scheme, worked out in collaboration with Mr. Pillsbury and the Kimbell trustees, calls for 104-foot-long wings on the north and south ends of the existing building, with 20-foot glazed passageways in between (fig. 4.4). Mr. Kahn's signature cycloid vaults, which define the galleries and wash them with cool, silvery light, will be replicated in both wings. The original building, except for the restaurant, will remain intact.

It is a conservative and deferential proposal inspired, says Mr. Giurgola, by Mr. Kahn's own early studies for a larger building.

"The fact that some of Kahn's early schematic designs for the museum included cycloid vault gallery spaces extending throughout the areas of the proposed design was a strong factor in defining the design approach. It was almost as if Kahn had left design intent instructions for how the museum should be expanded."

For Ted Pillsbury and Romaldo Giurgola, the combination of

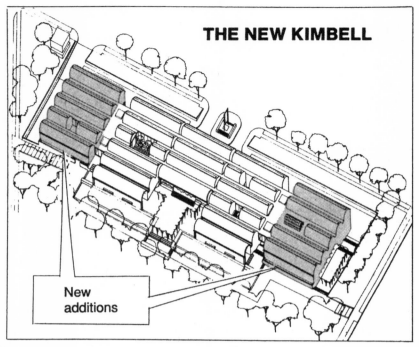

THE NEW KIMBELL

New additions

The Dallas Morning News

4.4. *Romaldo Giurgola's planned addition to Louis Kahn's Kimbell Art Museum consisted of an extension of the barrel vaults to the north and south of the original building. This illustration accompanied Dillon's article; courtesy* Dallas Morning News.

cycloid vaults, natural light, and fine materials is the essence of the Kimbell, far more important than square footage.

"We are not transforming Kahn's building," Mr. Pillsbury emphasizes. "We're putting something next to it, like bookends. You will still be able to walk around the walls of the 1972 building."

Mr. Giurgola has also said that Mr. Kahn's early studies are the main reason that alternative expansion schemes were not pursued. But this is slippery business, the intentional fallacy applied to architectural design. Whatever Mr. Kahn may have contemplated in his early sketches, there is no evidence he believed that the building that was finally constructed was compromised or incomplete.

And unlike the Whitney and the Guggenheim, the Kimbell has numerous options, from expanding under the great lawn to the west to constructing a separate building on an adjacent site—for paintings or traveling shows—that would allow Giurgola to be Giurgola and Kahn to be Kahn. I. M. Pei's East Wing at the National Gallery is only the most celebrated recent example of the latter approach.

Much will depend, of course, on how deftly the proposed addition is executed. Mr. Giurgola is a thoughtful and discriminating architect who is unlikely to do anything outrageous to his mentor's building. But he is also traveling a path more perilous than Michael Graves at the Whitney or the firm of Gwathmey Siegel at the Guggenheim. He is attempting to speak in another's voice without losing his own, to revise a masterpiece while appearing to do almost nothing. It is a balancing act that few architects have pulled off.

And, of course, no matter how faithfully the Kimbell's forms and materials are reproduced, our experience of the building will change. For we see it now not only as a sequence of rarefied interior spaces, but also as a harmonious structure on a landscape, set off by trees, water, and a great lawn, an elegant fragment of a larger whole.

The proposed addition will extend the building some 250 feet, stretching it across an entire city block and making it a cultural megastructure. The additions will not have Mr. Kahn's vaulted porches, or his refined symmetry. Nothing will be quite the same.

Add to this the absence of a truly compelling need, and this entire project, however well-intentioned and farsighted in the abstract, becomes difficult to support.

San Antonio museum:
A recycling success story

APRIL 21, 1991

The San Antonio Museum of Art combined historic preservation, adaptive reuse, and new construction, an approach that was atypical for Texas but, Dillon observed, appropriate for San Antonio's historic fabric. Since 1991, the museum has continued to expand and is now accessible from the River Walk's Museum Reach branch, which opened in 2009.

San Antonio thrives on improbabilities, and nowhere is this more evident than at the San Antonio Museum of Art. Originally a Lone Star brewery, then a cotton mill and a food warehouse, the building would have been demolished in many cities as a safety hazard. San Antonio transformed it into a palace of art. The museum opened in 1981 to widespread acclaim as a farsighted and remarkably inexpensive renovation. That's another part of the San Antonio way. Recycle as many old buildings as you can, for as little money as you can get away with.

What San Antonio got for its initial $7.2 million was a pair of castellated towers, spacious galleries with 20-foot ceilings and dramatic concrete vaulting, and a half-dozen small brick outbuildings that give the complex the character of a nineteenth-century industrial village. "I don't know another museum in the country with better raw material," says San Antonio architect Pat Chumney, who collaborated with

4.5. *Cambridge Seven designed the first of a series of modern interventions into the Lone Star Brewery as part of its transformation into the San Antonio Museum of Art. Photograph courtesy Cambridge Seven Architects.*

Cambridge Seven Associates on the original renovation and designed the new Ewing Halsell Wing for ancient art (fig. 4.5).

As a new museum in a poor city, SAMA had its share of problems.

Its operating budget was frequently slashed, and in the early years there often wasn't enough money to keep the heating and air-conditioning equipment operating. Some of the galleries had too much light, and the main lobby, with its large windows and meager wall space, is still virtually unusable except for occasional parties.

Yet in an era of aesthetic overstatement, the San Antonio Museum of Art remains engagingly unpretentious. Visitors wander from boiler room to brew house to storage towers, looking at paintings and sculpture in settings that no interior designer could duplicate. And when they get tired or bored, they can float up and down in glass elevators, which double as gigantic kinetic sculptures, or else step out onto the neon-lit sky bridge for dramatic views of the downtown skyline.

With the opening of the Halsell Wing last fall, and the arrival of *Mexico: Splendors of Thirty Centuries*, the museum has entered a critical new phase in its development. It has not only more space—and more recognition—but also an opportunity to clarify its curatorial agenda. Does it want to become a traditional civic museum, a Southwestern outpost of the Metropolitan, or will the *Splendors* exhibit be the catalyst for making the museum a center for Hispanic art?

This blockbuster consumed not only most of the existing gallery space, but also required the renovation of one of the warehouses almost overnight. Designed by Lake/Flato Architects of San Antonio, the William L. Cowden Gallery is a spare 7,500-square-foot space with many similarities to the Temporary Contemporary in Los Angeles, including high ceilings, wide spans, and a welcoming, "anything is possible" atmosphere.

For $650,000—a typically frugal San Antonio budget—the architects replaced the roof, repaired the original brick, cut several new entrances, and designed a connection to the main building.

Once *Splendors* departs, the Cowden Gallery will house traveling exhibitions and contemporary art.

The Halsell Wing was a more ambitious undertaking. San Antonio lawyer and philanthropist Gilbert Denman, a trustee of the Ewing Halsell Foundation, provided approximately $2 million to convert the brewery's engine and boiler rooms into galleries. He then donated his own collection of ancient art to fill them.

Mr. Chumney retained the industrial features of the original boiler room, including steel roof trusses, rough bricks, and vestiges of old coal chutes and other boiler room apparatus. The roof soars feet above the exhibit floor, and—combined with the rough brick walls and arched windows—gives the room the feel of an ancient Roman bath that has been restored.

Since the pieces in the Denman Collection are mostly small, exhibit designer Clifford LaFontaine placed them on pedestals so that they could hold their own in such a grand space. The result is stunning. Instead of a daunting forced march past rows of glass cases, visitors can walk among the sculptures, viewing them from different vantage points, as though they were in a courtyard instead of a gallery.

The Halsell Wing also contains two smaller spaces: the Arnold and Marie Schwartz Gallery for ancient glass and the Estelle Blackburn Gallery for ancient Mediterranean decorative arts, a gift of Nancy Hamon in honor of her mother. The collections are outstanding, but the galleries are no match for the boiler room, the best new "Oh, God!" exhibit space in the country.

The Ewing Halsell Wing and *Mexico: Splendors of Thirty Centuries* are like arrows pointing in different directions: one east, toward New York and Europe, the other south, toward Latin America. The Denman Collection is superb and no doubt curatorially irresistible. But given the museum's location and financial resources, its Latin American and folk art collections represent a more plausible future. It already has small pre-Columbian and Spanish Colonial collections, along with the enormous Nelson Rockefeller Collection of Mexican folk art, most of which is in storage or on loan. "It's bizarre that a state like Texas, with its roots in the Americas, should know so little about Mexico," says Marion Oettinger, the museum's curator of folk and Latin American art. "We see the exhibit as a chance to open up new possibilities for the city and the state. This is not simply my biased curatorial view. It is something that makes sense historically and in the context of the ethnic composition of San Antonio." Director Paul Piazza says that Latin American art is becoming "a major thrust" of the museum. "I don't envision us trying to become like Houston or the Met. We couldn't afford to do it anyway." Converting one of the remaining outbuildings into a Latin American art wing, discussed for years but never pursued, reportedly has become a priority. The museum will have to launch a major fund-raising campaign to pull it off, but if past is prologue, it probably will end up with more and grander space for less money than any other institution in the country.

Economy, additions revive Arts District: Backers hope area at last fulfills its potential

JULY 26, 1998

After the opening of the Dallas Museum of Art in 1984 and the Meyerson Symphony Center in 1989, progress in the Arts District seemed to stall. Nearly a decade later, Dillon covered a new surge of planning and construction in two articles published together, the one below and "New Foundation—Dallas's Arts District Stakes Out the Future," the cover story for the Sunday Arts section.

To a generation in Dallas, the Arts District is only a sign on Woodall Rodgers Freeway. They may drop into the Dallas Museum of Art or show up for a concert at Artist Square, but the sense of "district" remains elusive, like a rumor that can't be pinned down.

Now the combination of a booming economy and an explosion of arts groups needing space has revived interest in this tantalizing but troubled civic project. Within the last eighteen months, four major additions to the Arts District have been announced: the Nasher Sculpture Garden; a housing/shopping/performance development between Pearl and Olive Streets; the Trammell and Margaret Crow Collection of Asian Art; and a performing arts center. The Crow Collection will open in November and the Nasher garden in 2001. The timing of the other projects is unclear.

In May, Dallas voters approved $10 million to purchase land for

194

the performing arts center, a possible preview of a more substantial bond request in 2000 for construction. They also backed an additional $500,000 for a cultural facilities master plan. A second planning study, by Theatre Projects Consultants of Ridgefield, Connecticut, is assessing the needs of groups that want a home in the district. That report is expected in late August.

This rush of activity has convinced Dallas Opera general director Plato Karyanis that an Arts District renaissance is at hand. "The timing couldn't be better. The economy couldn't be better. We have more disposable income available than at any time in our history. This is the moment."

Mayor Ron Kirk predicts the Arts District is going to be crucial in making Dallas a vibrant city in the next century. "It helps give us an identity, it contributes to our bottom line and does something for the city's soul."

But Arts District supporters have heard such rosy predictions before, only to have their hopes dashed. One lesson in the tortuous history of the district is that nothing ever goes according to plan. A second is that arts alone do not a district make.

The idea of an arts district emerged from a 1977 study of Dallas's cultural facilities by renowned urban planners Stephen Carr and Kevin Lynch of Boston. The study pointed out the educational and economic benefits of clustering exhibition and performance spaces in one area. This in turn provided a rationale for the DMA and the Dallas Symphony Orchestra to leave Fair Park and begin converting twenty blocks of marginal real estate between Ross Avenue and Woodall Rodgers into an arts district.

A June 1978 arts bond referendum failed, a rare event in Dallas. But a year later voters had a change of heart, and the Arts District was born. The DMA snapped up a site for approximately $20 a square foot and began lining up donors. But within three years, land prices had soared to $200 a square foot—too pricey for them and for even the wealthiest developers. The district began to stall as soon as it started.

In 1981, Sasaki Associates of Watertown, Massachusetts, won a national competition to provide an urban design plan for the district. It was a quintessential '80s document, based on expectations of $50-a-barrel oil and an inexhaustible demand for office space.

The Arts District appeared as a forest of towers, most more than forty stories, arranged Monopoly-like along a grand boulevard amid

4.6. *Sasaki Associates, Dallas Arts District 1983 concept drawing showing a thriving pedestrian mall on Flora Street shaded by allées of trees. Courtesy Sasaki.*

cafes, restaurants, galleries, and specialty shops catering to "the affluent, casual metropolitan audience." By the year 2000, it would have 10 million square feet of office space, 250,000 square feet of retail, and three hotels.

"The whole city was riding this wave of optimism," recalls Stuart Dawson, who directed the plan. "We believed that the country was going to continue to build and Dallas would be in the center of things. We figured it would take ten years to build out the Arts District, fifteen if you were a pessimist. Nothing could stop it."

The Sasaki diagram is as revealing for what it omits as for what it includes: no parks or open space, no small commercial buildings that might be converted to studios or apartments, no mass transit (fig. 4.6).

"The original Sasaki vision was not attainable and probably not even desirable," says Arts District coordinator Howard Hallam. "Things needed to go in a different direction."

But before this vision could be realized, the economy collapsed and the district fell into a deep sleep from which it is only now beginning to stir. Except for the Morton H. Meyerson Symphony Center in 1989, virtually nothing happened in the Arts District for another decade.

"The story [of the Arts District] is a metaphor for Dallas's failures," wrote Neal Peirce, a syndicated urban affairs columnist, in his 1991 special report on the city. "Unwillingness to share, to risk public wealth with imagination or smart timing, to involve people who aren't already powerful. . . . Dallas ought to correct its error, reclaim the Arts District land and build a true arts community in place of an elegant collection of arts monuments."*

Arts District leaders insist that this time around things will be different. They will work to build a "true arts community" made up not only of major institutions but also of small groups, experimental groups, and minority groups, many of which have had to cancel or curtail their seasons for lack of space. It will be about $5 tickets as well as $50 or $100 tickets. Instead of another "arts monument," the proposed Dallas Center for the Performing Arts will consist of three or four smaller buildings linked by alleys, plazas, and a major outdoor public space, probably a reconfigured Artist Square (fig. 4.7).

For the Dallas Black Dance Theatre, a home in the performing arts center would mean a longer season and more visibility.

"We perform in the Majestic, which has fifteen hundred seats and is expensive to use," explains artistic director Ann Williams. "If we had a space with six hundred seats, we could give a week or two of performances for the same cost."

For the Dallas Children's Theater, it would mean an end to a gypsy existence in temporary quarters.

"Our goal," says executive director Robyn Flatt, "is to have a situation where children and families can come into the theater without feeling that they are interrupting something else. They are essential to the future of the Arts District, or else it will choke itself off."

"The vision was generated by this district, by the limited amount of land available, and the tremendous need for performance space throughout the city," adds John Dayton, chairman of the Dallas Center for the Performing Arts.

This revised vision reflects changes taking place throughout the country, as diversity, inclusiveness, and pragmatism become the focus of arts planning.

Although arts palaces are still being constructed—Bass Performance

---

* Neal Peirce's report, which focused on downtown rejuvenation through housing, education, and transit as well as offering a critique of Dallas's political power structure and lack of minority representation, ran in a special section of the *Dallas Morning News* on October 27, 1991. The report is also available in Peirce, *Citistates: How Urban America Can Prosper in a Competitive World* (Washington, DC: Seven Lock Press, 1991).

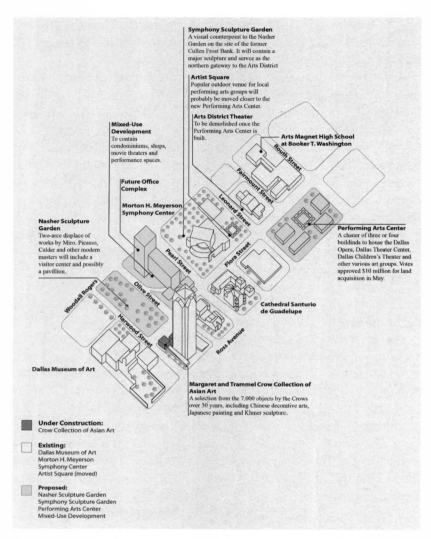

Symphony Sculpture Garden
A visual counterpoint to the Nasher
Garden on the site of the former
Cullen Frost Bank. It will contain a
major sculpture and serve as the
northern gateway to the Arts District

Artist Square
Popular outdoor venue for local
performing arts groups will
probably be moved closer to the
new Performing Arts Center.

Arts District Theater
To be demolished once the
Performing Arts Center is
built.

Mixed-Use Development
To contain
condominiums, shops,
movie theaters and
performance spaces.

**Arts Magnet High School
at Booker T. Washington**

Future Office Complex

**Morton H. Meyerson
Symphony Center**

Nasher Sculpture Garden
Two-acre displace of
works by Miro, Picasso,
Calder and other modern
masters will include a
visitor center and possibly
a pavillion.

Performing Arts Center
A cluster of three or four
buildinds to house the Dallas
Opera, Dallas Theater Center,
Dallas Children's Theater and
other various art groups. Votes
approved $10 million for land
acquisition in May.

**Cathedral Santurio
de Guadelupe**

Dallas Museum of Art

**Margaret and Trammel Crow Collection of
Asian Art**
A selection from the 7,000 objects by the Crows
over 30 years, including Chinese decorative arts,
Japanese painting and Khmer sculpture.

Under Construction:
Crow Collection of Asian Art

Existing:
Dallas Museum of Art
Morton H. Meyerson
Symphony Center
Artist Square (moved)

Proposed:
Nasher Sculpture Garden
Symphony Sculpture Garden
Performing Arts Center
Mixed-Use Development

4.7. *The state of development in the Dallas Arts District in 1998. Image by Karis Bishop, based on the original illustration from the* Dallas Morning News.

Hall in Fort Worth, Benroya Hall in Seattle, and the New Jersey Center for the Arts in Newark—many communities are opting for more modest facilities that respond to what a community needs instead of some abstract notion of culture.

Even some of the palaces are being stitched into the fabric of the city instead of placed on a pedestal. The new halls in Fort Worth and Seattle are located downtown, surrounded by stores, hotels, and offices. The proposed opera house in Toronto will occupy the site of an old law building in the business district.

According to Duncan Webb, a consultant on the Theatre Projects study, the new yardstick for arts facilities is whether they can survive, prosper, and serve the community over time.

"That's quite a shift," he says. "In the past we'd usually figure those things out after the fact."

Mr. Webb adds that prosperity doesn't necessarily mean turning a profit or playing only to full houses, but rather achieving a mix of activities that can be sustained by some reasonable combination of earned and contributed income. Theatre Projects Consultants is now analyzing the needs of the prospective Arts District tenants to determine, in Mr. Dayton's words, "whether we are way out on a limb and overly optimistic or more or less in touch with reality."

Constructing culture: New museums are springing up in all corners of Texas

APRIL 18, 1999

While there was a global boom in art museum construction and planning in the 1990s, Dillon took time to explore the context for the boom in Texas. It provided background for the development of the Arts District in Dallas, but also contributed to Dillon's understanding of a Texan culture and the role of intercity rivalries.

All of a sudden, Texas is hat high in culture. In the past five years, more than sixty museums have opened, broken ground, or been announced. That's better than one a month. Every corner of the state is represented, along with every kind of institution, from grand civic monuments, such as the Audrey Jones Beck Building in Houston, to an offshore drilling museum in Galveston and a proposed Cowgirl Hall of Fame in Fort Worth.

The Texas Association of Museums estimates the total cost of these projects at nearly $600 million, with another $100 million set aside for endowments. The obvious questions about this boom are "Why Texas?" and "Why now?"

The obvious, but only partly satisfactory, answer is money. Lots of money—in Texas and throughout the country. The US economy has been on a binge for eight years. Hardly a week passes without a new high for the Dow Jones, the NASDAQ, or the S&P 500. Unemployment is down, corporate profits are up, and inflation is flat.

All of this has produced record amounts of discretionary capital for individuals, corporations, and foundations. At a time when government support for the arts and humanities is dropping, private donors are lining up to fund art museums, science museums, and other high-minded cultural enterprises. Of the six hundred art museums built in the United States since 1970, nearly two-thirds have opened since 1985, ranging from the $1 billion Getty Center in Los Angeles to the $230,000 Museum of the Big Bend in Alpine.

Fort Worth's Modern Art Museum is about to break ground on its new $60 million building, while in Dallas the Meadows Museum and the Women's Museum are under construction and the Trammell and Margaret Crow Collection of Asian Art opened in December.

"If you've been in the stock market since 1982, you'd have to be an idiot not to have tripled your money," says Peter Marzio, director of the Museum of Fine Arts, Houston. "We're seeing one of the greatest transfers of wealth in history, which is producing a new collector class and a new patron class."

To understand what this means, consider that four of the first five names on this year's Forbes 400 list of the richest Americans are computer and telecommunications moguls. Microsoft chairman Bill Gates, first on the list, is a major benefactor of the Seattle Library and Seattle Museum of Art. Microsoft's co-founder, Paul Allen, is bankrolling that city's $100 million Experience Music Project, to be housed in a guitar-shaped structure designed by Frank Gehry.

Closer to home, Michael Dell (No. 4 on the Forbes chart) and other top executives at Dell Computer recently donated $13 million to the future Austin Museum of Art, the single largest gift to a local cultural institution by a factor of ten.

This is not old money, nurtured over generations like a case of Lafite-Rothschild. It is new money, made quickly by individuals who can't quite believe their good fortune and may even feel slightly guilty about it. They aren't traditional art people or philanthropists or members of the culturati. They are typically business people who view museums and other cultural attractions as investments in the future of their communities.

"Supporting world-class quality-of-life opportunities in greater Austin will benefit us all," Mr. Dell said in announcing his company's gift. These "opportunities" will undoubtedly make Austin a better place to live. They will also help Dell and Austin lure high-tech talent

4.8. *The San Angelo Museum of Art provides an anchor for the city's development of a cultural district on the south side of the Concho River, just across from a revitalized downtown. Photograph by Jim Bean, image courtesy the San Angelo Museum of Fine Arts.*

from Boston, San Francisco, and other culturally enfranchised areas. An outstanding museum or concert hall becomes an imprimatur of sophistication and civic ambition. It can put a city on the map, as Fort Worth and Sydney, Australia, found out years ago and Bilbao, Spain, is discovering today.

Before the Guggenheim Museum opened, nobody went to Bilbao; now nobody seems to go anywhere else. The city gambled that art would put it in the world's eye, and it won. By opening three museums in three years, Austin is placing a similar kind of bet.

Yet despite all the dramatic headlines, the Texas museum boom is no overnight phenomenon. The $80 million Beck Building in Houston, for example, is the product of fifteen years of donor wooing, collector cultivation, and audience massaging. The stock market explosion simply gave these orchestrated efforts greater focus and urgency.

The same is true of the new $6 million San Angelo Museum of Fine Arts, whose director, Howard Taylor, sees the museum boom as a critical moment in the state's cultural development (fig. 4.8).

"Texas is creating its culture now," he says. "Twenty years ago, there wasn't much here once you got past the Kimbell. Now a lot of communities are benefiting from this great upsurge in wealth and a corresponding dearth of cultural institutions. There's a strong desire to have the things that other parts of the country have had for a century. I call it the 'Everything's-up-to-date-in-Kansas-City syndrome.'"

Mr. Taylor and others believe the entire state is playing cultural catch-up, investing in museums and performing arts centers the way earlier generations invested in libraries, banks, and schools. It's the end of the frontier phase and the beginning of something else.

These new aspirations are reflected in the choice of architects, as well. The most prestigious museum commissions, with the biggest budgets, are going to name architects from out of state or out of the country: Rafael Moneo in Houston, Tadao Ando and Philip Johnson in Fort Worth, Herzog & de Meuron and Richard Gluckman in Austin, Hardy Holzman Pfeiffer in San Angelo.

Regardless of what boards of trustees say about choosing the most qualified architect for the job, reputation counts. It excites donors, generates publicity, and energizes fund-raising. Local firms will continue to get the smaller jobs, but they will have to claw their way onto the short lists for the big ones.

Fortunately, the impersonal market forces that are driving the boom have not eliminated the idiosyncratic or serendipitous element in museum building, the singular personal gesture that derives from passion instead of calculation and that can define the spirit of an undertaking.

One of the largest gifts to the Jack S. Blanton Museum of Art in Austin—$10 million in cash and $16 million in art—came from author James Michener and his wife, Mari, as a thank-you to the city and to the University of Texas for years of support.

The new Texas State History Museum down the street is the crusade of former Lt. Gov. Bob Bullock, who considers it his valedictory to Texas. The idea had been kicking around for years, but Mr. Bullock's vision made it real.

Similarly, the Women's Museum being constructed at Fair Park expresses the dreams and passions of a small group of committed women. Although most of the contributions have come from SBC Communications, Texas Instruments, Lucent Technologies, and other high-tech companies, the motivation for the gifts was often familial and communal: Honor thy mother or thy wife or thy female employees.

"These are very different projects, yet the timing was right for all of them to happen," says Dealey Herndon, project coordinator for the Texas State History Museum. "The state is doing well. There is money out there to be raised. People are willing to give more. In Texas, once the momentum kicks in, things move pretty quickly."

The big danger in the current boom, experts agree, is that things will move too quickly. Too much space, too much debt, a spate of mediocre museums that will drive audiences away. "If the economy were to go south, it could easily take some of these projects with it," says Jack Nokes, executive director of the Texas Association of Museums. "It's happened before."

In the mid-1980s, the Austin Museum of Art, then known as Laguna Gloria, had a celebrated architect in Robert Venturi, a sophisticated design, and an ambitious program, only to run afoul of local politics and a national real estate bust. Other Texas cities had similar problems with science museums and children's museums.

Directors insist that they are smarter about such things now. Few institutions are running big deficits; most have endowments and realistic expansion plans. They are also working hard to become part of everyday life through school programs and lectures and civic events. With their concerts, cafes, and shops, they are becoming more like community centers—malls in the worst cases—than palaces of culture. The American Association of Museums reported a record 868 million visits to museums of all kinds in 1997.

Museums are now part of the entertainment network through the introduction of computers and the latest information technology. Visitors, especially younger ones, are no longer willing to stand passively in front of elegantly displayed objects. They want to talk back, to interact with the exhibits and the spaces around them, to learn by doing.

Frank Gehry expressed this desire in his swirling, biomorphic design for the Guggenheim in Bilbao, and most new museums, even modest ones, are acknowledging it as well. The first thing visitors encounter in the new Rockefeller Center for Latin American Art in San Antonio is a resource room filled with computers explaining the historical and cultural background of the collection. The Admiral Nimitz Museum and Historical Center in Fredericksburg, in many ways an old-fashioned history museum, is using interactive exhibits to tell the story of World War II in the Pacific.

At the same time, museums are providing relief from technology by giving singular objects new importance. In the digital age, we have become starved for real things and memorable sensory experiences. The museum has become the domain of both.

Instead of virtual reality, it offers us things themselves. Studying a Jackson Pollock painting on a computer screen is no substitute for standing before one in a museum, which is why last fall's retrospective at the Museum of Modern Art in New York drew hundreds of thousands of people. Museums offer something unique and nonreproducible. Tangibility is their edge.

And this, as much as overnight wealth and a new collector class, will likely sustain the museum boom in the years to come.

Hidden riches: A calm exterior doesn't give away new Houston museum's interior surprises

MARCH 25, 2000

Houston's Museum of Fine Arts has expanded from its original Beaux-Arts footprint adjoining Hermann Memorial Park to a network of interconnected but clearly distinct buildings. Since the expansion Dillon reviewed here, the museum has continued to grow, with the latest additions and campus plan set to be completed in 2020.

"Cool," "sober," and "disciplined" are terms we associate with banks rather than art museums, yet they seem particularly appropriate for the new Audrey Jones Beck Building at the Museum of Fine Arts, Houston. This is an exceptionally controlled design that offers few exterior clues as to what is happening inside.

"I want people to be curious about what is going on behind the walls," explains architect Rafael Moneo.

His approach is the opposite of Frank Gehry's at the Guggenheim Museum in Bilbao, Spain, with its swirling forms and gleaming surfaces. Mr. Moneo is following an older Spanish tradition of massive walls and hidden delights—an architecture of intimation and innuendo rather than overt public display.

The $85 million Beck Building, opening Saturday, concludes twenty-five years of methodical expansion by the Museum of Fine

Arts—starting with the completion of Mies van der Rohe's Brown Pavilion in the 1970s and including new conservation and education facilities; a sculpture garden; the restoration of Ima Hogg's mansion, Bayou Bend, for American decorative arts; and finally, the Beck Building. Of its 192,000 square feet, nearly half is devoted to exhibition space—a ratio made possible by the museum's decanting most of its storage, workshops, and mechanical equipment into a new visitor center and parking garage on Fannin Street.

Mr. Moneo pays his respects to Mies by turning the Beck's front door toward the Brown Pavilion and by covering his building in the same Indiana limestone as its predecessors. But his intentions are entirely different. Whereas the Brown Pavilion reaches out to the city by means of sweeping transparent galleries, the Beck Building remains reticent and introspective.

"I put all of my interest into the interior," Mr. Moneo says. "I wanted it to be dramatic and scenographic, with each sequence of spaces and images being different."

In this effort he has succeeded brilliantly. The Beck is not just another boring parade of stark white spaces. It tells a complex story that begins in the ancient world and ends just after World War I.

Visitors enter the museum from Main Street or through an underground tunnel linked to both the Brown Pavilion and the visitor center. The central atrium, a grand space that at the moment overwhelms its art, is flanked by a museum shop and galleries for American art and temporary exhibitions (fig. 4.9). On the floor above are the Blaffer Collection of old masters and the Beck Collection of impressionist and post-impressionist art as well as several smaller collections.

The galleries are the high point of the museum, impeccably detailed in an intriguing blend of old and new. Vaulted and cove ceilings, similar to those in nineteenth-century salons, are combined with sophisticated roof lanterns that spread natural light evenly throughout the galleries. These lanterns are an updated version of those Mr. Moneo installed, with mixed results, in his Modern Art Museum, in Stockholm. In Houston, they cast a consistently soft and suggestive light that draws visitors through the building and shapes their encounters with the art.

This "collection of rooms" is packed with variety and surprise to reflect the diversity of the art. There are squares, cubes, and rectangles, painted in a variety of subtle colors. Ceiling heights vary from

4.9. *Rafael Moneo, atrium to the Audrey Jones Beck wing of the Houston Museum of Fine Arts. RG23-635 01-018, MFAH Archives.*

twelve feet in several of the lower galleries to eighty feet in the atrium and American sculpture court. Some of the best spaces are the smallest, such as the intimate rooms of Dutch still lifes and flower paintings. The floors are covered in limestone, terrazzo, granite, and wood, often in combination. Several galleries contain large windows that offer stunning views of the city; all have entrances framed by polished bronze jambs that allude simultaneously to the world of old master paintings, with their gold frames, and to modern technology.

Locating the main galleries on the top floor, where they can take advantage of natural light, was shrewd. They are the heart of the building and the climax of the narrative. Yet the farther one gets from the galleries, the less compelling the museum becomes. Except for the Main Street facade, with its reflecting pool and canopy of mature live oak trees, the exterior is stiff and uninspiring. Even the luscious bronze doors and panels, like slabs of Godiva chocolate, are not enough to make it memorable.

Mr. Moneo defends his introspective approach by saying that

Houston is a car city and a semitropical city, where nobody walks and nature can be enjoyed only indoors.

"Air conditioning is what allows you to recover nature here," he says. "This is not an Islamic garden. You need to be protected from the wet atmosphere."

He has accommodated the automobile with a long porte cochere along Main Street and a combination visitor center and parking garage on Fannin. Visitors who park at the center will buy their tickets in the lobby, then follow an underground tunnel into the museum.

The lobby is pleasant for a garage but not nearly special enough for the entrance to a major museum. And the tunnel is dreary except for a tour de force light installation by James Turrell. Located midway between the Beck Building and the original, it marks the transition from old masters to contemporary art, from the depiction of light to the direct experience of it.

For all its interior richness, the Beck Building is going to take some getting used to. Unlike many new art museums, it is not a piece of sculpture. It does not do pirouettes or deconstruct on the sidewalk. It is a rather old-fashioned box in which the container is less significant than its contents. For a city that likes to live on the edge, nearly out of control, such sobriety may come as a surprise—but a healthy one.

State of the arts in Fort Worth: Museum is latest gem in Cultural District, but area still lacks identity

NOVEMBER 17, 2002

Fort Worth's Cultural District traces its roots to the 1936 Will Rogers Memorial Center, designed for the city's celebration of the Texas Centennial and to compete with the Centennial Exposition grounds in Dallas at Fair Park. * *While Dallas moved its arts institutions away from Fair Park to the Arts District, Fort Worth instead added new arts and culture institutions adjacent to its historic fairgrounds beginning in the 1960s.*

On Monday, journalists from around the world will get their first look at the new Modern Art Museum of Fort Worth, architect Tadao Ando's $65 million addition to the city's Cultural District. Museum officials are touting it as one of his greatest buildings, the perfect complement to Louis Kahn's revered Kimbell across the street.

Even people suspicious of superlatives are likely to be impressed by its elegant detailing and sublime light. When the Modern opens to the public December 14, it will be the country's second-largest contemporary art museum. And, along with the Kimbell and the Amon Carter,

---

*   For more on the Centennial projects constructed across the state, see Kenneth B. Ragsdale, *The Year America Discovered Texas: Centennial '36* (College Station: Texas A&M University Press, 1987).

4.10. *The cultural district in Fort Worth began with the Will Rogers Memorial Coliseum and livestock barns in 1936 and grew across the decades to include art, culture, and science museums and theaters. This view shows the coliseum at top, center, and the triangle of art museums, from right to left: the Amon Carter Museum (opened 1961), the Kimbell Museum (opened 1972), and the Modern Art Museum of Fort Worth (opened 2002). Photograph by David Woo.*

it confirms Fort Worth's status as one of the premier art centers between the coasts.

"I feel that we've hit the trifecta on the art museum front," says director Marla Price, who has quietly shepherded the project for six years. "A major piece of the puzzle has been filled in. We expect people will now visit two, maybe three museums instead of just one. We also expect our attendance to double."

The new Modern's debut—the old one is being recycled into a grass-roots arts center—will cap five years of furious construction in the district (fig. 4.10). Among the additions are the National Cowgirl Museum and Hall of Fame, a $35 million expansion of Philip Johnson's Amon Carter Museum, major renovations to Will Rogers Coliseum, and a flurry of new boulevards, plazas, and sidewalks.

And it's not over. A new arena is being contemplated for the district's southwest corner, along Montgomery Street. The Cattle Raisers Museum may rise next to the Cowgirl Museum, creating a Western heritage village. Casa Mañana Theatre recently announced a $3.2 million renovation of its geodesic-domed space. There's even a chance that the Kimbell may dust off its plans for a second building across the street from the original.

DISTRICT CRITICIZED

Extremely impressive as far as it goes, but in the opinion of some observers it doesn't go far enough.

"The institutions are incredible, but as an urban place, the district stinks," says Phillip Poole, president of the Associated Businesses of the Cultural District, a nonprofit group promoting commerce and tourism in the district.

Tough talk about hallowed ground. The Cultural District has always been an uneasy blend of city and suburb—a collection of imposing civic buildings set among large trees and lush lawns, as in a Beaux-Arts rendering, yet without a clear overall identity or the kind of electricity now being generated downtown by Bass Performance Hall and neighboring attractions.

Within the district's 950 acres reside three superb art museums, designed by a triumvirate of Pritzker Prize winners and American Institute of Architects Gold Medalists. One of them, the Kimbell, is widely regarded as the finest museum building of the late twentieth century. Add to that a botanic garden, an expanding science and history museum, and a coliseum and equestrian center that draws 1.5 million visitors a year, and you have a uniquely American cultural collision. Calf ropers and Cézanne enthusiasts occupying the same block, sometimes the same building.

Yet if the visiting journalists venture beyond the museum precinct they will encounter a different landscape: streets lined with parking lots, billboards, and ramshackle buildings, few places to eat, shop, or hang out.

"Right now, it's an island," says Fort Worth's planning director, Fernando Costa, "but community leaders realize that developing the edges of the district is essential to fulfilling its promise."

FRAGMENTATION

One place to start might be Camp Bowie Boulevard near the Modern. Standing in the new building's monumental lobby, looking out toward the reflecting pond and sculpture garden, visitors will see a gigantic billboard for a restaurant's "lobster rodeo." Probably not the kind of public art the museum wants to celebrate.

The major edges and entrances to the Cultural District—Montgomery and Seventh Streets, University Drive, and Camp Bowie—are mostly fragmented commercial strips, providing no sense of anticipation or arrival. Visitors often don't know when they're in the district and when they're not. Highway signs don't identify individual institutions, so folks who show up at the Museum of Science and History thinking they're at the Amon Carter are not entirely to blame.

This is not so different from the Dallas Arts District, which is prefaced by a depressed freeway and pockmarked with parking lots. The Dallas Museum of Art, the Morton H. Meyerson Symphony Center, and the Arts Magnet High School are still separate enclaves. The Nasher Sculpture Center, opening next fall, is intended to be a green link in this chain. And architects Norman Foster and Rem Koolhaas aim to pull everything together with their master plan for the Dallas Center for the Performing Arts.

Fort Worth discovered the cost of isolation and fragmentation in 1994, when the celebrated Barnes Collection came to the Kimbell. A record 430,000 people flocked to see the Monets and Renoirs and other impressionist treasures, yet most left town without visiting the other museums, the Stockyards, or anything else that Fort Worth had to offer.

"That was a wake-up call for all of us," recalls Doug Harmon, president of Fort Worth's Convention and Visitors Bureau. "We saw the tremendous economic impact the arts could have, but we also realized that we needed more collaboration and cross-marketing to take advantage of it." The museums and the Cultural District are now prominently featured in the Bureau's magazine ads and billboards, and architecture has become its own marketing niche.

IN CITY'S HANDS

The next step is up to the city. Although the district's museums are private—the Kimbell and Amon Carter are essentially family affairs—most of its land is public, which means that the public can have a big say in what happens.

"We're committed to more balanced development in the Cultural District," insists Mr. Costa, "so that people will not only visit but stay." The current Cultural District plan, adopted in 1990, described the area as an archipelago of discrete attractions with ambiguous relationships to one another and their surrounding neighborhoods. It recommended additional sidewalks and tree-lined streets, better signs, and more gathering places. Most of this has been accomplished.

But the plan also showed several "urban villages" of houses, stores, and offices along the edges of the district. So far, none of this has occurred. According to a recent survey, the population of neighborhoods within a half-mile radius of the Cultural District has declined 32 percent since 1990—partly from the demolition of apartments and a small hotel on the Modern site.

More recently, a vintage movie theater on Seventh Street was torn down for a ceremonial roundabout that was later abandoned, and a block of small shops and restaurants along Camp Bowie was cleared for the expansion of the University of North Texas Health Science Center.

The Cultural District is quietly wrestling with how to keep the Health Science Center from overwhelming the district's northern edge. On one hand, it brings several thousand workers into the area; on the other, it is a big, detached, and tightly programmed institution that needs a lot of parking. In response to neighborhood concerns, the hospital hired James Polshek, architect of the acclaimed Rose Center at the American Museum of Natural History, as a consultant on its new biotech research center. He has reportedly recommended including shops and restaurants along Camp Bowie.

EXCITING CHANGE

One thing that many in the district are delighted about is the transformation of the old Modern into the Fort Worth Cultural Arts Center. Fairly or not, the district has long been perceived as "a West Side plaything" concerned mainly with the exhibition of traditional European and American art. The issue is not the value of Picasso or Matisse, but whether in a minority-majority city like Fort Worth the district's programming is sufficiently broad and inclusive.

"The museums are focused on the exhibition of great art," says the center's director, Flora Maria Garcia. "Outreach and education are not large components of their programs."

She refers to the new center as an "arts factory" and an "incubator," containing affordable studios, galleries, offices, and performance spaces; it will be managed by the Arts Council of Fort Worth and Tarrant County with a $300,000 city subsidy. "It will add a whole other dimension to the Cultural District and the city," Ms. Garcia says.

"There is virtually no nonprofit exhibition space in Fort Worth, no place where artists can go to try things out. The opera rehearses in a shopping mall. We need something like this."

This is precisely the kind of low-key, blue-jeans-and-barbecue place that the Dallas Arts District has talked about but hasn't delivered. Whether the new Modern turns out to be Mr. Ando's masterpiece or merely a very good building, it will undoubtedly propel the museum into the top tier of contemporary art institutions. Long the poor museum in a rich museum town, the Modern now has cachet and clout.

"It's an exciting moment for us and the district, with the museums being completed and so many other projects in the works," says Ms. Price, the Modern's director. She's not alone in thinking that the next wave of development will be mostly private.

A Dallas entrepreneur has optioned a large tract east of the Modern for a mixed-use development. There's talk of a small hotel and serious discussion about a light-rail system linking downtown, the Stockyards, and the Cultural District. If even a few of these proposals pan out, in ten years the Cultural District will no longer be an island or an archipelago but part of the urban mainland.

Thoroughly modern museum: The Kimbell's new neighbor is strong, simple building design at its best. Serene spaces, commitment to craftsmanship help reaffirm FW's standing as an oasis for art

DECEMBER 8, 2002

Walk into the lobby of the new Modern Art Museum of Fort Worth and space explodes upward and outward, toward a sculpture garden and reflecting pool that bounces light off walls and into corners. For a moment, the building dematerializes and all is earth, water, and sky. Inside and outside, nature and architecture appear to be one.

The lobby is more than an entrance: it is a summary of the entire building and of Japanese architect Tadao Ando's intentions. Monumental without being intimidating, it uses modern materials and technology to create spaces of timeless serenity—a building with some of the resonance of an ancient temple. No crown moldings, no historical bric-a-brac, only structure as architecture. In a period of hyperbolic museum design, it speaks in a quiet, assured voice about the values of construction and craftsmanship.

"It is difficult to maintain craftsmanship in this age of economy," says Mr. Ando. "People abandon it for profit, which is a mistake because craftsmanship is what holds the other parts of a building together. When it is present, you recognize it and appreciate it and grow more fond of the building."

The $65 million building, which opens Saturday, is the most significant addition to Fort Worth's Cultural District since Louis Kahn's Kimbell Art Museum in 1972. It reaffirms the city's standing as a mid-continent cultural oasis and vaults the Modern into the top tier of America's postwar art museums. Others may have more Picassos and Pollocks, but none can show them better.

At 153,000 square feet, the new Modern is four times the size of the old building, now a community arts center, and second only to New York's Museum of Modern Art in exhibition space. Unlike Frank Gehry's Guggenheim in Bilbao, Spain, or Santiago Calatrava's Milwaukee Art Museum, it is a builder's building rather than a sculptor's. What happens outside matters less to Mr. Ando than what happens inside, as indicated by the Modern's having four sides but only one real facade, along Darnell Street. Even that is somewhat corporate and predictable, like a brochure photo for a Fortune 500 company. All of which makes the interior so much more remarkable.

The Modern is a building within a building, an aluminum-and-glass shell enclosing a dense concrete core. Although its basic plan—five parallel pavilions framing a reflecting pool—implies repetition and uniformity, the Modern is neither. It is packed with surprises, created by Mr. Ando's playing one quality against another: solid and void, light and heavy, open and closed, East and West, matter and spirit. From some points, the museum looks like a brilliant floating ship; from others, it appears dark and cavelike.

Visitors will probably turn left, past the information desk and a remarkably unobtrusive museum shop, to a curving concrete wall that leads to the first gallery. The ellipse is a kind of side chapel devoted to a single work, Anselm Kiefer's sculpture *Book with Wings*. A large Kiefer painting dominates an end wall, with a smaller Francis Bacon self-portrait off to one side. That's it. Three islands of art in a sea of space.

A first impression might be that the Modern's permanent collection is too small for the building, but that's wrong. Out of more than 2,750 works, only 154 are on display. Instead of hanging as much art as the walls can hold, chief curator Michael Auping has focused on a few key pieces. In this highly calculated installation, less is more, subtraction more revealing than addition.

NOT AS THEY SEEM

The main exhibition galleries are large white rectangles appropriate to the scale of a Robert Motherwell or a Jackson Pollock. Yet as in the rest of the building, appearances are deceiving. These look-alike spaces turn out to be surprisingly varied in scale and proportion.

Some are self-contained while others suddenly open up with views of the reflecting pool or the downtown skyline. It is possible to look down from the second floor at a Morris Louis or up a long staircase to an Andy Warhol self-portrait. At no time is there a sense of being on a forced march through the landscape of contemporary art.

The exhibition highpoints are the aforementioned elliptical gallery, displaying Mr. Ando's fluid organic side, and the two-story concrete gallery revealing his minimalist inclinations. Concrete as clay, concrete as steel. The latter gallery is a stunning piece of construction containing only Martin Puryear's *Ladder for Booker T. Washington*. Ponder the foot of the ladder from below, the tip from above—museum-going as aerobic exercise.

A grand staircase rises beside the ellipse to galleries and class-rooms on the second level. Mr. Ando is a poet of vertical movement. His ceremonial stairs at the Chikatsu Asuka Historical Museum in Osaka, Japan, for example, recall the great Mayan pyramids at Tikal and Chichen Itza. Always the coupling of ancient and modern.

The Modern staircase is impeccably crafted, with concrete the tex-ture of silk and daylight washing gently down the walls from a vaulted ceiling. As in the Kimbell, this light has body and dimension; you feel you could cut it with a knife. At the same time, its sources are unobtru-sive, mysterious even. Individual fixtures are spare and recessed into walls and ceilings. The louvers that direct daylight into the exhibition galleries are nearly invisible.

Like Kahn, Mr. Ando wanted his museum to have as many moods as the day. The reflecting pool bounces daylight throughout the mu-seum; at night, its pavilions glow like gigantic Japanese lanterns. An *engawa*, a narrow transitional space between inside and outside, edges the first-floor galleries. Concrete on one side, glass and water on the other, the *engawa* underscores the Asian concern for integrating the natural and the man-made (fig. 4.11).

Much has been written about Mr. Ando's admiration for Kahn and the challenge he faced in building directly across the street from that masterpiece. For him and many others, the Kimbell is a summa of modernist craftsmanship, after which architecture devolved into a pastiche of gratuitous historical details and ironical private jokes. He said repeatedly that he wanted to "achieve the level of construction [Kahn] did."

He has done that. His building and Kahn's are both forty feet high. His original six-pavilion design—subsequently reduced to five for

4.11. *Tadao Ando, Modern Art Museum of Fort Worth, showing the galleries extending into the reflecting pool. Photograph by David Woo.*

budget reasons—responded to the Kimbell's six vaults. Using different technology, he made natural light the centerpiece of his design.

ONE MISTAKE

Mr. Ando's one serious blunder was turning the Modern's loading dock toward the Kimbell. The latter's dock is in a similar position, of course, but it is smaller and lower and concealed by a wall and berm.

Most visitors don't even know it's there. What you see from the Kimbell, on the other hand, is the business end of the Modern—shipping, receiving, and trash collection. It makes for a clunky composition and whatever the reason, a surprisingly rude gesture.

The west-facing sculpture terrace atop the loading dock seems equally problematical. However blissful on an April morning, it's likely to be an oven on a July afternoon.

Ultimately, the Modern's greatest tribute to the Kimbell is the quality of its own construction.

The elegance of the concrete, the structural inventiveness of the Y columns and floating restaurant roof, the extraordinary refinement of even the most ordinary joint—all honor Kahn without mimicking him.

The Modern possesses weight and dignity. It is lyrically literal and built to last.

Knitting together the Arts District: Master plan for performance center envisions an area linked by plazas, greenery, and people

SEPTEMBER 10, 2003

As construction finished on the Nasher Sculpture Center, another wave of construction began in the Arts District. A retooled collaborative master plan was intended to provide public space to connect these new projects. Dillon would later be disappointed in the outcome. Because he retired from the paper in 2006, most of his writing about the new additions to the Arts District appeared in national architecture magazines. *

The Dallas Arts District is a long, landscaped boulevard connecting four cultural institutions, a high school, and a string of vacant lots. In ten years, it could be a quilt of plazas, gardens, and outdoor performance spaces, ringed with shops and cafes and unified by a canopy of trees—a livelier and friendlier place where people might go just for the fun of it.

That's the future sketched by the new master plan for the Dallas

---

* One of Dillon's last articles as a full-time critic for the paper was "Room to Grow—Park doesn't measure up to ambitions of performing arts center's buildings," September 14, 2006. He continued to write on the subject for the national architectural press: Dillon, "Dallas Arts District," *Architectural Record* 198, n. 2 (2010): 50–51.

Center for the Performing Arts released Wednesday. The plan is a three-cornered collaboration among Foster and Partners of London, Rem Koolhaas's Office of Metropolitan Architecture (OMA) in New York, and Paris landscape architect Michel Desvigne.

It has been conceived as a setting and framework for the main components of the $250 million center: a 2,200-seat opera house by Foster and Partners; a 600-seat, multiform theater from Mr. Koolhaas; and a smaller, third venue for theater, dance, and music groups. The Margot and Bill Winspear Opera House would be on Flora Street, east and slightly north of the Morton H. Meyerson Symphony Center and fronting a grand plaza that includes an expanded Annette Strauss Artist Square. The other two buildings would share a facing block south of Flora.

"Today is the culmination of three years of hard work," said William Lively, president of the Dallas Center for the Performing Arts Foundation. "All of our primary goals for this phase of the project have been met, and we are looking forward to the next intervals."

So far the foundation has raised $132 million in cash and pledges for the arts center. Dallas voters approved an additional $20.2 million for site improvements and the design of the third venue in the May bond election. Mr. Lively said the foundation hopes to complete all architectural contracts by the end of the year and have preliminary designs for the opera house and multiform theater by spring. If that schedule holds, construction could begin in 2005, with a grand opening in 2009.

"It's a real step forward," said City Council member Veletta Forsythe Lill. "After so many plans and so much speculation, it's nice to get a glimpse of the future. But we can't just sit back and say, 'OK, it's all in the hands of the architects.' We have to see it through to the end and be sure that the edges are as well-designed as the arts facilities."

The master plan builds on the 1982 Sasaki plan, which established the original guidelines for the Arts District but, because of its emphasis on office towers and mega-blocks, is now considered outdated.

The new plan maintains Flora Street as the district's spine but gives added importance to cross streets such as Leonard and Routh. Leonard, for example, would become a major gateway from Ross Avenue.

"Resisting the temptation to establish a cultural ghetto," the planners wrote in their introduction, "[we have] placed an emphasis on opening up the area to create a lively and inclusive city quarter."

The heart of this new quarter would be a grand plaza linking the Meyerson with the opera house and a dramatically renovated Booker T. Washington High School for the Performing and Visual Arts. Artist Square, the setting for most of the district's outdoor activities, would expand into the site now occupied by the Arts District Theater, which would be demolished.

"Artist Square is the most crucial piece because it will attract a cross section of people and events," explained Simon Bowden, project director for Foster and Partners. "A folk concert and a high-end opera side by side, that's the kind of mix we want." He noted that the proposed plaza would be the same size as London's Trafalgar Square, while conceding that the similarities ended there.

The multiform theater and the third venue would be located south of Flora, on a block fronting Leonard and Ross. No architect has been selected for the third building.

Modifications to the master plan are inevitable once the architecture appears, but Spencer de Grey of Foster and Partners, who is co-directing the project with Joshua Ramus of OMA, insists that it must be about spaces as well as buildings.

"If it deals only with the immediate pieces of the performing arts center, it will fail," he said. "There has to be a strategy for the whole Arts District, and that can't come only from the architects. It requires a full-scale public debate."

A design so artful, you may not notice: At Nasher Sculpture Center, what you don't see is as impressive as what you do. Architect Piano creates a precise blend of light, texture, and mood

OCTOBER 19, 2003

The Dallas Morning News *dedicated an entire pull-out section to the opening of the Nasher Sculpture Center, with maps, site plans, interviews, and lush photographic spreads. Dillon contributed several essays to the section—the text here is compiled from that special issue.*

Italians have a word for it—*sprezzatura*—the art that conceals art. It's what Renaissance courtiers were expected to display in public, an effortless grace that subsumes sweat and strain in exquisite form. It's what the Nasher Sculpture Center is about as well.

The museum and the garden are both stunning exercises in concealment. The travertine walls of the galleries are crammed with ducts and cables and sophisticated electronic gear, but only pristine surfaces show. The architects didn't want drains and catch basins in the garden, so they built up layers of "designer dirt" to take care of the runoff. Even the loading dock is hidden, as though deliveries and trash collection were of purely hypothetical concern.

Developer and philanthropist Raymond Nasher says he chose Renzo Piano because he is a builder who understands materials and because of all the architects he interviewed, Mr. Piano understands art the best. His relationship to Mr. Piano is that of a patron, a Texas

Medici, rather than a conventional client. Clients get buildings; patrons get architecture. Mr. Nasher got architecture.

The $70 million center, a gift to the city, is a refined synthesis of art, architecture, and engineering in which bold form gives way to the pleasures of light, texture, and mood. It shows the Pritzker Architecture Prize winner at his most self-effacing, a building of lapidary precision in which every detail—from the arc of the vaults to the joints of the stone and the frames of the doors—has been thought through to the last millimeter.

Mr. Piano even carries a tape measure in his pocket so that he can instantly recalculate the width of a rib or the shape of a turnbuckle. Workers tremble whenever he pulls it out, knowing that another change order is on the way. "He never stops designing," one of them said wearily. Mr. Piano's tolerances range from impossible to nonexistent, yet in a building defined by the gradual accumulation of small sensory pleasures, they couldn't be otherwise.

"NOBLE RUIN"

Mr. Piano also carries around a crumpled photograph of an ancient ruin in Herdonia, Italy, that he says inspired his thinking about the center.

"We wanted to make something that is about the day-to-day life of the city yet is also outside of time," he explains. "It is absurd, really, this idea of a noble ruin in the middle of a busy downtown, but that is what makes it powerful."

On the exterior, the travertine is pitted and weathered, as though it had just come from the quarry, whereas in the galleries it has been polished and mitered like fine cabinetry so as not to upstage the art. Within these serene contemplative spaces, sculptures are set off by white oak floors, pale limestone walls, silvery aluminum, and glass. That's the entire tonal range. No bright colors or sharp contrasts, but no bland uniformity either. The walls and floors are subtly veined and streaked, and everything is washed in soft, even light.

Light is the soul of the Nasher Center, and the sunscreens its technological high point—straight sections of cast aluminum laid over curved glass that rests on 2-inch steel beams. Not easy to do. This is the level of craftsmanship that Mr. Nasher demanded. He challenged Mr. Piano to come up with something completely new.

Most architects would have opted for a proven solution over an experimental one, but as befits someone from Genoa, Italy, Mr. Piano is an inveterate explorer and adventurer who is always interested in what's just over the technological horizon. He doesn't have a distinctive style, like Frank Gehry or Richard Meier, or even a consistent look. From the Centre Pompidou in Paris to the Tjibaou Cultural Centre in New Caledonia, every building has been different.

Mr. Piano's best buildings tend to be gatherings of small sensory pleasures—a grille, a bracket, a light fixture, a staircase—that may be technically adventurous, but that also surprise and delight.

His three Texas projects make the point unequivocally.

The Menil Collection in Houston, completed in 1987, is a long wood-and-steel pavilion that nevertheless fits comfortably into a neighborhood of simple gray bungalows. It is a house for art rather than an imposing cultural monument. Its principal technological flourish is a roof of fixed concrete louvers, similar to gigantic leaves, that filter light to the porches and galleries below. Light becomes a basic building material and the soul of the architecture.

Eight years later, Mr. Piano designed the Cy Twombly Gallery across the street, an elegant concrete box with a leaner but more intricate roof—he once compared it to "a butterfly alighting on a firm surface"—that includes stretched fabric ceilings clearly inspired by sail making.

This shift from light to lighter to lightest continues in the Nasher Sculpture Center, a spare, transparent pavilion featuring aluminum sunscreens of extraordinary delicacy.

The sunscreens consist of 4-foot × 6-inch sections of cast aluminum, topped with oval scoops that allow soft northern light into the galleries. True to Mr. Nasher's instruction, they are smaller and lighter than the ferro-concrete "leaves" in the Menil Collection and far simpler than the computerized louvers in the Twombly Gallery or the Beyeler Foundation in Basel, Switzerland. They are only six inches thick and contain no moving parts that jam at inopportune moments. They took three years to design and install, causing an international run on Valium, but from all appearances are worth every minute.

From the beginning, Mr. Nasher insisted that the landscape be as important as the building, and as usual he got what he wanted. Peter Walker's garden is as refined in its own way as the galleries, extending their thin travertine walls with tight rows of live oaks and cedar elms. The live oaks occupy the center of the lawn and will gradually spread to form canopies over the walkways. The deciduous cedar elms, which can soar seventy feet, line the edges to allow sunlight to penetrate the garden during the winter.

Like everything else at the center, the garden went through numerous revisions—six at least. Mr. Nasher initially wanted to keep the collection at his home in North Dallas, until he realized that the grounds couldn't accommodate monumental pieces like Mark di Suvero's I-beam *Eviva Amore*. Yet Mr. Walker's first design played off this romantic domestic setting with groves and mounds and long serpentine borders. It didn't fit the building or the urban setting. Mr. Piano subsequently proposed an apple orchard, which nobody wanted except him.

"DUEL OF THE TITANS"

In the meantime, the placement of the building kept shifting, from Harwood Street to the edge of Woodall Rodgers Freeway to Flora Street.

"We finally decided to do the simplest thing we could and then complicate it here and there," says Mr. Walker, making the negotiations sound far more amicable than they were.

"It was a duel of the titans," says Vel Hawes, the owner's representative and one of the heroes of the project. "They kept filibustering each other over everything, to the point that we tried not to have the two of them in town at the same time."

In the end, simplicity and urbanity won. A gently sloping path teases from the terrace, through an enfilade of trees, to fountains and reflecting pools at the foot of the garden. As in the galleries, the color register is extremely limited—green to green with nothing flamboyant to compete with the sculpture.

The long, axial views are crisp and formal, but those side-to-side are more episodic and mysterious. From one spot, Roy Lichtenstein's *Double Glass* is only a spot of color; from another, Jonathan Borofsky's *Hammering Man* becomes only a head and upraised arm. These intimations are invitations to roam and explore. Unlike most sculpture gardens, the Nasher Center is not an art supermarket in which every square foot is claimed. There's room to relax and reflect (fig. 4.12).

Not even great design is flawless, however. Compared with the rest of the building, the large gallery windows look a bit flat and two-dimensional, as if Mr. Piano had temporarily misplaced his tape

4.12. *Renzo Piano and Peter Walker, Nasher Sculpture Center and garden, completed 2003. Photograph by Paul Hester.*

measure. A few pockets in the garden, around Jean Dubuffet's *Gossiper II*, for example, feel overcrowded, something that curatorial fine-tuning should take care of. And the bamboo, beautiful as it is, makes an odd companion for the native plantings elsewhere, as though it had mysteriously migrated from the Crow Collection of Asian Art across the street.

Yet these are minor blemishes in an exemplary project. Dallas is hoping, of course, that the center will finally put it on the international culture map. City officials have visions of limos and tour buses decanting onto Flora Street streams of out-of-town visitors, who will then fan out through the Arts District. Mr. Nasher typically takes the broader view that it's time for Dallas and Fort Worth to collaborate on creating a regional cultural center instead of behaving like dueling frontier outposts.

"SO MUCH TO SEE"
"People will now be able to come and spend a weekend or longer because there is so much to see," Nasher says.

The big winners, of course, will be the residents of Dallas.

From one perspective, the center is a refuge from the city, a soft green place in a hard brown environment, where the air seems fresh and the roar of the traffic is temporarily stilled. Yet from another, it represents a heightening and intensification of urban life. The walls of the garden frame and recompose the downtown skyline, making it appear new and surprising. Some buildings look better than they did before or than they really are. This is what architecture is supposed to do—change our perceptions of space and place, make us take a second look.

"A poet works with words," says Mr. Piano. "A musician works with notes. An architect works with gravity. Searching for lightness as I do is always a fight against nature."

It is this constant interplay between light and heavy, ancient and modern, tradition and innovation that makes Mr. Piano's buildings both provocative and accessible. He does not strive for the flashiest or trendiest designs, but for those that are rooted and resonant.

Standing in the Nasher garden at twilight, as the sun sets and the lights in the surrounding skyscrapers come on, it's hard to remember that five years ago this was a parking lot, that it's still surrounded by parking lots and unrealized dreams. Such moments reaffirm the transforming power of great architecture, and Dallas's deep need for it.

5

HISTORIC
PRESERVATION

Few architectural issues generate more public response than historic preservation. Decisions about whether to save or demolish historic buildings and neighborhoods are bound up in emotional and personal memories that are difficult for architecture critics to navigate. Dillon could be a tough sell on preservation issues, sometimes lukewarm to preservationists' desire to protect everyday architecture, but most often a champion of architecture and neighborhoods that provided a distinct sense of character and place. He saw preservation in a broader context of costs and benefits and did favor new construction if it was better than the building it replaced. The intense controversy over the efforts to preserve the Dr. Pepper bottling plant on Mockingbird Lane in 1988 is a good example of the complexities of historic preservation in a young city. Dillon was not a full-throated champion of the plant's preservation, but he was a critic of the results after its demolition.*

Dillon especially questioned demolition for demolition's sake and the tendency to demolish historic structures to make way for parking

---

* Dillon, "Dr. Pepper Site Needs a Tonic," *DMN*, April 4, 1993; "This Decision Is Peppered with Problems. Historic Building Has Much More to Offer than Shopping Mall Space," *DMN*, March 23, 1995. See also "Shock of the NEW" in this volume.

lots, a problem he saw as devastating to downtown Dallas, Oak Lawn, Deep Ellum, and Fort Worth. According to one report, 90 percent of demolitions in downtown Dallas during the 1980s was for parking lots.* Outside of downtown, private houses in high-value neighborhoods began to fall to the wrecking ball with startling frequency, and Dillon wrote to raise awareness of masterworks by Texas architects like O'Neil Ford, David Williams, and Charles Dilbeck. Buildings associated with significant shared cultural memories, like the Texas School Book Depository, the Stanley Marcus house, and the Juanita Craft house, also received his support.

Historic preservation came relatively late to Dallas and Fort Worth. While the Conservation Society formed in San Antonio in 1924 and the Galveston Historical Foundation and the Harris County Heritage Society both formed in 1954, similar organizations did not form in North Texas until after Congress passed the 1966 National Historic Preservation Act.† Historic Fort Worth formed in 1969 and the Historic Preservation League (now Preservation Dallas) formed in 1972. In their early years, both advocacy groups focused on neighborhood revitalization on Fort Worth's Southside and in Old East Dallas.

Conversations about the goals and meaning of historic preservation in such young cities are still developing, and Dillon's writing on the subject reflects these changing attitudes. By 2000, Dillon had shifted his perspective to reflect a broader understanding that a healthy mix of historic and new construction provided the substance of a city's character. Historic preservation is a tool that allows cities to capitalize on their own distinct stories as told through buildings, neighborhoods, and landscapes, and as Texas matures, more of its historic fabric will begin to tell those stories.

---

* Dillon, "Historic Buildings of Dallas Losing Battle with Parking Lots," *DMN*, March 20, 1988.

† For local histories of preservation in Texas, see Lewis F. Fisher, *Saving San Antonio: The Precarious Preservation of a Heritage* (San Antonio: Trinity University Press, 2016), and Minnette Boesel, "Historic Preservation in Houston ... A History?" *Houston Review of History and Culture* 3, n. 2 (2006): 4-9, 51, as well as Susan Wiley Hardwick, *Mythic Galveston: Reinventing America's Third Coast* (Baltimore: Johns Hopkins University Press, 2002).

Preserving a painful past: Controversial tower would bring people to Oswald's perch

AUGUST 16, 1987

The Sixth Floor Museum, dedicated to examining the history and context of the assassination of President John F. Kennedy in Dallas, opened in the Texas School Book Depository in 1989. While the subject of Dillon's article is ostensibly the proposal to build a new external elevator, his diplomatic take outlines the difficulties and negotiations informing the series of decisions that preserved the building and public access to the sixth floor as a historical site for future generations. Ultimately, an external elevator was built on the rear façade of the building.

To commemorate a tragic public event is inevitably to relive it. The nation refought the Vietnam War over the Vietnam Memorial in Washington, with every facet of its design becoming a referendum on American foreign policy and moral values. Rarely has the symbolic power of architecture been more forcefully demonstrated.

In quieter and less obvious ways, Dallas has been fighting a similar battle over the Texas School Book Depository. After wishing it gone for almost fifteen years, neatly excised from the community memory like a malignant tumor, Dallas began slowly to come to terms with the building and its traumatic history.

These efforts surfaced dramatically on Tuesday, when the city

5.1. *The Texas School Book Depository, shown with the controversial new elevator tower under construction during its transformation into the Sixth Floor Museum. Image courtesy the Sixth Floor Museum at Dealey Plaza.*

approved construction of a controversial 60-foot elevator tower for the north facade of the Depository. The tower will be the first new structure on the assassination site (fig. 5.1).

The Dallas County Commissioners saved the Depository from the wrecking ball in 1977, then renovated it for courts and offices and renamed it the Dallas County Administration Building. The government seal of approval, together with the blandly bureaucratic name, removed some of the stigma from the building and, in a sense, returned it to the public domain.

Simultaneously, a small group of preservationists, led by Lindalyn Adams and Conover Hunt, were working on plans for an educational exhibit on the Kennedy assassination to be located on the sixth floor, from which Lee Harvey Oswald fired the fatal shots.

It was an underfunded and amateurish effort at first, sustained largely by the conviction that, for better or worse, the School Book Depository had become an international landmark and that Dallas had a responsibility to accommodate the thousands of visitors who came each year to see it. This group evolved into the Dallas County Historical Foundation, a private, nonprofit organization with a prestigious board of directors and a mission to explain the events of November 22, 1963, to the world.

"It became part of my life for ten years," said Adams, president of the foundation. "I was willing to do whatever it took to get it done. It became a personal crusade."

Their efforts received a significant early blessing in the late '70s when the Dallas County Commissioners agreed to leave the sixth floor unrenovated. An even more crucial imprimatur came last January when newly elected County Judge Lee Jackson announced that he would do everything he could to make the assassination exhibit a reality.

The sixth floor, complete with documentary photographs, the model of Dealey Plaza and the grassy knoll, and the re-creation of the sniper's perch, would finally be open to the public.

Shortly thereafter, the county agreed to issue $2.2 million in revenue bonds to pay for the construction of an exterior elevator tower and visitor pavilion to serve the exhibition exclusively, with the money to be repaid from ticket revenues.

Last Tuesday, the Dallas Landmark Commission removed one more obstacle by approving construction of the tower and pavilion, with the fine points to be reviewed later.

But the foundation's success was hardly unqualified. The approval came after three months of intense controversy that pitted county against city, city planning staff against landmark commission, historical foundation against Texas Historical Commission, and preservationists against one another.

At a July review session, a Historical Commission member told his staff architects—present for an official site visit—to stop criticizing the tower design, that it was going to be approved no matter what they thought.

"It was a very bitter meeting," said Adams, the tower's prime proponent, who was alarmed that the consensus of four years was coming apart. "I walked out. I lost my cool and cried."

At one level, the dispute is primarily architectural, involving the scale of the tower, its impact on a landmark building, and its appropriateness for the West End Historic District. At another, it is psychological and philosophical, rooted in Dallas's lingering guilt over the Kennedy assassination.

Like the infantryman statue that was added to the Vietnam

Memorial, the tower provided an occasion for exploring the more troubling questions of whether Dallas should commemorate the assassination at all or, if so, how. Boldly? Circumspectly? As a full-blown tourist attraction? The tower is utilitarian, but also symbolic because it is attached to this particular building and because it leads to the sniper's perch.

The nascent Dallas County Historical Foundation stepped into a vacuum in the late 1970s when it first proposed an exhibit on the assassination. It saw a civic cause where others saw only a civic embarrassment.

Public response, however, was anything but enthusiastic. Although the group often got polite receptions from civic leaders and business groups, it seldom got money. Until Dallas County pledged $2.2 million, the foundation could raise only enough money to pay for an occasional workshop or study conference. (It recently appointed a committee to raise an estimated $600,000 to construct the exhibit proper.) Every November 22, the press would inquire how the project was going, and each year the answer was the same mixture of apology and regret.

"It's not an easy project to sell to Dallas people," was last November's explanation from Shirley Caldwell, chairwoman of the Dallas County Historical Commission, the unofficial keeper of assassination memorabilia. "The Dallas people who were living here when this happened still maintain so many hurts and scars and pain from the event that it's not something they want to commemorate in any way."

Even those who were required to review and comment on the foundation's design did so tentatively, guardedly, as though anything they said in public would be held against them.

The Texas Historical Commission gave conceptual approval back in 1983, with clear signals that the design was a compromise. The county had insisted that it didn't want crowds of tourists surging through the building, nor did it want to undo the restoration work it already had completed. Rather than get into a battle with the county, the state body went along. Staff members now say privately that they regret the decision, but are powerless to change it.

The Dallas Landmark Commission followed suit, giving conceptual approval in 1983 while avoiding a hard, critical look at the design. To this day, commission members can't agree on whether they approved a concept, a specific design, or some combination of the two. Like the

Texas Historical Commission, they waffled, taking refuge in vague recommendations and polite circumlocutions.

"We were much too polite on that first review," said commission chairman Ruthmary White. "We should have said flatly, 'Go back and find a way to internalize the elevator, then come back to us.' We thought they would come back anyway, but they didn't. We learned a hard lesson."

The Dallas County Historical Foundation, assuming quite reasonably that it had the green light, geared up to sell its idea to the public. It already had hired an exhibit consultant, Staples and Charles of Washington, to prepare designs for the sixth floor. Between 1983 and 1986, it installed a display model for the Depository lobby, commissioned a $10,000 promotional film called *One November Day*, and put together an automated slide presentation for the Chamber of Commerce, the Central Dallas Association board, and key community leaders, such as Stanley Marcus and John Stemmons.

The basic theme was that the time had come for Dallas to confront the past that hurt, to preserve the history that had been imposed upon it as well as that which it had made for itself. The tone was low-key and underplayed. "Our overriding concern was to avoid the feeling of controversy," Adams says. "We didn't want to go forward with a cloud hanging over our heads."

And yet, for all the promotion, public understanding of the project remained low. Tourists, not natives, viewed the display model. The infrequent newspaper stories dealt mainly with what was not happening. Even preservationists were only vaguely aware of what was being proposed.

"There's a big difference between educating the public and raising money," says one observer, "and the foundation was mostly doing the latter. It was widely perceived as a private, elitist undertaking, and probably was."

In the meantime, the context surrounding the project had changed. Preservation thinking in Dallas had matured to include more sophisticated ideas about what should and should not be done to historic buildings. The West End Historic District finally came into its own, creating heightened concern over the impact of new construction on existing buildings. Perhaps most crucial, the twenty-fifth anniversary of the Kennedy assassination was approaching. The foundation had done virtually nothing to commemorate the twentieth anniversary. If there was ever a time to act, it was now.

All of these pressures came to a head in the spring of 1987. After a four-year hiatus, the foundation went back to the landmark commission for a "certificate of appropriateness." The commission responded by criticizing the size of the proposed tower and its probable impact on the rest of the West End. The West End Task Force, an advisory group, examined the possibility of an internal elevator.

Suddenly the presumed consensus about the tower started to unravel and the controversy-free atmosphere coveted by the foundation evaporated. An architect on the task force, Craig Melde, drew up a quick plan for replacing the tower with an interior elevator. The foundation's architects, James Hendricks and Tony Callaway, countered with studies that they said proved that such a scheme couldn't work. A design that had remained virtually unchanged for four years was now being revised daily, with both sides digging in their heels.

"It was a strange situation," said Ron Emrich, the city's senior preservation planner. "This was not how we've ever dealt with property owners in the West End. There is always a lot of give and take, but on this issue there was no serious consideration of alternatives. They (the Dallas County Historical Foundation) presented us with a fait accompli."

"One thing about us is that we don't cave in," said Conover Hunt, project director for the foundation. "People don't like the design because they don't want to. It reminds them of something painful. They're reacting emotionally."

The West End Task Force recommended that approval for the design be denied. So did Emrich and the city planning staff. Despite these recommendations, the landmark commission approved the design once again, and did so without any substantive, critical discussion. It based its decision on a perceived moral obligation to follow through on the 1983 approval, even though no one was certain what had been approved.

"If we send people off with conceptual approval, we are required to work with that prior approval," explained Commissioner Sid Trest.

The central design issue—whether the elevator should be inside or outside—is not a black-and-white matter. It involves a subjective judgment about which part of the Depository is most significant historically. To opt for the tower, as the foundation and the county have, is to say that the sixth floor is sacred, to be preserved before anything else. To put the elevator inside is to say that the exterior of the building, the public face as it were, is most significant.

The city staff and the West End Task Force also objected to the height and bulk of the tower and expressed a fear that it would set a bad precedent for other buildings in the West End. The tower is not, as Hendricks claimed at Tuesday's meeting, a "subtle and sensitive solution." It is a massive, clunky structure that still needs a great deal of refinement. But neither is it without architectural precedent in the West End, as Hendricks correctly pointed out. There are several buildings in the district with elevator towers. They are as much a part of neighborhood vernacular as anything else.

Hendricks's design represents a reasonable response to a difficult problem. Its main drawback is that it's the only proposal under discussion. As the foundation has maintained from the beginning, the School Book Depository has international importance, like Ford's Theatre in Washington, so that every alteration, no matter how small, is going to be magnified a hundred times in the public's perception. Surely it deserves more intense critical scrutiny than it has received so far.

Whether this happens is finally up to the Dallas County Commissioners since the county owns the building and is the architect's client. Preservation choices aside, the county's space and budget requirements are dictating an exterior elevator. Would the county be willing to explore the other alternative?

Judge Lee Jackson says probably not, without slamming the door on the possibility.

"The county's investment in this building is not the largest issue," he says. "It's not impossible that if there were a solution that satisfied the task force and the consultants that we would wait and pursue it. But so far nobody has given us a reason to do things differently."

Which brings us back again to the larger question of what the tower is all about. It is clearly more than a public convenience. It is a kind of sign for an exhibition. It is also a statement about how the city wants the Kennedy assassination to be viewed. Informed, well-intentioned people on both sides have different views on the appropriateness of this structure.

The foundation now has permission to proceed with its plans. But, given the sensitivity of this undertaking, might it not make sense to explore all alternatives fully? To solicit a few more proposals, like Melde's, on the off chance that a better solution might be found?

There is nothing to lose at this point but a little time. The answer may turn out to be the same. But the public might be better satisfied that there had been no rush to judgment.

The storm over Mrs. Craft's house: The late civil rights leader's home offers a lesson in the politics of preservation

MARCH 13, 1988

Historic preservationists prefer that historic homes remain a part of their original neighborhoods or landscapes. In the case of the Juanita Craft house, which Craft willed to the City of Dallas after her death, controversy stemmed from competing plans to move the civil rights leader's home to a new location—to the Dallas Heritage Village in City Park, to Fair Park, or to another location. Dillon's article outlines the arguments for and against each proposal. Today the home is still owned by the City of Dallas, though it has never been managed by the Park and Recreation Department, which manages other historic city properties, and it remains on its original site on Warren Avenue, a historic landmark for the African American community of Wheatley Place in South Dallas. The house suffered serious water damage in 2018, and new plans are under way to restore it and reopen it to the public.

The Juanita Craft house sits discreetly among its Warren Avenue neighbors, a simple white wood-frame structure with an enclosed porch, a bit of decorative aluminum trim, and a low brick wall behind which Mrs. Craft once planted shrubs and flowers. Like most houses, it is significant as a setting for a life rather than as a piece of architecture. In this case, the life was remarkable.

In Juanita Craft's kitchen and living room, overflowing with books

239

5.2. *Juanita Craft was a visionary civil rights leader who used her home on Warren Avenue in Wheatley Place as an office and meeting place during the civil rights era. Photograph by Judith Sedwick, 1984.*

and cartons of correspondence, three decades of Dallas civic leaders went to civil rights school. Mrs. Craft organized NAACP chapters during the '20s and '30s, helped integrate Dallas schools and the University of Texas Law School in the '40s and '50s, marched with Martin Luther King in the '60s, and served two terms on the Dallas City Council in the '70s. She made her house a center for teaching others about the American civil rights struggle (fig. 5.2).

About Juanita Craft's achievements there is no dispute, but there are bitterly conflicting opinions about what to do with the house she willed to the city. No one wants to demolish it, and no one is claiming that it is synonymous with her legacy. Unlike most preservation fights, the battle over the Craft house is about site and use rather than physical survival.

To many, the house has become a symbol of her public life, and like all symbols, it is overlaid with broader political and social significance. In ways that nobody could have predicted, the Craft house has momentarily become inseparable from the commemoration of minority contributions to the civic life of Dallas.

Juanita Craft died in August 1985 at the age of eighty-three. Even before her death, the future of her house was murky. Initially she told friends that she wanted it left at 2618 Warren Avenue, near the intersection of Oakland and Martin Luther King Boulevard, to be used as a learning center and library. Later she suggested that it be moved to nearby Juanita Craft Park.

Then, in early 1985, Dallas Park Board president Billy Allen and Park and Recreation director Jack Robinson persuaded her that Old City Park, the Texas architectural museum just across Interstate 30 from Dallas City Hall, was a better location.

"The perception of crime in South Dallas is so widespread that we felt that visitors would not go to Juanita Craft Park," says Allen, who is no longer on the board.

"The mistake we all made was not asking them [Old City Park]," says Chandler Vaughn, the executor of the Craft estate and a participant in the negotiations. "We just assumed that they would be overjoyed to have it."

Mrs. Craft subsequently willed her house to the city with the hope, but not the requirement, that it be moved to Old City Park. On November 19, 1985, the Dallas County Heritage Society, which operates Old City Park, rejected the gift. The board's resolution stated that the Craft house, built in 1922, fell "outside the boundaries established as the educational mission of Old City Park." The park includes only structures built between 1840 and 1910, selected, the resolution says, "to reflect the changing lifestyles of North Central Texas residents during the period represented rather than on the accomplishments of specific individuals."

To Old City Park, therefore, the key questions presented by the Craft house concerned the park's policy and educational mission. Old City Park had rejected other houses left in wills, including the F. A. Brown homestead now being restored by the Historic Preservation League. It saw no reason to make an exception for the Craft house.

Between the fall of 1985 and the spring of 1988, the Dallas Park Board quietly studied alternative sites, including one adjacent to the proposed new building for the Museum of African-American Life and

Culture at Fair Park and the nearby South Dallas Cultural Center on Second Avenue. The museum board initially agreed to accept the Craft house, but the Dallas Park Board eventually decided against the Fair Park location, citing a lack of space and basic design incompatibilty. One board member reportedly said it would look like an "outhouse" behind the main building.

So almost by default the South Dallas Cultural Center became the site of choice. It is operated by the Park and Recreation Department, and in the Dallas Park Board's opinion, the site was sufficiently visible and secure to accommodate the Craft home. In April 1987, the Park Board recommended that the house be placed on the grounds of the center.

But that was not the end of the matter. The Cultural Center is just outside the gates of Fair Park. In the fall of 1955, Juanita Craft led one thousand black high school students to the State Fair there. "They couldn't get in because it wasn't Negro day," Mrs. Craft later recalled. "It was quite an experience."

To some members of the black community, including Park Board member Vivian Johnson, putting Juanita Craft's house at the South Dallas Cultural Center would dishonor her memory. She'd be outside the Fair Park gates again.

In February, Johnson asked the Park Board to withdraw its 1987 recommendation and put the house in Old City Park instead. "I asked whether the community had been consulted about this and was told no," Johnson explains. "So we got nine South Dallas organizations together to consider the issue, and the consensus was that the Cultural Center was inappropriate. Many people feel that it is a betrayal of the promise of a much larger and better-equipped center. A symbol of betrayal is not a place for the Craft house."

When the Park Board voted four to two to stand by its earlier recommendation, Johnson and her supporters stormed out of the meeting. Johnson then took the matter to the City Council, which urged the Park Board to reconsider its earlier recommendation and to consider strongly Old City Park as the site for the Craft house.

By now, all participants were feeling pressured and abused. Charges of racism and betrayal were flying on all fronts. On February 25, in an effort to defuse the controversy, the Dallas Park Board voted to postpone a final decision on the Craft house for thirty days, to allow a review of all options.

Preservation battles are never simple, and often, as in this one, they are only incidentally about buildings. The Craft house controversy is as layered as an onion.

One layer concerns institutional autonomy and public policy: Should cultural organizations such as Old City Park run themselves or be operated by political fiat?

A second layer, political and racial, is the need for minorities to have their contributions acknowledged publicly and prominently, even if that means challenging the white cultural establishment.

Yet another layer is historical and commemorative, finding a way to honor and perpetuate Juanita Craft's work.

To Tom Smith, executive director of Old City Park, policy and jurisdiction are the paramount issues. He agrees that Juanita Craft is a more important historical figure than any whose houses are now exhibited at Old City Park. He even concedes that the 1910 cutoff date is somewhat arbitrary, though not capricious. But what is not negotiable, in his view, is who runs the park.

"The issue is the integrity of this organization," he explains. "The Heritage Society had a contractual agreement with the Park Board to operate the park. Now the City Council has overruled the Park Board and tried to interfere in the management of a cultural organization. That is totally unacceptable. Is the council then going to tell the art museum what paintings to hang, or the opera what works to put on?"

Smith says that because of the controversy, Old City Park has already lost thousands of dollars in contributions and may even lose its accreditation from the American Association of Museums if it is forced to accept the Craft house.

However one views these problems, the underlying issue of institutional autonomy cannot be ignored. If the city has the right to tell an organization what it can exhibit, it also can tell it what not to exhibit. Dallas tried to establish an "official culture" in the 1950s, banning the work of Picasso (to name only one of the most celebrated cases) and succeeded only in making the city a laughingstock.

While sympathetic to Old City Park's jurisdictional dilemma, the Dallas preservation community generally decries such "house museums," which collect structures from scattered sites and bring them together in a new, concocted setting.

"From a philosophical standpoint we can't endorse a project like Old City Park," says Joe Wyman, executive director of the Historic

Preservation League. "A house is integral to its site, and once you separate the two the house loses most of its historical significance. Moving houses to create a museum is not what historic preservation is about. If that idea were dropped, this problem might get resolved."

Leaving the Craft house where it is would make it eligible for local and state historic designation, perhaps as a prelude to the creation of a national historic district. Wyman and others believe the area is important enough to qualify for such a designation. They also point to the economic benefits that have followed the preservation of the Martin Luther King birthplace in Atlanta and the home of Harlem Renaissance poet Anne Spencer in Lynchburg, Virginia. In both cases, keeping the house in the community spurred economic redevelopment.

"The house deserves to stay where it is," says Ruthmary White, one of two Park Board members who voted against moving the Craft house to the South Dallas Cultural Center. "I keep thinking what Juanita would have thought, and I believe she would have been pleased to think that her house could be a catalyst for redeveloping her old neighborhood. If it doesn't work out, you can always move it later."

But what precisely did Juanita Craft want? It's still not clear. Chandler Vaughn, her executor and a close friend for years, insists that the issue of where the house will be located clouds the more important issue of how it will be used.

"I want to execute the broadest wish of Juanita Craft to make the house do something, to carry on her approach to things. I have a problem with pulling it out of the community, but I can't take a narrow philosophical view of it. She said she wanted the house to be used, and as her executor I'm bound by that."

To Vivian Johnson, and many of those for whom she speaks, Juanita Craft's wishes are sacrosanct.

"We view the will as a contract between the city and Juanita Craft," Johnson says. "She died believing that her house was going to Old City Park, and that wish should be honored."

Johnson is challenging the legality of the master plan that governs the operations of Old City Park, as well as the criteria by which individual structures are selected.

"The more legal smokescreens they throw up, the more they kindle the desire to put the house there," she explains. "For too long people have treated as private, institutions that are public. And blacks haven't fought this. They've just let it happen."

Johnson denies charges made by her critics that she is motivated primarily by a desire to beat the Park Board and crack the predominantly white cultural establishment symbolized by Old City Park.

"There are good reasons for putting the house there," she responds. "Mrs. Craft wanted lots of visitors to see her house, for it to be a learning center for children. Because Old City Park brings school tours through, more young people could come through the house. It will also bring black families to the park, who don't come often now. So the park will gain as well."

Representatives of all interested groups, including the city staff, are now visiting the five potential sites. They will meet in workshops, and at nine o'clock Saturday morning they will gather at Dallas City Hall for a daylong public meeting. The objective is to come up with a final site recommendation for the Park Board. Whatever the result, the process will at the very least force all parties to answer tough questions.

The Park Board and the City Council will have to decide just how far they want to go in determining the programs of arts groups. Old City Park will have to determine if its educational mission is broad and deep enough. The black community will have to balance its need for a voice in the city's cultural policies against its desire to commemorate Juanita Craft's legacy.

It has been suggested that Juanita Craft would be dismayed to see her house the center of controversy. Maybe, but probably not. Hers was a political life, and she understood that the path of change is usually tortuous and unpredictable. The parties to this controversy have shown that they know how to approach a problem from many different directions. They have yet to demonstrate that, like Juanita Craft, they also know how to push through to a solution.

The state of State-Thomas: A once-vital downtown area is poised to come back to life. So why doesn't it?

DECEMBER 25, 1988

The State-Thomas neighborhood is a small fragment of what was once part of a much larger neighborhood of prosperous Dallasites and an adjoining African American neighborhood that traced its roots to North Dallas, one of the thriving Freedman's Towns formed by former slaves after Emancipation. While today "North Dallas" refers to the suburbs much farther north, the original North Dallas was eviscerated by highway construction from the 1950s to the 1980s, leaving only a tiny fragment intact in the State-Thomas Historic District.* The rebranding of State-Thomas as part of Uptown Dallas prioritized economic development over its history.

It's hard to find State-Thomas these days, even if you know what you're looking for. Most of the old Dallas neighborhood's houses are gone, marked only by crumbling foundations and neat rows of pecan and live oak trees along the property lines. The businesses have fled, too, leaving the area with one grocery store and one beauty shop. The small Catholic school, St. Peter's, is closed.

Only the restored Victorian houses along Fairmount and Routh

---

*   See the State-Thomas Historic District designation report, February 1984, written by residents of State-Thomas with the City of Dallas Urban Planning Department and the Historic Preservation League.

5.3. *2606 State Street, one of the surviving Victorian homes in the State-Thomas Historic District in the southeast corner of Dallas's redevelopment of "Uptown." Photography by Stefan Gorman for Preservation Dallas, 2012.*

Streets, the heart of the tiny State-Thomas Historic District, suggest what the neighborhood used to be (fig. 5.3). The rest looks like a turn-of-the century photograph of pre-urban Dallas—empty prairie and a few telephone poles.

But State-Thomas, named for parallel streets that run its length, once was a lively urban neighborhood, a center of black life and culture from after the Civil War into the late 1940s, when the new Central Expressway sliced it in half and precipitated its decline. It was called Freedman's Town even then because of its history as a haven for freed slaves; its later residents included preachers, merchants, and musicians.

As Dallas grew up around it, speculators arrived in the mid-1970s with offers too good to refuse. Gradually, a neighborhood of small lots on narrow streets evolved into a collection of large land assemblies controlled by large real estate investment corporations, such as Lehndorff USA and the computer giant EDS, as well as assorted trusts and pension funds.

A map explains why the 100-acre State-Thomas area brought a covetous gleam to the eyes of developers. Wedged against Central Expressway and Woodall Rodgers Freeway, with its back to McKinney

Avenue and buffered by Greenwood Cemetery on the northeast, it seemed an ideal location for new office construction.

But with office space now overbuilt, State-Thomas has become an ideal location for the kind of urban neighborhood—where eating, sleeping, shopping, and entertainment all take place within a few square blocks—that could lure the disaffected Dallas middle class back downtown to live.

So why, despite being an island of opportunity, is State-Thomas still so short of opportunists?

The conventional answer has been that nobody really wants to live in downtown Dallas. Dallas is pool-and-patio land, we hear, where a distant view of the urban spectacle is all most people can stand.

State-Thomas does include a residential enclave, a 15-acre historic district of Victorian and prairie-style houses near the Crescent. But it has no neighbors. The rest of the area remains 95 percent vacant land, a grim reminder of the social costs of speculation.

Now comes a two-volume tome, *Intown Dallas Housing Strategy*, that says Dallasites want to live downtown after all—at least some of them. The study was compiled and funded by Lehndorff USA and other major property owners in State-Thomas, so its conclusions are hardly unbiased. At the same time, they resemble the conclusions of similar studies in other cities and can't be ignored.

From a survey of fifteen thousand downtown workers, the study concludes that there is a demand for approximately forty-six hundred housing units in and around the downtown core. Most of these would be apartments in mid-rise buildings and should rent for $650 to $700 per month.

The study also indicates "a gap between what potential residents will pay and what development and operating costs require." In other words, downtown housing is a risky proposition. The cost of building housing is greater than the potential profit from rents; developers would like someone to underwrite some of their costs.

On December 14, the Dallas City Council helped to close that gap by passing a tax-increment financing plan for State-Thomas, exclusive of the historic district. In a nutshell, it provides that tax revenue from all new development will be used for streets, sidewalks, utilities, and other public improvements in the area, instead of going into the general tax fund. The plan will last for twelve years, at which point the city expects to have collected $17 million more in taxes than it would if it had not primed the development pump. The city also will lend the area $2 million up front for public improvements and has pledged an additional $7.5 million for parks and other amenities.

The State-Thomas plan, together with the funding strategies for the proposed downtown mall, mark a philosophical turning point for Dallas. After bowing to the tenets of laissez faire capitalism like Moslems to Mecca, the city is finally realizing that it is a developer, too, the biggest of the lot. Just like any private company, it has an obligation to protect its investment, in this case in an underperforming division that could be an asset.

But some property owners in State-Thomas insist that the city must do more.

Tom Lardner of Lehndorff USA, the largest property owner in State-Thomas, says that while "philosophically important," the December 14 action won't close the gap between rents and development costs.

"The plan reduces costs and increases the chances of an aesthetically pleasing neighborhood," he says, "but it doesn't allow us to build mid-rise apartment buildings with $700-a-month rents, which is what you need in State-Thomas."

Lardner is urging the city to put up an additional $8 million to $10 million or perhaps promise to buy back unsold lots in State-Thomas as it did in Bryan Place, the first and so far the only inner-city housing development, started fifteen years ago across Central and Woodall Rodgers from State-Thomas.

The city says it has done everything it can do.

"This is always going to be a joint-risk deal," says Assistant City Manager Jim Reid. "The ball is in the private court now. We've put our money up. Now let's see theirs."

"It's time for the developers to start building instead of just talking," adds Al Cox, an architect and a resident of State-Thomas. "None of them wants to do a deal that will devalue anybody else's property, but they're all a little too greedy to cut the price of their land for a time in order to get something started."

While the State-Thomas debate between the city and investors has focused on development costs and subsidies, a successful urban neighborhood is only partly an economic issue. Nobody is going to move into State-Thomas just because the price is right. The place must be right, too, meaning more varied and energetic than suburbia, offering real alternatives in housing and atmosphere.

The master plan for State-Thomas, drawn up in 1986 by RTKL Associates, a Dallas architecture firm, divides the neighborhood into three sections: the historic district on the west, a central area of six- to eight-story apartment buildings, and a buffer of tall office buildings along Woodall Rodgers and Central.

The master plan recommends some mixing of residential and commercial uses in the same buildings, proposing that Allen Street, now mostly bordered by trees and weeds, become a principal commercial street with apartments above shops and restaurants, as in cities in Europe and the Eastern United States. Affordable housing is mentioned by RTKL as an option for developers—as a trade-off for height or density concessions from the city—not as a requirement.

It is a broad-brush plan, reasonable enough in outline, but hard to grasp block by block. A first project is absolutely essential if State-Thomas is to get moving.

Lardner says that Lehndorff USA will build ten town houses at the corner of Allen and Thomas Streets next spring, each with a two-car garage, each to sell for $175,000 to $200,000. While the commitment is encouraging, neither the price nor the type of housing seems appropriate for this urban neighborhood. The proposed town houses sound like a mixture of The Village and Bryan Place, rather than Georgetown and Beacon Hill.

Dallas has no housing policy, nor is it overrun with developers who know how to construct urban housing. This has been an office building and shopping center kind of town, filled with what architect O'Neil Ford used to call "the raw land boys" who understand the economics of building on cotton fields but not the constraints, physical and social, of downtown development. It's easier, and usually more profitable, to pour concrete slabs for warehouses than to plumb one hundred bathrooms in an apartment building.

But Dallas doesn't need more office buildings or warehouses. It needs a thriving downtown, which means it needs downtown housing. To get it, Dallas may have to import architects and developers from St. Louis, Seattle, San Francisco, or any of a dozen other cities where downtown housing is a tradition instead of an anomaly.

This seems a good time to do it, while the development lull continues and building housing in places such as State-Thomas is still possible. The conditions may not be perfect, but then they never are. What's lacking is a developer willing to step forward and be first.

Urban History: Fort Worth's Southside has stayed in character

MARCH 23, 1989

The Fairmount/Southside historic district in Fort Worth remains Texas's largest neighborhood on the National Register of Historic Places. Formally approved in 1990, the district is primarily residential, with more than one thousand properties that contribute to its historic character.* Since 1990, the district has provided an anchor for gradual economic redevelopment of the city's south side and along Magnolia Street, the district's main commercial corridor.

When Katherine Anne Porter couldn't get a job at the *Dallas Morning News*, she moved to Fort Worth, took a room at 1627 College Avenue on the city's south side, and began writing theater reviews for the fledgling *Fort Worth Critic*. That was in 1918, twelve years before the publication of *Flowering Judas* made her one of the most acclaimed young writers in America (fig. 5.4).

---

*   The original National Register nomination form listed 1,016 buildings that contributed to the historic district. Ron Emrich, Tom Niederauer, and Niederauer Associates, National Register designation report for the Fairmount/Southside Historic District, 1990, https://atlas.thc.state.tx.us/NR/pdfs/90000490 /90000490.pdf.

5.4. *Writer Katherine Anne Porter lived briefly at 1627 College Avenue (at right) in 1918. The house is typical of the modest bungalows and cottages in the Fairmount Historic District, created in 1990 and still the largest historic district in Texas. Photograph by Kathryn Holliday.*

Nothing so memorable happened to her old neighborhood, however. Settled in the 1890s as Fort Worth was booming as a railroad and meat-packing center, the Southside remained a working-class district—a handful of puffy Victorian mansions and hundreds of modest bungalows and prairie-style houses occupied by tradesmen, factory workers, clerks, and secretaries. The area was convenient rather than chic, fewer than two miles from the Tarrant County Courthouse and crisscrossed by five streetcar lines. After Katherine Anne Porter, its most celebrated residents were one Mrs. Ninnie Baird, whose homemade breads eventually found their way into every supermarket in North Texas, and the Pangburn family of candy fame, creators of the Millionaire and other popular confections.

But anonymity has its advantages, one being that the Southside retained its indigenous character while most other city neighborhoods were losing theirs. Driving through the area, one can get a vivid picture of urban life in North Texas at the turn of the century: hundreds of unpretentious frame dwellings stretching out along broad, straight streets, with a grocery store every few blocks, a scattering of apartment houses, and a half-dozen schools and churches.

In late February, the Texas Historical Commission approved the nomination of Fairmount/Southside to the National Register of Historic Places, the official list of buildings and places important in American history and culture. The nomination has been forwarded to the National Park Service in Washington, and if it is approved—usually a formality at this stage—Fairmount/Southside will become the largest urban historic district in Texas—360 acres, 1,450 structures, all packed into 107 blocks south of the freeway mixmaster in downtown Fort Worth.

The National Register nomination culminates fifteen years of work by local residents and merchants. Although the Southside is not under intense pressure from developers at the moment, the residents recognized that the district could not retain its historic integrity without a major preservation effort. Already it has the abandoned buildings and vacant lots that can fuel decay.

A National Register designation will give residents various local and federal tax incentives for restoring and renovating their properties while also boosting civic pride.

"In the past, such recognition would have meant instant gentrification," says Jim Steely, director of National Register projects for the Texas Historical Commission. "Now people are seeking designation to maintain the quality of the neighborhood they have. They see it as a tool rather than as a green light for developers."

The appeal of Fairmount/Southside is its diversity. Three of the boundary streets—Hemphill, Magnolia, and 8th Avenue—are primarily commercial thoroughfares that grew up with the streetcars. Here the occasional Victorian relic, such as the Reeves/Walker house at 2200 Hemphill Street, are interspersed with stores and restaurants—some successful, some clearly struggling—and remnants of earlier commercial success, such as the Equitable Bank building at Magnolia and Fifth, formerly the Southside Masonic Lodge.

All of these streets are pockmarked by helter-skelter development, but the neighborhood within is packed with subtler pleasures. Chase Court is a tidy enclave of bungalows and prairie-style houses grouped behind a stone wall. On Lipscomb Street, ranks of grander houses are set on terraced lawns like pieces of sculpture. And Katherine Anne Porter's College Avenue is lined with simple craftsman bungalows that establish a pleasing streetside rhythm despite an obvious lack of architectural panache.

As in the past, Fairmount/Southside is racially and economically mixed, with large numbers of Hispanics, Asians, and African-Americans. The Anglo population is divided between elderly residents who have lived in the neighborhood for decades and young families with children who have chosen the area for its stability and proximity to downtown.

"You name it and we've got it," says Mike Patterson, president of the Southside Preservation League. "It's a city in microcosm." Ten years ago, the Fairmount/Southside area would not have been seriously considered for the National Register. The American preservation movement was still in its high-style architecture phase, meaning that it focused on the Swiss Avenues of America and ignored the less glamorous blue-collar districts.

All of that is changing, as the Register and other preservation groups have come to recognize the value of vernacular architecture and the enormous historical and cultural importance of areas such as Fairmount/Southside or Winnetka Heights in Dallas. In lieu of grand design, they offer a palpable sense of place.

"We're trying to be realistic about this," Mr. Patterson says. "Fairmount/Southside is not going to be (an upscale historic district like) Munger Place. It's culturally and economically varied. . . . That's the way we want it."

Library or parking lot? Time is running out for a downtown Fort Worth landmark

SEPTEMBER 1, 1990

This article provides a precis of the challenges that face historic preservation. In 1990, Texas was in the depths of the post–oil bust recession and little money flowed to civic history. While there was widespread consensus that Fort Worth's 1932 public library building should be saved, there was little formal apparatus to support that preference. Despite the appeals Dillon chronicles here, the building was demolished to become a parking lot and remains open space today. Ironically, the 1939 building had replaced the city's original Carnegie Library, which stood on the site from 1901 until it was demolished in 1938.

Fort Worth turned itself upside down to save Thomas Eakins's *The Swimming Hole,* but the building that housed the painting for decades may soon disappear with only faint protest.

The old Fort Worth Public Library, a restrained but impressive art moderne building on the south side of downtown, has been living on borrowed time since the early 1980s, when the city opened a new library and lost control of the old one in a legal dispute with the family that donated the land.

The present owners—Toronto investor Jack Pasht and Reilly

Brothers Property Co. of Arlington—plan to demolish the building for a parking lot, of which Fort Worth has an even greater glut than Dallas. Even so, they claim that the lot will generate $100,000 a year whereas the empty library is merely a cash drain.

Preservationists have been scrambling to find a buyer and tenants for the building. They have talked to theater groups, research libraries, and assorted nonprofit agencies. They have lobbied the city to buy the building as a home for some of its far-flung departments. The owners say they are also willing to lease the building to the city for $2 a square foot, approximately $110,000 a year. So far, no deals.

"Right now, I'm worn out and not very hopeful," says Paul Koeppe, chairman of the Tarrant County Preservation Task Force. "We just can't seem to get anyone interested."

"If times were better, it would be logical for the city to acquire the building," says assistant planning director Emil Moncivais. "But the timing is just wrong. We're laying off people. The city has other priorities."

Historic buildings have a low priority even in good times, and in a period of budget deficits and rampant bank failures, saving them can seem hopeless. Even the beloved Will Rogers Auditorium lost out in the July bond election, as Fort Worth voters put street improvements ahead of cultural facilities.

And yet tough times have frequently been the catalyst for inspired civic design. New Orleans saved the French Quarter in the early years of the Depression, at the same time that San Antonio was developing its River Walk. Now it's impossible to imagine the two cities without those attractions.

While the old public library is not in the same class, it is a handsomely proportioned example of 1930s civic design, of a kind that contemporary architects have forgotten how to do. Its fluted pilasters and crisp aluminum decoration make an impressive statement about the importance of books and learning on the prairie.

The library also doubled as the city's art museum, displaying major works by Eakins, George Innes, and other masters who later moved to fancier quarters in Fort Worth's major art museums. Until that time, Fort Worth culture was concentrated at Throckmorton and Ninth Streets.

The library is also part of a civic ensemble that includes the Lanham Federal Building, the Police and Municipal Courts Building, and City

5.5. *The 1939 Fort Worth Public Library, a project funded by the Public Works Administration during the Great Depression, was demolished in 1990 to make way for a parking lot. Star-Telegram Collection, Special Collections, University of Texas at Arlington.*

Hall. With all the publicity about Fort Worth's cultural district, it's easy to forget that such compact, architecturally integrated domains are among the city's genuine treasures (fig. 5.5).

Its downtown is still compact and comprehensible at a glance. Only nine blocks separate the Tarrant County courthouse on the north from the Convention Center on the south. And even today these blocks are mostly occupied by brick and stone buildings that create a comfortable, richly textured environment where walking is still a pleasure.

History and sentiment notwithstanding, finding a new use for an old library is not easy. The Fort Worth building is small (55,000 square feet), triangular, and without parking. Since the city lost control of it, it has been haphazardly maintained.

Owner Michael Reilly says that the legal fiasco is why the city has not tried to lease or buy the building.

"The city needs space," he argues, "but because it lost the property the way it did, it is embarrassed to get back into it. They wish it would go away."

Embarrassed or not, the city is the library's most logical tenant. It is next door to other major civic buildings, and the city currently spends $330,000 a year to lease space for city agencies. For that amount of money it could begin renovating the library and preserve a key piece of its past.

Another possibility, logistically more difficult, is to convert the library into a center for nonprofit organizations. The Meadows Foundation has done this on lower Swiss Avenue; perhaps a Fort Worth foundation could underwrite a similar venture.

If anything is to happen, it will have to happen quickly. The owners have a demolition permit, and without a solid offer they will level the building. Ironically, before the city demolished the old Carnegie Library in 1937, artists and patrons signed petitions, marched on City Hall, and generally carried on a high-minded debate about civic values. This time the discussion has been primarily about market forces and dollars per square foot. At the current exchange rate, one landmark is worth fifty parking spaces.

In Grapevine, everything old is news: City hopes efforts to preserve its past will be drawing card for business in future

NOVEMBER 3, 1991

Grapevine was one of the first suburban small towns within the immediate pull of Dallas and Fort Worth to begin to build its identity through a combination of historic preservation and the reconstruction of its Main Street. It has provided inspiration for other D/FW cities to follow, particularly in its emphasis on preserving a turn-of-the-century Main Street directly adjacent to contemporary development. Since 1991, the city's preservation efforts have expanded and now include the historic Nash Farm and The Hill, a historically African American neighborhood.

In the age of dueling suburbs, when competition for new airports and corporate headquarters makes the old range wars seem like games day at scout camp, Grapevine is selling Main Street and the pleasures of rocking on a Victorian verandah.

As the oldest settlement in Tarrant County (1844) and the site of the fourth busiest airport in the world, it promotes itself as a place "where you can get away from it all and still be in the midst of it all." And more and more conventioneers are buying the sales pitch. Not the Home Builders or the American Medical Association, but major corporations that want to introduce a new product to their salesmen in the morning and have them back home by midnight. The Association of Overseas Brats has met in Grapevine, as have veterans of the

USS *Missouri*, and more religious and fraternal organizations than anyone can count. "We give them the Hyatt with thirteen hundred rooms and the hometown they grew up in in the same package," boasts P. W. McCallum, executive director of the Grapevine Visitors & Convention Bureau.

And after lunch or dinner, the conventioneers can visit an endangered American icon: a working Main Street. Instead of a gaggle of antiques stores and gift shops, where expiring in a cloud of perfumed body powder is always a risk, downtown Grapevine has two hardware stores, a drugstore, a bank, several jewelers, and clothiers.

The town newspaper is located on Main Street, next door to the Grapevine Opry and close to half a dozen restaurants. Business is brisk and vacancies are few. "The whole retail thing gets rolling around buildings that have a period look," adds Mr. McCallum.

The buildings on Main Street are mostly turn-of-the-century prairie commercial, strictly utilitarian, with bumpy sidewalks and split-level curbs, all expressing Grapevine's farming and ranching past. The latest addition to Main Street is the Wallis Hotel, an 1891 drummer's domicile that is being recreated by Architexas of Dallas. The original hotel was demolished years ago, so the architects had to take calipers to a historical photograph to determine the hotel's dimensions and proportions. They are replicating the brick exterior faithfully, including the bold lettering and the second-story porch.

Only a few anachronistic details, such as stove flues on the roof, are being eliminated. The interior will be modernized for offices, with the Visitors & Convention Bureau the first tenant.

The hotel occupies the south side of Liberty Plaza, a new town square being created by Mesa Design of Dallas. In addition to the Wallis, the plaza will contain a restored log cabin, a windmill, and a grape arbor, all meant to recall a typical Texas downtown of 1900.

At the opposite end of Main Street, beside the Cotton Belt railroad tracks, the Grapevine Heritage Foundation plans to restore the original wood train depot as the centerpiece of a historic park that will include a museum, a farmer's market, and a craft center.

Eventually a steam train may run from Grapevine to Plano and Fort Worth.

The historic park is being funded by grants and private donations, while the $600,000 Wallis Hotel project is being paid for, in cash, with revenue from the city's 6 percent hotel/motel tax.

5.6. *Grapevine's Main Street mixes historic fabric, including the Palace Theater (1940), with some new construction that maintains the language of Texas vernacular architecture (Grapevine's City Hall with the tall cupola was completed in 1997). Image courtesy Grapevine Tourism and Convention Center Bureau.*

By the time these projects are completed—probably in the summer of 1992—Grapevine may have started construction on a new city hall, to be located on Main Street and designed in a nineteenth-century style. Grapevine officials are fundamentalists about new buildings (fig. 5.6).

They encourage owners and architects to stick to period styles, and they think that copying earlier buildings is fine provided the original can be thoroughly researched and documented.

They're also aware that this is a slippery aesthetic path, at the end of which could be Six Flags. "We hope to get new development that is compatible with existing structures," says Ron Emrich, director of the Heritage Foundation. "But we don't want to see a lot of quasi-historical buildings. We need to avoid the theme park at all costs." The cloud hanging over all of these preservation efforts is the proposed expansion of Dallas/Fort Worth International Airport. If the new west runway gets built, DC-10s will be thundering over Main Street Grapevine, rattling the windows of the Grapevine Opry and making small talk on the steps of the Western Auto store impossible.

City officials fear that the cultural fabric of the city will be destroyed and that Grapevine will turn into another faceless suburb. "Many people won't renovate their houses until they know what's going to happen with the runway," says Mr. Emrich. "We could lose a lot of historic buildings by neglect."

History has become a valuable chip for Grapevine to play in the regional economic sweepstakes. But clearly more than money is involved in the restoration of downtown. Residents see Main Street as the last little bit of old Grapevine, its identity, and they don't want it run over and demolished. "The environment today is so transient and so stressful," says Mr. McCallum. "So people come here to see something in America that is stable and relates to what it was in the past."

Preservation times two: New museum will hold history of women and Fair Park building

OCTOBER 18, 1998

Fair Park, the historic home of the State Fair of Texas in Dallas, is a beloved collection of art deco and streamline moderne exhibition halls arranged around a grand esplanade. While it is filled with people during the one month of the annual State Fair, for the rest of the year the grounds are disused by comparison. A continuing challenge for the city, and for preservation advocates, is the appropriate adaptive reuse of the fairgrounds and many of its exhibition halls for year-round activity. The opening of the Women's Museum in 2000 held promise—however, the museum closed in 2011.

It's not every day that an organization steps forward with $20 million to turn a crumbling arena/music hall/office building into a museum.

But that's what the Austin-based Foundation for Women's Resources plans to do with the Administration Building at Fair Park. In October 2000, it's set to reopen as The Women's Museum: An Institute for the Future and, the sponsors hope, a national center for the study of women's history.

"It has the potential to make Dallas the place to visit in the year 2000," says Cathy Bonner, president of the foundation board.

It also has the potential to re-energize Fair Park by introducing a stunning piece of contemporary architecture that is appropriate both to its subject and its historic setting. The proposed national women's museum is not just another tired retrofit; it is a reinvention. And last week, it cleared some last-minute roadblocks that threatened to scuttle the project.

The concept surfaced nearly three years ago as a vague longing on the part of Ms. Bonner and several others for a way to celebrate women's achievements on the eve of the millennium. Their original idea was a twenty-first-century Women's Fair, which evolved into a national women's museum once they saw the 1909 Administration Building at Fair Park.

With its tall windows and vaulted roof, "it was the perfect building," Ms. Bonner says.

It was also a wreck, with buckling floors, holes in the roof, and mounds of pigeon dung for decoration.

The original building had hosted everything from livestock auctions to grand opera. It was converted to an office building for the 1936 Centennial, with Raoul Josset's sublimely kitschy statue of Venus rising from a cactus guarding the front door. Since then it has been a warehouse, workshop, design studio, and maintenance nightmare—much admired but rarely used.

Having decided on a museum, the foundation quickly hired New York architect Wendy Evans Joseph, formerly of Pei Cobb Freed & Partners, to come up with a preliminary design that captured the spirit of the project while enticing potential funders. Her response was a building within a building that preserves the shell and the major architectural features of the 1909 structure while creating a contemporary space inside.

"I didn't want a complete break between inside and outside," she says. "I wanted a dialogue and a feeling of continuity between old and new, like the Musée d'Orsay in Paris."

The strengths of the building are its large arched windows, steel roof trusses, and dramatic two-story main room that resembles a turn-of-the-century train shed. Ms. Joseph's design celebrates all these elements, honoring the original building while giving it a late-twentieth-century openness and fluidity.

In her design, the main room is divided by a crisp diagonal wall. On one side are various storage and support spaces; on the other, the public areas: cafe, shop, temporary exhibition gallery, and a great room known as "The Gathering" for parties and special events.

A curving metal screen, probably of perforated copper, frames a three hundred-seat orientation theater near the entrance; at the rear, a grand staircase leads to the second and third levels.

From a shallow lobby, visitors will move directly into The Gathering, from which they can view the entire museum at a glance. In both its scale (about 210 feet long by 175 feet wide) and its crisp angularity, the room provides a contemporary counterpoint to the foursquare, steel-and-stucco architecture of the Administration Building. It announces that something new and unusual is happening here.

The permanent exhibits will be on the second and third levels, overlooking the great hall. Although the details are still sketchy, the overall intention is clear. These will be thematic rather than historical or chronological exhibits, focusing on such topics as diversity, generations, women's movements, technology and science, and women in the arts. Many will be computerized and interactive and will involve new telecommunications devices, such as wireless companion phones that provide additional information about the exhibits at the touch of a button. At the center of The Gathering will be an "electronic quilt" of video screens flashing images and messages about women's achievements.

Ms. Joseph's design is bold, appropriate, inventive without being mannered—and, it turned out, controversial. Several weeks ago, a small group of Dallas preservationists objected to the demolition of the Administration Building's art deco lobby and briefly persuaded the Texas Historical Commission, the state's preservation agency, to withhold approval. Without the commission's blessing, the museum would have died. Fortunately, cooler heads prevailed and a compromise was reached that preserves a portion of the 1936 lobby and makes a permanent exhibit out of the rest.

This is the kind of controversy that makes preservationists look silly and that casts doubt on serious efforts to rescue endangered buildings from the wrecking ball. What matters is saving the Administration Building and giving it a productive new life, not arguing about a few feet of warped paneling that was carelessly erected and not expected to last more than a few years. It was a forest-and-trees argument, and in the end someone saw the forest.

With that crisis passed, the Foundation for Women's Resources is racing toward an October 2000 opening. Starting this week, as soon as the State Fair closes, the building will be cleared of lead and asbestos,

5.7. *In 1936, George Dahl redesigned C. D. Hill's 1910 coliseum building for the State Fair of Texas to serve as its administrative building. Wendy Evans Joseph then repurposed the building to serve as the the Women's Museum, which opened in 2000 and closed in 2011. Photograph by Carol Highsmith. The Lyda Hill Texas Collection of Photographs in Carol M. Highsmith's America Project, Library of Congress, Prints and Photographs Division.*

with groundbreaking scheduled for March 1999. Nearly $20 million of the projected $25 million budget has been raised, including major grants from SBC Communications and Texas Instruments.

The Women's Museum will be the first institution of its kind in the nation and an extraordinary boon to Dallas in general and Fair Park in particular. For decades, park officials have been struggling to revive the main entrance at Parry and Exposition, which is rarely used except during the fair. The addition of the Women's Museum—as well as The Turn, a millennium extravaganza proposed for the esplanade—could be the catalyst.

The museum will bring life to a dark and derelict corner of the park; it will attract out-of-town visitors for something besides the fair and the Cotton Bowl. It will be a unique attraction instead of a clone of something found in a dozen other cities. Dallas is lucky to get it (fig. 5.7).

A tale of two houses: Notable buildings face different fates as preservationists and developers clash

JANUARY 4, 2004

The "tear-down" is not a problem unique to Texas cities, but in a state with a strong private property rights ethos, preserving the architecture of private homes presents a challenge. Mid-century modern homes are in particular jeopardy as their relatively modest scale and spartan décor are at odds with contemporary tastes. The examples here reflect these issues as they relate to high-end real estate in Dallas's most expensive neighborhoods, where the cachet of owning a historic home by a celebrated architect is still insufficient protection against demolition. The loss of the Zale house has not stemmed the tide of demolition of houses by Dallas masters like Meyer, Ford, and Dilbeck.

Most cities have eureka moments when latent creative energies erupt into something fresh and provocative. Routine stops, and new possibilities emerge. Think of Chicago in the 1890s, New York in the 1910s and '20s—or Dallas in the 1930s and '40s.

Its boomlet coincided with the triumphant Texas Centennial Exposition and the arrival of modernism in the persons of David Williams, George Dahl, O'Neil Ford, and Howard Meyer. Their architecture represented a search for honesty and simplicity in the face of rampant historicism that was transforming entire neighborhoods into stage sets. "We're just trying to do things that fit this country and that don't

267

look like all the stuff over on Armstrong Parkway," Ford said at the time. By which he meant houses that were clear, direct, and intimately connected to setting and place.

Now the set decorators are back, bigger and bolder than ever, and threatening to bury the legacy of Ford, Meyer, and other progressive architects under a pile of fake columns and looming mansard roofs.

In June 2003, a superb Howard Meyer house in Highland Park was demolished because of soaring land prices and no preservation plan. At the same moment, an equally significant O'Neil Ford house in Lakewood was making a graceful transition to the twenty-first century because a buyer and a seller understood its cultural value and joined hands to save it. Two outstanding examples of mid-century Texas modernism—one lost to market forces and regulatory indifference, the other rescued by enlightened stewardship—tell us where we've been and maybe where we're going.

LOST

The lost house, at 4400 Rheims Place, was completed in 1948 when Mr. Meyer was at his creative peak. It combined elements of Frank Lloyd Wright and Mies van der Rohe with the casualness of a Texas country house. Rooms looked out onto terraces and gardens, connected by clean shafts of space that allowed uninterrupted movement.

The house was built for jewelry magnate Morris Zale, who lived in it for nearly twenty years (fig. 5.8). Charles and Helen Storey bought it in the late 1960s and stayed for another thirty-five. Two owners in half a century is not unusual for Dallas's early modern houses, which were commissioned by adventurous clients who wanted to make a mark instead of a quick buck. Mr. Meyer counted the Zales, Sangers, Lipshys, and other business leaders among his clients, while Ford was virtually the resident architect for the founders of Texas Instruments.

The Storeys decided to sell because they were elderly and wanted a smaller house with less maintenance. Yet they weren't interested in deed restrictions, easements, or other mechanisms that would preserve the old one.

"I'm sympathetic to preservation," Mr. Storey said in October 2002, "but if it comes to a point where preservationists tell people they can't sell their house to anyone who will tear it down, that would be unfair. A house is a physical thing, and you can't control what a subsequent owner has a right to do."

5.8. *Howard Meyer's house for Morris Zale, formerly at 4400 Rheims Street in Highland Park, fell to the wrecking ball in 2003. Photograph by Meyer in the Howard Meyer collection, The Alexander Architectural Archives, The University of Texas Libraries, The University of Texas at Austin.*

Not in the Park Cities anyway, which have no preservation plans, historic districts, or landmark ordinances. The only way to stall or stop a demolition is through moral persuasion, which in a runaway real estate market means almost nothing.

"A Frank Lloyd Wright house in Highland Park could be torn down tomorrow with no difficulty," says architect Craig Melde, a board member of Preservation Park Cities, a fledgling advocacy group. "When you don't have a plan, developers control the land uses."

Preservation Park Cities is working on a plan, but it is still several years away and faces political opposition. In the meantime, the inventory of older houses in the Park Cities continues to shrink. Between 1990 and 2000, Highland Park lost 22 percent of its pre-1960 homes. University Park loses an estimated one hundred older houses annually. The communities are like teenagers going through a growth spurt. Suddenly, nothing fits. The houses are too big, and the lots are too small. Scale, proportion, and a sense of appropriateness are disappearing.

Ironically, these are precisely the qualities that have made the Park Cities such attractive places to live. Wilbur David Cooke's original plan for Highland Park emphasized the importance of trees and creeks and topography and included various deed restrictions to force developers to respect them. The result was an intimate, comfortable community where buildings and landscape struck a harmonious balance, and even grand houses seemed to belong.

"The trend now is to tear down and build new," notes realtor David Griffin, who negotiated the sale of the Ford house in Lakewood. "People who have money want to make their own statement, which often amounts to nothing more than a big house with all the latest appliances."

The trend doesn't seem to bother Park Cities officials, who take a strict property rights view of tear-downs.

"Nobody comes to us and asks whether it's better to demolish a house or save it," says University Park public works director Bud Smallwood. "It's strictly a homeowner's decision. The city shouldn't do anything to interfere with what a person wants to do with his property."

The Storeys put their house on the market for $2.45 million, a hefty price in a community where postage stamp lots sell for $1 million and older houses are worth more dead than alive. Real estate broker Ellen Terry offered it as a tear-down. The term wasn't used, but the message was clear. "A magnificent contemporary home situated on an enormous double lot that could also be a premier building site," the listing began. And for anyone who missed the point, there was a coda: "If you are a lover of contemporary homes or want to build your dream home on ¾ of an acre, look no further."

Ventura Custom Homes, from suburban Frisco, was eager to build in the Park Cities. The company eventually bought the Storey house for $1.6 million, intending to replace it with an 11,200-square-foot "Spanish Mediterranean mansion" containing six bedrooms, eight fireplaces, eleven full and half-baths, and three courtyards. If the original house, at 3,500 square feet, was a compact and understated expression of elegant living, the proposed replacement was a pseudo-historical monument to excess.

Preservationists rallied to the beleaguered house's defense, firing off letters and emails and conducting drive-by vigils. Preservation Park Cities brought a number of interested buyers to Ventura in hopes of a reprieve. Reportedly, there were several offers on the land, but none on the house. Ventura said that the house was deteriorating and needed at least $500,000 in repairs, a figure disputed by architect Wilson Fuqua, who inspected it and found the structure to be sound. "I wouldn't be surprised if the bulldozer broke its blade demolishing it," he says.

To its credit, Ventura delayed demolition several times and at one point offered to give the house to anyone willing to move it to a site where, in the words of co-owner Loy Lowary, "the dirt cost is more in line with the existing structure."

"I'd like to do more restoration and renovations," says the Ventura architect, Will Snyder, "but when owners insist on selling their old houses for $300 a square foot, which is the price of new construction, all you can do is tear down and start over."

Preservationists contend that Ventura could still have made a profit on the Storey house—the lot was big enough to accommodate a media center or weight room or other fashionable addition—though certainly not as much as on a new $4 million Spanish Mediterranean mansion with three courtyards and eleven bathrooms.

Construction will start in the spring, says Mr. Snyder.

PRESERVED

Over in Lakewood, a more inspiring story was unfolding.

Alan Bromberg grew up in a modern house on Wendover designed in 1938 by Ford and Arch Swank. It was a smaller and somewhat purer version of their Texas houses in San Antonio—long and low, with a line of decks and screened porches across the front and stunning craft details by Ford's brother Lynn and other artisans (fig. 5.9).

When Mr. Bromberg's mother died in 1999—another lifetime owner—he and his wife, Anne, began a slow, meticulous search for a new owner. To them, the house was much more than "a physical thing"; it was part of family history and community memory.

So they drew up a remarkably detailed set of deed restrictions requiring the new owners, among other things, "to respect and retain the natural character of the land," preserve "exterior features," as well as the "interior design and use of materials." They couldn't subdivide the lot or convert the house into apartments. All changes had to be approved by the Brombergs, who also insisted on holding mini-tutorials for prospective buyers on the history and significance of the house. Most vanished at the mention of deed restrictions, fearing they would kill the resale value.

5.9. *The Bromberg House, designed by Arch Swank and O'Neil Ford in 1938, showing the regionalist influence of Dallas architect David Williams. Photograph courtesy of Michael Cagle.*

"They just wanted to demolish the house and sell off the land," recalls Mr. Bromberg. "Several offered more than the asking price, but we weren't interested."

But not Dan and Gail Patterson, who were living on Swiss Avenue but looking for something smaller, simpler, and with a bit more land. As a former president of Preservation Dallas, Ms. Patterson was already familiar with deed restrictions and untroubled by them.

"We didn't have any problem at all," she says. "What the Brombergs wanted for the house we wanted, too. It was like a good marriage. And if we ever sell it, it will be to someone who loves it as much as we do."

As soon as the sale went through, the Pattersons hired Dallas architect Frank Welch, a protégé of Ford's, to restore not only the house but also the meadow and creek that were integral to the original design.

"It was like doing surgery on one of my own children," says Mr. Welch. "I didn't want to make a mistake and ruin the place."

He restored the windows and half a dozen carved fireplace mantels, along with Lynn Ford's intricate V-shaped paneling on interior walls and doors. He reclaimed a large screened porch on the first floor and a deck above. But since the overall goal of preservation is renewal, not pickling, he was allowed to modernize the kitchen and bathrooms and to add a long narrow gallery on the back to accommodate family living in 2003. Yet all of this was handled so deftly that new and old blend seamlessly.

The Brombergs approved every change, which sometimes sent construction into first gear but improved the final result. "That's how a project like this should be done," says Mr. Welch. "Carefully, lovingly."

All of this might suggest that responsible preservation is mostly for wealthy people with money and time to burn. The Brombergs left approximately $400,000 on the table to get what they wanted. Not every seller is in a position to do that.

But money and time are only part of the story. The rest is about respect, determination, and feeling.

"One of the things that pushed us was a sense of history," says Mr. Bromberg. "Our families were very active in the intellectual and cultural life of Dallas from the '30s on. It was a very frothy period, and we wanted to maintain a connection to that."

Ultimately, that is what historic preservation at its best is about—connection, continuity, and the reaffirmation of bedrock community values. It's what the Meyer and Bromberg houses represent, and the faux chateaux do not.

Saving beauty: The quirky glories of the Mercantile Building escape the wrecking ball

FEBRUARY 19, 2006

Developer Tim Headington comes across as a hero in this story of the mosaics rescued from the doomed Mercantile Bank Building in downtown Dallas and moved into his new Joule Hotel. But in 2014 his Sunday morning demolition of several nearby buildings sparked public outcry that resulted in the creation of a stronger preservation ordinance.*

The Hall of State in Fair Park may be Texas's greatest art and architecture ensemble, but the Mercantile Bank Building on Main Street is its most surprising—a stream of murals, mosaics, ceramics, and sculptures coursing up staircases, across lobbies and mezzanines, into boardrooms and executive suites.

---

* A sampling of coverage of the downtown demolitions can be found in Robert Wilonsky, "Before More Buildings are Razed, 'the way Dallas Does Historic Preservation Needs to Change,'" *DMN*, March 18, 2015; Peter Simek, "An Open Letter to Tim Headington Re: Forty Five Ten," *D Magazine*, June 3, 2015, https://www.dmagazine.com/frontburner/2015/06/an-open-letter-to-tim-headington-re-forty-five-ten/; Mark Lamster, "Has Dallas Had Its Penn Station Moment?," *DMN*, September 25, 2015. The Headington Company's response to criticism is included in Karen Robinson-Jacobs, "Developer Headington Nears End of 12-Year 'Vision Quest' for Downtown," *DMN*, January 17, 2015.

Most Dallasites have never seen, or can barely remember, this work, so its eleventh-hour rescue in January by a coalition of architects, preservationists, civic activists, and a lone developer qualifies as a small civic miracle, like opening a box of cornflakes and finding a Tiffany brooch inside. Or in this case life-size mosaics, stained-glass light fixtures, birds in flight, and galloping horses—playful, sparkly, eccentric work of a kind Dallas hasn't paid much attention to.

Tim Headington, a Dallas oilman-cum-hotelier, put up $270,000 to remove and store the art, just as wrecking crews were taking their practice swings.

"I was overwhelmed by the scale and beauty of the individual pieces," he says, "But it also seemed like a unique opportunity to save a part of Dallas history."

The Mercantile Building is a jumble of four bland brick structures cobbled together over thirty-five years. The tower—four clocks, four times, all wrong—was built in 1943, one of the few skyscrapers erected during World War II. It will remain while the three later additions, from 1947, 1958, and 1974, will be demolished to make way for a $250 million residential-office complex that city officials hope will spark a downtown turnaround. All the art is to be crated and removed by early March.

From Main Street, the Mercantile is banality itself, clumps of beige brick rising to a collective anticlimax. The interiors, however, exuded aesthetic sophistication worthy of a museum or a hip gallery. And the curator, amazingly, was Mercantile president and Dallas Mayor R. L. Thornton, a self-professed philistine who once said that he'd do anything to help the symphony "so long as you don't ask me to attend any concerts."

Yet Mr. Thornton was also a savvy entrepreneur who packaged and sold the 1936 Texas Centennial Exposition and therefore saw first-hand what good art could do for business.

"He was very influenced by the work George Dahl and others had done at Fair Park and wanted to continue that feel," recalls his grandson Robert L. Thornton III. "If he could have found a way to put an esplanade in the building, he'd have done it."

Instead of an esplanade, Mr. Thornton hired Millard Sheets, a prominent California industrial designer, to turn a run-of-the-mill banking hall into a head-turning work of art.

"We'll make it warm, friendly, contemporary but not cold," he promised.

At the time, Mr. Sheets was director of Otis Art Institute in Los Angeles and thus able to enlist former students for the project, along with Dallas artists such as Octavio Medellin. For the most part they worked from Mr. Sheets's drawings; occasionally they designed their own pieces under his supervision. The result was a colorful, dramatic, thoroughly integrated but delightfully quirky installation that reminds us how timid most contemporary collaborations have become.

The best pieces were located in the 1958 Dallas Building, which the *Dallas Morning News* breathlessly described as "monumentally opulent, a dazzling dynamic sweep of embellishment from sub-basement to the thirty-first floor." If that sounds more like the Bellagio casino than a bank, the idea of a carefully orchestrated sequence of special effects is not so far off.

The sub-basement contained cinematic vaults with massive round doors that only fit employees could open. In the upstairs lobby, customers were greeted by blazing tile sunbursts, an intricate Aztec calendar, and mosaics of stars and planets set in soaring travertine walls. The mezzanine, which served as the main banking floor, contained four free-standing mosaic grilles celebrating the art, science, industry, and agriculture of Texas. Adjacent walls were decorated with glass mosaics of the four elements—fire being the most dramatic—along with a series of eight mosaic birds circling above Main Street. The stained-glass light fixtures were all designed by Mr. Medellin. Cashing a check at the Mercantile thus became the occasion for an art walk.

"The project was primarily decorative," says Tom Van Sant, a California artist who designed a conquest of Mexico mosaic for the tower's executive lounge. "There was no real theme and no hidden messages from the client or the artists."

No messages, perhaps, but plenty of clever allusions to Maya and Aztec art, Renaissance frescoes, 1930s WPA murals, and much else. Several of the free-standing mosaic figures, with their round faces and flat features, look like misplaced Giottos—not far-fetched considering that they were fabricated in Venice. And the anomalous Tahitian maiden in the twentieth-floor boardroom could have stepped straight out of a Gauguin painting. So while Sheets and company were intent on reviving ancient crafts and incorporating them into architecture—Texan O'Neil Ford had similar interests—they didn't mind having fun either.

Why saving this unique art collection was not part of the city's agreement with Forest City Enterprises, developers of the Mercantile block, remains a mystery.

"It just wasn't on anybody's radar screen," Mayor Laura Miller said at the time.

And if it weren't for Mr. Headington and two attentive architects, Craig Melde and Jay Firsching of Architexas who coordinated the effort, it wouldn't be on anybody's mind today either.

Mr. Headington is currently looking for a downtown building, preferably near the old Mercantile, to exhibit the eighty to ninety pieces he salvaged from the bank. His future Joule Resort on Main Street is too small, he says, plus he wants the exhibit accessible to the public.

"I was overwhelmed by all the calls and letters from people I don't know whose lives had been touched by that building," he says. "They remembered the Mercantile as a vital piece of the Dallas skyline."

And that, of course, is another part of this tortuous story. The Mercantile belonged to the last golden age of downtown Dallas, before freeways and cheap home mortgages sucked the life out of it. It was an era when streets were crowded, stores and restaurants stayed open nights and weekends, and all the major banks were locally owned and fiercely competitive.

As president of the smallest of the big three, after Republic and First National, Mr. Thornton was constantly looking for the upper hand. He kept an office facing Neiman Marcus in hopes, says his grandson, "that anybody who could afford to shop there could be persuaded to bank with him as well."

Yet like the other dynamic leaders of Dallas in the 1950s and early '60s, he was also a tireless promoter of his hometown as a livelier and more sophisticated place than Fort Worth or Houston, a future St. Louis or Kansas City. New buildings were popping up all around him: the Statler Hilton, the Republic Bank Tower, a sleek new public library by his friend Dahl.

And on top of that, the city now had exciting modern art, done by people from Los Angeles and other faraway places. Here was further proof that Dallas was no longer a provincial backwater but a vigorous young city on the rise.

6

TEXAS ARCHITECTS
AND DEVELOPERS

Look in any textbook on modern American architecture and you'll be hard-pressed to find mention of a single Texas architect. Checklists of great American architects are formed in New York, Chicago, and Los Angeles and leave little room for the local practitioners who built the vast majority of our cities and suburbs. One of Dillon's central missions was to educate his readers about the individuals and firms, both exceptional and mundane, that built the local environments across the state. Especially as large commissions began to go almost exclusively to out-of-town architects by the 1980s, Dillon supported and praised Texas architects and firms. In preparation for his biography of O'Neil Ford, he spent long hours in conversation with the architect. He learned directly from Ford's tales of Texas to celebrate the lessons of vernacular architecture, and he delighted in sharing his own stories of contemporary designers who found new and inventive ways to continue that legacy.

Dillon reported on the annual Texas Society of Architects meetings, he covered AIA Dallas and AIA Fort Worth's annual awards, and he took the annual home tours offered by Preservation Dallas and AIA Dallas. He attended conferences and symposia and exhibits sponsored by architecture schools and wrote about their efforts to produce new generations of responsible designers. He acted as something of a translator between the professional world of architects and the public, summarizing professional concerns in ways that made it clear how architects affected everyday life. His article on new Americans with Disabilities Act compliance laws, for example, turned something esoteric and technical and outwardly boring into an essential primer for both architects and the public to see the world around them in a new way.* And Dillon did not ignore the primary influence of real estate developers as the most prominent patrons of good (and bad) architecture in Texas.

While some of these essays are reviews of good design work, in many cases Dillon wrote as a kind of local historian, plucking lessons about Texas history from the buildings that line city streets. He helped create a local canon, from the early work of architects like Hal Thomson and Lang & Witchell to high modernists like Howard Meyer, Charles Dilbeck, and O'Neil Ford to contemporary practitioners like Gary Cunningham, Max Levy, and Lake/Flato. Along the way, Dillon paid particular attention to the kinds of materials, construction, and landscapes that distinguished Texas architecture from architecture in other places, making the case that Texas has nurtured a rich tradition of informed regionalism.

---

*   Dillon, "One Step at a Time," *DMN*, January 26, 1992.

The education of Harlan Crow: The son of the world's largest developer wants to build a few good buildings and a liveable downtown. But first, he had to teach himself how.

NOVEMBER 11, 1984

Like Dillon's profile of Mayor Erik Jonsson, this profile of Harlan Crow uses a "people story" to illuminate the inner workings of the world of real estate development in Texas. The casual discussion of the merits of postmodern architecture in the context of high finance pulls the curtain back on the decision-making process.

Harlan Crow is sitting at his desk in LTV Center, jacket off, chain-smoking Merit Lights, talking architecture (fig. 6.1).

"Suppose you owned the land across Harwood from the museum," he says nonchalantly, because he does. "What would you build on it?" Conversation shifts to the prominence of the site, the need for compatibility with the new Dallas Museum of Art, and the importance of enhancing the character of the Arts District.

"Should I do another postmodern building?" he swerves, and without waiting for an answer skids a brochure across the conference table. "What do you think of Cesar Pelli?" he asks, pointing to photographs of Pelli's Four Leaf Towers in Houston and his plan for Battery Park City in New York.

"How about Helmut Jahn?" he presses, tossing in another glossy promotional piece. He follows with capsule critiques of the work of a half-dozen nationally prominent architects—Kevin Roche, I. M. Pei,

6.1. The Dallas Morning News *nominated Dillon for a Pulitzer based on his profile of Harlan Crow. Page image courtesy the* Dallas Morning News, *clipping from scrapbooks in the David Dillon Papers, Special Collections, University of Texas at Arlington.*

Edward Larrabee Barnes. It's a favorite Crow gambit, polling friends, visitors, and potential tenants for their views on his upcoming projects, gathering information that may work its way into the company's marketing campaigns.

Dallas architects are not mentioned. Without saying so explicitly, Crow indicates that for his major projects he's scanning distant horizons, where the Johnsons and Pellis reside. He acknowledges that a few years ago he was awed and terrified by celebrity architects. "I couldn't talk to them. But if I met Philip Johnson today, I'd be respectful, not scared," he says.

Outside his office window, like a made-to-order backdrop, stand the Trammell Crow Company's major downtown buildings: Diamond Shamrock Tower, San Jacinto Tower, 2001 Bryan Tower.

Diamond Shamrock was Harlan's initiation into office development, a gift from his father. It remains, on balance, one of downtown's worst office buildings. LTV Center, his latest project, is the best downtown building of the '80s and one of the best new skyscrapers in the country. The distance between them is more than two blocks and five years; LTV is a quantum jump in architectural understanding and sensitivity, marking, perhaps, Harlan Crow's emergence as the great blond hope of Dallas architecture. Having begun his career with enormous wealth, he's clearly not content to sit on it. He's determined to be known as a developer of great buildings, instead of just another real estate mogul.

The Trammell Crow Company has developed more than $5 billion in property, ranging from one-story warehouses to luxury hotels, trade centers, and fifty-story office buildings. It owns and manages major projects from Dallas to Dusseldorf to Sao Paulo. It is the lead developer for the upcoming New York Trade Mart in Manhattan and is planning a world-wide network of computer marts.

Harlan, at thirty-five, presides over the company's office building division, the most glamorous and adventurous. Besides projects in downtown Dallas and Las Colinas, he's responsible for InterFirst Plaza in San Antonio; a complex in Washington; projects in Denver, San Diego, and Charlotte; and a score of suburban developments too small to get more than a fragment of his divided attention.

But "presides" is too pallid and bankerish a verb for Harlan Crow's managerial style. "Stalks," "surrounds," or "envelopes" are closer to the truth. He roams the company offices like a bear in search of honey, downing corn chips and cheese sandwiches, peering over shoulders at sketches and blueprints, doing his best to track a hundred details on a dozen different projects. He's been known to hold meetings while lying flat on his back, throwing a ball of Silly Putty at the ceiling. Ideas fly from him like sparks from a Roman candle, some igniting fires, others fizzling out for lack of fuel.

Asked what he does to relax, he pauses, scratches his head, then points to his buildings on the far side of Ross Avenue.

"There it is," he responds almost apologetically. "That's what I do for relaxation."

Harlan Crow graduated from the University of Texas at Austin in 1974 with a degree in business and spent the next five years in Houston leasing warehouses for his father. It was the standard Crow Company apprenticeship, designed to teach prospective partners, sons included, the real estate business.

But in the course of knocking on doors, Harlan discovered that Houston's developers were different from Dallas's. Gerald Hines was rewriting the rules of commercial real estate with Pennzoil Place and Texas Commerce Tower, proving that good architecture was also good business. Hines believed that money spent up front on good design, high-quality materials, and what developers refer to as "the amenities package"—landscaping and art, for example—could be recouped many times over during the life of a building. No Dallas developer, Trammell Crow included, saw architecture in those far-sighted terms.

"Houston is a city of extremes," Harlan says, "the greatest laboratory for good architecture in the country and the greatest laboratory for bad architecture. Dallas architecture has been so conservative, so plain vanilla. Many buildings in Houston are far worse than ones here, but many are far better. I coveted the latter."

That desire wasn't immediately apparent, however. Harlan's first building, Diamond Shamrock Tower, opened in 1980. It was a leasing triumph and an architectural mediocrity. It has cheap materials, bad detailing, and a gimmicky, inward-sloping facade that creates the impression that the building is about to topple over onto the street. The building was roasted by critics as overscaled and inhuman.

Harlan defends Diamond Shamrock as "basically a good building. ... It was my first building and I had a lot to learn. I took my lumps and went on to do more buildings. The experience made me bulletproof."

His next venture was San Jacinto Tower (1982), somewhat more sophisticated architecturally without being in any way innovative.

Its three slab forms, laid up against one another like books on a shelf, are an obvious borrowing from Rockefeller Center, Embarcadero Center, and several other projects. The basic design was by Beran & Shelmire of Dallas (architects of the World Trade Center and the Anatole Hotel, among other Crow Company projects), in association with John Carl Warnecke of San Francisco. Warnecke was Crow's first experience with a nationally known architect, though one nestled securely in the second tier.

As usual, the building was a commercial success. Crow's biggest regret about San Jacinto, besides not having made it fifty stories tall, was substituting precast concrete panels for red granite on the exterior. "I chickened out," he says candidly. "I looked at the budget and decided to save $2 million by using the precast. It was a mistake."

While San Jacinto Tower was going up, Crow was already planning a companion building across Pearl Street for what he called his "Foo dog scheme," after the twin canine statues at the entrances to Chinese temples. Beran & Shelmire were once again the architects, in association with ex-Warnecke partner Emilio Arechaederra. Yet, aware of the growing need to make a statement and smarting from the criticism he and his father had received on earlier projects, Crow switched architects mid-stream.

"[Crow] told me that he needed an architecture firm with a national reputation and a proven track record on large commercial buildings." Beran & Shelmire continues to work on hotels and suburban office buildings for the Crow Company, but it is no longer involved in major office projects.

Harlan's new firm was Skidmore, Owings and Merrill, about as nationally prominent as one could get, with high-rise office buildings in virtually every major city in the world. The architect was a talented and aggressive designer named Richard Keating.

Keating was already working on a small Crow Company office building in Las Colinas and had been hired by Trammell Crow to design the Soundstage for the nearby Dallas Communications Complex. He later fired Keating for refusing to "draw up" one of his design ideas. The rift didn't bother Harlan, who would continue to hire Keating for his major office projects, including the highly regarded InterFirst Plaza in San Antonio (1983), LTV Center (November 1984), and the recently announced 2200 Ross Avenue (which ultimately replaced the Foo dog).

The collaboration of Crow and Keating has proven to be a study in the benefits of creative tension. Crow is impetuous and impulsive, operating on intuition and nervous energy; Keating is more measured and businesslike, with firm design and planning ideas and the slick arrogance needed to back them up in the board room.

In many respects, Keating is the perfect architect for an ambitious but uncertain client such as Harlan Crow. In LTV Center, he had the sense to recognize Crow's latent romanticism, and the skill to channel it into a building that is evocative and nostalgic, yet at the same time sufficiently straightforward and functional to satisfy the hard-nosed leasing demands of the Crow Company.

"Harlan and I have managed to develop mutual understanding and trust over several projects," Keating says. "If that hadn't happened, I don't know what the hell we would have done when we got a project as complex as LTV."

"We already had some idea of where we wanted to go," Crow explains, "but Keating gave these notions form and direction. He led us."

LTV Center is a conscious evocation of the romantic skyscrapers of the '20s and '30s, combined with the smooth surfaces and crisp, hard-edged detailing of orthodox modernism. It is formal and classical, with a three-part division into base, shaft, and top. The top is a rather sporty continuation of a series of bay windows that, in the right light, makes the facade jump and dance. It is an elegant, superbly proportioned building, dominant from virtually every direction, yet with enough restraint and self-possession to seem durable rather than trendy.

LTV's most revealing features are not on the skyline, however, but along the street and in the lobby. Here Crow's romanticism, his Gatsby-like delight in conspicuous consumption, gets full expression.

Around the base of the building are twenty bronze sculptures by Rodin, Maillol, Bourdelle, and other charter members of the French figurative school. Crow's original plan was to purchase a single major piece, preferably Rodin's *Burghers of Calais,* but after several visits to Paris and meetings with curators and dealers, he broadened the collection to include lesser-known artists. The sculpture is traditional—safe and appealing—and of high quality. It is not just more corporate "plop art," trucked in at the eleventh hour to dress up a hostile building. It is part of a conscientious plan to develop humane public spaces.

"I'm not doing all this for the architects," Harlan says of LTV.

"I'm not even building it for me. It's for everyone else. Maybe it's for the taxi driver."

"Harlan is doing something far more intimate than the sculpture garden at the Dallas Museum," says Fred Kent of Project for Public Spaces, a consultant on LTV's public spaces, as well as to the Arts District. "And he's doing it in a corporate setting. He's breaking out of the mold of Dallas corporate architecture with its austerity and stiffness."

The LTV lobby, in turn, is opulent bordering on orgasmic. The walls are kevazingo and bubinga wood from Africa, the fixtures and elevator cabs are finished in gleaming bronze, and the floors and rotunda are covered in white Italian marble and black Andes granite.

LTV is done in the venerable tradition of Rockefeller Center and the Fisher Building in Detroit. The lobby, like the building as a whole, dramatizes the freedom accorded clients and architects by the revival of interest in classical and historical architecture. Harlan Crow is enjoying the benefits of being in the right place at the right time, whereas his father was doing most of his building when modernism was dominant. They share similar humanist impulses, but Trammell never had the chance to bring them to fruition under the sanction of good taste. He was always swimming against the architectural tide, while Harlan is squarely in the mainstream.

Crow says that he relishes being able to "do an elitist building again," in which the delight in rich materials is not considered an offense against architectural purity. "I'm not unique in this," he says. "My whole generation is responding this way."

The cost of the lobby, art, and pavilion is staggering, $20 million by Crow's estimate. The pavilion behind the tower, which will contain shops and restaurants as well as free space for the performing arts, cost nearly $4 million. Crow is neither cavalier about the expense nor unrealistic about its commercial benefits.

"It costs a little more, but not that much. If you're going to spend $200 million on a building, you'll spend $210 million. That's only five percent, for God's sake. I'm already contemplating major changes in Diamond Shamrock and 2001 Bryan to bring them up to the market, but I don't expect to have to do anything to this building for fifty years."

LTV Center is part of the twenty-block real estate empire that Harlan Crow is developing in the northeast quadrant of downtown. 2200 Ross Avenue, with its dramatic sky window and semi-circular top, is now under construction. Planning has begun for the Arts District project at Harwood and Woodall Rodgers, a key chunk of which is owned by the DMA. Harlan refers to this modestly as "the most important site in the United States." It's a major one, obviously, and it's clear that Harlan believes his reputation is intimately connected to what he does with it.

His biggest challenge may not be the success of individual buildings, but whether they can be tied together to create a rich urban environment. Urban design is becoming as critical an issue for Crow as architecture.

On the back of a set of blueprints, Harlan quickly sketches the elements that will transform a collection of skyscrapers into an inviting urban environment: trees and flowers, pocket parks, shops and restaurants at the street level of all buildings, pushcarts (owned and operated by the Trammell Crow Company) for dispensing hot dogs and bagels. Great quotations will be inscribed on the pylons in front of San Jacinto Tower; tiny brass plaques commemorating historic events in the area will be placed on sidewalks and building facades.

Some of this may turn out to be cute and kitschy, but the basic impulse is sound: The developer of skyscrapers is learning how to think small.

"You don't make any money on the shops and the restaurant, but it's important to have them because they make downtown more inviting. Right now we call this the Central Business District, and that's right. It's the center for business and not much else. I don't know where the real center of Dallas is, but it's not here."

The influence of William Whyte and other street life evangelists is clear in all these proposals. In a letter to Whyte, Crow said that although he had recently pumped $1 million into the downtown skybridge system, Whyte had convinced him he was wrong. He refers to Whyte unequivocally as "the single most important influence on planning in Dallas at the moment."

But some of Harlan's thinking also comes from his father. Because Trammell Crow could never make his peace with the stark, abstract forms of modern architecture, he spent a fortune trying to work around it, often by being his own architect. The atrium in the Trade Mart and the sculptures in and around the World Trade Center are expressions of this impulse. So are the ornamental brick work on the Anatole and the bronze horses around 2001 Bryan Tower. While one can argue with taste and execution, it's impossible to question the basic intention, which is humane, civilized, and generous. It reflects an understanding that architecture must work on many levels, that it is more than line and volume.

No one can predict where all this energy and enthusiasm will lead, least of all Harlan Crow. "Will I be no good in twenty years?" he asks, and seems genuinely to wonder.

His taste at the moment is sumptuous and traditional, exemplified by the Rodin sculptures. He may never be on the cutting edge of design, but his example may force other developers to do better work than they otherwise would. Nobody, including his competition, seems to doubt the sincerity or impact of his current efforts.

"I believe his commitment to good architecture is fundamental," says Vincent Carrozza, developer of One Dallas Centre. "The city is fortunate that he's here and doing what he's doing."

"These guys (the Crow Company) are the most successful real estate entrepreneurs in the history of the earth," says Keating. "They can tell Dallas, 'This is what we're going to do,' and do it. They are the inheritors of (Trammell) Crow's success."

Crow is fond of reminding visitors that he was born in Dallas, that he's lived in Dallas, that he expects to die here. He's committed to taking the long view—to building a city, not merely projects.

His commitment sometimes leads him to make heretical statements. He would like to see a moratorium on development in Oak Lawn, for example: "I think this laissez-faire approach to things is going too far." He wants the city to be more aggressive about planning and land-use controls and supports the idea of land banking.

It's hard to know how deep this vein of liberal social thinking runs. Will he push on these volatile fronts, bringing others along with him, or fall back into a more conventional posture? The one sure thing is that anyone who has progressed from Diamond Shamrock to LTV Tower in the space of five years is capable of just about anything.

Dilbeck, Meyer, and Ford: Dallas architects of the forties and fifties and their enduring contributions

OCTOBER 6, 1985

Charles Dilbeck, Howard Meyer, and O'Neil Ford represent the iconoclastic, single-practitioner tradition of Texas architecture. While huge corporate offices are the norm today in Dallas, this trio remain heroic archetypes of individual practice.

The Dallas Morning News *previewed Dillon's 1985 book on Dallas architecture by excerpting passages.* This essay is edited and condensed from the article published in the newspaper.*

CHARLES DILBECK

The unique flavor of a city depends in large part on the architects who design its buildings.

The houses of Charles S. Dilbeck occupy a unique place in the history of Dallas architecture, being neither modern nor traditional but highly original hybrids. With their striking exteriors of brick, stone, and wood, topped with elaborate chimneys and whimsical towers and cupolas, they are unlike anything else in town. They've been called doll houses, troll houses, and houses that Jack built, but to their architect, they're all just "Dilbecks."

---

*   Dillon, *Dallas Architecture 1936–1986* (Austin: Texas Monthly Press, 1985), with photographs by Doug Tomlinson.

6.2. *Charles Dilbeck designed this weekend home north of Fort Worth for Ted Dealey in 1938, shortly before Dealey became publisher of the* Dallas Morning News. *It has been recently moved and restored by architect Nancy McCoy. Photograph courtesy Carolyn Brown.*

Dilbeck built hundreds of houses in the Dallas area between 1935 and his retirement in 1969, many of them in the Park Cities and Lakewood. The 4000 block of Bryn Mawr in University Park is a virtual Dilbeck museum, featuring everything from his early cottage styles to the later, more prototypical Texas ranch houses. The original R. E. Griffith house at 3817 McFarlin Boulevard is a superb early Dilbeck ranch house scaled down for a city lot (fig. 6.2). The Julian Meeker house in Fort Worth, now a school, is a sprawling frontier version more than 300 feet long.

Dilbeck was born in 1907 in Fort Smith, Arkansas, and grew up working in his father's planing mill. The family moved to Tulsa in 1915, where his father built apartment houses and churches. By the age of eleven, Dilbeck had already designed and seen built a small church complete with bell tower and Doric columns around the entrance. At fifteen, he went to work for a Tulsa lumber company adapting stock house plans to the needs of builders and developers.

In the fall of 1932, he opened his own office in Highland Park Village. "The clients who came to see me wanted something a little different,"

Dilbeck recalls. What many of them wanted, it turned out, was a picturesque period house, something that evoked an idealized vision of village life when idealized visions of any kind were in short supply. One of Dilbeck's first Dallas houses was an early Colonial mansion on Turtle Creek. He subsequently designed a French farmhouse for P. N. Wiggins on Preston Road (still one of the best traditional houses in Dallas), as well as a series of Irish and French provincial houses on Douglas and Stanhope Streets.

In the early 1930s, Texas architects David Williams and O'Neil Ford were calling attention to the simple limestone farmhouses of the Texas Hill Country, with their broad metal roofs and small, deep windows. They admired the clarity and directness of these houses and worked to abstract and refine their forms and details to create a simple yet elegant Texas house, of which the Elbert Williams residence at 3805 McFarlin is a superb example. Dilbeck, on the other hand, was attracted to a different type of indigenous architecture, the sprawling ranch houses of the Panhandle and West Texas.

"I was the first to develop Texas ranch houses," Dilbeck said in a 1979 interview. "Others had done city-type Texas houses, but not ranch houses. These usually started out as plain log houses, which were built onto as the family grew. The log house became the hog pen and so on. If the owners made a lot of money, they'd build a Colonial or a gingerbread up on top of a hill, and the original ranch house would become a second or intermediate house. But if you look closely, you can almost always find that original log house in there somewhere." The rambling, ad hoc plans of the originals led to updated Dilbeck versions in which rooms are laid out at odd angles to the rest of the house, mostly to catch the prevailing breezes but sometimes just for show. The roofs are slightly pitched, with deep overhangs for protection from the sun. The windows are usually large, the fireplaces enormous, and frequently there are porches on both the first and second levels, the latter an adaptation of the so-called lookout porch on ranch houses.

Dilbeck liked to cover his roofs with hand-split oak shingles, although he frequently used red Spanish tiles as well. O'Neil Ford used to say that "Dilbeck's houses look as though they need hair cuts." Other favorite materials included brick, adobe, limestone, and hand-hewn beams and lintels, all combined in a rugged rustic style. The surfaces of his houses are a medley of materials, textures, colors, and quirky architectural details. Sometimes his use of materials becomes careless and self-indulgent, but his best houses stand out as coherent and highly personal statements, full of visual delight and without the pointless picturesqueness that marks much period-revival architecture.

Dilbeck went on to design hotels, resorts, shopping centers, and hundreds of houses in all shapes and sizes. He retired in 1970 and now lives in a Highland Park house that he designed in the late 1960s. Except for an ornately carved front door, it bears little resemblance to his earlier work. Not that Dilbeck has gone conventional—or is mellowing toward contemporary architecture. "Contemporary houses leave me cold," he says bluntly. "White walls and black furniture, all that's just too stark for me. Roofs go straight up then just stop. They remind me of a dog with his leg in the air. I keep my guard up against it."

HOWARD MEYER

Howard Meyer is an architect of the old school, someone for whom architecture has always been more art than business. He brought modernism to Dallas in the 1930s, when the city was firmly entrenched in a period-revival/ranch house phase and over the next fifty years showed how modernism could be married to native materials and indigenous building traditions to create distinguished architecture.

In 1926, while still a student at Columbia University, Meyer worked with pioneer modernist William Lescaze on a design for the League of Nations competition. (Lescaze subsequently designed the Margo Jones Theater at Fair Park as part of the 1936 Centennial.) The experience was sufficiently enlightening that after graduation he made a pilgrimage to Europe to see the then-revolutionary work of Gropius, Mies van der Rohe, and Le Corbusier. Le Corbusier even provided letters of introduction to several of his most important clients, including Madame Savoye, owner of the Villa Savoye at Poissy, arguably the most influential modern house of the twentieth century. "Corbusier convinced me early on that the new forms had great meaning," Meyer recalled. "He knew how to get more wit and charm out of a square than anyone."

Returning to New York City, Meyer went to work for the firm of Thompson and Churchill, where Frank Lloyd Wright made his office when in town. In addition to having his sketches scrutinized by Wright, Meyer got glimpses of Wright's original plan for St. Mark's in the Bowery, a visionary skyscraper finally built as the Price Tower in Bartlesville, Oklahoma. Wright and Le Corbusier quickly became Meyer's main sources of architectural inspiration.

Meyer moved to Dallas in 1935. The Charles Storey and Lipshy-Clark houses, completed in 1949 and 1950, are Meyer's finest residences, imaginative syntheses of International modernism, Wright's prairie houses, and elements of indigenous Texas architecture. More abstract and austere than the Texas houses of David Williams and O'Neil Ford, they are nevertheless equally suited to a hot, dry, and windy climate.

The Storey house has a typically relaxed interior plan, with each cluster of rooms looking out onto its own terrace or garden. These clusters are connected in turn by clean shafts of space that allow virtually uninterrupted movement from one to the other. Most rooms have windows on at least two sides to offer pleasing cross views and an overall feeling of airiness. The colors, mostly the reds, browns, and tans of the desert Southwest, are Meyer staples, as is the combination of wood and stone on the exterior. The crab orchard stone on the facade is artfully continued in the living and dining areas as well, unifying interior and exterior spaces in the best modern tradition.

The Ben A. Lipshy house was clearly inspired by Wright's earth-hugging prairie houses, both in its overall form and its casual interior organization. The house is an ensemble of rich natural materials—brick, redwood, white birch, cork, oak—combined with streamlined modern details such as sliding glass doors and horizontal steel casement windows that are identical to those in Rietveld's Schröder house in Utrecht. The Lipshy house epitomizes an entire era of modern architecture in a few spare rooms.

Subsequent owners, unfortunately, weren't as dazzled by the clear hard light of modernism as the Lipshys. Meyer's crisp, uncluttered spaces were gradually obliterated by armoires, Louis XIV chairs, crystal chandeliers, and, during one bizarre interval, vast expanses of rough-cut barn siding.

The house was purchased in 1982 by Mr. and Mrs. James Clark, enthusiastic collectors of modern art, who promptly hired Meyer to restore it to its original condition. He followed orders literally, to the point of bringing a metal worker out of retirement to stamp replacement pieces for the casement windows and insisting that all the rounded switch plates in the house be replaced by ones having the original 45-degree bevel. The result won an award from Dallas's Historic Preservation League, the youngest house ever to receive such an honor.

The sensitivity to materials and siting evident in Meyer's houses carries over to his larger projects as well. One of Dallas's first high-rise apartment buildings, 3525 Turtle Creek continues to be a prestige address twenty-five years after it was built. The fourteen-story tower is constructed of exposed textured concrete and soft Mexican brick, a favorite combination of Meyer's. Most of the 120 units have three sweeping views of the city, and each has a *brise-soleil*, or sunscreen, with the size of the openings varying with the exposure. The original lobby was finished in teak and brass (largely obliterated in subsequent renovations), and the porte cochere featured metal sculptures by Heri Bartscht. Parking was concealed behind the building, a civility that new neighbors have frequently ignored, and the whole structure is so sensitively sited among large trees that it doesn't intrude on Turtle Creek Boulevard, or the rest of Oak Lawn.

Temple Emanu-El, completed in 1957, remains Meyer's finest building and, along with the Hall of State at Fair Park, the finest architect/artist collaboration in the Southwest. In its form and basic organization, it is a thoroughly modern structure—rigorous, logical, without a trace of trendiness or self-indulgence (fig. 6.3). Yet the generous use of teak, tile, travertine, and soft Mexican brick also gives it a richness and softness that we don't usually associate with modern architecture. It is dignified without being stiff, uplifting without being pompous and overbearing—in short, a place of worship that inspires reverence and a consciousness of sacred things.

O'NEIL FORD

O'Neil Ford and Dallas always were on speaking terms, but they rarely had a heart-to-heart conversation. Dallas had too many slick bankers and shiny glass boxes for his sturdy populist tastes. Compared to his beloved San Antonio, with its missions and River Walk and simple limestone houses, Dallas seemed an uppity, pretentious sort of city that cared more about image than history. He laughingly pronounced the name in flat sheeplike tones, as though it contained six *A*s, and often claimed that even a weekend visit gave him vertigo for months. Yet Ford began his architectural career in Dallas, and long after he had moved his practice to San Antonio, he returned to build elegant

6.3. *Temple Emanu-el, one of Dallas's purest high modern interiors, was executed by Howard Meyer in collaboration with György Kepes, Anni Abers, and a large team of artists, craftsmen, and craftswomen. Photograph courtesy Carolyn Brown.*

6.4. *O'Neil Ford completed the Haggerty House in 1958 as a family home for Patrick Haggerty, a founder of Texas Instruments, and his wife Beatrice. Photograph courtesy Tom Jenkins and Preservation Dallas.*

residences for old friends, landscape architects Marie and Arthur Berger and Texas Instruments founders Cecil Green and Patrick Haggerty (fig. 6.4). With Richard Colley and Arch Swank he designed TI's first semiconductor building, one of the most innovative industrial structures in the world. The bell tower and many of the classroom buildings at the University of Dallas are his. So are the planetarium and science quadrangle at St. Mark's School of Texas and several classroom buildings at the Greenhill School.

Pressed to explain the apparent contradiction between his opinion and his practice, Ford would respond, in a loud whooping laugh, that he was just trying to whip the city into shape, and with a few more good commissions he could probably do it.

Ford was born in 1905 in Pink Hill, Texas, a railroad flag stop just south of the Oklahoma border. His formal architectural training consisted of a few drafting courses at North Texas State University and a certificate from the International Correspondence School (ICS) in Scranton, Pennsylvania. Everything else was learned on the job.

In 1924, Ford and an uncle made a vacation jaunt in a Model T Ford through the German and Alsatian communities of Fredericksburg, Bracketville, and Castroville. Ford was astonished by the beauty and simplicity of the early Texas buildings he saw and equally astonished that Texas architects ignored them completely. Primarily limestone block, with deep windows and metal roofs, they were regional in the most basic sense of the term—built out of local materials in direct response to the imperatives of climate and local geography.

In 1926, Ford went to work for Dallas architect David Williams, another ICS graduate and by then the most prominent spokesman for Texas vernacular architecture. During the next six years, they criss-crossed the state, sketching and photographing old Texas buildings in the Hill Country as well as in the small towns along the Rio Grande such as Roma and San Ygnacio. Here was another stock of overlooked vernacular forms: low, chunky structures made out of stone or caliche, with thick walls, tiny windows, and massive end chimneys. In the late 1920s, local interest in things Spanish and Mexican focused mainly on the Mission and Colonial styles, the high styles, rather than on the plain, unaffected adaptations found along the Mexican border.

Ford and Williams collaborated on a number of houses in Corsicana and Dallas in the late 1920s and early 1930s, including the Warner Clark house on St. Johns Drive and the Elbert Williams house on McFarlin Boulevard, although Ford always gave Williams full credit for the latter. They were not nostalgic copies of older houses but abstracted blends of the indigenous forms and materials that showed what the vernacular house might have become had it developed unin-terrupted from pioneer days.

The shapes were generally simple and straightforward, with pitched roofs, broad overhangs, porches on the first and occasionally the sec-ond level, and massive end chimneys. The houses were carefully sited to catch the prevailing breezes and to offer maximum protection from the parching Texas sun and wind.

The interior plans, while respecting the traditional division of rooms, were typically relaxed and open, in keeping with the informal living habits of the region. Native brick, stone, and wood were used throughout, with regional decorative detailing provided by a small repertory company of artists and craftsmen. Lynn Ford, O'Neil's brother, carved doors, beams, and mantels, while Jerry Bywaters and Tom Stell stenciled walls and did mosaics.

In their integration of architecture and crafts, Williams and Ford were following the example of the English Arts and Crafts movement and the work of some of its American disciples, such as the Greene brothers in California. To Ford, the idea that architecture and the other visual arts were neatly divisible was heresy, and in projects such as the Little Chapel in the Woods in Denton, designed in 1938 with Arch Swank, he showed how rich the synthesis could be.

Of Ford's Dallas residences from the 1940s and 1950s, the Berger house on Stonebridge (Scott W. Lyons, associate architect) epitomizes his attempts to graft modern architecture onto sturdy regional roots. In plan, it is a crisp, contemporary bi-nuclear house, with living and dining areas in one wing, bedrooms in another, joined by a glass-walled gallery that merges interior and exterior spaces in the best modern manner. But the basic materials are pink Texas brick, unpainted Douglas fir, and a lightly colored concrete—hardly modernist staples. Also, the house is so discreetly sited among trees and fingers of ledge that we never see more than a fraction of it at any one time. The Bergers, landscape architects who often worked with Ford, added many native trees and shrubs for shade, plus a network of pergolas and pathways that, as in an Oriental garden, make the small site seem large.

The house is styleless in the conventional sense, having far less to do with formal geometry and sidewalk pyrotechnics than the careful accommodation of architecture to surroundings. Yet thirty years after it was built, it remains one of Ford's freshest and most illuminating designs.

Throughout his career Ford struggled to translate his intimate, essentially residential style into larger institutional and corporate structures. His major successes were Trinity University in San Antonio, carried out over a twenty-five-year period, and his bold design for Texas Instruments's first semiconductor plant in Richardson.

The Semiconductor Building at Texas Instruments was completed in 1958, during the first great transistor boom. With electronics technology changing overnight, scientists who previously got along nicely with AC-DC and tap water suddenly discovered they needed four grades of current, five kinds of gas, and six types of water. And they usually needed them at a moment's notice.

Their solution was an innovative three-level structure, with manufacturing located on the top floor, offices and laboratories on the bottom floor, and a 10-foot-high utilities corridor sandwiched in between.

This "upstairs basement," as it became known, consisted of a series of concrete trusses, called tetrapods, that supported the top floor without impeding the flow of men and equipment below.

The entire structure was covered with thin concrete shells known as hyperbolic paraboloids, which had been developed in Mexico by architect Felix Candela. They were light, easy to cast, simple to erect, and surprisingly beautiful. Each shell spanned a 63-foot-square area, creating the kind of large flexible open spaces necessary for manufacturing.

As important as these technological breakthroughs is the humane way in which the entire structure was planned. By locating workers, scientists, and bosses in the same building, separated only by the service corridor, Ford and Colley created opportunities for collegial exchange among groups that otherwise seldom met. They even provided the settings—a series of open interior courtyards planted with native trees and enhanced with ceramic wall reliefs by Tom Stell.

Ford made crafts an essential part of his designs, as did Greene and Greene and Frank Lloyd Wright. Their presence helps distinguish the Semiconductor Building from conventional factories. It is as compelling today as it was twenty-five years ago, a model union of form and function and an even rarer marriage of humanism and high technology.

Dream houses: Rediscovering Hal Thomson's legacy of architectural eclecticism

JANUARY 25, 1988

While Dillon's personal tastes ran to the modern, in his columns he did elaborate on the talents and skills of Beaux-Arts, moderne, and eclectic architects from the late nineteenth and early twentieth centuries. He took pains to distinguish their accomplished inter-pretations of historical ornamental detail from the more shallow and copyist impulses of contemporary architects. This can be a dif-ficult distinction to make, but Dillon's discussion of Hal Thomson and, later Lang & Witchell, specifically distinguishes turn-of-the-century eclecticism from postmodern drudgery.

Hal Thomson traveled widely in Europe at the turn of the century and, judging from his houses, he never met a facade he didn't like. His town mansions in Dallas and Austin are a gazetteer of continental forms and styles, including Tudor, Georgian, neoclassical, Italianate, and Spanish. There's even a French farmhouse on Mercedes, complete with picturesque outbuildings.

Thomson was born in Austin in 1882 and set up practice in Dallas in 1908, first under his own name, later as Thomson & Swaine. Although he remained active into the 1950s, his best work dates from the teens and '20s, the Gatsby era, when every ambitious American city was trying to enhance the local vernacular with a veneer of cosmopolitan elegance.

He was a typical eclectic, who reacted to the perceived ugliness of the new city by turning to the architecture of the past and adapting it, with personal flourishes, to modern needs.

Like many of his contemporaries, Thomson specialized in housing for the overprivileged, many of whom belonged to his own social set. The Aldredge house at 5500 Swiss was designed in 1915 for Dallas banker and civic leader George Aldredge. Just down the street, at 5314 Swiss, is a gleaming confection of Georgian, neoclassical, and Italianate elements designed for John Sealy, the first president of Magnolia Petroleum Co. The intersection of Gillon and Drexel in Highland Park is a miniature Thomson enclave, featuring several excellent quasi-Mediterranean houses designed for members of the town's business and political establishment.

Not long ago, work such as Thomson's was routinely dismissed as simple-minded nostalgia served up by copycat architects with no ideas of their own. Now, of course, pediments, arches, and capitals are not only fashionable again but also coveted as icons of sophistication.

In such altered circumstances, Thomson becomes more contemporary than perhaps we realized. Compared with the current perpetrators of so-called traditional architecture—pick a block, any block, you can't escape it—he might even be considered a model.

But there are reasons other than shifting fashion to examine Thomson's work more closely.

He was trained in the Beaux-Arts tradition and consequently had an exhaustive introduction to the architectural sources from which he cribbed. He saw through the facade to the plan within so that, even though his houses are typically collages of historical elements, they transcend mere mimicry to express appropriate scale, proportion, and massing.

The Aldredge house is a massive rectangular volume set on a broad lawn, with two balancing wings, large end chimneys, and an assortment of colonnades, pediments, and medallions across the façade (fig. 6.5).

There is no point in trying to classify the style; it is a hybrid of a half-dozen sources assembled in an orderly yet individual manner. Thomson knew how to work within architectural conventions without being hobbled by them. And anyone who thinks that is easy should look at the neo-Georgian hodgepodges being thrown up in the Park Cities. Any similarity between copy and original is purely accidental.

6.5. *The Aldredge house, one of Swiss Avenue's finest homes, designed by the prolific and eclectic Hal Thomson. Photograph courtesy of Steve Clicque, as published in Virginia McAlester's* A Field Guide to American Houses.

Diagonally across the street from the Aldredge house, at 5439 Swiss, is a more sprawling horizontal mansion that integrates a scattering of Georgian details with arches and colonnades more characteristic of Mediterranean villas. The facade is a striking combination of brick, stone, and wood, as assertive as the Aldredge house is sober and decorous. Large projecting wings with open galleries balance the central portion of the house. Above are sleeping porches, a popular Southern feature found on most of Thomson's houses.

In adapting traditional styles, he acknowledged harsh realities of the Texas climate. His houses are well sited to catch the prevailing breezes, and even some of the largest are only one room deep to increase cross ventilation. For the same reason, casement windows and French doors are standard.

The craftsmanship of Thomson's houses stands out, even for a period that routinely integrated architecture and the other arts.

His interiors are predictably spacious and formal, designed as settings for grand social events more than intimate family gatherings. (The Aldredge house, now owned by the Dallas County Medical Society Auxiliary, was used in the pilot for *Dallas*, proving that it is as appealing to the nouveau riche as to old money.) Most are organized around a tall central hallway, decorated with pilasters and other Classical features, with a broad staircase sweeping up to the second floor.

Living and dining rooms are typically finished in dark, bankerish paneling, which is made less lugubrious by the use of white ornamental plaster, ornate fireplaces, and deep, intricate wood carving around doors and windows.

Surrounding the formal central spaces Thomson frequently placed tall-ceilinged garden rooms and galleries that bring light into the house while drawing interior spaces out into the landscape.

The current revival of interest in historical architecture, whether fad or prelude to the future, has shifted attention from architecture as response to purely functional needs—which in part it must always be—to architecture as the expression of dreams and fantasies.

To be Georgian or Classical or French was not the point for Thomson or most thoughtful eclectic architects. Rather, it was to create houses that were comfortable and inviting, using anything and everything that served the purpose.

One doesn't have to accept all the premises to recognize the appeal of such an approach, or in Thomson's case, to enjoy the results.

Young guns: A new generation of architects is redrawing the Texas landscape

JUNE 23, 1991

In this take on contemporary Texas architecture, Dillon uses the varied landscapes of the Gulf Coast, the Hill Country, and the North Texas prairie to draw connections among Texas architects.

The word "Texas" brims with instant associations: big, brash, rich, expansive, folksy—the adjectives roll on and on. But no comparable associations surface for "Texas architecture." Some people may think of the compact limestone buildings of the Hill Country. Galveston calls to mind white clapboard cottages with high front porches, shuttered against the sea. The Valley is a province of adobe and bleached wood. Yet no single architectural image fits the entire state, the way it does in Virginia or Vermont.

Texas is bigger than those places, and scale is obviously one reason for its architectural diversity. The Piney Woods are to the Big Bend as Sweden is to Bahrain. Nor is there any longer a common architectural culture that serves as a unifying factor. Twenty years ago, O'Neil Ford and William Caudill presided over Texas design like Old Testament prophets, haranguing their colleagues about scale and materials and regional design imperatives—although, it should be noted, without achieving consensus.

Within a few decades, Texas has gone from a predominantly rural state to one of the most urban regions of the country. Three of the ten largest cities in America are here. The courthouse square has given way to the shopping mall, and connections to the past have become more tenuous. Texas architects now work anywhere in the country, even outside the country. For many of them, common ground has come to mean membership in the same professional organizations or subscriptions to the same design magazines.

Younger Texas architects—those thirty- to forty-something—are taking a broad range of design approaches, from pristine modernism to rugged, industrial-strength urbanism and poetic evocations of historic Texas architecture. There is no dominant style or widespread concern for orthodoxy, a condition that is generating vigorous work by small firms.

KEEPING THE PEACE

Houston architect Carlos Jiménez works in a clean, spare studio, attached to his equally spare house with an intense blue facade and an almost monastic interior. He is a private person who prefers to work intensely on a few projects rather than turn over control to someone else. Calm and repose are themes and goals of his work—whether in a house or an industrial building. "I try to create contemplative spaces," he says. "I'm never happier than when I am sitting quietly in my house reading, or just looking out the window. If that is important to me, it may be important to others as well." Born in Costa Rica in 1959, Mr. Jiménez arrived in Houston in the late 1970s and stayed on, receiving an architecture degree from the University of Houston in 1981. Where others are fascinated by the city's paradoxes and wild juxtapositions of scale and mood, Mr. Jiménez is most intrigued by its lushness and its rich, filtered light. "When you have no mountains or ocean, and a lousy climate, you celebrate trees and light," he says candidly. The Beauchamp house in Houston, for example, is close to freeways and only ten minutes from downtown, yet it has the qualities of a sanctuary. Behind an intense blue wall—another homage to Luis Barragán and Ricardo Legorreta—the house opens up on three sides to embrace Buffalo Bayou. Mr. Jiménez describes it as "an exercise in how to bring light into a house," which could stand as a description of most of his projects.

The workshop for the Houston Fine Arts Press has many of the qualities of his residential work: simple geometric forms, inexpensive materials, and planes of primary color. From the street, it looks as serene as a chapel.

REASON AND ROMANCE

The work of David Lake and Ted Flato in San Antonio is as solid and foursquare as Carlos Jiménez's is private and ethereal. Both architects worked for Mr. Ford in the 1970s and early 1980s and absorbed their mentor's devotion to history, natural materials, and painstaking craftmanship. They consistently borrow the forms of Texas vernacular buildings, abstract them, and then enrich them with meticulous modern detailing.

Mr. Lake describes himself as the romantic of the firm and his partner as the rationalist. "I prefer eccentricity, and he doesn't," he says matter-of-factly. "My approach is to try to get a simple, straightforward design, then pull back and enrich it," replies Mr. Flato. "I have a great fear of doing something trendy that I won't like after ten years." Partners since 1985, they have produced an impressive body of work that includes houses, banks, and museum additions, mostly in Texas and New Mexico. The Frost Bank in Fair Oaks, Texas, near San Antonio, is a dense, craftsmanly building that with its thick limestone walls, deep windows, and silo-like roof recalls Texas pioneer architecture.

The firm's ranch houses in South Texas are unequivocally romantic evocations of earlier prototypes, combining simple materials and at times almost skeletal forms with sensitivity to the harsh realities of Texas weather and topography. "People go out into the country to be close to nature," says Mr. Lake, "so doing ranch houses is a great way to learn how to handle climate." But the Carraro house in Buda, between Austin and San Marcos, is the best recent example of their design intentions. The steel frame was salvaged from an abandoned cement plant in San Antonio. Out of it, the architects made three pavilions. The largest contains a small stone house with kitchen and living room, surrounded by a screened porch the size of the flight cage at the Dallas Zoo. The second pavilion, covered in corrugated metal, contains a study and master bedroom, while the third serves as a garage. The completed house is part Texas farm, part pristine modern abstraction—in short, a perfect marriage of reason and romance.

STARTING OVER

It is harder to classify the work of Dallas architect Gary Cunningham, mainly because he has made such an effort not to repeat himself. "For some architects, maintaining a stylistic thread in their work is very important," he explains. "I like to start over every time. I couldn't handle consistency. These days, we spend a lot of time avoiding architecture and trying instead to get the clients to talk in philosophical terms about what's important to them." The result is a remarkably diverse collection of projects that typically cuts against the grain of prevailing fashion. Mr. Cunningham's early office buildings were plain brick boxes, self-effacing, yet painstakingly detailed. He referred to them as "stupid," but in the context of the hyperkinetic, style-of-the-month '80s, they come across as highly intelligent. Several early houses were taut, abstract compositions of flat, intersecting planes of brick and stone that pay discreet homage to the German modernist master Mies van der Rohe. In North Dallas, this is not the way to get standing ovations. And in the "Power House" in Highland Park, completed two years ago, Mr. Cunningham pushed his tough, "take that" aesthetic to new levels of sophistication. In an abandoned 1920s electrical substation, he created a dazzling contemporary residence using steel, glass, and industrial staircases, even reinstalling the substation's original traveling crane and chain fall. It is an aggressive, pit bull kind of design that grabs your attention and won't let go. It is also, without question, the most provocative new house in Dallas, maybe in the Southwest.

As if to confirm his reputation as an architectural chameleon, Mr. Cunningham is designing a chapel for Cistercian monks at the University of Dallas, commemorating centuries of scholarship with traditional liturgical forms and walls made of 6,000-pound blocks of limestone.

WIDE-OPEN SPACES

After lengthy apprenticeships, made even longer by the recession, these architects are beginning to receive more prestigious public commissions. Mr. Jiménez is designing the new classroom and office building for the Houston Museum of Fine Arts. Mr. Cunningham is completing a new theater and conference center for Addison.

Lake/Flato recently finished the temporary exhibition gallery for the San Antonio Museum of Art. In enumerating the plusses of working in Texas, many young architects mention openness, not simply geographical but psychological. Even in bad times, they insist, Texas is more tolerant of invention—and artistic independence—than the coasts. The pressure of fashion, which classifies architects as either with it or out of it, is not as intense here as in New York or Los Angeles. "Nobody is looking over your shoulder here," says Houston architect Albert Pope. "You have the freedom to work without having to live up to other people's expectations about what is serious architecture." The attrition rate among Texas architects over the last five years has been high. Many were forced to move to keep working, and many have not returned. The fallout from that is still unclear.

More encouraging is that some of those who stayed are producing accomplished, at times exhilarating, architecture, as good as anything being done elsewhere. Even if times are still tough, the future of Texas architecture looks bright.

Art and Commerce: Dallas architects Lang & Witchell left a legacy of eclectic designs

JULY 5, 1992

Dillon's essay on Lang & Witchell was sparked by the discovery in 1992 that the original Dallas Cotton Exchange building, designed by the firm, was still intact inside a later addition. The discovery, made during the demolition process, sparked an urgent public campaign to find a way to save the building. Sadly, the campaign failed and the Cotton Exchange was demolished in 1994.

One of the nicer surprises surrounding the rescue of the Dallas Cotton Exchange was that the building had been designed by Lang & Witchell.

"Lang and who?" you might ask. But for the first half of this century, the question would have been impertinent. Lang & Witchell were the premier commercial architects in town, responsible for the Lone Star Gas Co. headquarters, Fair Park Music Hall, the Dallas Power & Light Building, the vast Sears, Roebuck warehouse and the Sanger Bros. department store at Main and Lamar (now the home of El Centro Community College). Much of the fledgling downtown skyline belonged to them, the way it now belongs to the Resolution Trust Corp.

Otto Lang and Frank Witchell were eclectics when the term still stood for something good. Trained in the classical Beaux-Arts tradition, they could draw like demons. They were also on sufficiently cozy terms with historical architecture to escape the cardboard cutout malady that afflicts so many contemporary postmodernists. Pick a style, any style—Classical, Spanish Colonial, Romanesque, Sullivanesque—and they could render it with grace and authority. They appreciated materials and craftsmanship, and even when a building was strictly utilitarian, such as a warehouse or market, they usually provided a stylistic edge that raised it above the ordinary.

Otto Lang was born in Freiburg, Germany, in 1864, and first saw Dallas on his wedding trip in 1888. He recognized it for what it was: an incipient boomtown in which a talented young architect could make a mark. He worked fifteen years as chief designer for the Texas and Pacific Railroad, then in 1905 teamed up with Frank Witchell to start a firm.

Mr. Witchell had been working for Sanguinet and Staats in Fort Worth, another accomplished commercial architecture firm responsible for, among others, the handsome Wilson Building at Main and Ervay.

By most accounts, Mr. Lang was the driving creative force, with Mr. Witchell superintending the work and keeping the growing office humming. Together they possessed the necessary talent and business savvy to rise quickly in a young city.

The firm's early work was often in the Chicago style—the skeletal, discreetly decorative architecture pioneered by H. H. Richardson and Louis Sullivan. Their Southwestern Life Building, now a parking lot at Main and Akard, was a superb example of the type, with its crisply articulated base, shaft, and top and its exfoliating ornament creeping along the cornice line. It possessed clarity and grace and for decades was one of Dallas's finest tall buildings.

The El Centro Community College block at Main and Lamar exhibits many of the same qualities in attenuated form. An ornate cornice was stripped off years ago, but the broad, Chicago-style windows and intricate terra-cotta trim on the facade remain to recall what a handsome commercial building this once was.

Lang & Witchell, rarely out of the mainstream, experimented with all the popular period styles, along with a few exotic ones. During their Spanish Colonial phase in the early 1920s, they designed the Auditorium at Fair Park (now the Music Hall), complete with mission bell towers capped with scrolls and friezes. Even leaden additions haven't diminished its appeal.

The Highland Park Town Hall, completed in 1923, contains equally fanciful examples of Spanish Colonial detailing, including a front door that might have been lifted whole from a church in Guadalajara.

But for sheer whimsy, nothing topped their Hippodrome Theater at Elm and Field Streets. With obelisks at the corners and splashes of neo-Egyptian detail in between, it was as far out on a stylistic limb as Lang & Witchell wanted to get. The Hippodrome's demolition [in 1960], together with those of the other downtown movie palaces, drained Dallas's shallow reservoir of fantasy almost dry.

Over the years, Lang & Witchell worked for many wealthy and influential clients, for whom they frequently designed several projects. They designed a gigantic warehouse for R. W. Higginbotham—it's the red brick hulk with the white suspenders at Lamar and Jackson, now known as Founders Square—and in 1913 a prairie-style house for the Higginbothams on Swiss Avenue. They did such a convincing copy that a subsequent owner told everyone the house had been designed by Frank Lloyd Wright.

But Lang & Witchell were clearly most comfortable with art deco, the racy, hard-edged style that became wildly popular in the late 1920s and had disappeared by the end of the next decade.

The Southwestern Bell Building at 308 S. Akard has a compact lobby, fitted with gleaming stainless steel trim and a vaulted ceiling with elaborate plaster inlays of vaguely heraldic intent.

The Lone Star Gas Co. headquarters on Harwood Street has more flair, particularly the stenciled sunburst ceiling and the engraved silver and black doors that look like Aubrey Beardsley drawings executed in metal.

But their deco gem is the Dallas Power & Light Building at 1506 Commerce. Into a prototypical wedding-cake skyscraper, Lang & Witchell poured all their decorative expertise (fig. 6.6). From the black marble facade with ornamental spandrels to the various elevator lobbies, sparkling with brass trim and ornamental light fixtures, it is a superior example of commercial art deco. And the leaded glass window over the entrance, showing electricity flowing to the city through the outstretched arms of some supercharged classical deity, is terrific period art.

Though rarely original—this was Dallas, after all, which wanted to look like the big Eastern cities, not stick its neck out—Lang & Witchell's work had range and integrity. They were knock-off artists rather than just two guys in the back shop cribbing details from history books.

6.6. *Lang & Witchell designed multiple skyscrapers in Dallas and commercial properties in Fort Worth and across the state—the Dallas Power & Light Building, completed in 1930 on Commerce Street downtown, is one of the best. Photograph by Jim Parsons.*

And even though theirs was mainly a commercial firm, they aimed higher than merely hitting the numbers on some developer's spreadsheet. Their work had texture, color, resonance, and sensory appeal. So much contemporary historical architecture is like bad painting, no deeper than the pigment. Lang & Witchell, though hardly profound, knew how to make the familiar hum, and sometimes sing.

Artists in residence: A handful of architects champion modern flair amid retro-house Dallas

JUNE 23, 2002

Dillon was an advocate for modern design and actively promoted contemporary architects whose work had the "clarity," "honesty," and "bite" of the modernist tradition. In this essay, he spotlights the work of six Dallas architects and argues that they should be getting commissions for more than houses, addressing a long-held concern of Dallas and Fort Worth practitioners.

Modernism has always been a guerrilla movement in Dallas, a hit-and-run attack on pretension and nostalgia carried out by contrarian architects in the name of honesty, economy, and the future. In the 1920s and '30s the leaders were David Williams and George Dahl. After the war came Howard Meyer, O'Neil Ford, and California émigré Harwell Hamilton Harris, followed by Bud Oglesby, James Pratt, Frank Welch, and a small supporting cast. Modernists didn't triumph here the way they did in Los Angeles or Chicago. There was no explosion of pristine white buildings with glass walls and flat roofs and no ornament. Yet Dallas modernists produced enough significant work to persuade younger, like-minded architects to stick around for the renaissance to come.

That moment, deferred for decades by pell-mell development and the historicist craze known as postmodernism, may finally be upon us. And not only because Renzo Piano, Norman Foster, Richard Meier, and Rem Koolhaas have all come to town. It's what's happening away from the celebrity spotlight, in places where good design rarely surfaces, that justifies the optimism.

DART, with its sleek trains and muscular stations, is a hit with the public, as is the raw yet engaging Mockingbird Station. Maverick developer Diane Cheatham has raised the standards for apartment and townhouse design—and lived to tell about it. Even a few good suburban office buildings have popped up, such as Lionel Morrison's elegantly controlled International Business Park in Carrollton.

Along with the buildings has come an elevated public awareness of design. Last fall's competitions for the Dallas Center for the Performing Arts and the arts magnet high school provided a crash course in European modernism, which the Dallas Architecture Forum supplemented with regular lectures by avant-American designers. A small but stimulating exhibition at the University of Texas at Dallas called *Five Dallas Modernists* gave a group of talented local architects the attention they deserve. Tours of mid-century modern houses sponsored by Preservation Dallas have sold out. There's even a fledgling "save the '50s" movement, and not a moment too soon.

And then there are all the new modern houses, far fewer than the bloated North Dallas specials—our own particular species of kudzu—but full of ideas and aspiration. Some recall the work of earlier Dallas modernists; others subtly transform tired Texas vernacular motifs into something fresh and provocative or give the widespread fascination with industrial materials and digital technology a local twist.

"Modernism only works in places where the future looks better than the past," insists University of Texas at Arlington professor Edward Baum, "and Dallas has generally felt that way. Compared to many American cities these days, it's a pretty lively place."

That's so in part because there is now a substantial body of sophisticated modern work, created by architects in their forties and fifties who have chosen to dig in and make their careers here. These include Gary Cunningham, Max Levy, Cliff Welch, Graham Greene, Joe McCall, and Ron Wommack. They like one another, support one another, and are growing a genuine architectural culture together.

CHAPEL HILL/CLIFF WELCH

Mr. Welch's clients wanted a modern house, but not an abstract white box. So he took them to see a vintage Howard Meyer house in Highland

Park, with its crab orchard stone walls, gently pitched roof, and large windows. They were hooked and eventually decided to build their own version on Chapel Hill, near White Rock Lake.

The house sits among large trees, with a creek on one side and a broad lawn on the other. The exterior consists of brick, glass, and the same mellow stone as the Meyer house, laid thick and tight to create a sense of mass and rootedness. Balconies and screened porches reach out into the landscape, protected by a broad sheltering roof that slides through the house like a great bird. The living and dining spaces are open and flowing, and thanks to the subtle interweaving of stone, brick, cherry, fir, and cork—a favorite Meyer material—the house has a warmth that defies all preconceptions about modernist sterility.

DEVONSHIRE/MAX LEVY

Mr. Levy is a romantic who believes that one of his architectural responsibilities is to "reframe the Dallas landscape." With his long slender house on Devonshire he has done precisely that. It is a natural house with a Texas accent, celebrating the magic and mysteries of sun, shadow, wind, and rain. A screened porch overlooks a quarry pond where one of the owners swam as a child. To either side are narrow Texas dogtrots through which cooling breezes flow on hot summer days. One of them contains a shallow cistern that collects rainwater from the roof and sends it coursing down a stone channel into the pond (fig. 6.7). The gutters are even suspended below the roof to dramatize the process.

The interiors of the house are elegant but spare: concrete floors, plain plaster walls, fir and mahogany woodwork, and a galvanized metal ceiling to suggest a Texas thunderstorm. "Architecture isn't just about some dazzling new look," Mr. Levy says. "It's about raising your sensitivity to commonplace things."

SHADYWOOD LANE/SVEND FRUIT

Mr. Fruit, of Bodron + Fruit, inherited a similarly lush site on Shady-wood Lane, except that his also contained a crumbling 1950s ranch house that obscured most of the natural features. So he demolished the original and replaced it with a fluid, glassy house of exceptional grace and refinement.

Transparency is the central theme, with everything revolving around views of trees, hills, and creeks. A single gallery runs the full

6.7. *Max Levy's house on a pond extends the Texas regionalist tradition into a new generation. Photograph courtesy Max Levy.*

length of the house, the main living and dining areas on the first floor and the bedrooms above. The ceilings are tall, the windows large, the materials quietly elegant (limestone walls, teak floors, mahogany trim), and the mood meditative, like a weekend in the Norwegian woods. If your goal in life was to read, listen to music, and contemplate nature, this would be the perfect place to do it.

ARMSTRONG AVENUE/DAN SHIPLEY

Mr. Shipley's house on Armstrong Avenue is a lively collage of materials and colors that reflects his own playful sensibility. His clients, a painter and her executive husband, wanted a modern house but not one that was pushy or self-conscious. So Mr. Shipley designed a simple two-story brick volume, with a hipped roof, and set it among large live oaks and cedar elms. The trees established the plan of the house and provide a kind of frame within which he manipulates shapes, textures, and decorative details.

From the street, the house looks as if it has been around for years—the stone wall in front could almost be a relic of an earlier habitation—while in back it breaks out into a series of wings and porches and odd projections that reflect the variety of family life. Here the house seems to be looking at itself instead of the street and the neighborhood.

WEST LAWTHER DRIVE/MARK DOMITEAUX

Mr. Domiteaux's industrial-strength house on West Lawther Drive started out, conceptually, as a romantic Mediterranean villa that would have fit right in with all the other grand period pieces around White Rock Lake. But after several fruitless revisions, he succeeded in turning his clients 180 degrees toward a denser Jiffy Lube modern house with spectacular views of the lake and plenty of architectural bite.

The main elements—living area, bedroom wing, and guesthouse—feature concrete block, steel siding, and rolled metal roofs. The centerpiece is the long vaulted living and dining room, with a kitchen at one end, a massive concrete fireplace at the other, and bursts of intense color in between. As with most modern houses, structure becomes decoration. Here that means textured concrete, exposed steel beams, and wood trusses and the occasional solitary column. There is some handsome architectural stained glass by Bert Scherbarth and a graceful, intimate staircase lined with tiny niches for the owners' collection of Japanese tea urns.

Modernism may still be a minority report in Dallas, but now there are enough committed architects and clients to make it more than an intriguing aberration. The people who are buying modern houses are typically young, well educated, well traveled, and curious about the next new thing. Some are wealthy, but many are not. The tenants of developer Ms. Cheatham, for example, are often artists, photographers, and software designers who appreciate the clarity and directness of modern design and wouldn't trade it for anything.

At the same time, modernism in Dallas is more conservative than on the East and West Coasts. Clients feel perfectly comfortable with modern interiors and furnishings, the stuff of the shelter magazines, yet balk at bolder structural expression that might be construed as brash or iconoclastic. Likewise, except for Mr. Cunningham and Mr. Shipley, there's little experimentation with new or unusual materials, a staple of older modernism. Buying a sink or shelving at Home Depot is not the same as exploring new uses for canvas or corrugated metal or cullet glass.

An obvious next step is for some of these talented Dallas modernists to get a shot at designing a school, library, museum, courthouse, or other important civic building. On this front, the past is assumed to be brighter than the future. In Europe, young architects get public work through juried competitions, which are both a way of life and an instrument of policy. Here it's a crapshoot in which most of the best designers don't win.

All of which makes the current modernist renaissance sound a bit provisional, which it is. Yet being on the cusp rather than on the cutting edge has its advantages. Relentless innovation can produce spectacular individual objects but lousy places to live. Appropriateness and continuity and a commitment to nudging things a bit further along each time can be more valuable, because in the end you can make a city out of them.

Dallas developer builds reputation for creativity: Cheatham's eclectic mix of modernity has trusted foundation

JUNE 23, 2002

Dillon recognized the power real estate developers held as patrons of architecture. In a state where developers like Gerald Hines, Trammell and Harlan Crow, and Ross Perot Jr. have an outsized impact on city building, Dillon paid special attention to the ideas and processes that informed their work. In this essay, he praises the smaller-scale work of developer Diane Cheatham, whom he holds up as a model of informed investment.

Diane Cheatham's houses don't stand on one leg or do cartwheels or romp about in period costumes. For the most part they nod politely to their neighbors and step back. Yet architects admire them, and sophisticated clients are lining up to buy them.

"No one buys my houses who doesn't like modern architecture. They're not for everybody."

Ms. Cheatham, fifty-two, says this with a mixture of pride, determination, and disbelief, as though she's not entirely sure how she got into the development business. Even though she has completed only two dozen projects—invisible by the standards of Centex or Trammell Crow—her reputation has soared.

Realtors refer to edgy projects as "the sort of thing Diane Cheatham might do," and most of the best young architects in Dallas compete to work for her: Gary Cunningham, Lionel Morrison, Graham Greene, Robert Meckfessel. In a city that stands resolutely behind the curve in residential design, she has been a one-woman avant-garde, trying things that other developers wouldn't attempt and pushing clients and architects to go along for the ride.

"I'm in love with all the latest building technologies, metals to plastics" is how she explains her enthusiasms.

That's not what you'd expect to hear from a former CPA who started out working for a Big Five accounting firm and then spent several years in Wichita, Kansas, doing tax returns and financial planning. Yet she was always more builder than bean counter. Her father and uncle were in the construction business in Shreveport, Louisiana, and she recalls spending many hours in their woodworking shop making fishing lures and go-carts. She even did cost estimates and floor plans for fun.

A PROJECT MANAGER

When she and her husband, Chuck, moved back to Dallas in the late 1970s, she decided to go into real estate, eventually working as project manager on the Belo Building and the Doubletree Inn at Campbell Centre at a time when women were considered Jonahs on a construction site. When she turned forty, she quit to build houses because "it was the only thing I really wanted to do."

She began by renovating duplexes in the Park Cities, living in one half, leasing the other, then selling and moving on to the next one. She admits she was winging it and credits Dallas architect Lionel Morrison with teaching her the difference between design and mere building.

After he refused to redecorate her sprawling builder special on Chevy Chase—"It gags me to think about it now," she says—they teamed up to renovate a contemporary townhouse on Travis Street by the late Bud Oglesby. It was the first of half a dozen collaborations over the next fifteen years.

"Her taste was totally undefined in the beginning," recalls Mr. Morrison, "but she was open and willing to let the architect be the architect. And there was this sense of adventure that you don't often find in Dallas."

By the standards of Los Angeles or Barcelona, Spain, Ms. Cheatham's houses would be considered mainstream modern. No radical forms or inscrutable theoretical pronouncements; just clean contemporary spaces with crisp detailing and a shrewd blend of pragmatism and experimentation. Inventive but not crazy, in other words.

Some of her experiments are virtually invisible. Her own townhouse on Travis, designed by Mr. Morrison, looks like a conventional stucco box except that it is built of insulated foam blocks filled with concrete and then stacked like Legos.

SHORT ON AESTHETICS

Although interiors are cool, quiet, and reassuringly solid, there is comparatively little aesthetic payoff on the street. This doesn't bother Ms. Cheatham, who appreciates things that are well-built and easy to maintain. "When I'm an old woman, I don't want to worry about peeling paint and crumbling foundations," she says.

A far bolder project is the concrete tilt-wall apartment building on a neighboring block that she did with architect Gary Cunningham. Although the technology has been around since the 1920s, it is used mainly for warehouses, where speed and economy are essential. The more doors and windows, the heavier and more expensive the panels because of all the steel bracing that must be added.

At the sight of a crane swinging the first 20-ton slab into place, she nearly passed out.

"I remember thinking that I got through the '80s without bankruptcy, and now I was risking everything I had, and everything my husband had, on this crazy project. If I'd been a little bit smarter, I wouldn't have built it. It was so out there that it could have ruined me," she says.

But it didn't. The apartments rented quickly, and profitably, and she and Mr. Cunningham went on to do two more housing projects on Cole Avenue, using more conventional construction methods but including several inventive bits, such as tapering concrete counters running the entire length of a wall and glass-block parking garages that glow like lanterns at night.

"With Diane, you get to do exciting work," notes Mr. Cunningham, "but you also earn your money. She's not interested in cranking out two hundred of the same thing. Every project is different, which makes it hard to hit the market and make a profit at the same time."

That's the consensus of others who work for Ms. Cheatham: great ideas, energy to burn, tough negotiator.

She explains the "tough negotiator" part as a necessary response to

6.8. *In the 1990s, developer Diane Cheatham built a reputation for high-quality, small-scale modernist residential development. She built on that success with the creation of the Urban Reserve, a multi-site, sustainable project developed with landscape architect Kevin Sloan and houses by a wide range of Dallas architects; the one shown here is by DSGN studio. Photograph courtesy Robert Meckfessel.*

tract builders who work with captive subcontractors and hire space planners instead of architects.

"When you work with architects, you're going to get more expensive details. No way around it. If you don't have molding, that wall had better be damn near perfect."

Countering her architectural bravado is an accountant's understanding of balance sheets and cash flow and how to wring the most out of every dollar in projects that range from $100,000 to $2 million. This gives her credibility with bankers, who typically aren't enamored of female developers or modern architecture.

"MORE RELAXED"

In the early days, they sometimes insisted that she take out a life insurance policy and make them the beneficiary so that if something happened to her, they could at least finish her "way out" houses. Things are more relaxed these days, she says.

Yet as impressive as her business savvy is her commitment to building in town, in redeveloping urban neighborhoods instead of suburban subdivisions. Her early projects are all clustered along Travis, Cole, and Buena Vista, within walking distance of one another and the booming Knox/Henderson neighborhood.

Lately, she's been branching out, with a small townhouse development in Oak Lawn in partnership with architect Edward Baum and a concrete duplex on Edgewater, which is being designed by Mr. Greene. "She pushes you all the time," says Mr. Greene. "She wants you to do architecture."

A passion for serious architecture and a willingness to take chances on its behalf set Ms. Cheatham apart from most Dallas developers. Although she enjoys being in the spotlight and can name every design award she has won, she's the first to admit that she's still a novice. She reads constantly, travels widely, and routinely hires architects who she thinks can teach her.

Right now she is working on a Mediterranean house in Greenway Parks with Mr. Meckfessel—a diversion rather than a change of heart, she insists—and is also shopping for a site on which to build a dozen or so modern houses designed by a dozen architects.

This is somewhat reminiscent of the housing expos that modernists were doing all over Europe in the 1920s and '30s. It's an experiment that Ms. Cheatham wouldn't mind repeating (fig. 6.8).

Stately grace: Meadows exhibit celebrates Mark Lemmon's landmarks

APRIL 11, 2005

The exhibit reviewed here resulted in a catalogue on Mark Lemmon that extended the conversation about Texas architecture and the development of a culture of competent if aesthetically conservative corporate architecture firms in Dallas. *

In our post-Bilbao world, in which high style and big statements are routinely confused with quality, it is instructive to examine the work of an architect for whom boldness mattered far less than civility, appropriateness, and quiet reassurance. Mark Lemmon was that kind of architect, and *Crafting Traditions*, a retrospective exhibition of his work at Southern Methodist University's Meadows Museum, demonstrates the power of those values.

In a career that began in 1920 and continued through the mid-'60s— he died in 1975—Mr. Lemmon designed more than one hundred major projects in Texas, including Woodrow Wilson High School, the Tower Petroleum Building on Elm Street, some twenty buildings at SMU, and a collection of meticulous historicist churches such as Highland Park Presbyterian and the Third Church of Christ, Scientist, in Oak Lawn.

---

* Richard Brettell and Willis Winters, *Crafting Tradition: The Architecture of Mark Lemmon* (Dallas: Southern Methodist University Press, 2005).

Most of the time he was a staunch traditionalist, inspired by historical precedents and a conviction that good architecture should be an extension of the past rather than a clean break with it, as modernists of the day were claiming.

Educated at the University of Texas and Massachusetts Institute of Technology, Mr. Lemmon spent eighteen months in France during World War I and returned to Europe every year thereafter to absorb historical architecture.

"He went back for renewal the way people today go to Outward Bound," says his son Mark, a Dallas plastic surgeon. "He felt that European architecture was more durable than the storefront stuff being done in America at the time, and he wanted to know as much about it as he could."

He mastered most of the traditional architectural languages, from Greek and Latin to Gothic Revival, Romanesque, and Georgian. His own house on Mockingbird Lane is a romantic Norman cottage, while the Tower Petroleum Building downtown is textbook art deco. He handled massing and proportion with a sureness that can't be faked and, like most of his contemporaries, could draw like a dervish.

Crafting Traditions is curated by Richard Brettell and shrewdly designed by David Gibson, with large color photographs by Carolyn Brown and an excellent catalogue by Willis Winters. It focuses appropriately on Mr. Lemmon's churches and schools, his most familiar and sophisticated designs.

His first important ecclesiastical commission, the 1924 Highland Park United Methodist Church, shows a deft command of Gothic forms and details, from the harmonious relationship of sanctuary and tower to the tracery around the arched windows and the delicate finials on the roof.

Highland Park Presbyterian, finished three years later, is even more accomplished. The basic design derives from a Pittsburgh church by Bertram Goodhue, a Beaux-Arts master, but the details are all Mark Lemmon, from the ornamental stonework to the vaulted sanctuary with an acoustical plaster ceiling that resembles wood and a tall, slender spire that recalls a fléche or arrow.

Mr. Lemmon's most memorable church, in part because initially it seems so implausible, is the Third Church of Christ, Scientist, on Oak Lawn Avenue. One of his few attempts at Romanesque Revival, it combines a weighty, rooted sanctuary and tower with delicate arches, small windows, and flecks of color in the masonry—in short, refined historical copying untainted by the academy.

Mr. Lemmon's schools—he was consulting architect to the Dallas Independent School District for nearly thirty years—are more conventional, though always skillful. The Alex W. Spence Junior High School, completed in 1940, is a pleasing exercise in art moderne, while the 1957 W. W. Samuell High School on Palisade Drive shows Mr. Lemmon's latent modern streak. In between came another dozen or so schools designed with conviction and a refreshing lack of ego.

As Mr. Winters points out in his catalogue essay, Mark Lemmon was not an innovator or a form giver. He had many styles, not one, and always put tradition and continuity ahead of self-expression. History was his guide and his camouflage.

7

AESTHETICS AND ARCHITECTURE

The roots of architectural criticism lie in aesthetics, the look and feel of a finished building. Montgomery Schuyler, one of the first writers who can truly be called a critic of architecture, saw himself as an arbiter of taste, someone who could educate the public about the merits of good design and the humiliations of bad. Perhaps even more importantly, Schuyler and other early American critics like Mariana Griswold Van Rensselaer saw their role as chastising architects for their mistakes and helping to build a new and confident American aesthetic culture. Through both these roles, critics wrote about buildings as examples of architectural art that could succeed or fail based on judgments of taste alone. Beauty in architecture was an end unto itself, evidence of growing cultural and intellectual maturity. Criticism could thus help usher in a "living, a progressive, a real architecture—the architecture of the future."*

---

*   Montgomery Schuyler, "The Point of View," in *American Architecture* (New York: Harper Brothers, 1892), 5. On Schuyler, see William Jordy, ed., *American Architecture and Other Writings* (New York: Atheneum, 1964), and on Van Rensselaer, see David Gebhard, ed., *Accents as Well as Broad Effects: Writings on Architecture, Landscape, and the Environment, 1876–1925* (Berkeley: University of California Press, 1996).

While the criticism of buildings forms the core of an architecture critic's trade, this group of essays comes last in this collection intentionally. Even as Dillon's criticism of buildings follows in the early traditions of aesthetic criticism, his assessments of buildings also formed in a broader context than the purely artistic. His sense of how individual buildings fit in to the development of the city as a whole and could contribute to Texas's growing cultural maturity is a recurring theme. How they served the purpose of their clients and the public, how they used scarce resources responsibly or rashly—all these broader questions of social and civic responsibility informed Dillon's interest in "good design." A building review was more than simply a thumbs-up or thumbs-down.

Dillon wrote at the height of postmodernism in the 1980s and his reviews reveal an ambivalence about the often cartoonish borrowing and pastiche that characterizes architecture of the period. His writing is particularly useful in reconstructing the spread of a kind of vernacular postmodernism in the work of commercial architecture firms and the vast market for suburban developments. His responses are reflective rather than reactionary, appreciating the thoughtful revisiting of historical precedent but rejecting insipid imitation.

The reviews included here contain a mix of the positive, negative, and all points in between. Reading Dillon's praise for pure material choices and intricate construction details as well as for more abstract architectural qualities like light and space makes his own taste for refined, minimalist aesthetics very clear. The Nasher Sculpture Center and the Modern Art Museum of Fort Worth received his most ebullient praise. But Dillon could be unexpectedly flexible in embracing more populist approaches—the postmodern brick of the Ballpark in Arlington, home of the Texas Rangers, had its own kind of appeal as well. Those catholic tastes were informed by Dillon's sense of whom he wrote for—not just for architects, but also for the people who used buildings everyday. The point of encouraging "good design" was not just to reinforce architects' professional preferences, but also to empower the public to develop its own informed voice.

Built fast: But they last. Avion Village was built as temporary wartime housing in 1941, but its sturdy, prefab walls are standing strong forty-four years later

JULY 28, 1985

Especially in the first few years he wrote for the Dallas Morning News, *Dillon visited the "greatest hits" of architecture in Texas and provided reviews of existing buildings. These reviews contributed to the development of a canon of Texas architecture and they also helped bring attention to remarkable places, like Grand Prairie's Avion Village, that remain largely off the radar for most Texans.*

Two thousand people gather on a flat dusty field in Grand Prairie, surrounded by circus tents, stacks of prefabricated wall and roof panels, and small mountains of gleaming bathroom fixtures. Mayors and judges are present, along with a jazz band and photographers from *Life* magazine.

In the middle of the field, decked out in blue or white shirts with numbers on their backs, like rodeo cowboys, stand one hundred construction workers.

At the sound of a starting gun, the workers break into two competing teams, and within minutes, they have hefted, hammered, and hoisted themselves into a frenzy. The sponsor of the competition, the Central Contracting Co. of Dallas, has promised to produce a finished house—with model family in place, hot meal on the table, and belle in the bathtub—in less than one hour.

Fifty-seven minutes and fifty-eight seconds later, the captain of the white team hoists his level in victory. All promises have been kept except for the hot meal, which was prepared at a nearby cafe. A Fuller Brush man even shows up in the model living room, peddling his latest dusters and whisk brooms.

The date is May 16, 1941. They worked faster then. Within three months, three hundred units had been completed, and Avion Village was on the map.

The project was funded by the Federal Works Agency (FWA) to provide emergency housing for defense workers at the nearby North American Aviation plant (now LTV Aerospace). The government expected the houses to last for five years, ten at the most. Every one is still standing, and dozens are occupied by their original tenants.

"Hammering on those old beams is like driving a nail into concrete," says A. J. Owens, a resident for thirty-two years. They built things better then.

Avion Village is the kind of unpretentious development that one could pass a dozen times a week without really noticing. Located on Belt Line Road, a few miles south of White Water and the Wax Museum of the Southwest, it is a vestige of another era—not only in the sturdy simplicity of its construction but also in the clear-headed practicality of much of its planning.

The principal architects—Richard Neutra of Los Angeles and David Williams and Roscoe DeWitt of Dallas—combined extraordinary economy with sophisticated architectural and planning ideas. The houses had sliding doors and windows to improve cross ventilation; adjoining houses were staggered to increase privacy; large open spaces were set aside for baseball, croquet, and other forms of communal recreation (fig. 7.1).

A typical two-bedroom Avion cottage cost $2,300 to build and originally rented for $20 to $25 a month, utilities included.

Avion Village was a direct response both to a national housing shortage and a critical lack of affordable housing close to burgeoning defense plants. The government purchased the 75-acre Avion Village site in 1940 for $22,000, and, through the efforts of Col. Lawrence Westbrook, a Texan and former head of the FWA, persuaded Neutra, Williams, and DeWitt to collaborate on its design.

Neutra, by that time one of the country's foremost modern architects, had previously designed a number of innovative community

7.1. *Richard Neutra and David Williams designed Avion Village in Grand Prairie as workers' housing sponsored by the Federal Works Agency. Its first residents were employees of the North American Aviation Company and it remains a mutually owned housing development today. Image courtesy Avion Village, as published in* Pencil Points *(November 1942).*

housing projects—including one for Westbrook in Jacksonville, Florida—and was eager to experiment with new prefabrication techniques.

Williams, then head of the National Youth Administration, was a talented advocate of Southwestern vernacular architecture, especially the architecture of the Hill Country and the Rio Grande Valley. Like Neutra, he had designed workers' housing projects and was fascinated by the possibilities offered by prefabrication. They made an ideal design team.

The two-story apartment buildings, built for only $9,000, were erected on concrete slab foundations, with flat roofs, brick end walls, and pine board and batten siding—nothing extraordinary but, given the tight budget, extremely functional. Williams's touch is visible mainly in the two-story gallery porches, a staple of Central Texas residential architecture, and in the careful siting of the buildings to take advantage of the prevailing southwest breezes. The apartments also were constructed on the perimeter of the development, giving it a firm outer edge that acted as a buffer for the one-story houses on the interior.

Those smaller houses—most containing a kitchen, living/dining room, and two bedrooms—were more clear-cut expressions of

Neutra's crisp modernism. Typical units had horizontal sliding windows and movable wall panels to promote cross ventilation. Walls and roofs were prefabricated. Some models were equipped with carports, which doubled as modest architectural links between units.

"It is fitting," Neutra told the *Dallas Morning News* at the time, "that the workers in the most advanced branch of modern technology should be housed in modern homes."

The master planning of Avion Village remains one of its most impressive features. The entire development takes the shape of a large teardrop, with a park or commons in the center and finger-like cul-de-sacs radiating outward toward the surrounding streets. The layout was not original—Williams had designed a similar central green for Greenway Parks in Dallas—yet it gave the sprawling project both a central focus and an atmosphere of rural spaciousness. Utilities were placed underground, and each house had its own crepe myrtle tree.

In the original plan, all houses faced the park, with the back door on the narrow cul-de-sacs. This arrangement ensured privacy as well as a modicum of safety for the many children who lived in the development. With the growing hegemony of the automobile, that arrangement was slowly reversed; now, the front door opens onto the street in the best Dallas fashion.

In the early years Avion Village was an island apart from Grand Prairie. It had its own grocery store and its own community recreation center, which was the scene of dances, birthday parties, and watermelon festivals. The central green, like those in older New England villages, was the setting for baseball games and public celebrations of various kinds. A few vegetable gardens crept into the public space, and an occasional horse or goat was allowed to graze there. All of this was dutifully recorded in the village newspaper, *Prop Wash*.

The defense housing crisis ended with the war in 1945. But the need for affordable worker housing did not. Avion Village remained 100 percent occupied, with the sons and daughters of charter members often taking over their parents' quarters.

"Good moral character and the ability to pay are what we've always been most concerned about," explains Owens, currently the manager of the residents' association.

In 1948, the federal government sold the project to the residents for $750,000—80 percent of its original investment of $920,095. Avion Village is now a mutual ownership corporation, the only defense housing

RT

project to survive in this form. The residents own the corporation, but the corporation owns the houses.

Residents are assessed monthly fees based on the size of their houses and the annual maintenance costs of the project. The highest rent, for a three-bedroom house, is $246 a month, including all utilities except gas. Rents for smaller units are proportionally lower.

If economy is one reason for the undiminished appeal of Avion Village (the waiting list currently numbers 168), it is far from the only one. The village is quiet, with many retirees, and the houses are generally in excellent condition. The original pine siding is only now being replaced on many units with aluminum siding—forty-four years after it was applied.

"The houses have stood up real well," says Haskell Dodd, who's lived in his since it was built. "It's an ideal place for old people because there's not a whole lot of trouble with (people) selling dope, and there aren't a lot of stairs to climb."

"It's still home to me," says Mrs. Jerry Burnett, another charter member. "It's not like it used to be, of course. Everybody used to work at the aircraft plant. We all had that in common. There are lots of different jobs now. But I wouldn't want to live anywhere else."

Owens, currently manager of the Avion Village Mutual Ownership Corporation, says that the village is having minor problems with vandalism and trespassing, and that it is trying to sell some unused parkland on the edge of the project to pay for a new water system. The fact that the village has any extra land at all is evidence of the foresight of the planners.

Architectural historians will probably not be flocking to Avion Village to measure the buildings and document the latest changes. But with virtually all such projects having long ago succumbed to the wrecking ball, they might give an approving nod to one that has survived and, in its own quiet way, continues to prosper.

Borrowing from the past: Industrial-age Crystal Palace influences computer-age Infomart

JANUARY 13, 1985

The Infomart is a landmark of North Texas's development as a tech and telecommunications hub. The region has also served as home for the headquarters of Texas Instruments in Richardson and the new corporate hubs for MCI and GTE, built during the 1980s. AT&T's corporate headquarters moved to downtown Dallas in 2008 and continues to expand its media and hi-tech footprint in the city.

Its inspiration is the Crystal Palace, designed by Joseph Paxton for the Great Exhibition of London in 1851. Paxton, a botanist turned architect, created a mammoth iron and glass greenhouse for displaying the technological marvels of the Industrial Revolution—and, not incidentally, the imperial might of Britain. It was the first large iron-frame structure in the world, the first to use prefabricated structural units, and among the first buildings with a glass curtain wall. The construction methods were so efficient and economical that the Crystal Palace soon became the prototype for countless exhibition halls of the nineteenth century, as well as many grand railway stations in Europe and the United States.

"The idea of the Infomart," says its architect, Martin Growald, "was to construct a big metal and glass greenhouse to celebrate the (computer) technology of the 1980s, the way Paxton celebrated the technology of the 1850s."

At a time when architects borrow freely from hundreds of historical sources—when a Chippendale highboy can inspire a skyscraper—such thinking is not only familiar but also almost orthodox.

Two earlier designs for the Infomart, not by Growald, show a squat, nearly windowless box similar to the existing Market Hall, and an equally ponderous, if less crudely detailed red brick version that appears to stretch all the way to downtown. Compared to these, this latest addition to the Dallas Market Center complex seems supple and sporty.

The original Crystal Palace was a vast three-tiered structure, more than 400 feet wide and nearly 1,850 feet long. It would have stretched the entire length of the Dallas Arts District, from the Dallas Museum of Art east to Routh Street.

It was dramatic, but its basic configuration would hardly have met the needs of a harried computer software salesman on a two-day buying trip. The Infomart is much blockier, 400 feet square, with 1.5 million square feet of showrooms and exhibition space on seven floors; that's nearly the volume of the new seventy-two-story InterFirst Plaza downtown. The bottom two floors are taken up mainly by exhibition halls, while the top floor contains two large lecture halls and dozens of meeting rooms. In between are some 225 showrooms for manufacturers of computer hardware and software, a universe of modems and microchips.

The Infomart represents the latest application of the lessons developer Trammell Crow learned from the Apparel Mart and the World Trade Center. His simple but revolutionary insight was that bringing buyers and sellers together under one roof would generate far more business with far less effort than having the parties scattered among separate buildings.

But while this concept makes perfect marketing sense, it often produces architecturally unmanageable buildings. Floors must be enormous, to reduce the time customers spend riding elevators, yet sufficiently regular to prevent chronic disorientation. The solution to both problems is usually a gigantic box with an overscaled central atrium that functions as the building's principal public space. As with convention centers, the architect's creative energies must then be expended trying to disguise the box.

7.2. *The Infomart was built in 1985 to house information technology systems and support the region's growing tech industry. Photograph by Kathryn Holliday.*

Growald's approach was to decorate the exterior of the building with lacy white cast-aluminum panels, bolted to the building's steel frame. They are replicas of Paxton's and the Infomart's most distinctive architectural feature (fig. 7.2). Without them, the building would be just another box.

Growald also copied the semi-circular vaults and numerous exterior structural details from the Crystal Palace, with the intention of making a broad, bulky building appear more vertical and animated. The effect is significantly undercut, however, by the use of silver reflective glass. During the day, we can't see what's happening inside this technological greenhouse. A building that should have been light and transparent, a festive celebration of computer wizardry, became solid and two-dimensional.

The central atrium may turn out to be the building's most successful feature, an intriguing fusion of nineteenth- and twentieth-century technologies. Again, many elements are copied directly from the Crystal Palace, including the large fountain on the ground floor, the ironwork on the balconies, even the pattern of the wood floor. Paxton's atrium contained enormous elm trees in which birds nested, to the dismay of the gentry parading below. There will be trees in the Infomart atrium, but no aviary.

Yet these nineteenth-century details are set against a background of gleaming, high-tech elevators and escalators, creating the kind of ironic juxtaposition of old and new that is missing on the exterior of the building. There the historical details are labored and self-conscious, without the witty detachment one would hope for; on the inside, they may come together to create a unique public space—Charlie Chaplin meets the computer age.

Contemporary and historical details are mingled on the adjacent parking garage as well. The small arches on the walls mimic the arches on the nearby Commerce Street viaduct. But this massive structure, with spaces for 1,250 cars, belongs underground rather than right on Oak Lawn Avenue. Given the Crow Company's commitment to making the surrounding area part of an inner-city greenbelt system, with parks and artificial lakes, the placement of the garage seems self-defeating.

Whatever the merits of the Infomart, everyone in Dallas seems to have an opinion about it. It displays frontier bravura, a reckless disregard for architectural protocol, that is more typical of Houston than Dallas. And in the architectural sculpture garden that is the Dallas Market Center, the Infomart is not really out of place. When one's neighbors are the hulking, windowless World Trade Center (jokingly referred to as "the box that the Infomart came in"); the elliptical Wyndham Hotel, floating on the horizon like a gigantic Bic lighter; and Loews Anatole Hotel, whose dormer windows and mansard roofs may be the largest in the world, fitting in is hardly the issue.

In such surroundings, the Infomart is a step up. On the other hand, it is finally less a piece of architecture than a huge, momentarily diverting stage set that may not wear well once the first few performances are over.

Instant history on the prairie: In drawing on the past, architects have achieved the hopelessly eclectic in the new land north of LBJ

JANUARY 19, 1986

"Instant history" provides a capsule overview of the postmodern exurban vernacular of the 1980s. Today, thirty years later, many of the developments Dillon describes here are now anchors for continued growth in the northern suburbs.

No one knows what the architectural future of Richardson, Plano, and Far North Dallas is going to be, but right now the emerging style is Spanish Georgian Early-Texas Romanesque, with heavy doses of Greek Revival and Roman Triumphal.

On land that was cotton fields and grazing land five years ago, a historical theme park has sprung up. All the above styles are on display—frequently on the same street, occasionally on the same building. This is not run-of-the-mill roadside history—the hamburger stand with the mansard roof or the gas station with the Palladian windows. This is mainstream corporate America design, the leading edge of the city's northerly business migration.

A crash course in instant history is available on Preston Road near Plano and along Campbell Road through Richardson. At the corner of Preston and Campbell, for example, sits a neo-Georgian complex known as The Summit at Preston Trails (Stephen S. McGinnis Architects). It looks like a North Dallas branch of SMU, but in fact it's a collection of office buildings. From a distance, The Summit has a certain charm. The basic shapes are adequately re-created, and the brick and stone work displays at least an elementary grasp of basic Georgian detailing. If one must do a Georgian office building on the Richardson prairie, this isn't a terrible example.

Until, that is, you take a peek at the buildings in back. There the illusion comes apart. Brick and stone give way to stucco and green shutters and cheap wood details. Behind the period front and the straight face is a stage set, like the back lot at Warner Bros. Except that Warner Bros. isn't so serious and self-conscious.

A mile or so farther north sits Georgetown, an office development that exhibits similar confusions on a far grander scale. Once again, the basic intention isn't so bad. Instead of scattering the buildings willy-nilly across the site, the architects (Wheeler & Stefoniak) chose to create an office village, placing the individual buildings around cobblestoned squares and along tapering alleys, illuminated by reproductions of old-fashioned street lamps. Making the office less like an office and more like a home is not a foolish concept.

But the execution is a parody of its historical sources. The individual buildings are all bloated versions of Georgian mansions, monotonously similar in proportions and details. The major stylistic variation seems to be the number of dormer windows. The buildings aren't grouped to create interesting exterior spaces; they are simply lined up in rows. Nor is there any evident understanding of how historic villages like Georgetown were formed. (Hint: Some buildings were made big and some small, some met the street, some were set back.) Georgetown is a vast design paradox—historical architecture that looks as though it came off the assembly line.

A few miles north of Georgetown is Preston Park Village (O'Brien, O'Brien & Callaway), a rambling, arcaded shopping center designed in some indecipherable combination of styles. It looks like a genteel livery stable with Romanesque, New England, and Colonial Williamsburg trimmings. This project isn't cheaply or shabbily executed. There's an abundance of brick, cast stone, and slate, even though the historical details stop at mid-roof, leaving the backside of the building bare. But architecturally it's bonkers, a muddle of historical details and allusions that doesn't evoke any period or style.

A major criticism of modern architecture was that it referred only to itself and to technology, not to things that most people already know.

We can't tell what many modern buildings are or how they should be used. While that criticism is largely true, a project like Preston Park Village hardly seems like the answer. It is so encrusted with historical messages that it's difficult to say what any of them are.

But what's wrong with having a little fun? "Architecture's not supposed to be fun," O'Neil Ford used to bellow whenever someone asked that question. "It's serious business." Ford could be a bit puritanical on that subject, however. Wit is fine and welcome, and ironically, that's what is so often missing in these supposedly whimsical designs. They are frequently solemn and literal-minded, downright polemical in their architectural intentions. Ironic detachment appears to be in short supply.

A small, otherwise innocuous strip shopping center on West Campbell Road (Urban Architecture) has been inflated into something resembling a branch of the Federal Reserve Bank. The facade consists of large, round columns with capitals (Doric perhaps?), which support a stair-stepped pediment with a frieze of glazed tile. That's a lot of historical baggage tacked onto a building that may eventually house a florist or a donut shop. It may just sink from sight under the weight of history.

But if excessive, at least the architectural language of this project is consistent. The same can't be said of Richardson Commons (Pierce, Goodwin, Alexander Architects) at the other end of Campbell Road, just east of Central Expressway. Here is a building that makes nonsense of the word "eclectic." The sloping metal roofs and awnings and the small balconies recall, sort of, the early Texas architecture of the Hill Country, Castroville maybe. The large, blank office windows, however, are textbook commercial modern, totally at odds with the rural and rustic implications of the sloping roofs. And at the front door is a potpourri of pseudo-classical elements. Such confusion is regularly excused in the name of visual interest; less forgivable is the disregard for scale, order, and proportion, the basics of sound design no matter what the period.

So what shall we make of all this instant history? On the positive side, the revival of interest in historical architecture has freed designers to explore new ideas and to work with new and richer materials. Color and ornament are back; the glass box is gone, which is not to say it won't be "rediscovered" next month and made into the trend of the future.

Yet even the best new modern buildings in the area, such as the Dallas Museum of Art and the new Frito-Lay headquarters in Plano, have become richer and more inviting because of the historical revival. Would Edward Larrabee Barnes have done a barrel vault ten years ago? Likely not.

So the issue clearly isn't whether to use history or ignore it. The search for a usable architectural past has been a national obsession since the early settlers saved up enough money to put classical pediments and columns around their front doors. The desire to make buildings more familiar and approachable by relating them visually to what we already know is entirely commendable.

And yet much of the historical architecture being perpetrated these days is having just the opposite effect. To start with, it's *CliffsNotes* history, bits and pieces got up quickly to fool the examiners. Cheap materials and cute shapes are thrown together in loose imitation of imperfectly understood originals.

In reaching for timelessness, architects are regularly coming up only with a different kind of trendiness. The simple-minded equation of old and good is as provincial and narrow as the "-ism" it replaced.

The Crescent: Dallas's newest, glitziest high-rise promises us a great building, but does it deliver the goods?

MARCH 30, 1986

Dillon appreciated much of Philip Johnson's architecture, especially his Kennedy Memorial in downtown Dallas and the Amon Carter in Fort Worth. But that did not mean that he spared the criticism for a project he did not like. Dillon's intense dislike for the postmodern historicism of the Crescent is made palatable by his acerbic humor.

The Crescent is contemporary architecture on an imperial scale, corporate America and Napoleon Bonaparte together on one site. In a single stroke, Dallas got three French Classical office towers, a 226-room hotel, and a retail pavilion with fifty shops and galleries, all sitting atop a 4,100-car parking garage that is a kind of vehicular Grand Canyon.

Whatever else one can say, the Crescent is not cheap or faint-hearted. It has the largest cut slate roof in the world; only the Empire State Building has more Indiana limestone. Along with LTV Center and the Allied Bank Tower, it epitomizes Dallas's new fascination with its skyline and with architecture as a municipal symbol (fig. 7.3).

The Crescent's greatest strength is its clear, rigorous plan, compared to which the conventional mixed-use development resembles the House that Jack Built. But between the big idea and the particular details lies enough hedging and backstepping to rob the Crescent of

7.3. *Philip Johnson, the Crescent, uptown Dallas, completed 1985. Photograph courtesy Crescent Real Estate.*

its clarity and conviction. It seems the product of several architectural visions, which often as not conflict rather than complement one another.

The grand vision is the clearest. Architects Philip Johnson and John Burgee, in association with Shepherd & Boyd, have placed the tallest buildings, the eighteen- and nineteen-story office towers, along the Pearl Street or downtown side of the project. The project then steps back and down to a three-story retail pavilion at the intersection of Maple and Cedar Springs. This arrangement gives the Crescent a dramatic skyline and freeway profile while respecting the low-rise residential character of adjacent Oak Lawn.

The project's three major components—retail, hotel, and office—are connected by a pedestrian spine that runs north to south, starting at

the arched entrance to the Stanley Korshak specialty store and terminating in the soaring lobby of the central office tower. What is now
the Korshak entrance originally was to be part of a public passageway
with shops on either side. ("You don't rent the front door," Johnson
said after learning of the change.)

But even the commercialized version makes an attractive prelude
to a walkway featuring an open-air rotunda with an elaborate, three-
tier fountain, an intimate courtyard with gardens and reflecting pools,
and a grand interior street known as Crescent Court Boulevard that
is only slightly narrower than New York's Park Avenue. The arrangement is both formal and flexible, keeping office workers out of the path
of shoppers and allowing hotel guests to remain blissfully unaware
of both.

Because the site lies midway between downtown and Park Cities,
part urban and part suburban, the architects attempted to keep a foot
in both worlds. The office towers and the grand interior street speak
the language of the city, though in a somewhat self-absorbed and in-
troverted manner. Everything else speaks the patois of loopland and
strip shopping centers, where the automobile rules.

Along Cedar Springs and Maple—potentially lively pedestrian
promenades—the Crescent shops are separated from the sidewalk
by several rows of parking. There is no edge, no sharp delineation of
street and building. Along Pearl Street, the main link to downtown,
the project moons the public with ramps, parking lots, loading docks,
and what is probably the world's first French Classical drive-in bank.
A grove of trees at the intersection of Pearl and McKinney is inad-
equate to screen this clutter from view. In working so hard to create a
private interior world at the Crescent, the architects have haphazardly
treated the edges where the project meets the rest of the city.

Inside is Johnson/Burgee's best design stroke: Crescent Court
Boulevard, a combination ceremonial boulevard and public square
that gives the project a symbolic center while connecting it to the
outside world. It is sufficiently grand—140 feet across—to mediate
the dramatic differences in scale between the office buildings and
the five-story hotel. Unfortunately, the office towers are so massive
and monolithic that little sun penetrates Crescent Court during the
winter months.

Worse, Crescent Court has been turned into a parking lot, in which
the fountain and trees—the urban grace notes—are overwhelmed by

limos and sports cars. Johnson/Burgee's master plan allows for some parking, but using every square foot for vehicles is obviously not what they had in mind. With 4,100 spaces underground, and an army of solicitous car parkers, why would anyone do this?

On the north side of the street, between the office towers and the retail pavilion, stands the Crescent Court Hotel, the most architecturally accomplished of the three sections. Here the project's Pharaonic budget—estimated at $300 million—has been used to good effect. The lobby, designed by Kalef Alaton of Los Angeles and Shepherd & Partners, has tall windows and ceilings and massive columns, yet exudes the kind of old-fashioned grandeur that makes guests feel more important than the space.

The Beau Nash restaurant and bar, also designed by Alaton, is an equally impressive mixture of tall, painted ceilings, massive mahogany columns, with a bar the size of a yacht in the center. These interiors are among the most knowing and sophisticated in Dallas, the equal of the Manhattan and European versions to which they clearly allude.

Elsewhere, however, confusion reigns. If God is in the details, as Mies van der Rohe reportedly once said, then the office towers are at best agnostic. They are certainly as eclectic as anything Johnson/Burgee has designed of late, mixing contemporary and period details in sometimes baffling ways. The mansard roofs, with their finials and frilly ridges, make pleasant if somewhat kitschy skyline decorations. At least they are designed to be seen against the sky, as François Mansart intended, instead of being pushed down over the brow of the building like oversized hats.

But the metal-and-glass bay windows in the center of each tower look like cheap afterthoughts, especially in combination with the elegant Indiana limestone. And the base of the building is a complete flop, too slight and unarticulated for such a massive facade. It's as though the weight of the towers has pressed it into the earth, leaving only a narrow band of polished granite showing. On a building that works so hard to evoke older architecture—in which the clear division of a building into base, shaft, and top was axiomatic—this is not a minor slip.

Spreading over, above, and around the Crescent, like a kind of architectural psoriasis, is the cast-aluminum grillwork. Whatever value it has as a decorative or scaling device is offset by its riotous proliferation. No surface or shape has been spared, with the retail pavilion getting the most heavy-handed treatment. Some shop fronts are virtually obscured by swirls of vines and clusters of grapes.

The architects and the developer, Rosewood Corporation, explain these details as a grander expression of early Texas architecture and point to precedents along the Texas Gulf Coast, such as Nicholas Clayton's Ashton Villa in Galveston. But most of these older structures are fewer than four stories tall, and their ironwork was manufactured on the East Coast and shipped in. It is about as indigenous as the mansard roof on the neighborhood McDonald's.

For the past decade, Johnson/Burgee has led the march away from the cool, unembellished architecture of the modern movement toward romantic buildings that evoke memories and tell stories. AT&T in New York, Transco Tower and RepublicBank Center in Houston, and PPG in Pittsburgh—to cite only the most familiar examples—are all plays on historic forms, adapted to the needs of today's corporate clients.

The Crescent is another link in that chain, a grand period piece with monumental spaces, rich materials, and a romantic flair. To protest that a pseudo-French Classical building with cast-aluminum tchotchkes is inappropriate for Dallas is to miss the point. On this front, the Crescent is almost quintessentially American, no quirkier than the old neoclassical Dallas City Hall or Highland Park Village. Style is a minor issue.

Compared to the Infomart, Dallas's latest architectural stage set, it is a model of resolve. Its historical intentions don't stop with the application of a few decorative panels to a conventional glass box. They are expressed in the plan and, to some extent, in the detailing.

But the Crescent fails in its attempt to reconcile the competing claims of city and suburb. Its grand plan is compromised by Dallas's obsession with the automobile and the strip shopping center. Intermittently brilliant and always entertaining, the Crescent ultimately cannot deliver on what it has promised.

A prism on the skyline: Allied Bank Tower adds a unique and changing shape

SEPTEMBER 28, 1986

While frustrated by much postmodern architecture of the 1980s, Dillon found antidotes to its excesses in late-modern projects like the Allied Bank Tower and its public plaza, Fountain Place.

Allied Bank Tower is to modern skycraper design what a laser-cut diamond is to an ornate brooch. It is the ultimate minimalist skyscraper, a virtuosic essay in the architecture of subtraction.

Preliminary plans and models suggested that it would be redundant and regressive, Dallas's entry in the "Let's Top Pennzoil Place" competition. The results prove otherwise. Allied Bank Tower, which opens October 8, is superior to Houston's breakthrough Pennzoil. If glass skyscraper design has further leaps to make, it is hard to imagine what they could be.

When Criswell Development Co. hired Henry Cobb of I. M. Pei & Partners—who had previously given Dallas Arco Tower and One Dallas Centre—it demanded a building that would dominate the downtown skyline yet also be welcoming on the street. Their model was the Eiffel Tower, which is a dramatic steel skeleton from afar but dissolves into a tranquil urban park close up.

Cobb had played the now-you-see-it-now-you-don't game ten years before on the John Hancock Tower in Boston, though in a different way. By using non-reflective glass and making window and frame virtually a single plane, he caused a sixty-story building to dematerialize on the skyline. Instead of a three-dimensional object, it became a gigantic mirror suspended above the city by invisible threads.

Along the street, unfortunately, this seemingly weightless form comes crashing into the sidewalk without relief, consoling pedestrians only with their own shimmering reflections. The transition from skyline sculpture to city building never came off.

Allied Bank Tower at Fountain Place (to use the full name) would be inconceivable without the Hancock Tower, even though it turns the technology of that building on its head. Here Cobb uses flatness and smoothness to turn a sixty-story building into a dramatic, three-dimensional object. A continuous surface of glass, even more subtle and restrained than the Hancock's, encases the building's steel skeleton like a sheet of blue-green Saran Wrap. The glass is folded around the frame, not cut and fit, to maintain the smoothness. The grid of green mullions carries the eye across the building's dramatic planes (fig. 7.4).

The result is a stunning prism that changes shape from different angles and at different times of day. From one side, it looks like a gigantic rocket ship about to lift off its pad; from another, it is a towering green gable or an intricate collage of slopes and planes. Surfaces advance and recede as the light or one's physical position changes. All of this animation makes it one of Dallas's few successful freeway buildings, a great "quick read" when viewed at sixty miles an hour. What pierces the sky is what's left after Cobb's deft whittling and not, as in LTV Center, what has been added on.

"I was determined to show that you could have a true skyscraper without all the figurative details of those in New York," says Cobb. "I didn't want a building with a hat on it. I'm just not interested in that kind of thing."

Allied Bank Tower rises to such a balletic point because it has an enormous base—192 feet square, the same as each of the World Trade Center towers in New York. Without some alteration of the scale of the base, Allied would have loomed even more menacingly over the street than the Hancock Tower.

Cobb, working closely with Chicago architect Harry Weese, chose to carve away a portion of the building's base to accommodate a plaza and water garden. Visitors walk beneath the legs of the building, as they might walk beneath the legs of the Eiffel Tower, to discover an oasis of water and trees.

7.4. *Pei, Cobb, Freed's Allied Bank Tower, with Dan Kiley's Fountain Place at its base, brought new development to the northwest end of downtown. Photograph by Carol Highsmith. The Lyda Hill Texas Collection of Photographs in Carol M. Highsmith's America Project, Library of Congress, Prints and Photographs Division.*

Designed by landscape architect Dan Kiley, the Allied Plaza is a cross between a pond and a European public park, with its angular walkways and soldierly rows of trees. Seventy percent of its surface is water, so that from some angles the building appears to float. Some of the water is dark and tranquil, while other sections are animated by bubblers, jets, and cascading waterfalls. In between stand hundreds of bald cypress trees planted in a regimental grid that complements the crisp geometry of the building.

Kiley had no interest in creating picturesque natural effects that provide only a green counterpoint to the architecture. His goal at Allied was to carry the landscaping through the building so that the plaza became, in effect, the true lobby.

This, unfortunately, did not come off. Kiley, Cobb, and Weese all wanted the lobby left spare and open to underscore the unity between building and plaza. Weese even proposed a "see-through" lobby with nothing below the sixth floor except a pair of escalators. But the developers insisted on a warmer and cozier place for their tenants and chose to dress it up with dark green marble, brass trim, and intricate patterns etched over the elevators.

This produced an extremely sophisticated result by conventional office building standards. The lobby nevertheless undercuts the more ambitious idea behind the entire project. It is a piece of stylish interior decoration rather than an element in the grand orchestration of building and landscape that makes Allied so unusual among contemporary skyscrapers.

The promotional brochures from Allied tout the intersection of Ross, Field, and Munger Streets as an exceptional site for an office building. From the point of view of freeway access, that may be true, but in other respects, it is really no-man's-land—blocks from the center of downtown, buffered by parking lots and drive-in banks and mediocre commercial buildings.

Ironically, these deficiencies are one reason the building works. If it were located a few blocks to the south or east, among well-established neighbors with a clear relationship to one another, it would be a disaster, disrupting the harmony of scale and materials that makes urban spaces work. It needs its own world, which is what it has got. Given the current economic slump, it's unlikely to have any competition for a few years.

Allied Bank Tower at Fountain Place was originally designed as two towers, the second (now on hold) identical to the first but turned 90 degrees. It seemed to some observers, this one included, that without the second tower the project would be at best a curiosity. It's now clear that while the second tower would create an intriguing dialogue of planes and angles, the first stands quite squarely, or prismatically, on its own.

Buildings conceived of as isolated objects in space are potential dangers; in inept hands, they can become a source of urban misery. Fortunately, Allied was in the hands of Cobb, Weese, and Kiley. The result is not simply another large object on the Dallas skyline, but a work of art.

The new skyline: Once it looked like Everytown, USA. Now Dallas has grown up

DECEMBER 13, 1987

In the previous essay, Dillon considers the Allied Tower as a single object—and in this follow-up piece, he considers it as a part of a changing, evolving skyline.

A tantalizing word, skyline, calling up images of a thin gray band far off in the distance, where earth and sky come together. That's the rural meaning of the term—the horizon, the place you never seem to get to when you drive across West Texas.

But a skyline is also the mark tall buildings make against the sky, a work of art rather than of nature. That's the urban meaning, the one we all know from postcards and T-shirts and the lead-in to the ten o'clock news. Cities have skylines, whereas towns have only views (fig. 7.5).

We love skylines for their drama and their assurances of progress and sophistication. Nothing boosts community pride like a tall building, which is why even the Abilenes and Big Springs of the world have their twenty-story hotels, in apparent defiance of all economic logic. They are expressions of hope as much as statements of fact.

Most of all, we love skylines because they make sense. The city in its maddening complexity always eludes us, whereas a skyline is the city as cut-out, a two-dimensional abstract of qualities that we rarely comprehend in their particularities: money, power, political ambition, all rendered in a sharp silhouette that implies a coherence that may

7.5. *The Dallas skyline changed dramatically during the building boom of the 1970s and 1980s. The singular forms of the mirrored Hyatt, Reunion Tower, First Republic Bank Plaza (now Bank of America), and the Allied Bank Tower redefined the city. Photograph by Carolyn Brown.*

not exist but that we need anyway. Skylines are real and ideal at once, an image of the city as we would like it to be.

In the shorthand of the imagination, New York City is its skyline, just as Paris can be condensed into the Eiffel Tower and Sacre-Coeur. Certain skylines are considered so precious—Washington's, for example—that they are protected by law, as though any major alteration would scramble the collective memory.

Dallas finally has a compelling skyline, far more compelling than the familiar opening shot from *Dallas*, in which the camera loops around the Hyatt Regency Hotel and Reunion Tower and zooms in on the high-rise offices of Ewing Oil Company. That was a skyline of money and raw power expressed in slick reflective glass.

The new skyline has architectural conviction as well, conveyed through a green glass prism and a rolltop tower with a gigantic skywindow punched through the middle. It is far more up-to-date than Kansas City's and is closing fast on Houston's.

At night, it surpasses both.

It has taken Dallas fifty years to reach these giddy heights. Over my desk hangs a photograph of the downtown skyline from the 1940s, with the Magnolia Building in the center, flanked by the Mercantile Bank Tower and the Adolphus Hotel. It is a compact and orderly image, like a child's drawing of a mountain, with the tallest buildings bunched up in the center and the warehouses and smaller commercial buildings fanning out toward the edges.

That's how most skylines used to look. Back then, ours was largely imported, from New York and St. Louis and Chicago. The distinctive local touches came in the fanciful rooftop decorations, of which the Magnolia Building's flying red horse was only the most conspicuous. The Davis Building had its classical temple, Mercantile its glowing neon spiral, and the Santa Fe Building its rounded ends, like the padded shoulders on a military uniform. More imagination went into the tops than into many of the buildings, yet it was this innocent State Fair exuberance that made the downtown skyline appealing, if not especially memorable.

That was the Dallas skyline until the mid-1950s, when the Republic National Bank Building appeared with its pulsating weather beacon, intended to be a replica of the Statue of Liberty until the board of directors apparently got cold feet. Already some of the sport was departing the downtown skyline—and most others in America, for that matter.

The new skyscrapers of the '50s and '60s were crewcut, trim, and square. They meant business. Often that's all they meant.

A few Dallas towers tried to break the mold. Southland Center got decked out in aquamarine tile, the International Style as filtered through Southern California. The First National Bank added white marble banding and fluorescent pinstripes for a bit of boardroom flash. But mostly this was the era of the good gray skyline, the skyline that said, "We're clean and upstanding. Your investments are in good hands."

In the mid-1970s, following decades of cautious anonymity, the downtown skyline began to look like more than a row of milk cartons. Reunion Tower arrived with its flash-dancing ball, and suddenly the western edge of town had a visual anchor. The skyline no longer dribbled off into blackness as it approached the Trinity River. It now had a boundary, a frame, and with it a potential for composition.

The Reunion ball showed up instantly on matchbooks, cocktail napkins, and other basic urban documents, irrefutable evidence that

Dallas had a new landmark. Even now, people aren't sure they're in Dallas unless the ball is in view. A photo of the downtown skyline without it is unfinished, like London without Big Ben.

By the early '80s, the area between Reunion and Central Expressway had started to fill in with a succession of notched, saw-toothed, nipped-and-tucked boxes that added no drama to the skyline but like foothills marked the transition to loftier peaks. Next came buildings with more distinctive shapes and more sophisticated architectural pedigrees, such as the three-volume San Jacinto Tower, which is packed with quotations from San Francisco's Embarcadero Center.

As competing skylines mushroomed in North Dallas and Las Colinas in the mid-'80s, downtown responded with pyramids and mansard roofs and monumental cross vaults. The most banal of the '70s skyscrapers was renamed Renaissance Tower and fitted with an intergalactic headdress that could be a launching pad for the sleek green rocket ship known as Allied Bank Tower. The thrusting LTV Center met the seductively rounded Texas Commerce Tower in a purposefully erotic embrace. Dallas went from crew-cut to R-rated in a single decade.

With the addition of the last three towers the skyline developed a rhythm, with distinctive sharps and flats. One could almost sing it, the way Indians sing mountains. Those towers without architectural presence submitted to cosmetic surgery in the form of demure white-light halos and brash green argon stripes.

The old night skyline was largely a grid of lights that revealed the internal structure of buildings. It was disciplined and logical. The new one reflects the quirky competitiveness of owners and developers as well.

But if a skyline were only bright lights and exotic shapes it would be mere fashion, no more durable than the shoulder pads on a Norma Kamali dress. It is because a skyline is also a collective symbol, an expression of community values, that it holds our attention.

The London skyline used to be dominated by church spires and government buildings, expressing the partnership of church and state that ruled the realm. Modern Hong Kong is a phalanx of technologically sophisticated towers, rising willfully out of the sea in defiance of difficult environmental conditions—just what one would expect of a financial center perched on the boundary between East and West.

Dallas has more of Hong Kong in its skyline than London. Except for the Old Red Courthouse, its civic buildings are nearly invisible, and among its churches only Guadalupe Cathedral has any claim to being a focal point.

We have cathedrals of commerce instead. All the tallest downtown buildings belong to banks. By drawing a line from the peak of Texas Commerce Tower to the peaks of Momentum Place, Allied Bank Tower, and First RepublicBank Plaza, one neatly maps the dominant values of the city.

The oil companies are next in prominence—Arco, Maxus (formerly Diamond Shamrock), Placid (ThanksGiving Tower)—followed by major hotels such as the Adolphus, the Sheraton, and the Hyatt. It's not a perfect map—Neiman Marcus isn't visible, for example—but it's close enough.

Dallas is a business and banking city, and its skyline says that. It is a city of competing entrepreneurs, and its skyline says that as well. The image is not egalitarian, with each segment of the community clearly represented, but hierarchic, with capital at the top.

The public realm is less clearly represented than the private. Dallas has not preserved views of its monuments and public buildings, as have Washington and Austin. Visitors cannot find City Hall without a map. It is barely visible even from freeways, perhaps our truest public spaces.

But as downtown has grown more dense and matted, its skyline has acquired a texture and complexity that it lacked before. In older photos, one view of downtown is pretty much like another: an uncluttered foreground, an eruption of buildings, then a falling off toward country at the edges. One could take it all in at a glance.

Now there are few places where this is possible. It has become a skyline of surprising juxtapositions, where old and new are laid upon one another as in a collage, where the very meanings of old and new are inverted. The newest towers, Texas Commerce and Momentum Place, take their stylistic cues from classic masonry skyscrapers of the '20s and '30s. Downtown is engaged in an animated architectural conversation between masonry and glass, past and future.

A decade of dazzle: At its ten-year mark, the Hyatt says "Dallas" like no other building

MAY 10, 1988

Dillon's review of Dallas's most recognizable skyline landmark mixes aesthetics with storytelling and appreciates the "good show." The Hyatt makes a prolonged appearance in the introductory credits to the Dallas *TV show and, like the Golden Gate for San Francisco or the Space Needle for Seattle, serves as a memorable stand-in for the city.*

One test of a landmark building is whether it's possible to imagine the landscape without it. In the case of the Hyatt Regency and Reunion Tower, the answer is no.

Ten years old this month, the Hyatt and its dancing ball have given Dallas a more memorable civic symbol than any city hall has come up with. To the driver on the freeway and the passenger in an airplane, the Hyatt epitomizes what Dallas is all about: style, motion, entertainment, the future.

Within months of its opening, it had made its way onto matchbooks, cocktail napkins, postcards, and airline posters, unimpeachable evidence that the city had found a self-portrait. Taller and better buildings have been erected since but none have captured the spirit of the place more convincingly.

The downtown skyline of the mid-1970s barely hinted at what it has become. It lacked form and drama; on the west it dribbled off into blackness. The Hyatt provided a visual anchor, an exclamation point that terminated the westward drift of buildings.

Standing by itself in a sea of space, it had to be bold, and is—a cluster of glass cubes and cones mounting into an image of the Emerald City of Oz (fig. 7.6). It also does what a glass building in the Southwest must do—capture and reflect the sky. It isn't just a flat, reflective mirror but a collection of sculpted and faceted forms that mold the light. At sunset the west facade becomes a gigantic television screen, bending the image of the landscape at the edges and by this distortion creating high visual drama.

Astonishing as it may seem now, the Hyatt wasn't supposed to be a glass building at all. Welton Becket and Associates of Los Angeles originally proposed a conservative concrete and glass structure, a squat version of One Main Place with balconies.

This design evolved into an aluminum and glass building, and only after months of discussion between the architects and the client, Woodbine Development Corporation, did the silvery glass version emerge.

The original master plan also called for six office towers, a vast water garden, and a long shopping arcade connecting the entire complex with Union Station. All of this has been on hold for years.

By the time the Hyatt Regency was built, architect John Portman and the Hyatt Corporation had parted company. Portman had become the king of hotel architects through the single-minded application of a few powerful ideas concerning the humanizing value of water and greenery and the theatrical importance of a soaring atrium. In a Portman lobby the space is on view—not the guests, as with older hotels. You are expected to be dazzled, even humbled by a succession of grandstanding moves. Tranquility and repose are not part of the package.

The Dallas Hyatt is better than many Portman clones, without avoiding entirely the usual clichés. The lobby features waterfalls and simulated pastoral niches, along with a soaring skylight supported by a massive steel truss, and chrome and glass elevators with tracer lights that zip up and down the wall like pieces in an electronic board game.

But it is also less of a mine shaft than many comparable spaces. The ceiling tapers as it rises, and there are pleasant bridges and terraces from which to view the passing scene.

7.6. *The Hyatt Regency and Reunion Tower, defining landmarks on the Dallas skyline, were finished in 1978 as part of a major redevelopment of the southwestern quadrant of downtown. The Lyda Hill Texas Collection of Photographs in Carol M. Highsmith's America Project, Library of Congress, Prints and Photographs Division.*

Grand as it is, the Hyatt's lobby always has taken second place to its exterior. If the facade is a television screen, Reunion Tower is the antenna; 560 feet tall, it beams its message for thirty miles around.

Like the hotel, it underwent a long evolution. Initially, the revolving restaurant sat atop the hotel like a flying saucer. Determining that a flying saucer was not the look it wanted, Woodbine pressed for a free-standing tower with a restaurant and bar.

Client and architect visited space needles in San Antonio, Seattle, and Toronto to determine the proper proportions. The first version was a cross between a golf tee and a clothespin, flat on top with a horizontal window slot and a triangular base containing apartments. Someone suggested crowning it with a statue of a Longhorn steer, but consensus broke down over whether the rear end should face Fort Worth or Houston.

The tower design faltered until Becket's design architect, Victor Chu, came across a book about Buckminster Fuller's geodesic domes. Inspiration hit. The golf tee with a Longhorn became a sphere with a lacy enclosure of lights. The architects built a 100-foot model of the new design on contractor Henry C. Beck's farm, to see if it sang. It did, and a civic symbol was born.

"What could be Dallas's Golden Gate Bridge—that was our mission," recalls Woodbine chairman John Scovell. "We were brash enough to think that we could provide a symbol for Dallas. Later I was watching the wrap-up to the (1980) Olympic Games, and in the concluding footage was an image of Reunion Tower. I said to my wife, 'We've achieved our goal.'"

I once accompanied Buckminster Fuller to the top of the ball, assuming that he'd be outraged to see his most famous invention, the essence of economical containment, used as decoration for an observation tower.

Bucky was unperturbed. Having designed geodesic domes for space stations and moon landings, what was 560 feet to him? He was more intrigued by the revolving bar and restaurant, for which the life of genius apparently had not prepared him. We sat through two complete revolutions as Bucky, smiling benignly on the city below, calculated the speed at which the restaurant would have to spin for the Manhattans and Chicken Divan to splatter against the windows.

The ball brings out the Bucky in many of us. It's a gigantic toy, an amusement park on a stick, a place to take relatives from out of town to give them the lay of the land. Every city needs a vantage point. Lacking mountains and promontories, Dallas makes do with the Hyatt and Reunion Tower. If it is not profound architecture, it is always a good show.

Painting the prairie: IBM's splashy new headquarters brightens a gray flannel image

OCTOBER 9, 1988

Architecture essays can sometimes be most powerful in reminding us what we have lost. The intense color that Dillon celebrates at the Solana campus in the far north suburbs of Fort Worth is now gone, replaced in 2015 with a toneless buff and beige in a developer-driven remodel that also jeopardizes the minimalist prairie landscape designed by Peter Walker.* Dillon's building review was originally accompanied by a second article, published the same day, that discusses the suburban development of Westlake as a new "satellite city" ("Dallas's Newest Satellite City Is Launched").

Westlake sounds like a resort or a country club, but until two years ago it was just a sleepy little farm community on the northern fringe of D/FW Airport. It had horse farms and hayfields, one convenience store, a Dairy Queen, and 253 residents.

Much of Westlake's rural character remains intact, but right in the middle of where the hay and the horses used to be sits IBM's new regional headquarters, straddling Highway 114 in northeast Tarrant County, with one foot in the neighboring metropolis of Southlake, population 3,602.

---

* Nicholas Sakelaris, "Once Bright and Bold, Solana is Now Down to Earth, with Plenty of Space for Lease," *Star-Telegram*, February 3, 2018.

Fifteen buildings have been completed so far, and at least another dozen will be finished by the turn of the century, when the workforce is expected to reach fifteen thousand. In addition to desks and parking spaces, employees will have shops and restaurants, a health club, hiking and jogging trails, and other blue chip benefits, all spread over nine hundred acres of scrub oaks and rolling prairie midway between Dallas and Fort Worth.

Corporate headquarters in rural settings are nothing new. American companies have been forsaking downtown problems for pastoral bliss for decades, using the change of scene as an occasion to refurbish the corporate image. Headquarters become "villages" and "campuses," calling up images of cloistered retreats safely beyond the reach of winos and gridlock.

Sometimes the move to utopia has produced distinguished architecture, such as the John Deere headquarters in Moline, Illinois, and the Connecticut General Life Insurance offices in Bloomfield, Connecticut. But overall the architectural quality of these "campuses" has been dismal. Either the buildings are bland boxes that pay no attention to their special settings, or they are so grandiose that they overwhelm the tiny communities around them. The new General Foods headquarters crunches the small town of Rye Brook, New York, like a potato chip.

IBM-Westlake is an exception to this pattern and, for a white-shirt, salute-when-you-speak corporation, a daring experiment.

The project's colorfulness has received the most attention, but an even bolder stroke was deciding to subordinate individual buildings to the site. The client, the developer (Maguire Thomas Partners), and the four architecture firms involved—Legorreta Arquitectos, Mitchell/Giurgola, Peter Walker/Martha Schwartz, and Barton Myers—worked together on a master plan that called for building on only 10 percent of the available land. The rest would be left in its natural condition, with 150 acres being planted with wildflowers and native grasses to restore the original prairie landscape.

The development at present consists of the Village Center and the Marketing and Technical Support Center, both designed by Legoretta, and the IBM complex by Mitchell/Giurgola. The landscaping and fountains were designed by Walker/Schwartz.

The firms agreed to keep all buildings below the tree line—roughly five stories—so that they are always seen against a background of woods and hills. They appear to be floating in the landscape, like villas or haciendas rather than conventional suburban offices (fig. 7.7).

To link these far-flung pieces, Walker/Schwartz created a network of lakes, streams, ponds, and groves that pull the site together without entirely remaking it. The landscaping has a logic and an integrity of its own that make the buildings better.

The architecture at IBM is forceful without being arrogant or overpowering. The boldest hand belongs to Ricardo Legorreta, who is best known for his Camino Real resort hotels in Cancun and Mexico City. Legorreta designed the IBM Marketing and Technical Center in Southlake, as well as the office buildings, shops, and hotel in the Village Center across the highway in Westlake.

His is an architecture of smooth, flat walls and square windows, of enclosed gardens and hot colors. Yellow, pink, and magenta pylons mark the entrance to the complex, rising out of the landscape like psychedelic obelisks. The sunscreens on the Marketing Center are magenta; the walls red, yellow, and brown; the barrel-vaulted reception area a deep, cool blue.

The residents of the nearby Trophy Club think his colors are outrageous, but Legorreta replies that they are just Mexican. Color is a starting point, not something added, he explains. "I do not say that I will make a wall and paint it red. I say I will make something red and it will be a wall."

Everything that Legorreta has done fits the place without being narrowly regional. His style is a highly personal synthesis of Mayan pyramids; Taos Pueblo; the iridescent houses and garden walls of his countryman, Luis Barragán; and Mexican vernacular buildings, all abstracted into something that is more an attitude than a look.

These qualities come through clearly in the nearly completed Village Center, a low, walled complex of shops, restaurants, and office buildings with the relaxed character of a Mexican town. It is designed to be an escape from the world of modems and VDTs, the little town at the edge of the army base.

The same ideas are present in more refined form in the National Marketing and Technical Support Center. This is where CEOs from around the country come to see and test IBM's latest products. It is a technological compound, as secure as the Johnson Space Center, that turns forcefully in on itself.

Legorreta's challenge was to make it more than a neurotic warren of

7.7. *Ricardo Legoretta and Peter Walker collaborated on the suburban corporate campus for IBM in Westlake, the far northern suburbs of Fort Worth. Image courtesy Peter Walker Partners.*

offices and showrooms. Working with Peter Walker/Martha Schwartz, he designed an extraordinary series of patios and courtyards, each different in style and mood, yet coming together to create almost a corporate Cancun.

The main entry courtyard, with its magenta walls, cedar trees, and misting fountain, provides a brilliant contrast to the cool, dark, barrel-vaulted lobby. Another garden, consisting of slender reflecting pools clearly inspired by Barragán, sits directly outside a row of windowless seminar rooms, an antidote for eyestrain and boring sales pitches. The patios and courtyards are connected by arcades and bright, wide corridors with wooden ceilings and framed views of the outside.

Compared to Legorreta's relaxed architecture, the buildings of Mitchell/Giurgola in the Westlake complex seem formal, classical almost, with everything plotted on a grid and crisp right angles everywhere. If Legorreta's model is the Mexican village, Mitchell/Giurgola's is the baroque town square.

The automobile entrance is like the entrance to a chateau, a grand boulevard lined with double rows of trees and framed by two long, low parking garages. It's impressive that IBM chose to put cars in garages instead of surface parking lots; it is ingenious that they then used these garages to form grand public spaces. They are part of the overall architectural plan, not utilitarian appendages hung off the back ends of office buildings. Every developer in North Dallas should study this design.

The basic design of the complex is low and compact so that it rests in the landscape. Instead of one monolith, Mitchell/Giurgola broke the building into six identical pieces, each five stories tall, with arcades at the base and white, semiclassical columns on the facade. But whereas both the Marketing Center and the Village Center look inward to gardens and fountains, these buildings look outward to the landscape. There are no offices on the perimeter, only wide corridors, so that everyone can have a view of the woods and prairie. Between the two rows of buildings is a long, symmetrical courtyard with trellises and reflecting pools.

Mitchell/Giurgola's buildings are covered in deep red stucco that ties them visually to Legorreta's Village Center and Marketing Center over the hill. The one conspicuous touch of traditional elegance is the employee dining hall, a granite and glass building with a grand stairway and a formal reflecting pool. In this remote, bucolic setting, lunch is the major social event of the day, the only chance to mingle. So Mitchell/Giurgola has given the dining hall the finish of a parliament building.

All corporate campuses are concoctions; the challenge to architects is to make them inviting places as well. Because they are far from the center of things, they inevitably suffer from isolation and homogeneity. The lively public realm that is a given in the city is often reduced to a cafeteria and a parking lot.

To compensate, IBM is providing restaurants and health clubs and exploring the possibility of extension courses and joint art programs with area museums. As the project develops, a trolley service will be added to carry office workers from one part of the project to another.

If IBM-Westlake hasn't solved all the problems of being an enclave, a world apart, it has done better than most in asking the right questions. The conventional office park is little more than a collection of discrete architectural objects, arranged like figurines on a vast coffee table. Each building is designed to be as conspicuous as possible and has almost nothing to do with its neighbors or its surroundings. Even the most farsighted projects, such as Las Colinas, have succumbed to this arbitrary planning. There are no *colinas* visible anymore at Las Colinas; the hills have disappeared behind or beneath buildings and with them most traces of the original landscape.

At IBM-Westlake, the buildings have a clear relationship to the roads and hills. There are edges and boundaries and a clear underlying logic to the planning—which is not that of the city, with its grid, but of great villas and haciendas, where house and stables and roads and paths are precisely, but not stiffly, related.

The real test for IBM-Westlake will come five or ten years down the road, when another generation of corporate tenants arrives.

Almost inevitably, a few of them will ignore the original plan and try to make their buildings ten stories tall, or fifteen, and turn them 45 degrees to the street so that they will stand out more from their surroundings. If they succeed, the significance of the scheme will be lost, as it was at Los Colinas.

The developer, Maguire Thomas, insists that they are prepared to hold out for tenants who understand the idea behind the development and will respect it. If they follow through on the pledge, IBM-Westlake will be not only a place to visit, but also one to emulate.

A sound beginning: The Meyerson— elitist enclave or municipal monument?

SEPTEMBER 17, 1989

Between 1985 and 1989, Dillon wrote a deeply researched series of articles about the Meyerson Symphony Center, reporting on cost overruns, construction problems, and issues with management. The review here is the culmination of those years of reporting and reflects that depth of knowledge. *

The Morton H. Meyerson Symphony Center has been open a week and the chorus of "I told you so's" is swelling. Those who insisted all along that the majesty of the hall would make up for the mistakes of its creation feel vindicated. Those who argued that the Meyerson would be just another elitist enclave believe that their fears have been realized.

Both sides have a share of the truth, but neither has a monopoly. And ultimately, the Meyerson is too complex architecturally and politically to be summed up by labels such as "world class" and "elitist." It is a grand building that cost too much, that satisfies certain civic aspirations and ignores others, that is powerful and problematical at the same time.

---

* See especially two lengthy stories, both published on page 1: "Where's the New Concert Hall? DSO Facility Falls Victim to Murphy's Law," *DMN*, October 28, 1984, and "The Meyerson Center: Saga of a Symphony Hall. Arts District Landmark Built on Big Dreams, Big Budget," parts 1 and 2, *DMN*, August 6, 1989.

Architecturally, the Meyerson is among I. M. Pei's most adventurous projects. Few seventy-two-year-old designers, with presidents for clients and closets full of professional honors, would have taken so many chances. In his first and only concert hall, Mr. Pei stretched himself like his conoid window and in the end achieved a kind of comfortable monumentality that has eluded him in many earlier buildings.

Compared to the Meyerson, the grand interior concourse of Dallas City Hall is stiff and static—all volume and no heart. The same could be said of the atrium of John F. Kennedy Library in Boston and even of the acclaimed lobby at the East Wing of the National Gallery in Washington, which for all its obvious drama has a touch of the classy shopping mall about it.

The Meyerson lobby, on the other hand, is an extremely fluid and energetic public space, and the secret is the curve, which wraps the rectangular concert room on three sides. Ordinarily an architect of squares, triangles, and crisp straight edges, this time Mr. Pei turned to sweeping staircases and gracefully arcing windows and balconies to create spaces that are as surprising as they are grand (fig. 7.8).

His geometry puts us in an exploratory mood by not revealing everything at once. As we wander through the lobby, we wonder what's around this corner or at the top of that stair. Levels change, lines dissolve. Concertgoers will doubtlessly arrive early just to hobnob and survey the passing scene from a balcony or staircase.

It's worth the $4 to park in the Arts District garage just to ascend the grand stairway to the lobby. Lights! Camera! Action! It's the most cinematic space in town.

The only dead spot is the southeast corner, behind the point where the garage staircase meets the main lobby. Even with two thousand people milling about, it looks deserted, cut off from entrances and the golden flow of patrons into the Eugene McDermott Concert Hall. The Dallas Mavericks could practice there and nobody would notice. To bring it to life, the area needs something as large and bold as the knockout Ellsworth Kelly painting that hangs on the northeast wall.

The lobby is a majestic overture to the intimate McDermott concert hall. Mr. Pei and associate Charles Young have carefully orchestrated the passage from one space to the other; limestone gives way to wood, asymmetry to regular geometry, hubbub to respectful silence.

The use of color and pattern in the concert hall also marks a new twist for Mr. Pei, who usually considers three shades of gray granite as

7.8. *The lobby of the Meyerson Symphony Center in 1990. Photograph by Thorney Lieberman.*

borderline gaudy. Here he has combined African makore wood, American cherry, brass, and onyx to create an interior that is both traditional and unlike any concert room in the world. Several critics have pointed out the influence of Josef Hoffmann and the Vienna Secessionists, particularly in the gridded panels on walls and balconies. But Frank Lloyd Wright's style is also evident behind the stage and on the underside of the canopy.

There are no bad seats in the McDermott Concert Hall, although the early consensus is that acoustically the orchestra level is inferior to the Grand Tier (that's symphonyese for the top balcony). Yet one disadvantage of sitting high up is the visual intrusion of the rigging for Russell Johnson's acoustical canopy. Another is having to crawl over twenty pairs of legs if you happen to have a seat in the middle of a row. Another aisle or two would have eliminated the problem.

But these are minor matters: Most of the pieces in McDermott Hall snap neatly together, like exquisite cabinet work. The room shows Mr. Pei at his refined best.

The same cannot be said of the Meyerson's exterior, an intricate Rubik's Cube of squares, rectangles, and half-circles. If inside Mr. Pei is essentially a classicist, outside he is a budding deconstructivist who breaks his building into its geometric parts for our examination.

Each side is different. The Woodall Rodgers facade is flat and unexpressive, as though Mr. Pei decided that here he couldn't tame Mr. Johnson's box and settled for a classy office building exterior.

On the west side, facing the Dallas Museum of Art, Mr. Pei heightened the architectural drama by installing a sweeping conoid (literally, cone-shaped) window that looks out on the downtown skyline. Close up, the conoid appears somewhat overwrought, like fabric that has been stretched too tight. But seen from a distance, and at night, the space gives off a warm, festive glow.

The remaining facades are combinations of advancing and receding planes, some flat and solid, others curved, notched, or indented. The result is more confusing than compelling—a case of trying too hard to offset the vast blankness of the rectangular concert chamber.

The main pedestrian entrance on Flora Street is especially disappointing, a reflection of money troubles and institutional priorities rather than Mr. Pei's original intention. His first scheme contained a *piano nobile*, a spacious upper floor that would have served as the entrance to the concert room, with ticket booths, boutiques, a music museum, and other public attractions located at street level. When the first budget crisis hit, the *piano nobile* was eliminated and all the public attractions relocated to the basement.

The Meyerson opening last weekend coincided with Montage, an annual street festival of the arts. The juxtaposition of jugglers and street musicians with tuxedoed and tiaraed couples raised hopes that the Arts District was finally becoming the cultural melting pot that its backers have been touting for years.

It was a lively urban scene, and also one that is unlikely to recur except on such special occasions. Dallas lost that kind of arts district ten years ago, when it ignored its consultants' recommendations to bank land in the area while it was still affordable.

So if an Arts District finally develops, it will be along the lines of upper Madison Avenue rather than a working, living artists' district like SoHo or the Left Bank—an area of office buildings, boutiques, galleries, fancy restaurants, a museum, and now a stunning new piece of civic architecture.

An old friend triumphs anew:
The Hall of State redo affirms the
power of great architecture

NOVEMBER 14, 1989

*Since this 1989 article, the Hall of State and Fair Park have re-
mained at the center of public discussion about the value of the
historic fairgrounds in the contemporary city. Many of the issues
discussed here are echoed in ongoing policy discussions.* *

In 1986, the National Park Service placed Fair Park on the National
Register of Historic Places and the Friends of Fair Park, a nonprofit
advocacy group, was born. With support from the Friends group, a
combination of public and private fund-raising allowed a three-year
restoration of the Hall of State, the centerpiece of Fair Park, transforming it into the home for the Dallas Historical Society. Today the
Hall of State awaits a second, much-needed restoration campaign.

---

* For the continuing discussion of Fair Park, see the variety of viewpoints
expressed in Mark Lamster, "What's Fair for Fair Park (and Dallas)," *DMN*,
June 14, 2014; Rex Curry, "What's the Proper Revitalization Mission for Park
and Recreation and the Fair Park Task Force?," *DMN*, January 22, 2015; Robert
Wilonsky, "Why It's Good that Two of Dallas's Most Powerful, Prominent Men
Are Tussling Over Fair Park," *DMN*, June 7, 2016; Peter Simek, "A Scathing Look
at Fair Park's History and Why Dallas Needs to Finally Fix the Park," *D Magazine*,
August 3, 2017, www.dmagazine.com/frontburner/2017/08/a-scathing-look-at
-fair-parks-history-and-why-dallas-needs-to-finally-fix-the-park.

When the Hall of State reopens Saturday, it will have a new research library, new archives, a refurbished auditorium, and staff offices where more than two adults can gather at one time. This two-year renovation project has been carried out thoughtfully—in the case of the new research library, stunningly—at a cost of $3.5 million, nearly three times the price of the original building.

More importantly, the rededication affirms the power of great civic architecture to elevate our spirit and our appreciation of where we live. The Hall of State was the centerpiece of the 1936 Texas Centennial Exposition at Fair Park, and it summed up better than any other building the paradoxes of that era.

Texas was simultaneously one of the fastest urbanizing states in America and a deeply provincial place clinging to its agrarian roots and a Judge Roy Bean sense of frontier bravado. The Hall of State speaks to both aspects. Its monumental classical facade, squared up and stripped down in a modern way, was as "international" and "world class" as anything going in the Depression year of 1936, while its elaborate, handcrafted interiors confirmed the vigor of the regional arts and crafts tradition with a grain of insight. For like a cathedral, the Hall of State reflects a broad popular consensus about Texas's values and aspirations. It celebrates land, labor, willpower, and native resourcefulness.

It does all this with pictures and stories that make sense to anyone who walks through its massive bronze doors. From Eugene Savage's murals in the Great Hall, executed in the robust proletarian style of Orozco and Rivera, to Joseph Renier's golden medallion in the Great Hall—an altarpiece, really—and the mosaics of armadillos and rattlesnakes in the floors, the building is a compendium of Texas life, presented in the most direct and accessible form.

The materials are mostly local and familiar—granite, marble, and limestone from Central Texas, timber from the Piney Woods—while the iconography is drawn from the experiences and aspirations of ordinary people.

Originally a nameless building on an esplanade, the Hall of State was christened by an appreciative public, which felt it said everything there was to say about Texas.

The Hall of State is also one of the few truly successful architect-artisan collaborations in the West. Moving from Allie Tenant's heroic Tejas Indian over the entrance to the meticulous detailing of the Great

7.9. *Allie Tenant's powerful sculpture of a Tejas Indian is the centerpiece of Donald Barthelme's 1936 Hall of State. Photograph by Carolyn Brown.*

Hall and the four regional rooms, visitors are enveloped in sensory details executed by accomplished artists and craftsmen (fig. 7.9).

Lynn Ford, artisan brother of the architect O'Neil Ford, carved figures for the North Texas room, while Tom Lea painted murals for the West Texas room and Dallas artist Olin Travis did the same for the East Texas room. Not every artist came from Texas—a fact that ignited the provincial wrath of some Dallas painters—but they were all of one mind about the significance of the task in front of them.

The so-called collaborations of today typically involve one architect and maybe one or two artists, who are called in at the eleventh hour to dress up a forlorn space. The spirit of the Hall of State is closer to Renaissance Florence, where group efforts were taken for granted.

Could we possibly achieve a similar consensus in Texas in 1989? Not likely. We can't even agree on a motto for a license plate. Consequently, much new civic architecture is little more than empty posturing about space and volume instead of an affirmation of communal life. We tend to identify civic buildings by their architects rather than by their constituents. I. M. Pei's city hall or Edward Larrabee Barnes's museum of art.

Few Texans know who designed the Hall of State—it was Donald Barthelme of Houston, assisted by ten other architects—yet fifty-three years after it opened it continues to stir us. It is a building of exceptional individual pieces held together by a powerful central idea—an exemplary period piece that reminds us what public design used to be, and what much contemporary civic architecture is not.

A way of life set in stone: Cistercian Abbey's church evokes history

MAY 29, 1992

Father Denis Farkasfalzy welcomes visitors to the Cistercian Abbey by asking if they'd like to see the "medieval part" first. He's referring to the new abbey church, a mass of rugged limestone blocks with the rooted character of an ancient peasant church.

The Cistercian monks came to Irving from Hungary in the 1950s, so the Old World associations are hardly accidental. Yet to construct a solid stone chapel in an era of cheap stone veneer takes both courage and great technical sophistication.

Architect Gary Cunningham, a 1972 graduate of Cistercian Preparatory School, had initially designed a simple fieldstone church for the community of 26 monks and 315 students. But when a benefactor donated $300,000 toward the cost of limestone, he rethought his original design.

He and Father Denis, the abbot, made a quick trip to Europe last December, visiting a dozen medieval Cistercian churches in Italy, Austria, and Hungary. Their immediate purpose was to learn more about materials and scale, but what most impressed Mr. Cunningham was the durability of the order itself.

"The Cistercians have been around for nine hundred years," he says, "so it became clear that whatever we built had to last. The roof may give out after a hundred years, but the walls will remain."

The modern technology part included $100,000 saws with tungsten blades and diamond drill bits, and air bags inserted into the cracks to split the stone with surgical precision. Some 427 limestone blocks, averaging 5,000 pounds each, were cut from a Garden City, Texas, quarry and trucked to the site, where they were erected one by one by Metro Masonry of Dallas—a lackluster name for such skilled crafts-men. The stones are held in place by thick mortar and by their weight, without any steel reinforcement. The entire process took two months, about the time required for medieval masons to build one interior cor-ner support.

Set against a low hill, its copper roof hidden behind weathered stone parapets, the church already has some of the character of a romantic ruin. The natural irregularities in the color and texture of the stone ac-count for most of its decoration. Cream-colored blocks alternate with layers of weathered surface stones to create a banding effect typical of Romanesque churches. The rough surfaces and sharp angles function like bas-reliefs, casting dramatic shadows across the walls. (Just what students need to get them through long sermons.)

The exterior creates such a powerful impression of weightiness and strength that the lightness of the interior comes as a surprise (fig. 7.10). A pitched roof of polished fir beams floats above the sanctuary, forming a space of unexpected exuberance and grace. The gap between the roof and the walls is covered with glass tiles, through which light washes into the sanctuary below. Three narrow windows in both the east and west facades—one higher than the other two—capture the drama of sunrise and sunset.

This subtle trinitarian symbolism extends even to the dimensions of the blocks of stone, which measure 9 × 6 × 3 feet. All the traditional associations of enclosure, refuge, and security are expressed by the sanctuary. It's a great place to hide in a thunderstorm.

And yet the Cistercian abbey church is not a nostalgic period piece. The pitched roof is attached to the stone walls by steel beams and tensile cables. The side walls sit upon massive concrete columns that are finished in spare industrial style. And whenever possible, Mr. Cun-ningham has exposed the church's structure so there can be no doubt that it's a modern building.

Some of the juxtapositions of old and new work better than others, however. The fir roof is stunning, a burnished complement to the rough limestone. But the concrete columns seem cold and lumpish for their

7.10. *Gary Cunningham's austere design for the church for Cistercian Abbey and Preparatory School in Irving. Image courtesy Gary Cunningham.*

setting. While stone veneer would be unthinkable, some type of covering would have given them more presence. The pews and choir stalls are appropriately spare, and the altar is a slab of limestone balanced on a single column. But the light fixtures are small and insubstantial, like decorated coffee cans.

What sings is the space itself, in the rich, sure tones of a Gregorian chant. Unlike many new suburban churches, obsessed with flexibility instead of sacredness, the Cistercian church evokes nine hundred years of history, scholarship, and prayer. It has nothing to do with current liturgical fashion. It can't be turned into an auditorium or a dining hall at a moment's notice. It reaches back across time to recall a culture and a way of life and memorializes them in stone.

Score it a hit: The Ballpark in Arlington may not be a home run, but it's pleasing enough to drive in plenty of fans

APRIL 10, 1994

The Texas Rangers built their new stadium in Arlington using a controversial mix of public funding and eminent domain that condemned houses and displaced residents. Dillon's review of the resulting nostalgic design points to the fan experience as the most critical measure of its success.

Rising from the plains, The Ballpark in Arlington seems apparitional, like a floating fragment of the Renaissance. The corners evoke the bell tower at St. Mark's in Venice; the columns and patterned brickwork are faintly Moorish, while the soaring arches might be remnants of a Roman aqueduct.

Even the hill on which it sits has been made up to convey an image of monumentality and civic importance in a place where the nearest town is the frontier village at Six Flags. At first glance, the ballpark could be just another ride (fig. 7.11).

There's no rational justification for a period ballpark in Arlington, Texas, the epicenter of the new American landscape of freeways and strip shopping centers and amber waves of satellite dishes. If ever a place was made for bold, contemporary architecture, this is it.

Except that the Rangers' owners wanted a design that had "the feel and character of the old parks," and "the look of Texas." And they also had seen Oriole Park at Camden Yards in Baltimore, which has sent so

7.11. *The Ballpark in Arlington was one of a generation of "traditional" ballparks. Photograph by Carol Highsmith. The Lyda Hill Texas Collection of Photographs in Carol M. Highsmith's America Project, Library of Congress, Prints and Photographs Division.*

many owners into a nostalgic swoon that the Orioles could franchise the design and pay for all their free agents.

Given these sentiments, bold modern architecture was out of the question, and David Schwarz shrewdly sensed that when he entered the ballpark design competition in 1991.

"I knew that if I made some kind of object for the stadium I would have lost," he says. "I was more interested in winning the commission than in doing something experimental."

Mr. Schwarz, who strives to be contextual even when there's no context, placed the ballpark on an imaginary urban block, gave it a rusticated stone base, a brick facade, and wide sidewalks.

That premise aside, the building wrapping the ballpark is skillfully done. Mr. Schwarz understands materials and proportions and knows how to manipulate historical motifs. He also is capable of more than postmodern legerdemain, though he is capable of that, too. The arches, for example, are deliberately overscaled so that when fans finally see the field it will seem smaller and more intimate than it really is. He also designed a lofty concourse that he's occasionally compared to

Chartres (once you start talking this way, it's hard to know when to stop), but which turns out to be scaleless and static compared with the web of structural steel that supports the grandstand.

IN THE OLD STYLE

This is old-fashioned ballpark architecture—flat-flanged steel girders, painted deep green, with just a trace of decoration. The classic early parks were designed mostly by bridge engineers, eager to show off their materials and technical skills. It's good to see that tradition celebrated behind the stage-set facade. In general, The Ballpark in Arlington is most compelling when it is most direct and unembellished.

The question for fans is not just how the ballpark looks but also how it works. The public, after all, is footing $140 million of the project's $189 million bill, in what may be the last of the sweetheart deals.

And the answer is that it works pretty well, though not as well as the Rangers and civic boosters would have everyone believe. To play the ratings game for a moment, The Ballpark in Arlington is a notch below Camden Yards but miles ahead of the new Comiskey Park in Chicago. It is also generally better than Jacobs Field in Cleveland, though the two parks are so different conceptually that fans should see both.

The seating in the lower deck at Arlington is excellent—close to the field, with superb sight lines, including even the seats in deep left and right fields, which are marginal in most parks. The architects achieved this by rotating or "cranking" the lower seating bowl anywhere from 22 to 45 degrees, so that fans sitting down the foul lines can see home plate or first base without having to look around or through their neighbors. These seats are superior to their counterparts in Baltimore and Cleveland, where the bowl rotation is 20 degrees or less.

"Home Run Porch" in right field, the Rangers' "sans overhang" version of the Tiger Stadium landmark, is terrific on the lower level, where the combination of steel girders and metal roof captures the feel and sound of the old-time ballparks better than anywhere else. But the upper deck is another matter. For most fans here, plays in deep right and center are only a rumor, and nobody can see the scoreboard. Also, the presence of a restaurant, with window seating no less, is likely to make purists whoof.

REMOTE UPPER DECK

To this point, The Ballpark in Arlington would probably be the best of the new parks. But its vast upper deck, where most of the displaced bleacherites will end up, is ordinary at best, particularly when you move a few rows back from the rail. At this altitude, the term "intimate" takes on an Alice in Wonderland quality. For perspective, the first row in the upper deck at Camden Yards is approximately 152 feet from home plate, compared with 176 feet in Arlington. In Cleveland, the distance is about 169 feet, compared with 155 feet in the disparaged Municipal Stadium, where the Indians previously played.

No matter what owners claim, new parks never can be as intimate as the old ones because of the addition of luxury suites, which raise the height of the grandstand, and the general absence of interior columns, which block some views but also allow the upper deck to be drawn closer to the field. The classic example of the problem is Comiskey Park in Chicago, where the first row of the upper deck in the new park is farther from home plate than the last row of the upper deck in the demolished one. How's that for progress?

The Ballpark in Arlington has some columns, which makes the comparative remoteness of its upper deck even more puzzling. One possible explanation is that while the Rangers wanted the upper deck closer to the field, they didn't want it so close that it created large overhangs above the luxury suites.

Such suites are the new gold mine of baseball. The 120 suites at The Ballpark will generate at least $8.5 million annually for the Rangers, enough to keep slugger Juan Gonzalez smiling. Mr. Schwarz has inserted them discreetly, particularly the lower tier, which appears as a thin dark ribbon running between the foul poles.

Yet together with the club seats—where waiters stand at your elbow with food and drink—the suites create an impenetrable layer of privilege in the middle of the ballpark. A fan who inadvertently wanders onto the elite concourse is made to ride the escalator to the top of the park, then walk back down the ramps, a trip that can take fifteen minutes. That's bad service in any league.

One consolation is that the top of the park has a large plaza (perhaps we should say "belvedere") where fans can take a break, sip a beer, and enjoy the view. So what if it's only of the GM plant.

BYE-BYE, BLEACHERS

In the new baseball economics, bleacher seats are a liability. Too cheap, so out they go. Arlington Stadium contained some seventeen thousand bleacher seats, while The Ballpark has only fifteen hundred. The pattern is the same in other new parks. The new bleacher seats in Arlington are better than the old ones, lower and closer to the field, but their alleged equivalents in the upper deck for the most part are not.

After suites, the trickiest design problem in any ballpark is center field. It must provide a sense of enclosure, yet not be so dominant that it distracts hitters. Some parks solve the problem with a scoreboard. Kansas City uses dancing fountains. Baltimore and Cleveland rely on the downtown skyline.

The Rangers started out with what looked like giant baseball cards on sticks, then graduated to a four-story office building that contains the team offices as well as lease space and the Legends of the Game baseball museum. It's an improvement, though the building is not as transparent as it should be, and the lacy metal work is disturbingly reminiscent of Philip Johnson's pseudo-Texas froufrou on The Crescent complex.

Off the field, things are immeasurably better. The clubhouse has risen to Club Med standards, and the concession stands are more numerous (fifty-two—count 'em—fifty-two) and more varied. At times, the game seems more like an appetizer than the main course.

It will take a season or two to know how the field plays. Whether it favors hitters or pitchers. How balls carom off the walls. Where the breezes blow on a hot summer night. Yet one of the trademarks of the old ballparks was that they welcomed the public instead of daring it to enter. They were places rather than anonymous sites, and they fostered memories and tradition.

Though some of the tradition at The Ballpark in Arlington is laid on with a trowel, it is still an attractive and welcoming place. And already it is developing some character of its own. In the first exhibition game against the Mets, kids piled out of the bleachers to scoop up home run balls in the grassy center field backdrop. It was the kind of spontaneous event that old parks encouraged and that the cyclotrons and soup tureens built in the 1960s and 1970s nearly killed. Something to build on.

The Rachofsky residence is an artistic triumph: Meier's world-class design achieves his utopian ideal

NOVEMBER 10, 1996

There has always been something utopian about Richard Meier's houses. All those white panels and shimmering glass surfaces call up visions of perfection, of the way things ought to be. Elegant, rational, pristine—and just a bit eerie, as though they are not intended for human habitation.

Mr. Meier's new house for Dallas investor Howard Rachofsky expresses all of these qualities. The architect describes it as "an ideal, an investigation into all of the possibilities of house as a building type, without many of the usual compromises."

For "compromises" read children, in-laws, mud rooms, and basement workshops. Mr. Rachofsky, a bachelor and avid contemporary art collector, calls the house "a one-bedroom apartment over a public space."

Both are right.

The idealizing elements are immediately apparent from the street, where the form sits on the land like an elegant white box on a black table. Is it a house? A museum? An office building? The headquarters of a foundation?

The stark white facade with its ribbon window and slender supporting columns declares the house's pedigree to be early twentieth-century European modernism, Le Corbusier and the Villa Stein in particular. It is cubic and continental rather than linear and American.

Mr. Rachofsky commissioned Mr. Meier after seeing his High Museum of Art in Atlanta in the mid-1980s. A problematical setting for art, the museum nevertheless possesses the kind of luminosity, day and night, that Mr. Rachofsky was looking for.

It took another ten years to complete the house (there were several false starts), during which Mr. Rachofsky's art collection grew dramatically. He wasn't interested merely in owning art; he wanted to live with it—day by day, week by week—constantly moving pieces around in search of ever more surprising juxtapositions. For this, he needed a house that functioned as a gallery; Mr. Meier had been designing them for years.

The Rachofsky house makes no concessions to traditional ideas of welcome. There is no walk or front stoop. The front door is a discreetly pivoting white panel without handle or knob. No conventional hardware anywhere, for that matter. The entire house is an essay in flushness.

Directly inside the front door is a long gallery featuring paintings by Mark Rothko, Elizabeth Murray, Julian Schnabel, and others. The house is organized as a series of zones, running from public to private, formal to semiformal, solid to transparent.

The gallery is a kind of lobby, and, while conceptually intriguing, is too narrow for the art it contains. It's impossible to get back far enough to study the paintings.

But the procession through the gallery to the main staircase is magical. Having been confined, we are suddenly released into a landscape of magnolias and red oaks and dramatic Texas sky, as though we had entered a crystalline aerie in a nature preserve.

No contemporary architect captures the landscape better than Richard Meier. His houses are not frames for viewing nature; nor do they suck up to it with soft colors and materials. Instead, they reach out and appropriate it by means of staircases, projecting planes, and free-standing walls.

In the Rachofsky house, an axis runs from the driveway through the front door and the kitchen to an outdoor staircase and finally to the pool house, pulling house and site together like an architectural drawstring (fig. 7.12).

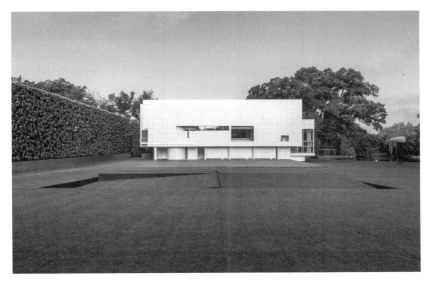

7.12. *Richard Meier, Rachofsky House. Photograph courtesy Rachofsky House.*

The architects also went to extraordinary lengths to protect the magnificent trees, including underground fans to aerate the soil. Mr. Meier even skewed his own grid—the ultimate sacrifice—in order to keep piers away from the roots.

But Mr. Meier has chosen to defy the Texas sun. The rear or west facade is virtually all glass, exposing the layers of space like a sectional diagram, but requiring special glass, mechanical sun shades and tons of air conditioning to keep from quick-frying the occupants.

The main staircase leads to the piece de resistance, the two-story living room. Twenty-three feet high, it is punctuated by dramatic cantilevered balconies, including Mr. Rachofsky's office on the third level that resembles the bridge on a battleship. Right full rudder!

In this one grand space Mr. Meier has concentrated the major themes of his architecture: light, abstraction, the play of solid and void, containment, and transparency. Unlike most of his contemporaries, who have changed their "isms" as often as their underwear, he has focused single-mindedly on a few central issues. The line from his early houses in the Hamptons to the Getty Art Center in Los Angeles is straight, narrow, and often deep.

Spatially, the Rachofsky living room is lyrical, its light varied and hypnotic, its engineering computer precise. Yet, as in the house as a whole, its relentless formality can become oppressive. We search in vain for a fireplace and an easy chair, or for a space where we can flop in a non-orthogonal heap. Even in the private third floor, where the art is edgy and confrontational, the spirit of cool control prevails.

"In this house I finally got to do exactly what I want," Mr. Rachofsky says triumphantly.

The Rachofsky house, like many of Mr. Meier's earlier houses, is a modern villa in which all the individual pieces—house, gallery, pool, landscaping—have been calibrated into an ensemble. It's the kind of commission that architects dream of—an enlightened client, total control, nothing left to chance.

"Howard made it clear that he wanted a total composition, not just a house," explains project architect Don Cox. "That meant that everything from the facade to the soap dishes had to be of a piece. It was the ideal situation."

The final piece of the composition, an art gallery along Preston Road, will be finished next year. In addition to providing a buffer for the house, the gallery will give Mr. Rachofsky the chance to share his collection, and his enthusiasms, with the public.

"I want to make contemporary art user-friendly," he explains. "You shouldn't have to go to a museum to see it. I want it to be part of daily experience."

This is an extraordinary civic gesture in a private city such as Dallas, where houses by celebrated architects are seen by appointment only, if at all. Mr. Rachofsky estimates that he will host nearly thirty benefit events over the next twelve months.

Similarly, Deedie and Rusty Rose have viewed their house in Highland Park, by Antoine Predock, as a public resource as well as a private domain. Dallas now has half a dozen contemporary houses of international distinction, as well as slightly earlier modernist jewels by Howard Meyer, O'Neil Ford, Bud Oglesby, and others. With its public realm largely bulldozed or brutalized, Dallas's architectural legacy may well be its exquisite private houses.*

---

* Public functions of the Rachofsky House have now been transferred to The Warehouse exhibition space in Preston Hollow.

Routine flight: By playing it safe on design, the new arena misses the chance to soar

JULY 30, 2001

For the Texas Rangers' home at the Ballpark in Arlington, Dillon mustered sympathy for the nostalgic quotations of historic ballpark architecture. But in the case of American Airlines Center, home to the Dallas Mavericks and Dallas Stars, he was less patient. A series of articles critiquing the development process, the selection of the site, and the choice of architect preceded this disappointed review. **

From the opening whistle, American Airlines Center has been touted not just as a place for basketball and hockey but also as a "civic building" where the community can come together. A laudable goal except that good civic buildings are more than public gathering places. In their forms and details they express a community's values and aspirations—how it sees itself and what it hopes to be.

I. M. Pei's thrusting Dallas City Hall provided an image of municipal confidence and stability in the grim aftermath of the Kennedy

---

* Dillon, "Arena Master Plan Lays Groundwork for Better Ideas—DART Rail Line, Power Plant Remain Major Sticking Points," *DMN*, October 9, 1998; "Future Arena Mostly Looks Backward—Revised Plan Remains Centered on Nostalgia," *DMN*, July 29, 1999.

7.13. *The American Airlines Center anchors the redevelopment of Victory Park, just northwest of downtown Dallas.*

assassination. Frank Gehry's swirling Guggenheim Museum in Bilbao, Spain, lifted the economic and cultural expectations of an entire region.

The $420 million American Airlines Center, which opened this weekend, sends less inspiring messages about Dallas: that it is more comfortable with the past than the present, that it is better to be big than bold (fig. 7.13).

Nostalgia without history is set design, and there is a lot of that in the new arena. It is a monumental period piece in a setting of freeways and railroad tracks and glittering steel-and-glass skyscrapers. Yet instead of engaging its immediate surroundings, it serves up a hybridized past that tells us where we've been—perhaps—instead of where we're going.

Architect David Schwarz shrugs off such criticism by saying that he is "a populist architect who designs buildings that people like." And in this case, he may be right. Fans probably will like the new arena—in part because it solves many of the problems of Reunion: too few bathrooms, not enough concession stands, an infinitely curving concourse that defeated anyone's navigational system, especially after a couple of beers.

The concourses in American Airlines Center are bright, airy, and logically organized, with rotundas at the corners, wide connecting hallways, and tall rounded windows that bring natural light in and offer views out. At the opening night Eagles concert Saturday, with twenty thousand bewildered fans milling about, foot traffic flowed smoothly, with bottlenecks and long bathroom lines confined to the top concourse.

The south lobby, facing downtown, features a mobile of American Airlines planes that looks like a gigantic mockup of a ten-year old boy's bedroom ceiling. The other lobbies are more restrained, with buff walls and silvery trim reminiscent of the suites at The Ballpark in Arlington and your local Marriott. Not the typical rough-and-ready arena décor but effective in its own way. Each lobby is crisscrossed with bridges and escalators that provide views of the passing parade as well as fleeting glimpses of the corporate aeries to which Joe Fan will not be admitted.

The new arena is the product of a 1998 design competition organized by the Stars and Mavericks, with the city as a complacent third party. Mr. Schwarz's design was the most readable and in many respects the most complete of the five submissions, though no match for Helmut Jahn's stunning steel-and-glass hangar that captured the energy of the freeway and the downtown.

Mr. Jahn's proposal disturbed partners Tom Hicks and Ross Perot Jr., who complained that it was unbuildable. Mr. Schwarz, on the other hand, gave them something reassuringly familiar: arches, pilasters, red brick, and zigzag deco details. He was also a known quantity, having previously designed The Ballpark.

Yet, like concert halls, arenas must be judged by how they play as well as how they look. With exhibition games still six weeks away, first impressions will have to do.

Although American Airlines Center has roughly the same number of seats as Reunion—18,000 for hockey, 19,200 for basketball—it is considerably less intimate. Like new baseball parks, new arenas must digest luxury suites, restaurants, bars, and other revenue enhancers, which invariably increase their height and girth along with the rake of their seats. Getting the lower half of the bowl right is a snap compared to keeping the fans in the upper deck from getting vertigo and nosebleeds.

That's certainly the case at American Airlines Center. The lower sections are tight, with graceful turns and excellent sight lines, while the third concourse should be reserved for fans with binoculars and their own oxygen supply.

The arena is the centerpiece of Victory, an urban neighborhood that doesn't exist, and that depending on the economy, the market, and the plans of its developers may or may not emerge. (This is hardly unique in downtown Dallas, which is sprinkled with such aborted grand designs as Cityplace, Fountain Place, and Reunion.) Its plan is a conventional blend of long ceremonial boulevards and shorter cross streets, with the taller buildings clustered on the downtown end of the site. It is all quite reasonable except for the massive parking garage slammed up against a residential neighborhood on the east side. That is insensitive urban design.

From the beginning, Victory's developers have insisted that it will be a catalyst for downtown development instead of a siphon. Given its remote location, that will take some doing. At the moment both it and the arena are severed from downtown by an elevated freeway and a *Blade Runner* landscape of parking lots and an abandoned power plant. Bad pedestrian connections could mean a repeat of the Reunion syndrome—drive in, drive out, and never set foot in the city.

At Friday's ribbon-cutting, Dallas Mayor Ron Kirk derided arena opponents and insisted that its completion was a sign of Dallas's "maturation." Yet, among other things, maturation involves taking risks. The city shelled out less money—$125 million—than many cities for a new arena, but didn't get the building it deserved. When push came to shove, and critical design decisions had to be made, the city deferred to the owners, who thought big but not boldly.

A monument to heroes: Dallas Police Memorial is an edgy, contemporary tribute that's a triumph

APRIL 8, 2001

Dillon served on the National Capitol Planning Commission in Washington, DC, and authored its memorials and museum master plan issued in 2000; he also wrote a monograph about Lawrence Halprin's design for the Franklin Delano Roosevelt Memorial in DC.* In other words, he was particularly interested in and informed about memorials and how they could transform public space through thoughtful combinations of space and art.

Rusting steel, chunks of concrete and blacktop, badge numbers reflected on the pavement—these are the images that greet visitors to the new Dallas Police Memorial.

And they are emphatically urban images, derived from the mean streets where police officers spend much of their lives. No bronze statues, classical inscriptions, or other conventional commemorative devices. The memorial is a contemporary tribute to sixty-eight Dallas police officers killed in the line of duty and to thousands more who have served the city since its founding.

"Our intention was to go beyond symbol as the device of memory," explains architect Edward Baum, who, with University of Texas at

---

*   Dillon, *The FDR Memorial: Designed by Lawrence Halprin* (Washington, DC: Spacemaker Press, 2006).

Arlington colleague John Maruszczak, designed the memorial. "We used the idea of a relic or authentic fragment to extend the memorial's meaning."

The $1.6 million structure, to be dedicated Wednesday, occupies the intersection of Young, Akard, and Marilla Streets, in the shadow of Dallas City Hall and across from Pioneer Cemetery, where many of Dallas's founders are buried.

The memorial borrows some of its crisp geometry from I. M. Pei's plaza and its softness from the cemetery. And by being located in the civic heart of the city it also acquires a resonance it would never have as a solitary object in a park. The design's asymmetry and suggestions of precarious balance become a commentary on Dallas and its ambivalent attitudes toward its police (fig. 7.14).

The Police Memorial consists of a series of low, broad terraces that rise gradually from Akard Street to an inclined stainless steel wall inscribed with the names, ages, and death dates of the officers. The sequence is random so that visitors will have to pause and examine the entire wall to find a specific name. Badge numbers are cut like stencils into the canopy above, to be projected onto the pavement or the stainless steel back panels as the sun moves from east to west. The shadow of the canopy falling on a number recalls the mourning bar worn over a police badge.

Planning for the Dallas Police Memorial began in the 1980s when officers Don Flusche and Jessie Lucio rallied support for a permanent tribute to their comrades. But the initial designs were rejected as having nothing to do with police officers or their work. Former Chief Billy Prince characterized one as "a giant crab with columns."

A second competition in 1995 was won by Mr. Baum and Mr. Maruszczak, with Kevin Sloan as the landscape architect. And this time the architects succeeded in being both evocative and intimate.

If one end of the contemporary memorial spectrum is the proposed World War II Memorial in Washington, DC, a vast sunken plaza surrounded by classical columns and laurel wreaths, the other is the Vietnam Veterans Memorial, which makes monumental statements with the simplest means. As they walk along a sloping path, visitors are invited to run their fingers over the names of the dead, to reconnect briefly through touch, while at the same time seeing their own images reflected in the glossy, black granite. A silent conversation takes place, based on sensation and a personal sense of loss.

7.14. *The Dallas Police Memorial along S. Akard Street with Reunion Tower in the distance. Dallas Municipal Archives, City of Dallas.*

The Dallas Police Memorial is about local rather than national history, but it aspires to a similar kind of intimacy. Here too, visitors are encouraged to touch names, to feel broken pavement, to connect the life of an individual to the life of the city. This intricate layering of stone, steel, grass, and sky makes the memorial dynamic, like an unfolding geological event. In plan, Akard Street looks like a fault line, with the memorial pulled to one side and City Hall Plaza to the other. Squint and their lines reconverge.

The memorial is edgy and unconventional, which may partially explain why it took five years to raise the $1.6 million to build it. In the beginning, it was the rank and file who kept the project alive. "They got it immediately and kept urging us on," recalls Mr. Maruszczak. Later, the Belo and Meadows Foundations and Communities Foundation of Texas came through with major donations.

The money has been well spent. If a few details don't quite work—the imbedded fragments are so small that they look more decorative than commemorative—the overall design is powerful. And unlike many modern memorials, it doesn't get so wrapped up in itself and the details of its own making that it loses track of its subject. Here the focus remains squarely, and movingly, on the twin themes of service and sacrifice.

Let it be: Don't move it or redesign it. The JFK Memorial is what it is

APRIL 10, 2006

This was a review with a single purpose—an argument to keep the much-maligned Kennedy Memorial in place across from Dealey Plaza. It is Dillon at his best, calling up images of "cowboys discussing Aristotle," while insisting on modest, commonsense additions to its settings in the west end of downtown Dallas.

Why do questions that aren't worth asking seem to get the most answers? Will Jennifer survive the breakup with Brad? Who is the most obnoxious celebrity on television? And, what should we do about the Kennedy Memorial?

Actually, few people had given the third question a second thought until *Slate*'s architecture critic, Witold Rybczynski, came to town recently and declared the memorial "poorly done." He compared its concrete walls to "mammoth Lego blocks" and the commemorative granite slab in the center to "a coffee table."

"Kennedy was not a notable patron of architecture," he wrote, "but he deserved better than this."

Now, Witold is a good colleague, a fine critic, and as entitled to an off day as anyone else. Yet, for whatever reason, his comments became rhetorical catnip for readers, editorial writers, and unsuspecting tourists trapped into giving street-corner critiques of architect Philip Johnson's concrete box.

"It reminds me of a European public lavatory," replied one. "It's weird, strange," said a second. "I don't get it," added a third. Not everyone was negative; there were scatterings of praise and appreciation. But the consensus seemed to be that Philip had put one over on Dallas.

Now the sensible response would be say *"de gustibus"* and move on. Yet, given the volume of empty attitudinizing on the subject, much of it sounding like cowboys discussing Aristotle, a few basic architectural points and a couple of polemical ones may be in order.

The Kennedy Memorial is a cenotaph, or empty tomb, part of an ancient commemorative tradition that goes back to the Greeks and the pharaohs. Mr. Johnson borrowed his design from an unbuilt World War I memorial in Berlin by his friend and mentor Mies van der Rohe. Like the prototype, it is a tall square box with massive walls and an inscribed black granite slab in the center. The walls rest on eight slender legs, a metaphor for the delicate balance between power and failure implicit in public life, and at night the entire structure seems to float on a bed of light.

The memorial is intentionally and unapologetically modern, an austere, contemplative room with no decoration or narrative, and only a simple inscription to remind visitors of the life and work of President Kennedy (fig. 7.15).

"Its modesty is its virtue," Mr. Johnson explained. "You walk in and there's that empty space and all that sky. Call it God if you like; when I'm there, I think of Kennedy."

For those who want something more—wreaths, garlands, statues, heroic quotations, anything!—the answer is that memorials should reflect their time, in this case the pre-post-modern '60s, when less was still considered more. Also, the Kennedy family asked that the memorial be as simple and unadorned as possible, and that's what Mr. Johnson gave them.

Moving, embellishing, or redesigning the memorial, as some have recommended, is risky business. Tastes change. What's in today is passé tomorrow, and vice versa.

The French hated the Eiffel Tower at first, only to embrace it later as an icon of their native technological genius. Washingtonians felt the same about Robert Mills's monumental obelisk on the Mall,

7.15. *Philip Johnson's John F. Kennedy Memorial, located adjacent to Dealey Plaza, was dedicated in 1970. Photograph by Carol Highsmith. The Lyda Hill Texas Collection of Photographs in Carol M. Highsmith's America Project, Library of Congress, Prints and Photographs Division.*

stripped as it was of colonnade, statues of Revolutionary War heroes, and George Washington himself in a chariot. Now, of course, it is universally admired as a timeless work of art.

And who can forget the abuse heaped on Maya Lin for her minimalist Vietnam Memorial, which led to the placement of a figurative tableau of infantrymen near the entrance? Many visitors walk right past it; those who pause probably wonder why it's there.

The Kennedy Memorial, on the other hand, is ideally located only two hundred yards from the Texas School Book Depository and assassination site, and in the middle of a civic crossroads that includes two courthouses, a jail, and several federal and county office buildings. It is one of the few spots in downtown Dallas with a dependable pedestrian count.

It is not a masterpiece, or even Mr. Johnson's best work. Those who complain of it being hot and hard are right. But the solution is not to move it or redesign it, but to enhance its surroundings.

A county park proposed for the adjacent block is a perfect opportunity to create a softer, more welcoming setting for the memorial as well.

Regrade the sloping site, and replace the concrete pad with a mixture of gravel and turf. Add water, comfortable benches, and trees that repel grackles.

Make these simple moves, and the Kennedy Memorial will do the rest.

THE TRADITION OF ARCHITECTURE CRITICISM IN TEXAS

Stephen Fox

This essay was originally presented as a paper at the inaugural 2012 David Dillon Symposium, "Architecture Criticism Today," organized by the David Dillon Center for Texas Architecture and held at the Nasher Sculpture Center.

When Kathryn Holliday invited me to participate in the first David Dillon Symposium in 2012, she asked that I talk about his work in relation to the historical framework of architectural criticism in Texas. Doing so compelled me to ask: What is criticism? What it is meant to achieve? And how useful is it as a medium for effecting change? Exploring these questions in a Texan historical context gave me a much more profound appreciation of David Dillon's legacy as an architectural critic and a public intellectual. It also made me aware of how Dallas architecture and urbanism changed between the late 1970s—before David Dillon— and the early twenty-first century, as he questioned architectural and planning decisions in print, evaluated proposals, and compared what was happening in Dallas to other cities, informing his readers about the critical issues and personalities that had shaped, and were proposing to reshape, Dallas and its metropolitan sphere.

The twentieth-century Italian critic and historian Manfredo Tafuri criticized what he called "operative criticism": criticism whose agenda is to validate an architectural position rather than disclose the conflict of historical forces detectable in a work of architecture.[1] In examining the history of architectural criticism in Texas, it is apparent that operative criticism is a type of criticism that offers critics a tempting advantage because it is motivated by the desire to effect change. Criticism—the search for truth through the processes of questioning, comparing, evaluating, and judging—serves a public purpose when it elevates cultural production to the level of social discourse. Although produced by individual critics, criticism is an inherently social project, evidenced by the practice of publicizing criticism in different forms of communication media.

Architecture in Texas began to be publicized in nationally circulated architectural periodicals in the late 1870s, commencing with the Galveston Cotton Exchange Building by the Galveston architect John Moser in the *American Architect and Building News* of August 3, 1878, two years after the Boston-based journal began publication.[2] In the 1880s and 1890s, articles about buildings in Texas's major cities— some designed by local architects, some by well-known out-of-state architects—were published sporadically in architectural journals based in New York, Chicago, Minneapolis, and Atlanta.[3]

Articles about new buildings in Texas in nationally circulated periodicals, although indicating recognition that architecture was being produced in Texas cities, did not advance critical discourse in those cities. I've encountered only three instances in which Montgomery Schuyler, now regarded as the most perceptive American architectural critic from 1880 to 1910, evaluated buildings with Texan connections: J. Riely Gordon's Texas Building at the World's Columbian Exposition of 1893 in Chicago and Cram, Goodhue & Ferguson's campus plan, and buildings for what is now Rice University in Houston of 1912.[4] The Houston-based *Southern Architectural Review*, published between September 1910 and October 1911, was the first architectural journal in Texas.[5] Signed commentaries on buildings were written by the architects; Montgomery Schuyler had no Texan counterpart. An issue of the *Southern Architectural Review* devoted to the design of the Rice campus did introduce as commentator William Ward Watkin, whom Cram, Goodhue & Ferguson sent from Boston to Houston to administer construction of the initial buildings. As the first professor of architecture at Rice after the university opened in 1912, Watkin would emerge as a critical voice in the 1930s.[6]

In the 1920s, architectural criticism in Texas began to take form around the question of cultural identity. This addressed a concern that emanated not from the periphery of American culture but from its metropolitan centers. Because metropolitans produce metropolitan architecture, the expectation that those dwelling on the periphery needed to distinguish themselves culturally by producing what, ten years later, would be called "regional architecture" was one way to define what was distinctive about the periphery from the perspective of the center.[7]

Beginning at the time of World War I, writings were published intermittently in response to the metropolitan judgment that peripheral regions, such as Texas, needed to claim their own architectural identity. These articles were not critiques of new buildings but stories about historical architecture in Texas. More news report than architectural history, they reflected the ways American eclectic architects from the 1870s through the 1940s wrote about historical buildings that, according to their judgment, possessed the potential to become models for new design. During the 1890s, the *American Architect* twice published images of the eighteenth-century Spanish missions of San Antonio.[8] Samuel E. Gideon, one of the first members of the architecture faculty of the University of Texas at Austin, published a pair of articles in 1917 on mid-nineteenth-century architecture in Austin and the Hill Country town of Mason in the *American Architect* and the *American Institute of Architects Journal.*[9] The San Antonio architects Harvey P. Smith and Atlee B. Ayres published articles on the missions and vernacular architecture of San Antonio in the *Western Architect* in 1917, *Architecture* in 1918, and the *American Architect* in 1924.[10] Between 1919 and 1926, I. T. Frary, an industrial designer and architectural journalist based in Cleveland, Ohio, wrote occasional reports for *Architectural Record* that focused on eighteenth- and nineteenth-century buildings in San Antonio, the picturesque landscapes of San Antonio, and Mexican vernacular architecture in the border village of San Ygnacio, Texas.[11] Written in the manner of travelogues, these stories emphasized charm, romance, and legend, rhetoric customarily invoked to stimulate interest in recovering new "traditions" for contemporary architectural revival. The Houston architect John F. Staub made this appeal explicit in a polemic published in *Civics for Houston,* a monthly magazine produced for one year in 1928.[12] Titled "Latin Colonial Architecture in the Southwest," Staub's manifesto promoted the adaptation of the Spanish Creole architecture of the French Quarter of New Orleans as a regionally appropriate alternative to Georgian, Tudor, or Spanish Colonial models.

A page of sketches of "early Texas" buildings, published in the short-lived, Fort Worth-based journal, *Southwestern Architecture* in September 1927, marked the emergence of a regionalist discourse in Texas and with it an operative line of architectural criticism.[13] The regionalist movement in American architecture was the vehicle linking appreciation of historical vernacular buildings to the production of new architecture. The Dallas architect David R. Williams advanced a Texas-oriented variant of Staub's argument in two essays published in 1928 and 1931 in the *Southwest Review*, a Dallas-based journal of culture that John H. McGinnis, its editor from 1924 to 1942, transformed into a platform for regionalist discourse.[14] Williams admired the range of Texas historical vernaculars that Gideon, Smith, Ayres, and Frary wrote about. He mobilized the simplicity, environmental responsiveness, and material integrity he ascribed to these buildings to criticize contemporary eclecticism.[15]

In 1931 and 1932, the *Southwest Review* published additional essays by the Dallas architects Roscoe DeWitt, Ralph Bryan, Thomas D. Broad, and O'Neil Ford that questioned the architecture of stylistic eclecticism, although only Ford went so far as to advocate for modern functionalist practices.[16] In 1933, the Dallas artist Jerry Bywaters followed with a summary essay in the *Southwest Review* that framed Williams's and Ford's architecture as Texas Regionalism and provided an "operative" history to legitimize it.[17] But although the *Southwest Review* would publish architectural projects by Ford in subsequent issues, it failed to become a forum for critical discourse in Texan architecture.

The most sustained critical writing during the 1930s came from William Ward Watkin of Houston. In seven essays published in the New York-based *Pencil Points* in 1931 and 1932 and in *American Architect* in 1932 and 1933, Watkin surveyed the rise of modern architecture in the United States and Europe.[18] Although conservative, Watkin's assessments were measured and reflective. His writing was addressed to a broad professional audience rather than to a regional audience and did not mention Texas buildings or architects. Williams, Ford, Bywaters, and their colleagues, unlike Watkin, engaged in operative criticism. The usefulness of taking a position was evident in the publication of their architectural work in nationally circulated house-and-garden magazines and architectural journals because it enabled writers to interpret their buildings within the rhetorical framework of Texas Regionalism and the modern ranch house and satisfied the appetites of metropolitan critics for a distinctive local architecture.[19]

John Rosenfield, the theater and music critic of the *Dallas Morning News* from 1925 to 1966, revolutionized the concept of operative criticism in Texas by becoming an architectural impresario.[20] Rosenfield seems to have been instrumental in getting Frank Lloyd Wright the job to design the unbuilt Rogers Lacy Hotel in Dallas in 1946 and 1947. He promoted Wright as architect for a theater for Margo Jones in 1951 and succeeded in getting the Dallas Theater Center to build Wright's design for the Kalita Humphreys Theater of 1955–1959.[21] Rosenfield seems to have been involved with the design of Temple Emanu-El (1955–1957 by Howard Meyer and Max Sandfield with William W. Wurster) after a 1951 project by Erich Mendelsohn was derailed.[22] Rosenfield mobilized his authority as a critic to secure commissions for architects he championed. He demonstrated the potential of cultural capital to effect change and advance Dallas's standing as a city of more than regional cultural distinction.

Houston had no counterpart to John Rosenfield and his fellow *News* critics, John McGinnis and Lon Tinkle, as cultural arbiters in the 1950s. Instead, it was the Houston architects Howard Barnstone and Burdette Keeland who sought to draw public awareness to architecture with their exhibition, *Ten Years, Ten Buildings*, organized at the Contemporary Arts Museum in 1959.[23] The show displayed work by Houston modern architects (and also by Philip Johnson and Ludwig Mies van der Rohe) built between 1949 and 1959. Barnstone invited the architectural historian and critic Henry-Russell Hitchcock to write an introductory essay for the catalogue, a ploy to ensure that Hitchcock became aware of architecture in Houston.[24] A similar strategy can be inferred from the workings of the Texas Society of Architects' annual program of statewide design awards, which began in 1952. By stacking the juries with prominent, out-of-state modern architects and architectural critics, the competition organizers, who were Texas (usually Dallas) modern architects, guaranteed that trendsetters whose influence was national in scope were exposed to new architecture in Texas.[25] The power of criticism—its mixture of observation, historical interpretation, subjective reaction, and judgment—was evident in an essay titled "Lockhart, Texas," published in 1957 in *Architectural Record* and written by two design critics at the University of Texas at Austin, Colin Rowe and John Hejduk.[26] Rowe and Hejduk's analysis of Lockhart's courthouse square displayed the power of criticism to galvanize critical thinking about landscapes, the buildings that occupy them, and the social patterns that these combinations spatialized.

A landmark of these mid-century efforts to raise critical consciousness about the cultural significance of architecture was the first architectural guidebook produced for a Texas city, *The Prairie's Yield: Forces Shaping Dallas Architecture from 1840 to 1962.*[27] Written by the Dallas architects Hal Box, James Wiley, James Reece Pratt, and Bill C. Booziotis, *The Prairie's Yield* was not simply a catalogue but a critical interpretation of the development of architecture in Dallas—critical because the authors framed their observations within a modern regionalist perspective. The publication of Drury Blakeley Alexander's *Texas Homes of the Nineteenth Century* in 1966, Howard Barnstone's *The Galveston That Was* the same year, and Clovis Heimsath's *Pioneer Texas Buildings: A Geometry Lesson* in 1968 represented a culmination of the regionalist impulse.[28] These books were aimed at the general public. They completed the foundation work, so to speak, for constructing a knowledge base about architecture in Texas, capped by the architect and historian Willard B. Robinson's publication of *Texas Public Buildings of the Nineteenth Century* in 1974.[29] These historical works complemented the expansion of *Texas Architect,* the journal of the Texas Society of Architects, which began publication in 1950. In 1961, during the tenure of its first full-time editor, Don Edward Legge, *Texas Architect* was transformed from a newsletter into a monthly magazine featuring buildings that won Texas Society of Architects (TXA) design awards. *Texas Architect*'s coverage was not critical. But it did advance architectural publication in Texas, although it was primarily addressed to a professional audience.

In 1970, work on raising a superstructure atop this critical foundation began in earnest. Two professors of architecture at Rice University, William T. Cannady and Peter C. Papademetriou, produced critical analyses of architecture and urban development in Houston for the London-based journal *Architectural Design.*[30] Papademetriou critically examined Houston's sprawling, low-density, unzoned suburban fabric and characteristic building types to question the relevance of the role of the architectural profession in producing contemporary

American urban spaces. As author of Houston's first architectural guidebook, the 1972 *Houston: An Architectural Guide*, he became a target for criticism in Houston because of his commentary on the sectors in which the guide's listings were located, remarking (with supporting photographs by Paul Hester and William Lukes) on the decay of inner-city minority neighborhoods, the spatial anarchy of retail strips, and the repetitive monotony of middle-income residential subdivisions.[31] Papademetriou ignored Regionalism (which never exerted the appeal in Houston it exercised in Dallas, San Antonio, and Austin) to imply that kitsch was the characteristic architecture of the suburbanized capitalist metropolis, further enraging Houston architects. From 1975 to 1989, Papademetriou was the first Texas regional correspondent for *Progressive Architecture* magazine. He also wrote about Houston in national and international architectural reviews and became a point of contact for such visiting critics as Ada Louise Huxtable of the *New York Times*.[32] Although he occasionally contributed to local publications, Papademetriou's writings were primarily circulated in the professional press.

Papademetriou's role in Houston was reinforced by two contemporaries who expanded and deepened the scope of architectural criticism in Texas. One was Larry Paul Fuller of Austin, who served as editor of *Texas Architect* from 1975 to 1985. By recruiting Papademetriou, among others, to serve as contributing editors to that journal, Fuller introduced critical commentary and reflection on issues of urban design, historic preservation, architectural education, and architectural history. *Texas Architect* brought architectural debate to a statewide professional readership. Subsequent editors—Joel Warren Barna, Vincent P. Hauser, John Davidson, Stephen Sharpe, Catherine Gavin, and Aaron Seward—have continued Fuller's practice of expanding the magazine's critical perspective.

The second contemporary was David Dillon, an English professor who wrote a 1980 cover story for the monthly *D: The Magazine of Dallas* provocatively titled "Why Is Dallas Architecture So Bad?"[33] In 1983, the *Dallas Morning News* hired Dillon to serve as its first full-time architecture critic, a position he retained until he retired in 2006. Like Papademetriou, Dillon also became a contributing editor of *Texas Architect* and a regional correspondent for *Architecture* magazine from 1983 to 1996 and *Architectural Record* from 1998 until his death in 2010.[34] Dillon demystified architectural criticism in Dallas.

He demonstrated that the goal of criticism was not stylistic commentary but a clarification of the processes through which decisions are made about how the public landscape is shaped. Dillon's writing about architecture, landscape architecture, urban design and planning, and historic preservation made it possible for work in these fields to be debated and discussed intelligently in Dallas, not simply within professional circles but by a wide public audience.

The sequential collapse of the Texas economy after 1982 had an inverse relationship to the emergence of new organs of architectural criticism. In 1982, the Rice Design Alliance in Houston, founded in 1972 to promote a public culture of architecture, began publication of *Cite: The Architecture and Design Review of Houston*. Although *Cite*, like the programs of the Rice Design Alliance, was addressed to a general audience, it drew heavily on the architecture faculties of Rice University and the University of Houston for its editorial direction and content.[35] At the University of Texas at Austin, the dean of architecture, Hal Box, launched *Center: A Journal for Architecture in America* in 1984. Its volumes, appearing at intervals under the editorships of University of Texas architecture professors Lawrence W. Speck, Michael Benedikt, Anthony Alofsin, and Kevin Alter, have covered a wide range of topics, from Regionalism to Value to God.[36] Joel Warren Barna demonstrated the existence of an architectural-critical network in Texas as he moved from the editorship of *Cite* (1983–1985) to that of *Texas Architect* (1985–1995) to the post of regional correspondent for *Progressive Architecture* (1988–1995) and author of one of the most acclaimed, and critical, books on architecture in Texas, *The See-Through Years: Creation and Destruction in Texas Architecture, 1981–1991*.[37]

As this survey shows, the "tradition" of architectural criticism in Texas consists in random, fragmented, and disconnected events, initiatives, and personalities that depended on cultural networks, primarily architectural journals published outside Texas, to gain sufficient momentum to become self-sustaining. Out-of-state journals bestowed recognition on Texan buildings and played a role in formulating a consensus on the existence of a Texas architectural culture. The contingencies of the historical cycles of architectural production, such as the dominance of stylistic eclecticism before World War II and the encouragement it offered for discovering regionally distinctive architectural practices, played a crucial role in shaping the contours of architectural criticism in Texas. But what the center-periphery dynamic of media coverage demonstrates is that architectural culture is local. Distant media cannot sustain cultural initiatives, which need to be locally grounded. University schools of architecture are of enormous benefit in that they support a culture of architectural expertise and discourse that can be externalized to address the public outside the academy. Documenting the history of architecture is an essential task because such knowledge underpins reasoning and judgment. Yet for criticism to function effectively as an instrument of public consciousness, it cannot be the preserve of specialized academic or professional constituencies nor is it subordinate to architectural history.

Criticism can externalize processes of conception and construction and explore the consequences of design on those who occupy buildings or come into contact with them, the impact of buildings on urban spaces, and the quality of life those urban spaces contain. Criticism, as Tafuri maintained, tests works to determine what their contradictions are. David Dillon's career as the *Dallas Morning News* architecture critic demonstrates the value that accrues to an entire city when this process of critical testing occurs as public discourse.

Reflecting on Dillon's legacy makes me realize how instrumental he was in the constitution of a network of remarkable people shaping a culture of architecture and design excellence in Dallas during the thirty years he was in action. Key contributors are Virginia McAlester and Deedie Rose, two women who saw no contradiction between caring passionately about the quality of life in Dallas and connecting their city to the wider world. Virginia McAlester achieved this by using Dallas as her base for writing books about American domestic architecture aimed at a general readership. Deedie Rose, who credits her uncle, Fort Worth architect John Wilson Floore, with kindling her interest in architecture, not only commissioned exceptional architects (Antoine Predock and Samuel Mockbee) for her own projects but also gave Dallas's civic and cultural leaders the courage and determination to bring the world's most challenging architects to Dallas and then actually build the structures they designed. Art historian and museum director Richard Brettell has invested his expertise and knowledge in interpreting Dallas's architectural culture, institutionalizing this work in the Dallas Architecture Forum, which he co-founded in 1997 with a large group of compatriots that included Gabriel Barbier, Edward Baum, Russell Buchanan, Vincent Carozza, Mary Ellen Degnan, Barbara Einspruch, Kathryn Greene, Irwin Grossman, Susan

Matusewicz, Lee and Virginia McAlester, Marlene Meyerson, Raymond Nasher, James Pratt, Howard Rachofsky, Deedie Rose, Cynthia Schwartz, David Stock, and Emily Summers.

During the 1980s, 1990s, and 2000s, Dillon may have commanded the broadest forum for reporting on architecture, design, and planning, but his voice was amplified by architectural historian Jay C. Henry and his students at the University of Texas at Arlington; Willis C. Winters, architect, historian, and director of the City of Dallas Park and Recreation Department; architect and historian Frank D. Welch; and architect and historian Ann Abernathy as they commented on, criticized, documented, and chronicled the architectural and cultural history of Dallas and Texas. Fort Worth architect W. Mark Gunderson has functioned as a singular and sustained advocate for architecture as a public culture in the Dallas-Fort Worth metroplex. Through public programs, lectures, classes, tours, and civic advocacy, Preservation Dallas, founded in 1972, and the Dallas Institute of Humanities and Culture, founded in 1980, have peopled the ideal Dallas that Dillon's writings envisioned, where citizens can learn about their city, its history, and populations in order to make wiser, more discerning, and more humane choices about its future.

Dallas entrepreneur Diane Cheatham projects this ideal Dallas through the projects of her Urban Edge Developers corporation, which commissions Dallas's most talented architects—Cunningham Architects, Max Levy, Oglesby Greene, DSGN, Russell Buchanan, Lionel Morrison, Sharon Odum, and Shipley Architects, as well as Vincent Snyder, Kieran Timberlake, and Tod Williams and Billie Tsien from beyond Dallas—to construct this new Dallas one modestly scaled project at a time. Complementing Diane Cheatham's business entrepreneurship is the cultural entrepreneurship of the College of Architecture, Planning, and Public Affairs at the University of Texas at Arlington. Its former dean, Donald Gatzke, and architectural historian and associate professor Kathryn Holliday masterminded organization of the David Dillon Center for Texas Architecture in 2011, and in 2013 brought Mark Lamster to the college as assistant professor in practice in order to facilitate his accession to David Dillon's role as architecture critic of the *Dallas Morning News*.

The word "criticism" does carry with it a negative connotation, as though to criticize involves passively chipping away at and undermining what more vigorous actors have labored to construct. History suggests otherwise in the case of David Dillon. In hindsight, his criticism was essential in helping to construct the foundations on which a better, more ambitious, and more distinctive Dallas architecture and urbanism took form in the 1980s, 1990s, and 2000s. As a recitation of the names of just a few of those who built this civic platform implies, this was a collective enterprise; no one person can claim primacy. Yet Dillon's contribution to this effort stands out because, as the essays in this book make clear, he consistently identified the critical shortfalls and articulated the critical goals that had to be negotiated in order to promote public understanding of what building a great city, and a good city, requires.

NOTES

1. "What is normally meant by *operative criticism* is an analysis of architecture (or of the arts in general) that, instead of an abstract survey, has as its objective the planning of a precise poetical tendency, anticipated by its structures and derived from historical analyses programmatically distorted and finalised . . .
   "Its attitude is contesting toward past history, and prophetic towards the future." Manfredo Tafuri, *Theories and History of Architecture*, trans. Giorgio Verrecchia (New York: Harper and Row, 1980), 141.
2. *American Architect and Building News* 4 (August 3, 1878): plate 136 and p. 40. The building's architect, the German-born John Moser, earlier published a reflection titled "Whither Are We Tending?" in the *American Architect and Building News* 4 (July 20, 1878): 23–24.
3. These journals included *Architectural Record* (New York), *Inland Architect* (Chicago), *Western Architect* (Minneapolis), and the *Southern Architect and Building News* (Atlanta).
4. Montgomery Schuyler, "State Buildings at the World's Fair," *Architectural Record* 3 (July–September 1893): 65, 69; Schuyler, "The Work of Cram, Goodhue & Ferguson: A Record of the Firm's Representative Structures, 1892–1910," *Architectural Record* 29 (January 1911): 30, 76–78; and Schuyler [pseud. Franz Winkler], "The Administration Building of the William M. Rice Institute, Houston, Texas," *Brickbuilder* 21 (December 1912): 321–324.
5. The Houston Public Library has the only known run of the *Southern Architectural Review*, although it is not complete. Publication began with the September 1910 volume; the last volume in the library's collection is dated October 1911.
6. William Ward Watkin, "Architectural Development of the William M. Rice Institute, Houston, Texas," *Southern Architectural Review* 1 (November 1910): 110–115 and plate section.
7. See Vincent B. Canizaro, ed., *Architectural Regionalism: Collected Writings*

on Place, Identity, Modernity, and Tradition, (New York: Princeton Architectural Press, 2007).

8. "Window of Mission San José," *American Architect and Building News* 30 (December 20, 1890): plate section; Arthur Howard Noll, "The Texas Missions," *American Architect and Building News* 57 (August 28, 1897): 71.

9. Samuel E. Gideon, "Early Architecture in Texas," *American Architect* 111 (January 24, 1917): 49–53; Gideon, "The Architecture and Incidents of a Texas Frontier Town," *Journal of the American Institute of Architects* 5 (June 1917): 285–298. See also Gideon, "Landmarks in Austin, the Capital of Texas," *Journal of the American Institute of Architects* 14 (June 1926): 306–312; Gideon, "A Little German Town in the Lone Star State," *American Architect* 139 (April 1931): 44–47, 88, 90.

10. Harvey Partridge Smith, "The Baptistery Window of Mission San José de Aguayo," *Western Architect* 26 (November 1917): 7–9; Smith, "An Architect's Impression of Old San Antonio," *Architecture* 37 (June 1918): 157–159; Smith, "Spanish Traditions of San Antonio," *California Arts and Architecture* 38 (August 1930): 34–35, 72; and Atlee B. Ayres, "The Earliest Mission Buildings of San Antonio, Texas," *American Architect* 131 (August 27, 1924): 171–178.

11. I. T. Frary, "The River of San Antonio," *Architectural Record* 44 (April 1919): 380–381; Frary, "Picturesque Towns of the Border Land," *Architectural Record* 44 (April 1919): 382–384; Frary, "The Carved Window of San José," *Architectural Record* 47 (March 1920): 286–287; Frary "The Passing of a Unique Office Building," *Architectural Record* 48 (November 1920): 462–464; Frary, "A Group of San Antonio Cottages Showing Spanish Influence," *Architectural Record* 51 (June 1922): 538–542; Frary, "The Stairway of Mission San José," *Architectural Record* 53 (January 1923): 87–88; and Frary, "A Group of San Antonio Houses Showing Classic Influence," *Architectural Record* 60 (September 1926): 281–283.

12. John F. Staub, "Latin Colonial Architecture in the Southwest: Exotic in Design and Color Blends With Colonial Type," *Civics for Houston* 1 (February 1928): 9–10. Staub's essay was reprinted in *Southern Architect and Building News* 56 (August 1930): 33–35.

13. David R. Williams and O'Neil Ford, "Architecture of Early Texas," *Southwestern Architecture* 1 (October 1927): 5.

14. On the *Southwest Review*, see Henry Nash Smith and Willard Spiegelman, "Southwest Review," *Handbook of Texas Online*, www.tshaonline.org /handbook/online/articles/kqs01.

15. David R. Williams, "An Indigenous Architecture: Some Texas Colonial Houses," *Southwest Review* 14 (October 1928): 60–74; Williams, "Toward a Southwestern Architecture," *Southwest Review* 16 (April 1931): 301–313.

16. Roscoe DeWitt, "After Indigenous Architecture, What?" *Southwest Review* 16 (April 1931): 314–324; Ralph Bryan, "Twelve Texas Buildings," *Southwest Review* 16 (April 1931): 325–328; Thomas D. Broad, "Toward A New

Architecture: I. What Is Modernism?" *Southwest Review* 17 (January 1932): 209–215; and O'Neil Ford, "What is Modernism? II. Organic Building," *Southwest Review* 17 (January 1932): 215–229.

17. Jerry Bywaters, "More About Southwestern Architecture," *Southwest Review* 18 (Spring 1933): 234–264.

18. William Ward Watkin, "Impressions of Modern Architecture," *Pencil Points* 12 (May 1931): 355–362; 12 (June 1931): 421–429; and 12 (July 1931): 521–530. Also by Watkin, "Are We Making Progress in Our Church Architecture?" *Pencil Points* 12 (March 1931): 193–196; "For the Future: Fitness and Harmony," *Pencil Points* 13 (February 1932): 73–74; "Whence Comes This Modernism?" *American Architect* 142 (September 1932): 22–23; and "Make No Little Plans," *American Architect* 143 (September 1933): 67.

19. Operative criticism can be seen at work in the articles by Violet Richardson, "Rambling Texas Home of Elbert Williams," *American Home* 13 (January 1935): 70–72; Wayne Gard, "The Ranch-House Goes to Town," *Better Homes and Gardens* 15 (June 1937): 32–33; and S. B. Zisman, "The Architect and the House: 5—O'Neil Ford of Dallas, Texas," *Pencil Points* 21 (April 1940): 195–210. See also Peter Papademetriou, "Nationalism-Regionalism-Modernism: In Search of a Texas Architecture," *Texas Architect* 18 (May–June 1978): 17–21, and "Regionalism: An Elusive Sensibility, 1925–1950," *Texas Architect* 31 (July-August 1981): 36–41.

20. Ronald L. Davis, *John Rosenfield's Dallas: How the Southwest's Leading Critic Shaped a City's Culture, 1925–1966* (Dallas: Three Forks Press, 2002); and John Rosenfield, "The Show: Music Appreciation at Taliesin, FLLW's Shangri-La," *DMN*, August 17, 1947.

21. "FLLW's Dallas Theater," *Architectural Forum*, 112 (March 1960): 130–135; also Ann Abernathy, "Kalita Humphreys Theater Designation Report" (2005), http://dallascityhall.com/departments/sustainabledevelopment/historicpreservation/HP%20Documents/Landmark%20Structures/Kalita%20Humphreys%20Theater%20Landmark%20Nomination.pdf. In addition, see "Margo Jones Off to See the Wizard," *DMN*, December 8, 1950; "Director Visits Dallas," *DMN*, December 29, 1950; and "Architect for Theater," *DMN*, July 29, 1955. On Wright's design of the unbuilt Rogers Lacy Hotel, see "Outstanding Architects to Visit Dallas," *DMN*, March 25, 1946; "Architect Arrives for Hotel Parley," *DMN*, March 27, 1946; "Famed Architect Confers On New Dallas Hotel Plans," *DMN*, March 28, 1946; "Deal Pending on Lacy Hotel," *DMN*, March 29, 1946; "Wright Chosen to Design New Dallas Hotel," *DMN*, April 21, 1946; "47-Story Windowless Dallas Hotel Designed by Celebrated Architect," *DMN*, July 28, 1946; John Rosenfield, "Dallas' Dream Hotel Soon Coming to Life," *DMN*, August 11, 1946; Peggy Louise Jones, "Wright Plans Arrive Here for Fair Show," *DMN*, September 25, 1947; and "Rogers E. Lacy, Oilman, Passes," *DMN*, December 10, 1947.

22. "A High-Domed Temple in Texas," *Architectural Forum* 108 (March 1957): 92–95. Also Stuart M. Doss, "Rebuilding Set For Emanu-El," *DMN*, May 29,

1951; "Congregation Plans to Build on Tract," *DMN*, April 30, 1952; "Work to Start on Temple's New Building," *DMN*, June 5, 1955; Rual Askew, "Splendid Vision Realized," *DMN*, February 3, 1957.

23. *Ten Years of Houston Architecture*, (Houston: Contemporary Arts Association, 1959). Exhibition catalogue.

24. Henry-Russell Hitchcock, "Introduction," in *Ten Years of Houston Architecture* (Houston: Contemporary Arts Association, 1959), n.p.

25. Stephen Fox, "TSA Design Awards, 1952–2005," *Texas Architect* 55 (September-October 2005): 30–31.

26. Colin Rowe and John Hejduk, "Lockhart, Texas," *Architectural Record* 121 (March 1957): 201–206. See also Alexander Caragonne, *The Texas Rangers: Notes from an Architectural Underground* (Cambridge, MA: MIT Press, 1995). The cultural geographer John Brinckerhoff Jackson also began to highlight the landscapes of Texas in the 1950s in the journal he published, *Landscape*. See, for instance, his essay "The Almost Perfect Town," *Landscape* 2 (Spring 1952): 2–8, as well as J. B. Jackson, "Regionalism in Architecture: An Essay," *Texas Architect* 31 (July–August 1981): 33–35.

27. John Harold Box, James Wiley, and James Reece Pratt, eds., *The Prairie's Yield: Forces Shaping Dallas Architecture from 1840 to 1962* (New York: Reinhold Publishing Corp., 1962).

28. Drury Blakeley Alexander and Todd Webb, *Texas Homes of the Nineteenth Century* (Austin and Fort Worth: University of Texas Press and the Amon Carter Museum, 1966); Howard Barnstone, *The Galveston That Was*, photographs by Henri Carter-Bresson and Ezra Stoller (New York and Houston: Macmillan Co. and Museum of Fine Arts, Houston, 1966); and Clovis Heimsath, *Pioneer Texas Buildings, A Geometry Lesson*, illustrations by Maryann Heimsath, (Austin: University of Texas Press, 1968).

29. Willard B. Robinson and Todd Webb, *Texas Public Buildings of the Nineteenth Century* (Austin and Fort Worth: University of Texas Press and the Amon Carter Museum, 1974).

30. William T. Cannady, "Houston Airport," *Architectural Design* 40 (January 1970): 20–25; Cannady, "TET-Center, Houston," *Architectural Design* 41 (April 1971): 217–218; Cannady and Jonathan King, "One Shell Plaza, Tallest Building West of the Mississippi," *Architectural Design* 42 (January 1972): 22–23; Cannady and King, "Galleria," *Architectural Design* 43 (November 1973), 695–697; Cannady and Jeffrey Karl Ochsner, "Boom City," *Architectural Review* 48 (November 1978): 298; and Peter C. Papademetriou and Peter G. Rowe, "The Pope and the Judge," *Architectural Design* 40 (July 1970): 345–349; Papademetriou, "Architecture in Houston: A Heritage and a Challenge," *American Institute of Architects Journal* 136 (April 1972): 18–22; Papademetriou, "Notes from A Billboard Culture," *Architecture in Greece* 7 (1973), 104–111; Papademetriou, "Memorandum—Dateline: Houston," *Domus* 537 (August 1974), 1–3.

31. Peter C. Papademetriou, *Houston: An Architectural Guide* (Houston: Houston Chapter, American Institute of Architects, 1972).

32. Ada Louise Huxtable, "Pennzoil: Houston's Towering Achievement" and "Houston: Deep in the Heart of Nowhere," in *Kicked a Building Lately?* (New York: Quadrangle, 1976), pp. 67–70, 143–149.

33. Dillon, "Why Is Dallas Architecture So Bad?" *D: The Magazine of Dallas* 7 (May 1980): 102–109.

34. Dillon, *Dallas Architecture, 1936–1986*, photos by Doug Tomlinson (Austin: Texas Monthly Press, 1985), and Dillon, *The Architecture of O'Neil Ford: Celebrating Place* (Austin: University of Texas Press, 1999).

35. Barrie Scardino, William F. Stern, and Bruce C. Webb, eds., *Ephemeral City: Cite Looks at Houston* (Austin: University of Texas Press, 2003).

36. By 2014, twenty volumes of *Center* had been published.

37. Joel Warren Barna, *The See-Through Years: Creation and Destruction in Texas Architecture, 1981–1991* (Houston: Rice University Press, 1992).

INDEX

415

private versus public interests in, 2–3, 12, 20, 22–23, 45–46, 92, 94–95, 357; skyline, 23–25, 54, 348, *354*, 354–357. *See also* Dallas, development programs; Dallas, downtown; Dallas/Fort Worth metropolitan area; *and specific buildings and neighborhoods*

Dallas, development programs. *See* Dallas Arts District; DART (Dallas Area Rapid Transit); *Forward Dallas* (2006); Goals for Dallas program (1965); Trinity River Parks Plans

Dallas, downtown: architecture culture of, 22–28, 32–33, 277; demographics, 66–68, 79, 82, 103; freeways and, 53–54, 121–123, 246, 351; housing and residential development, 56, 66–72, 78–79, 80–83, 248–250; peer cities and models for, 27, 29, 30, 55–58, 59–61, 85–88, 95, 97; private versus public interests in, 39–40, 83, 104, 248–249; public needs and pedestrian spaces in, xiii, 25–27, 53–55, 64, 71–72, 88–89, 106, 161–162, 392; public transit in, 55, 60–61, 62–64, 71, 100–101, 113; race and urban division in, 52–53, 55, 64, 72, 92–94, 98; revitalization plans, 2–3, 40, 50–51, 52–55, 70–72, 83, 88–89, 90; suburban flight from, 52–54, 67, 72, 120. *See also* Dallas: development plans; *specific buildings and neighborhoods*

Dallas (1978), 3, 302, 354, 358

Dallas Alliance, 96

Dallas Apparel Mart, 31, 336

Dallas Architecture Forum, 36, 315, 408

Dallas Area Rapid Transit. *See* DART (Dallas Area Rapid Transit)

Dallas Arts District, 2, 7, 51, 163–165, *164*; arts programming and diversity, 13, 165, 167–170, 197–199, 222; commercial interest and public space in, 32, 165, 167–171, 172–174, 176–177, 195–197; development plans, 56, 88, 166, 194–197, *196*, *198*, 213, 220–222, 227, 372; as isolated, 75, 89, 213, 228; location, 163, 166, 221–222. *See also* *specific buildings and institutions*

Dallas Arts District Foundation, 169

Dallas Black Dance Theater, 13, 197

Dallas Center for the Performing Arts, 84, 89, 197, 315; master plan, 165, 220–222

Dallas Central Business District, 63, 166, 287

Dallas Central Business District Association, 44

Dallas Children's Theater, 197

Dallas City Council, 50, 95, 239–241; decisions by, 47, 48, 109, 248; and the Juanita Craft House, 242, 243, 254; and the Trinity Parks Plan, 133, 134, 145, 148, 152, 154, 156. *See also* Dallas: civic participation in

Dallas City Hall, 31, 41, 45, *48*, 54, 389–390, 395; access to, 26, 357; design of, 46–47, 50, 347, 370. *See also* Goals for Dallas program (1965)

Dallas City Theater, 163

Dallas Convention Center, 27–28, 54, 87–88

Dallas Cotton Exchange building, 309

Dallas County Commissioners, 232, 233, 238

Dallas County Courthouse, 28, 357

Dallas County Heritage Society, and the Juanita Craft House, 241, 243

Dallas County Historical Foundation. *See* Texas School Book Depository (Dallas): preservation conflict